The Reconciled Life

A Critical Theory of Counseling

R. PAUL OLSON

HENDRICKSON PUBLISHERS

Hendrickson Publishers, Inc.
P. O. Box 3473
Peabody, Massachusetts 01961-3473

Printed in the United States of America

First printing — February 2001

Library of Congress Catalog Card Number: 97-11084
ISBN: 1-56563-608-2

Original cloth edition first published in 1997 by
Praeger Publishers, 88 Post Road West, Westport, CT 06881,
an imprint of Greenwood Publishing Group, Inc.

Duane Charles Olson
father, physician, friend
for his service beyond self
in a ministry of healing

Contents

Acknowledgments

I wish to thank several esteemed scholars and colleagues for their critical and constructive reviews of this manuscript. They include Lyn Cowan, Ph.D., David B. Kachel, M.Div., Jack Schaffer, M.Div., Ph.D., and Clyde Steckel, M.Div., Ph.D. I am grateful also for Clare Lee's assistance in my search for correct references and for Madelyn Thomas' expert transformation of this manuscript into book format under the guidance of my very professional editors, Leanne Jisonna and Lynn Zelem. I wish to acknowledge as well my wife's understanding and support throughout this project. Mary's patience and insights are an inspiration. Finally, I am grateful to the graduate students in clinical psychology who participated in my seminars on religious anthropologies and on psychotherapy and spiritual direction. Their own creative struggles to relate psychology and religion in psychotherapy and counseling have challenged and encouraged me to engage in a reconciling dialogue that preserves the uniqueness and independence of each discipline, while fostering their creative interdependence.

Chapter One

Introduction

This is a book about the reconciled life. I have written it to express a view on the meaning of the teachings of Jesus of Nazareth for both contemporary counseling and Christian living. By writing this book, I am joining the dialogue between Christian theology and clinical psychology. My primary purpose, however, is not to think Christianly about psychology, nor to think psychologically about Christianity. My intent is to utilize the spiritual wisdom Jesus taught as a theoretical foundation for a practical approach to counseling.[1] Stated another way, I want to construct a theory of counseling grounded in the teachings of Jesus and relevant to clinical practice.

Is this a legitimate undertaking? I believe that it is as valid to derive a theory of counseling from the teachings of Jesus as it is from the teachings of Freud, or for that matter, from any other contemporary psychological theorist. Those of other religious persuasions may wish to assert the same validity for a theory of counseling based upon Eastern religions or Native American traditions. My roots lie within the Judeo-Christian heritage. That is an obvious bias of this work.

By grounding my theory of counseling in the teachings of Jesus of Nazareth, I am providing a theological perspective on an area that is construed by most mental health professionals as primarily a secular, psychosocial experience. My theory is informed more by a theological anthropology than by the dominant biopsychosocial model of human behavior. Thus, while constructing a theory of psychotherapy, I am presenting simultaneously an affirmation of my faith in the loving presence and sovereign power of the living God revealed in human experiences of reconciliation.

Atheistic and agnostic psychologists will object to this approach since they have no need for either the hypothesis that God exists or that God plays an active role in human life. Hence theological insights are judged irrelevant to psychological theory. Their preference on several grounds is to exclude religious perspectives altogether in favor of other empirically based psychological theories. How else can we advance the science of psychotherapy?

Psychological explanations of human behavior in general, and counseling in particular, may be complete in their own terms and provide satisfactory answers to one set of questions. For example, how do thoughts influence behavior and vice versa? But psychological explanations do not answer other relevant questions that arise in human experience, one form of which is the experience of counseling. These other questions address religious issues of ultimate concern, that is, matters of faith. They include such questions as the meaning of suffering and the purpose of life, the nature of the good life, basic values and commitments involved in ethical decisions, sources of courage and hope, and the nature and relevance to one's life of divine self-disclosures in both historical revelation and religious experience. These are questions of meaning and values that involve the risk of personal decision. It is these types of questions that are addressed in a theology of counseling.

This chapter includes preliminary remarks about integrating psychology and religion, about the historical Jesus and his message and ministry, and a discussion of theoretical sources, norms, and limitations. Thereafter I discuss the relevance of Jesus' teachings to counseling, present a critique of contemporary counseling theory, and I define the purpose of psychotherapy as reconciliation. Following discussion of the role of psychological theory and personal experience in the construction of this theory, I present an overview of my theological and ethical perspectives and the definition of reconciliation that provide the foundation for the dialogue between psychology and religion presented in this book.

PRELIMINARY REMARKS

Cautions about Integrating Psychology and Religion

By seeking to discover the purpose of counseling in the teachings of Jesus, I am risking a compromise of psychological theory in favor of a theological and scriptural emphasis. I consider that to be a risk worth taking in light of the opposite positions taken in the past, at both personal and theoretical levels.

At a personal level, I have viewed myself for several years as a Christian *psychologist*. By that I mean both my theory and practice were anchored more in psychology than theology. So was my professional identity and my license to practice. The two areas just did not seem to interconnect meaningfully and practically. I functioned like a psychologist who happened to be a Christian. Over the past few years I have begun to see myself more as a *Christian* psychologist, that is, more as a Christian who happens to be a psychologist. There is a difference in these identities, one expression of which is this book.

At a theoretical level, psychology as a discipline has resisted relating with any religion, except as the latter is an object of psychological investigation. After all, psychology defines itself as the science of behavior, not as a metaphysic of the soul. Neither is psychotherapy the same as spiritual direction. There is, however, Division 36 within the American Psychological Association for psychologists interested in religion, that was renamed to reflect the subspecialty called the psychology of religion.[2] There is no subspecialty called the religion of psychology, that is, a field of inquiry that considers psychology itself as a worldview expressing the ultimate concerns of its members.[3]

In addition to the risk of subordinating psychological theory to theological interpretation, a second risk involved in any effort to articulate a theologically informed psychology is the potential misrepresentation of the religious wisdom used as its source, due largely to significant omissions of its truths. It is essential that the truth of Jesus' message be preserved in any application that demonstrates its relevance. I have attempted to discover and apply the truth and meaning of Jesus' message in this theory of counseling. New Testament scholars and Christian theologians can help to evaluate the accuracy of this representation of his message.

In my view, psychological counseling is a specialized form of the Christian ministry of reconciliation.[4] As such, it is both informed by and accountable to the Christian tradition. Consequently, those of us in the counseling field are obliged to consult with other individuals, besides our professional colleagues, for a reading of both the truth and relevance of what we teach and do. This is especially important for anyone claiming to base one's theory of counseling on the teachings of Jesus. Here the appropriate peer review is provided by other disciples who take seriously the teachings of Jesus.[5]

Non-Christian psychologists are likely to view this whole approach as foreign to the secular scientific approach they learned in graduate school. Even more strange is the turn to a wise and holy man of ancient times for insights into counseling and human relationships. After all, Jesus was not a graduate of an APA approved program in either clinical or counseling psychology. He had no advanced formal education beyond his religious training in Hebrew scriptures at the synagogue in Nazareth, which was probably not a regionally accredited school by contemporary standards. Were he living today it is unlikely that he would be admitted to a doctoral program because he lacked the prerequisite bachelor's degree and basic courses in scientific psychology. From a reading of the records about him, one is likely to infer that Jesus spoke in the New Revised Standard English, but his native tongue was most likely Aramaic,[6] hence his foreign language would be an obstacle to obtaining an American graduate education in psychology.

Moreover, this man from Nazareth lacks the professional credentials expected of psychologists today. He never took the EPPP exam, hence he was not licensed to practice. Nor did he achieve diplomate status with the American Board of Professional Psychology. (But then, neither did Freud, Adler, or Jung.) His trade was actually wood-working,[7] and he switched careers early in life to become of all things, an itinerant teacher of a reformed Hebrew faith. By most standards today he had a brief and unsuccessful career even as a teacher—no publications, no promotions up the academic ranks, no academic honors as a distinguished and tenured faculty member in a research-based program at a prestigious university. Judged by contemporary professional standards this Galilean charismatic figure seems to be an unlikely source of psychological insight and wisdom.

Furthermore, his view of the world was both religious and prescientific, hardly compatible with the scientific, biopsychosocial model that dominates secular psychology today. And he wasn't even accepted by the religious establishment of his own place and time. In fact, he got into serious trouble with both the religious and political rulers of his day, and he was executed like a criminal before he was thirty-five years old. These are hardly the credentials for even honorable mention in the obituary column in the *American Psychologist*.

The Jesus of History

Who was this man called Jesus of Nazareth? This is a historical question, the answer to which proves not to be so easy. There is tremendous diversity in the portraits of Jesus that have emerged since D. F. Strauss wrote *The Life of Jesus* in 1835.[8] As Witherington noted recently, "there are almost as many portraits of Jesus now available as there are scholarly painters, a testimony to acute scholarly subjectivity."[9] The scriptural records about Jesus seem to function like a projective test, for they elicit such diverse responses.[10] Among the answers that have emerged are views of Jesus ranging from a marginal Jewish peasant to the Jewish Messiah; a non-Jewish peasant; a teacher of noneschatological wisdom; an itinerant philosopher who was cynical about both Roman rule and the religious establishment; a sage who taught and embodied the wisdom of God; an eschatological prophet; a prophet of social change; an egalitarian social reformer; an instigator of a class struggle; a Jewish charismatic holy man (*hasid*); a man of the Spirit; an exorcist, miracle worker, and healer.[11]

The existence of so many diverse portraits of Jesus appears to support a reader-response theory, to wit, that the answer to the question of who Jesus was lies not in Scripture, but in the mind of the reader. This view reflects a subjectivist epistemology that is anti-historical and denies any objectivity to the meanings inherent within a text.[12] It seems legitimate to assert instead that historical facts are objective and separate from their interpretation, and also that some facts are more meaningful than others. For example, Jesus' authentic message about the kingdom of God is much more meaningful to me than the legendary stories about his virgin birth as a preexistent divine being, his alleged miracles, or his fantastic physical resurrection. His message matters more to me than all the mysteries and myths that have arisen about him. Moreover, the truth and value of his message can be judged apart from the mythical worldview in which it was presented, as Bultmann rightly noted.[13]

Of the variegated portraits presented by contemporary New Testament scholars, the views of Jesus as a man of the Spirit (Borg), a charismatic teacher of spiritual wisdom (Vermes), and prophet of social change (Theissen) seem most compatible with my own view of Jesus as a unique agent of reconciliation. These multiple images of Jesus are neither contradictory nor mutually exclusive. For example, while Borg[14] emphasizes that Jesus was (1) a spirit person with an experiential awareness of a transforming relationship with God, he views Jesus as also (2) a teacher of an unconventional wisdom, (3) a social prophet who criticized privileged elites, and (4) the founder of a Jewish renewal movement which shattered traditional social boundaries. I would affirm these same images of Jesus, though my own encounter with the Jesus of history presented in the Synoptic Gospels leads me to view him as a unique representative of God's realm of reconciliation. In this regard he is both a mediator between the human and divine,[15] and the exemplary reconciled personality, the archetypal reconciling life. For me Jesus is also a reconciling reformer. I look to Jesus to understand what the experience of reconciliation is like with God, self, and others, and for a vision of both personal transformation and social reformation.

Jesus' Message and Ministry

While the various portraits of Jesus address the question of who he was, and implicitly his qualifications to provide insights about the meaning and purpose of life, my own attempt to provide a foundation for counseling theory grounded in his teachings expresses the conviction that his message matters more than his personality profile, the biographical details of his life,[16] or speculations about his person, his work, or his pre- and post-existence. The real value of historical research concerning his message is that it serves to protect both faith and theology from distortions, superstition, and absurd claims about his person and work.[17] Moreover, I believe his message may be judged on its own merits irrespective of one's answers to the questions about his nature, person, origin, or destiny. Finally, it seems a mistake to divorce an interpretation of who Jesus was from what he taught, or to substitute teachings about the person of Jesus for Jesus' teachings about the kingdom of God.[18] It is the latter error that has been paramount in American Protestantism, for it seems to consist of a curious mixture of the religion of the apostle Paul via Luther, Calvin, or Wesley combined with a civic religion of democratic capitalism in contrast to Jesus' prophetic, ethical monotheism and his theology of the kingdom of God.[19] As a corrective balance, I have chosen to emphasize what Jesus taught as the foundation for the theory of counseling presented in this book, rather than to attempt to develop a theory of therapy by grace through faith.[20]

By deriving the purpose of psychotherapy from the teachings of Jesus I am also asserting the present relevance of his message. A similar emphasis on the relevance of his message was characteristic of the second quest for the historical Jesus in the 1950s and 1960s based in part upon the existential hermeneutic of Rudolph Bultmann.[21] I believe Jesus' message speaks to our existential present, not primarily or exclusively to a heavenly future. But my focus on the present relevance of Jesus' message need not be taken as a rejection of his equally authentic teachings about the future fulfillment of the kingdom of God. However, I do not endorse the apocalyptic interpretation of Jesus as one who expected an imminent end of the world as portrayed by Albert Schweitzer and others.[22]

Although the purpose of Jesus' actions can be understood only through his teaching, as Bultmann rightly noted,[23] my emphasis upon his message need not detract from an appreciation of Jesus' ministry. Especially informative for understanding his gospel of reconciliation is the way in which he related to people. Jesus lived what he taught—he lived a reconciled and a reconciling life.[24] How he related to people is particularly relevant to a theory about the process of psychotherapy. The focus of this book, however, is on the purpose of psychotherapy. By discussing the psychological dimension of reconciliation, I attempt to show the relevance of his gospel of reconciliation as a foundation for a psychotherapeutic theory.

Sources and Norms

My objective in this book is to address the following question: What truths and principles did Jesus teach and live that are relevant to understanding the purpose of counseling? I have looked to the Synoptic Gospels of Matthew, Mark, and Luke as the primary sources for the answer to this question. This has been a deliberate decision based on two convictions: first, the Synoptics are the earliest and the most reliable records of Jesus' teachings within the New Testament,[25] and second, much of what has been written by other Christians about counseling has been based more on the theology of the apostle Paul than upon Jesus' central teachings about the kingdom of God.[26] It is not my desire to rely upon the apostle's point of view.[27] I am more interested to know what Jesus taught than what Paul thought. Nevertheless, the apostle made explicit references to reconciliation, and these references provide a broader New Testament perspective.[28]

It is my conviction that the teachings of Jesus are normative for his disciples, not subsequent interpretations written about him by other disciples, including other letters canonized as part of the New Testament or theological opinions codified in ecclesiastical creeds. I consider the Church's confessions particularly as subordinate standards of faith. They serve as expressions of earlier Christian understandings, but they do not constitute the authoritative witness to either Jesus' teachings or his person, which scripture provides.[29] The authority of theological tradition is subordinate to the authority of scripture, though both are essential, in addition to reason and experience.[30]

In order to look for corroboration among the three gospel accounts of Jesus' teachings, I have used as a reference the *Gospel Parallels: A Comparison of the Synoptic Gospels*,[31] which in turn uses the New Revised Standard Version of the Bible. Wherever a passage in one gospel is paralleled to another, I have attempted to include them, separated in the text by a slash.

Some Limitations

I accept fully the predictable criticism that my theory of counseling grounded in Jesus' teachings recorded in the Synoptics is at best incomplete. Of course it is a limited theory. At the same time, any theories of counseling that rely primarily upon Old Testament wisdom, on the theology evident in the letters of the apostle Paul, or James and John, or upon other sacred texts such as the Koran or Bhagavad Gita, or on secular psychological literature are all less likely to express the message of Jesus of Nazareth than a theory based on the earliest known and most reliable records of his teachings. I think my approach is both valid and reasonable relative to my purposes. It is also more achievable than attempting to present the counseling theories implicit within the New Testament as a whole, or to attempt at this stage a comprehensive synthesis of Jesus' complete message with contemporary psychological theory. The history of efforts to integrate psychology and theology reflects both the enormous scope and rich diversity of approaches taken.[32] The existence of both numerous and diverse theologies and more than 250 approaches to psychotherapy make any efforts at integration a complex and daunting task.[33] Fortunately, a theory may be judged as good without being considered valid in any complete or absolute sense at C. H. Patterson noted.[34]

I elect this approach, however, with the recognition that other writings in the Bible, such as Proverbs and Psalms, are gold mines of both wisdom and consolation relevant to counseling. Other writers have already shown this relevance in very creative and inspiring ways. For example, Donald Capps[35] applied the structure of the Psalms of lament as a paradigm for grief counseling, Proverbs to premarital counseling, and Jesus' parables to marriage counseling. Jay Adams[36] used Proverbs extensively as a foundation for a more directive, cognitive-behavioral approach to counseling grounded in conventional Jewish wisdom of Jesus' time. According to Borg, an alternative wisdom about the world and how to live in it was taught by the authors of Ecclesiastes, Job, and Jesus of Nazareth.[37] Creative and relevant applications to counseling have been made by both William Oglesby[38] and Donald Capps[39] of biblical themes evident throughout the Old and New Testaments. Howard Clinebell[40] provided biblical roots for six dimensions of human wholeness as a foundation for Christian counseling. I have elected a different approach in this book. I ask the reader to suspend judgment until its implications have been fully drawn.

There is another potential limitation associated with my selection of reconciliation as the purpose of psychotherapy. This metaphor has been criticized by some liberation theologians as connoting a compromise of justice or a civil concession by those in power to placate marginalized minorities demanding their rights.[41] My response is to note that reconciliation involves a struggle for justice as well as peace. While grounded in God's prevenient grace, the experience of reconciliation is a liberating experience that persons must work to attain for the welfare of all, not merely for the benefit of a privileged few. Nor is the meaning of reconciliation limited to either a past historical event or to a personal, religious experience of repentance and forgiveness. Reconciliation has political and economic implications, for it expresses a vision of the good society and aims toward a reconciling world, both of which require continuous, effective action to overcome systemic sources of alienation and injustice in order to liberate the poor and oppressed. Reconciliation without liberation is appeasement, as surely as love without justice is hollow. Jesus' gospel of reconciliation is about a liberating justice as well as a healing peace. His teachings are relevant socially to issues of political liberty and economic equality just as they are relevant psychologically to counseling and psychotherapy. In this work I focus upon the psychological implications in the context of psychotherapy.

THE RELEVANCE OF JESUS' TEACHINGS TO COUNSELING

I have learned from others in the fields of pastoral counseling and biblical studies that the meaning and intention of Jesus' teachings and their relevance to counseling are not found by asking the question: "What does this text tell me to do in response to client A with problem B in situation C?" It was not Jesus' mission to teach the ABCs of counseling. Jesus never provided a series of lectures on the theories and principles of counseling. He did not write a manual or a "cookbook" of counseling procedures, nor for that matter, a text on civil law, architectural engineering, or orthopedic surgery.

Recognizing Jesus' purposes to be other than these has led many to conclude that his teachings are simply irrelevant to applied fields in general and to counseling in particular. But counseling addresses human problems in living, both personal and interpersonal, and these were also the subjects of many of Jesus' teachings. Moreover, every theory of counseling rests upon certain presuppositions about the world and human nature and how we know anything about both. These are ontological, epistemological, and even ethical assumptions implicit in all psychological theories of psychotherapy. Jesus taught about the nature of reality and human nature, about how we know what we know, what we ought to do, and who we are called to become. Thus his teachings are relevant to the very foundations of counseling theory, to its purpose, presuppositions, and basic principles.

Some consider the relevance of Jesus' teachings to end there. They are relevant at the level of theory, but not at the level of practice or counseling procedures. It is a responsible position expressed by those concerned about the inappropriate approaches to Scripture taken in the past, evident in citations of "proof texts" to substantiate a particular counseling procedure. The concern is legitimate, but it also errs in assuming that counseling is essentially a matter of techniques much like engineering is the technical application of the laws of physics. If instead one comprehends counseling as primarily a therapeutic relationship, then the unique contribution of the counselor is the way one relates to the client. Being a counselor is a way of being with others. The numerous narratives and teachings of Jesus all reflect his way of being with people.[42] Therein lie important clues to counseling as a Christian way of relating to those who are distressed.

The distress that humans experience is another reason for judging Jesus' teachings as relevant to counseling. While his first noble truth was not the Buddha's "all life is suffering," Jesus' realistic message was addressed to a suffering world. To paraphrase this in more theoretical terms, the question of alienation that arises from an existential analysis of the human predicament is answered by a theological interpretation of Jesus' gospel of reconciliation. One cannot take seriously the teachings of Jesus without realizing their power to bring about healing experiences of reconciliation. His message was therapeutic and practical; his religious symbol of the kingdom of God has healing and liberating consequences for the human condition, as I shall attempt to show throughout this book.

Jesus' reconciling message must be presented accurately in order to discover its therapeutic relevance. I have attempted to address the risks of potential misrepresentation of Jesus' message caused by omissions, subjective interpretation, and the dominance of psychological theory by asking repeatedly: What did Jesus teach about these matters? and What does his religious message about the kingdom of God mean? As a result of my efforts to listen empathically and faithfully to what Jesus taught, in order to discern both his meanings and their relevance, I discovered that his teachings constitute a compelling critique of contemporary theories of counseling.

A CRITIQUE OF CONTEMPORARY COUNSELING THEORY

This critique is relevant at several levels. First, it is relevant to the *goals of counseling* explicit and implicit within all theories of psychotherapy. In contrast to the goals advocated in several contemporary theories, it is my view that Jesus' teachings are most compatible with reconciliation as the primary purpose of counseling.[43]

Second, Jesus' teachings suggest an alternative *theory of personality structure* with an emphasis upon the whole person. At the same time, I believe he appreciated that human experience is multidimensional. Nevertheless, it is particularly his *holistic* emphasis that serves as an important critique of both reductionistic theories of personality and a myopic focus upon observable behavior, as if who we are could be defined by what we do.[44]

Third, Jesus' teachings about human motivation proved to be both enlightening and refreshing. In contrast to many psychological theories, his views highlight our experience as volitional beings oriented toward the future. Unlike those who stress the determining roles of either one's past history or present circumstances, Jesus keeps our eyes upon the future and upon human strivings, upon acts of will, and self-determining decisions. His clear and consistent focus reminds me of the saying that I once saw on a poster in a bakery: "As you amble on through life, dear friend, wherever you may go, keep your eye upon the doughnut and not upon the hole." Much of secular psychology has been preoccupied with doughnut holes.

In contrast to psychological determinism based on physiological drives, psychological needs, or environmental contingencies, Jesus taught that the human will is what directs human destiny. What matters most is not what pushes us or drives us, but what pulls us and what we are striving for, and that includes our values and intentions, our own freely chosen goals and self-directed actions for which we are responsible. It also includes the beckonings of the Spirit of God through faith and love to transform our selfish desires into sanctified strivings. Jesus' teachings appear most compatible with a *teleological theory of motivation*, which emphasizes the individual's intentions and focuses on the future.[45]

Fourth, many psychological theories of psychotherapy include notions about how both normal and abnormal behavior develop. There is an entire field of specialization called developmental psychology that is devoted to the study of normal processes and stages of human growth. Some theories of counseling are more influenced by this developmental perspective than others, and so are some mental health professionals.

I have not found in Jesus' teachings much discussion devoted to understanding developmental stages, but I'm not trained as a developmental psychologist. Other Christian psychologists and educators[46] have been more insightful in this regard. I did find that Jesus' teachings were very relevant to understanding the development of human distress and to what we construe today as mental disorders. Within his teachings are significant notions about the *etiology of psychopathology* (i.e., the causes of distress), construed primarily in spiritual and ethical terms. It is a spiritual model rather than a medical model. It is an ethical model rather than a psychological model. I think it is also an enlightening model.

Fifth, I also found within Jesus' teachings *an experiential model* in contrast to cognitive or behavioral models of human behavior. Jesus spoke a great deal about human experience, especially about our experiences of repentance and forgiveness and the transforming and healing power of both. It is our actual experience of reconciliation that matters, not merely what we believe or do. Based on his teachings, I consider "experience" to be a unifying construct for both a theory of personality and psychotherapy. The concept of experience also provides a bridge between psychology and theology, since we can speak of both psychological and spiritual dimensions of common human experience. The experience is one though our understanding of it may be diverse, depending upon the dimensions emphasized.

Sixth, counseling procedures rest on a particular *theory of cure*. In analytic therapy the key to cure is insight. In evocative therapies the key is a corrective emotional experience called an abreaction or catharsis. In systems approaches cure is effected by changing dysfunctional rules, roles, and communication patterns into more functional ones in families and other groups. In behavioral approaches cure results from the direct modification of overt, maladaptive behaviors. In existential approaches cure is effected by changes in meaning and being through responsible decisions and healing relationships.

Jesus' theory of cure was not a social psychological theory like those just mentioned. He presented a spiritual and ethical perspective. Recovery from the human suffering associated with alienation from God is brought about by reconciliation with God. Repentance is the key to this new life with God, along with the central experience of divine forgiveness and healing. Accepting God's acceptance of us leads to a grateful life of loving service sustained by a life of faithful prayer. Since this is a therapeutic experience,[47] it is relevant to the theory and practice of counseling.

By way of summary, the teachings of Jesus are relevant to understanding the goals of counseling, theories of personality structure and human motivation, the causes of distress, the nature of experience itself, and the cure of human suffering. With respect to each of these areas, Jesus' teachings constitute a critique of contemporary theories of counseling and a viable alternative to them.

THE ROLE OF PSYCHOLOGICAL THEORY
AND A WORKING DEFINITION

In addition to the teachings of Jesus of Nazareth, psychological theories of personality, psychopathology, and psychotherapy, and the standards of professional practice for clinical psychologists constitute a second general source of this book. Thus, while aware of its limitations, I also appreciate the contributions of psychological theory to our understanding of the meaning of persons and human experience and to the development of therapeutic interventions for those who suffer mental disorders. I will not be discussing these theories and standards in detail (to the relief of most readers), but they constitute a significant part of my background and are lenses through which I attempt to comprehend what it means to be a person and how to be of help to those experiencing distress. It is particularly existential-phenomenological theories that have been most meaningful to me. I also believe these psychological theories are compatible with Jesus' experiential teachings and his emphasis on human relationships.[48]

It is not psychological theory, however, that has shaped my current view of psychotherapy as much as the message of this rabbi of Galilee. Based on my understanding of both Jesus' message and his way of relating to people, the *purpose of psychotherapy* is to experience reconciliation in social, psychological, and spiritual dimensions through the process of compassionate confrontation of client incongruities in the context of a Spirit-centered therapeutic relationship.[49] I shall develop a systematic *definition of reconciliation* in chapter four, and draw out its implications in subsequent chapters. I present it here without discussion so the reader may anticipate my direction. Reconciliation is a multidimensional, unifying experience of resolving conflicts within and among alienated persons, whose being and relations are transformed through the power of forgiveness and the process of compassionate confrontation into a healing reunion of love, justice, and peace for the sake of which one decides to intentionally act.

THE RELEVANCE OF PERSONAL EXPERIENCE

A third general source of this work is my own education and life experience. I have formal education in sociology, theology, and clinical psychology. From my undergraduate sociology major at Carleton College, I learned to appreciate the social dimensions and cultural determinants of human behavior, primarily through the writings of functionalists such as Talcott Parsons.[50] One of my college professors, William Kolb, helped me understand the crucial role of values and the importance of preserving human freedom in social theory.[51]

At Yale Divinity School I learned an existentialist approach to the study of the Bible based on Rudolf Bultmann's work. It was also existentialist theologians such as Paul Tillich and Søren Kierkegaard who provided interpretations of the Word that have been most meaningful to me. The writings of Carl Rogers and Viktor Frankl have informed my approach to counseling. It was several years later that I learned an existentialist and experiential approach to spirituality from the writings of Thomas Merton,[52] a Catholic priest and Trappist monk, and from Douglas Steere,[53] a Quaker theologian. The influence of their thinking on my own will be evident throughout this book, but I doubt that any of them would want to be held accountable for my thoughts, and none should. There are both omissions and revisions for which I assume responsibility.

During a pastoral clinical training experience at St. Elizabeth's Hospital in Washington D.C., I discovered that what I really wanted to do was not to be a parish minister but to specialize in a ministry of counseling. Upon the advice of my seminary professors, I pursued additional education in a graduate school of clinical psychology. I applied to the University of Illinois in Champaign, primarily because Hobart Mowrer was there, and he seemed at the time to be like a voice in the wilderness of psychology addressing the role of values in human struggles and mental health. I learned as one of his research assistants that even Integrity Therapy[54] has its limitations, not the least of which are its atheistic premises and relative absence of grace.

In graduate school I learned primarily a cognitive-behavioral approach to counseling, an approach I have subsequently left behind in favor of a more Christian experiential approach. My graduate school experience did not help me to integrate theology and psychology. It was a period of separation and compartmentalization, with psychology as the dominant discipline upon which I based my professional identity and clinical practice for several years.

While working toward my doctorate in clinical psychology, I was ordained to the Christian ministry in the United Church of Christ, a liberal Protestant denomination, and served part time as a youth minister and a supply preacher. I have spent most of my professional career in a lay ministry of counseling in secular settings. I worked for about fifteen years as a clinical psychologist in two large multidisciplinary clinics. I have pursued continuing education in psychology and religion, pastoral counseling, and Christian spirituality. I have led seminars for lay persons on the Christian faith and mental health, on the reconciled life, and graduate courses on religious anthropologies, and on integrating psychotherapy and spiritual direction. For nine years I served as dean at a school of professional psychology, whose mission is to educate clinical psychologists. Happily I was able to continue teaching part time in the areas of psychology and religion, health psychology, professional ethics, and integrative psychotherapy until assuming recently a full-time faculty position.

I share this background because it provides the context in which my perspective on both psychology and theology is situated,[55] and it shows some of the influences on my views about both psychotherapy and spiritual direction. It also accounts for my attempts to integrate social, psychological, and spiritual perspectives. Moreover, it helps to explain my relative neglect of historical, political, economic, medical, and legal perspectives on problems in living.

Throughout my education and work experience, I have not related theological and psychological perspectives in a manner that has been satisfactory to me at either a theoretical or practical level. I have a need to do that now, perhaps in part because I have passed the landmark age of fifty, and partly because there is more time to reflect upon it now in my current academic position. Additionally, graduate psychology students with religious affections have responded so favorably when I have encouraged them to integrate their own spirituality and psychology into their theory and practice of counseling that their enthusiasm has inspired me to practice what I teach.

OVERVIEW OF THIS BOOK

My practical aim in this book is to construct a theory that will help me to reconcile my personal identity as a Christian with my professional identity as a clinical psychologist. More specifically, I am striving to relate my liberal Protestant faith with my experiential approach to psychotherapy. I believe that the detached objectivity of scientific psychology needs to be related to both the passionate self-transformations and the compassionate social reformations of religious faith in order to establish certitude and significance in the theory and practice of psychotherapy. In my view counseling is both a scientific process and a religious experience of reconciliation.

While reconciliation may be comprehended from a psychosocial perspective, I understand it primarily from both biblical and theological points of view. Biblically I rely upon Jesus' gospel of reconciliation; theologically I am coming from a liberal Protestant tradition. This tradition encourages a theology that is empirical as well as biblical, both prophetic and realistic, reasonable and intellectually honest, existential and relational, inclusive and nondogmatic, inspiring and reconciling.

This theological perspective is not the kind of rational liberalism of nineteenth-century Protestant theology, though its roots are firmly grounded there. While reason and experience are counted here as criteria and media of truth, so are scripture and tradition, by which I mean both religious and scientific tradition. In form, my theology is more in keeping with a prophetic, evangelical, and existential liberalism as others have defined these terms.[56] In content it varies from these forms by virtue of my theological norm. Its content is shaped by the theological norm of reconciliation grounded in the religious symbol of the kingdom of God taught by Jesus of Nazareth as recorded in the Synoptic Gospels.

I will discuss the meaning of this theological norm in chapter three. Here I wish to introduce it as a way of distinguishing my liberal theological perspective. I do not believe that the truth of the Christian faith rests upon the Logos doctrine as recorded in John 1:14 ("the Word became flesh"),[57] nor upon a doctrine of objective, vicarious atonement or exclusive salvation suggested by Romans 5 and John 3:16. I do not affirm as my theoretical norm the Pauline principle of "justification by faith" emphasized by Martin Luther.[58] Neither do I adopt the Apostle's Creed or other church confessions as the content for my theological norm. I consider historic creeds as testimonies of faith, not tests of faith.[59] While I am indebted to Paul Tillich in many ways, I do not affirm as my theological norm, "The New Being in Jesus as the Christ as our ultimate concern."[60] My theological norm is *"the kingdom of God in Jesus' gospel of reconciliation as our ultimate concern."*

This norm unites both the universal claim of Christianity in the concept of the kingdom of God with the concrete historical figure of Jesus of Nazareth as the one who proclaimed this reconciling gospel for the world. This theological norm also combines the material and essential Christian content with the formal and general definition of faith as ultimate concern.

In advocating this norm I make no claim to be presenting *the* Christian theology or that this is the necessary and indispensable norm to consider a theology Christian. Nor would I use this norm to support absolute or exclusive claims for the superiority of the Christian religion over others. I do claim this norm as grounded in the teachings of Jesus of Nazareth and as a foundation for the liberal Protestant theology developed in this book. Readers who prefer a more conservative theology may not find the discussion in this book congenial with their own perspectives, but hopefully it will be stimulating as an illustration of both a dialogical and constructive method of interaction between theology and psychology and in terms of content, that is, both methodologically and materially.

In this book I am engaging in theological reflections about the purpose of psychotherapy. Stated another way, in the process of constructing a normative theory of psychotherapy I am also developing a theological position. As a result, I have not written in a detached, impersonal style, but in a more existential manner as an expression of my faith informed by the Judeo-Christian tradition. This becomes evident particularly in chapters five and six. I have done so with the awareness that others find their root metaphors for life in different religious and philosophical traditions, and I have attempted to speak respectfully of other views in a manner consistent with the theme of this book. Where readers find my comments critical, hopefully they will also sense compassion and my willingness to take seriously other points of view.

In expressing my own point of view, I hope that I will not be like the cheerful dogmatist who said: "In controversial moments my perceptions rather fine; I always see both points of view: the one that's wrong—and mine."[61] Though my writing expresses deep convictions, I offer this work as an invitation to dialogue, not as a dogmatic position. One meets others in dialogue with the expectation that points of view initially presented may change over time. At best, dialogue serves as a medium of reconciliation, and in this context, a reconciliation between theology and psychology both theoretically and methodologically.

I have selected the concept of reconciliation as a bridge for dialogue, but not for a synthesis between an empirical Christian theology of ethical monotheism and an existential clinical psychology. I am leery of substituting a synthesis for a dialectic, lest the creative dynamic of ongoing dialogue be lost. The value of the idea of reconciliation is precisely that it serves as a medium for dynamic dialogue by virtue of its social, psychological, and theological meanings.[62] I believe the unique theories, methods, and findings from both psychology and theology may be related in a way that is more than a mutual tolerance or peaceful coexistence in a marriage of convenience called "integration." Informed by the rich nuances of this concept of reconciliation, psychology and theology may enjoy a genuine inter-action grounded in a common mission or purpose—contributing to the reconciled life.

As applied to the relation between psychology and theology, the metaphor of reconciliation connotes a rapprochement characterized by a mutually respectful engagement. This is a more limited connotation and different from the existential and theological meanings of reconciliation as the reunion of a divided self, a restoration of broken human relationships through love and justice, or as a healing communion between the human and divine. Nevertheless, the term is used con-sistently to distinguish this relation from both continued separation and from integration into one, unified discipline. The adjectives theoretical and method-ological help to circumscribe the meaning of reconciliation in chapters two and three as it relates to the autonomous disciplines of theology and psychology. Using this metaphor emphasizes that as persons, psychologists and theologians have experienced alienated relationships that are in need of healing.

I want to contribute to the reconciliation between these disciplines and groups of professionals without losing the distinctive scientific theory and empirical methodology of psychology, and while affirming simultaneously the gospel of reconciliation taught by Jesus of Nazareth. I leave it to my readers to decide whether or not I have met this challenge, to what degree, and in what ways. My intention is to illustrate one viable way of achieving the goal of reconciliation between psychology and religion, and thereby, to encourage others to find their way.

Neither a continued separation of these disciplines based upon hostile inter-actions in the past and mutual indifference in the present, nor some of the contem-porary struggles for theological domination of psychology under the guise of "integration" are satisfactory alternatives to me. Both separation and integration are positions distinct from the genuine reconciliation I am advocating based on a

continuous dialogue to build understanding and mutual respect of both their similarities and differences. This reconciliation is grounded particularly in the points
of convergence between these two disciplines evident in shared attitudes, philosophical foundations, empirical content, and ethical perspectives, which I discuss
in chapter two. Hopefully my own efforts in this direction will be received as an
invitation for others to feel the freedom to make their own creative contributions.
The goal of reconciling psychology and religion is commendable. The paths to
achieving it are diverse. Some will prove more fruitful than others. Let us judge
them by their fruits, including this one.

Using reconciliation as the central hypothetical construct, I am presenting one
form of a critical psychological theory. By "critical" I mean to say that my theory
is both descriptive and prescriptive, both objective and normative, both empirical
and philosophical. I concur with Don Browning's view[63] that clinical psychologies
cannot avoid a philosophical and ethical horizon and for this reason we need to be
self-conscious and explicit about the ontological premises, epistemological assumptions, and principles of moral obligation that undergird and shape our theories of
personality, psychopathology, and psychotherapy. I acknowledge that theories of
psychotherapy serve counselors and clients alike as systems of practical, moral
philosophy. They are not simply detached, scientific theories grounded solely in
objective, empirical research.

I apply linguistic, existential, and phenomenological analyses in chapters four,
five, and six to describe reconciliation as an experience and to understand the
meaning of this experience. I am attempting to explore the essence of this experience without identifying it with any particular dimension (social, psychological,
or spiritual), without limiting it to a specific psychological domain (cognitive,
behavioral, affective, or conative),[64] and without restricting it to a particular therapeutic modality.[65] I want to speak of reconciliation in a manner that does justice to
its inner nature as a lived experience.

My personal concern as a Christian is to understand my immediate experience
of reconciliation with God and its existential and social implications. My
professional concern as a clinical psychologist is to understand and facilitate the
experience of reconciliation in the context of the therapeutic relationship. I am not
writing about the actual experiences in psychotherapy reported by Christians;
rather, I am expressing a normative *theory* of psychotherapy informed by the
concept of reconciliation derived from the Judeo-Christian tradition.

I ground my theory philosophically in the monotheistic realism of the Judeo-
Christian tradition and in an empirical theology within the liberal Protestant
tradition. While I derive reconciliation as the goal of psychotherapy from Jesus'
teachings about the kingdom of God recorded in the Synoptic Gospels, I also
commend reconciliation as a norm independent of its religious roots. I adopt an
ethical point of view[66] to advocate reconciliation as the rational core of morality
and as both a value and moral obligation. This ethical perspective is implicit in the
descriptions of changes that occur in individuals who become more reconciling
persons.[67] Consequently, the changes occurring in a person who becomes more

wise, compassionate, courageous, thankful, and so forth are descriptions of ethical virtues, not simply psychological traits. I make more explicit ethical arguments for reconciliation as a normative concept in chapters six and seven.

In addition to viewing psychotherapeutic theory from an ethical perspective, I am viewing it also from a theological point of view. I endorse Paul Tillich's position that theology must be both kerygmatic and apologetic,[68] though I have a different conception of what constitutes the kerygmatic message, that is, the central Christian content. In my view kerygmatic theology must be guided by the criterion of Jesus' gospel of reconciliation. While expressed in both scripture and tradition, this message is not identical with either one, and both include much additional material that is even contradictory to Jesus' reconciling message about the kingdom of God. It is Jesus' teachings about the kingdom of God that I consider the essential Christian kerygma and the authentic foundation of the Christian faith, and it is this message that provides the norm for the theology of counseling presented here.

Theology must be kerygmatic, but it must be apologetic as well. By the latter term I mean that theology must be relevant as well as true. As Tillich noted, theology cannot merely announce its message irrespective of the situation addressed.[69] The "good news" will not be well received if it is dropped on our heads like a stone. Theology must be engaging: it must answer the questions raised by the contemporary situation. In the present period in which a therapeutic interpretation is salient,[70] a dialogue between theology and clinical psychology is crucial. Theology must be genuinely concerned with psychological interpretations of human experience, and insofar as these interpretations have implications for our understanding of self and the world, theology has both the right and the responsibility to address them.

Among the psychological domains theology needs to address are explanations of the structure and dynamics of personality, theories of human development and psychopathology, and theories about the purpose and process of psychotherapy. Among the significant questions raised in the current situation by psychological theories of psychotherapy are these: What does it mean to be a person? and What does it mean to say that an experience is therapeutic? Theological anthropology[71] addresses both questions by providing normative descriptions that may both inform and transform psychological understandings without dominating or controlling them. Theology must attempt to answer these psychological questions if it is to fulfill its apologetic function and avoid being judged as irrelevant by the professional, psychological community.

My own apologetic goal is to show that the historical gospel of reconciliation taught by Jesus of Nazareth in the religious symbol of the kingdom of God has power for present life and provides direction for it. One of the realms to which Jesus' gospel is relevant is the province of psychotherapy, particularly in defining its purpose, and that is the focus of this book. However, Jesus' teachings are relevant beyond the context of psychotherapy. They are relevant to life, both individually and collectively. Implicit in this statement is my view that while the concept of reconciliation is rooted in the particular teachings of Jesus about the kingdom of God, this compelling concept and his religious symbol have universal meanings that transcend the location and context in which they first appeared. The power and purpose of Jesus' gospel are relevant to all persons, places, and times. This observation does not prove Christianity as the final revelation of absolute truth. Such a position cannot be proven either logically or historically; nor as a Christian pluralist[72] do I feel obliged to attempt such proof. An apologetic theology need not be an arrogant theology; it may be offered in an invitational tone as a personal confession of faith for others to consider and try for themselves. This is a process akin to testing empirically the validity of a reasonable hypothesis. In this case, however, the test is existential, not merely a controlled, analogue experiment.

These introductory comments indicate the theoretical nature of this work. But this is not merely a theoretical treatise. I speak from a personal vantage point as well as that of a professional psychologist. While the first half of this book is theoretical in content and discursive in tone, subsequent chapters reflect my specific Christian convictions derived from the teachings of Jesus of Nazareth presented in a more personal and existential tone. Both my selection of the dimensions of reconciliation and their meanings are influenced by my understanding of Jesus' experience of reconciliation expressed in his teachings recorded in the Synoptic Gospels in the religious symbol of the kingdom of God. While Christian pastors will find homiletical material in these descriptions of the reconciled life, others may view them as somewhat parochial. I ask the reader to keep in mind my phenomenological approach. I have selected Jesus' experience of reconciliation as a particular example in which to discover the more general structure of reconciliation as a lived experience. From a scientific perspective, the dimensions described may be considered as hypotheses subject to further research. Subsequent phenomenological and experimental studies are likely to provide other elements as well. I encourage my readers to discover the salient dimensions of reconciliation in other religious and non-religious sources more congenial to their own worldview. As a Christian psychologist, I consider Jesus' experience of reconciliation to be normative and his teachings about reconciliation to be true, hence it is to his experience and teachings that I turn for a general understanding about the structure of this therapeutic and liberating experience.

One more personal remark brings this introduction to a close. When I think about what has sustained me through my own personal and professional struggles, I realize it has been my faith in God and love of family, not my psychological theories. This book is written as a gift of gratitude for the beatitude God has granted me. I hope that it will help mental health professionals, Christian ministers, pastoral counselors, and lay Christian counselors to proclaim through their counseling the good news of great joy—the kingdom of God has come near to you (Lk.10:17–20).

NOTES

1. I shall be using the terms psychotherapy and counseling interchangeably throughout this work. While legitimate distinctions have been drawn in the past, their differences are less salient for the purposes of this book than the fact that they are both guided by general therapeutic goals. In this formal sense, personal counseling and depth psychotherapy are similar, though their specific goals may differ as well as their strategies and procedures. Several definitions of therapy are provided by Carson, R. & Wedding, D. (1989). *Current psychotherapies.* Itasca, IL: F. E. Peacock Publishers. For a discussion of the similarities in the goals and structures of psychotherapy and counseling, see Patterson, C. H. (1980). *Theories of counseling and psychotherapy.* New York: Harper Collins, pp. xvii–xxii.

2. For a review of literature in this area, see Gorsuch, R. (1988). Psychology of religion. *Annual Review of Psychology, 39,* 201–221. A recent text is by Wulff, D. (1991). *Psychology of religion: Classic and contemporary views.* New York: Wiley.

3. Examples of conservative Christian critiques of psychology as religion include Vande Kemp, H. (1986). Dangers of psychologism: The place of God in psychology. *Journal of Psychology and Theology, 14,* 97–109; Wallach, A. & Wallach, I. (1983). *Psychology's sanction for selfishness.* San Francisco: W. H. Freeman; and Vitz, P. C. (1977). *Psychology as religion: The cult of self-worship.* Grand Rapids, MI: William B. Erdsman.

4. Tillich views counseling as one of the personal areas in which the church's constructive function is expressed. The constructive function is distinct from the constitutive, expanding, and relating functions of the church. See Tillich, P. (1963). *Systematic theology* (Vol. 3). Chicago: University of Chicago Press, pp.188–216, especially 196–212. The apostle Paul used the phrase "ministry of reconciliation" in 2 Corinthians 5:18-20. Disciples of Christ may be described appropriately as ambassadors of reconciliation.

5. H. R. Niebuhr observed that revelation cannot be considered a subjective or individualistic affair because God's self disclosure always occurs to persons in history, that is, to persons in a social, communal context. Since it is mediated to us through a community, every view of the universal from the finite standpoint of the individual is subject to the test of experience on the part of companions who look from the same standpoint in the same direction. See Niebuhr, H. R. (1960). *The meaning of revelation.* New York: Macmillan, pp. 20–21.

6. Witherington, B. (1995). *The Jesus quest: The third search for the Jew of Nazareth.* Downers Grove, IL: InterVarsity Press, pp. 27, 38. Jesus is likely to have known and spoken Greek as a second language according to Funk, R. W. (1996). *Honest to Jesus: Jesus for a new millennium.* New York: HarperSanFracisco, p. 79.

7. For the distinction between a wood-worker and carpenter, see Borg, M. (1994b). *Meeting Jesus again for the first time.* New York: HaperSanFrancisco, p. 26. As one who worked with wood (in Greek, *tekton*), Jesus was most likely at the lower end of the peasant class, more marginalized than a peasant who owned a small piece of land.

8. Strauss, D. F. (1835). *Das Leben Jesu.* Cited by Witheringon, B. (1995). *The Jesus quest: The third search for the Jew of Nazareth.* Downers Grove, IL: InterVarsity Press, p. 9. See also Borg, M. (1994a). *Jesus in contemporary scholarship.* Valley Forge, PA: Trinity Press International, p. 3; Borg, M. (1988). A renaissance in Jesus studies. *Theology Today, 45,* 280–292; Borg, M. (1994c). Reflections on a discipline: A North American perspective. In B. Chilton & C. Evans (Eds.), *Studying the historical Jesus: Evaluations of the state of current research* (pp. 9–31). Leiden: E. J. Brill; and Wright, N. & Neill, S. (1988). *The interpretation of the new testament.* New York: Oxford University Press, pp. 379–403. One bibliography of scholarly books about the Jesus of history lists

over fifty titles, forty-two since 1980. See Charlesworth, J. (1986). From barren mazes to gentle rappings: The emergence of Jesus research. *Princeton Seminary Bulletin, 7,* 221–230. Equally impressive is the burgeoning literature on the use of social science methods in New Testament studies. More than 250 publications were recorded between 1980 and 1988. See Harrington, D. (1988). Second testament exegesis and the social sciences: A bibliography. *Biblical Theology Bulletin, 18,* 77–85. For another assessment of the major scholarly contributions to the current quest for the historical Jesus, see Wright, W. T. (1996). *Jesus and the victory of God: Christian origins and the question of God* (Vol. 2). Minneapolis, MN: Fortress Press.

9. Witherington, B. (1995). *The Jesus quest: The third search for the Jew of Nazareth.* Downers Grove, IL: InterVarsity Press, p. 77. Crossan introduced one of his books by characterizing historical Jesus research as "something of a scholarly bad joke." His book is a very scholarly example of contemporary Jesus research. See Crossan, J. D. (1991). *The historical Jesus: The life of a Mediterranean Jewish peasant.* New York: HarperSanFrancisco.

10. Witherington, B. (1995). *The Jesus quest: The third search for the Jew of Nazareth.* Downers Grove, IL: InterVarsity Press, pp. 82, 253 n.2.

11. These various portraits of the historical Jesus have been summarized by Borg, M. (1994a). *Jesus in contemporary scholarship.* Valley Forge, PA: Trinity Press International, pp. 18–68, and by Eckardt, A. (1992). *Reclaiming the Jesus of history: Christology today.* Minneapolis, MN: Fortress Press, pp. 25–134. Borg presented a fourfold portrait of the pre-Easter Jesus as (1) a charismatic holy man of the Spirit, (2) a teacher of wisdom (sage), (3) a prophet in the sense of the classical prophets of ancient Israel, and (4) the founder of a movement to reform and revitalize the Judaism of his time. Borg, M. (1994a). *Jesus in contemporary scholarship.* Valley Forge, PA: Trinity Press International, p. 12. A similar view was expressed in his less technical book. See Borg, M. (1994b). *Meeting Jesus again for the first time.* New York: HarperSanFrancisco, p. 30.

12. Witherington, B. (1995). *The Jesus quest: The third search for the Jew of Nazareth.* Downers Grove, IL: InterVarsity Press, p. 264, n.65. A current a-historical perspective is presented by L. Johnson, who argues that the Christian faith should be based not on the historical Jesus but on the resurrected Christ proclaimed by the New Testament. See Johnson, L. T. (1996). *The real Jesus: The misguided quest for the historical Jesus and the truth of the traditional gospels.* New York: Harper Collins.

13. Bultmann, R. (1958). *Jesus Christ and mythology.* New York: Charles Scribner's Sons. For theological appraisals of Bultmann's program of demythologizing the New Testament records see Bartsch, H. W. (Ed.). (1961). *Kerygma and myth: A theological debate.* New York: Harper and Row, and Macquarrie, J. (1960). *The scope of demythologizing. Bultmann and his critics.* London: SCM Press. Paul Meier suggested that even the location of Jesus' birth is legendary. His birthplace was more likely Nazareth than Bethlehem. Meier, P. (1991). *A marginal Jew: Rethinking the historical Jesus* (Vol. 1). New York: Doubleday, pp. 214–216.

14. Borg, M. (1994b). *Meeting Jesus again for the first time.* New York: Harper-SanFrancisco, p. 30.

15. Borg's view of Jesus as a spirit person finds a parallel in Macquarrie's portrait of Jesus as a mediator, namely, a human being who is immersed in the Spirit of God. Macquarrie prefers Schleiermacher's term of "mediator" to other terms such as savior, prophet, redeemer, or revealer to describe spiritual geniuses such as Moses, Jesus, Buddha, Krishna, and Muhammad, whose profound encounters with Holy Being have served as the basis of visions of the divine preserved in sacred scriptures, and whose visions have been the most powerful factors shaping human life. See Macquarrie, J. (1996). *Mediators between*

human and divine: From Moses to Muhammad. New York: Continuum, pp. vii, 7–8, 103, 140, 147. The biblical witness records that Jesus was received as one who came in the name of the Lord (Mt. 21: 9, 23, 39; Lk. 11:9). Sanders portrays Jesus as a charismatic autonomous prophet and viceroy of God by virtue of Jesus' immediate relationship to God. Sanders, E. P. (1994). *The historical figure of Jesus.* New York: Penguin Books, pp. 238–239. He writes, "in the view of all three gospels, Jesus was following the guidance of the Spirit of God" (Ibid., p. 112).

16. It was Bultmann's conclusion that "we can know almost nothing concerning the life and personality of Jesus since the early Christian sources show no interest in either, are moreover fragmentary and often legendary, and other sources about Jesus do not exist" (Bultmann, R. [1958]. *Jesus and the word.* New York: Scribner's, p. 253). Both the form-critical method upon which his conclusion is based, and his premise that the Synoptics present the preaching of the early church (kerygma) have been challenged (Witherington, B. [1995]. *The Jesus quest: The third search for the Jew of Nazareth.* Downers Grove, IL: InterVarsity Press, pp. 79, 143–144, 253, 274 n.23). One may acknowledge these challenges while accepting both Bultmann's key emphasis upon Jesus' teachings as indications of Jesus' purpose (p. 10), and his method of separating Jesus' message from the mythical worldview in which it was presented.

17. Tillich, P. (1957). *Systematic theology* (Vol. 2). Chicago: University of Chicago Press, pp. 107–108. It is important to note, however, that Tillich argues that the New Testament is the witness to Jesus as the Messiah, not merely as a historical person called Jesus of Nazareth. For Tillich, the foundation of faith is not the Jesus of history as fact, but the reception by faith of Jesus as the Christ. Ibid., pp. 101–117. As a counterpoint, Funk notes that one need not be an empiricist or positivist in order to affirm that answers to such questions as what Jesus taught should be informed by historical facts bearing on that question. To reject the findings of reliable historical investigation is to risk a religion of myth and fantasy, superstition, and magic. See Funk, R. W. (1996). *Honest to Jesus: Jesus for a new millennium.* New York: HarperSanFrancisco, p. 2.

18. This distinction between the religion of Jesus and the religion about Jesus was made explicit in the nineteenth century by the liberal Protestant theologian, Adolf von Harnack (1986). *What is Christianity?* Philadelphia: Fortress Press. Harnack summarized the essence of Christianity in terms of Jesus' teachings about (1) the kingdom of God and its coming, (2) God the Father and the infinite value of the human soul, and (3) the higher righteousness and the commandment to love (p. 51). This he judged to be "the Gospel within the Gospel" (p. 14). His most controversial view was that "the Gospel has to do with the Father only, not the Son, as Jesus proclaimed" (p. xv). A contemporary expression of the distinction between the gospel of Jesus and the Jesus of the gospels is Funk, C. W. (1996). *Honest to Jesus: Jesus for a new millennium.* New York: HarperSanFrancisco, pp. 20, 41, 58, 197–216. See also Mitchell, S. (1991). *The gospel according to Jesus.* New York: HarperCollins. While Jesus' own theology was different from later theologies in the New Testament, we can find his theology within the Synoptic Gospels as noted by E. P. Sanders (1994). *The historical figure of Jesus.* New York: Penguin Books, pp. 2–6, 57, 63, 66–75.

19. It was H. R. Niebuhr's critique that Western Christianity manifests both henotheistic and polytheistic expressions of faith, just as it contained implicit trends toward the radical monotheism which Jesus taught (Niebuhr, H. R. [1960]. *Radical monotheism and Western culture. With supplementary essays.* Louisville, KY: Westminster/John Knox Press, pp. 38– 64).

20. The phrase is a reference to Martin Luther's summary of Pauline theology as "justification by Grace through faith." Luther used this norm to interpret the Bible as a

whole based upon Paul's letters as his primary source (Tillich, P. [1951]. *Systematic theology* [Vol. l]. Chicago: University of Chicago Press, p. 50).

21. An existential interpretation of Jesus' message emphasizes its value in helping us to understand our own existence, including the contingencies and necessities of our own life purpose. It expresses also Jesus' call to a decision of repentance and obedience to the will of God. This is not, however, substituting an existential philosophy for Jesus' teachings. As Bultmann noted: "When we encounter the words of Jesus in history, we do not judge them by a philosophical system with reference to their rational validity; they meet us with the question of how we are to interpret our own existence" (Bultmann, R. [1958]. *Jesus and the word.* New York: Scribner's Sons, p. 11).

22. Witherington, B. (1995). *The Jesus quest,* p. 10. A contemporary expression of an eschatological view of Jesus' message is Reiser, M. (1997). *Jesus and judgment: The eschatological proclamation in its Jewish context.* Minneapolis, MN: Fortress Press. While Sanders affirms that Jesus had an eschatological message, it was not an apocalyptic vision of the destruction of the world, but of God's creation of an ideal world. See Sanders, E. P. (1993). *The historical figure of Jesus.* New York: Penguin Books, pp. 95, 182–185, 189. Members of the Jesus Seminar have rejected the apocalyptic interpretation of Jesus' message. See for example, Funk, R. W. (1996). *Honest to Jesus: Jesus for a new millennium.* New York: HarperSanFrancisco, pp. 167–168, 314.

23. Bultmann, R. (1958). *Jesus and the word,* p. 10. Bultmann noted that Jesus' purpose can be comprehended only as teaching, and his teachings are historical events in time, not super-historical, rationalistic propositions about truth (p. 10). Furthermore, our own existential encounter with the Jesus of history occurs primarily in response to his message, not as a response to the biographical details of his life or to an interpreted personality profile, nor to fantastic theological claims about his person or work (p. 6).

24. Paul Tillich uses the term "New Being" to refer to the reality and power of reconciliation manifested in Jesus as the Christ. Tillich, P. (1951). *Systematic theology* (Vol. l). Chicago: University of Chicago Press, pp. 49–50.

25. For this conclusion I have relied upon New Testament scholars such as Bultmann, R. (1956). *Theology of the new testament* (Vol. 1). New York: Charles Scribner's Sons; Bultmann, R. (1958). *Jesus and the word.* New York: Scribner's Sons; Bultmann, R. (1963). *The history of the synoptic tradition.* Oxford: Basil Blackwell; *The interpreter's dictionary of the bible: An illustrated encyclopedia* (Vols. 1–4). Nashville: Abindgon Press, 1962; Sanders, E. P. (1993). *The historical figure of Jesus.* New York: Penguin Books; and Vermes, G. (1993). *The religion of Jesus the Jew.* Minneapolis. MN: Fortress Press. Biblical scholars associated with the Jesus Seminar have dated the Sayings Gospel Q and the Gospel of Thomas as earlier and reliable sources of Jesus' sayings. See Funk, R. W. (1996). *Honest to Jesus: Jesus for a new millennium.* New York: HarperSanFrancisco, pp. 124–125, 134–135. Further discussion of the Synoptic sources is provided in chapter three.

26. For example, judging from the frequency of biblical quotations of the Pauline corpus, Jay Adams seems to base his nouthetic counseling mostly upon Paul's teachings in addition to the Book of Proverbs. See Adams, J. (1970). *Competent to counsel.* Nutley, NJ: Presbyterian and Reformed Publishing Company, pp. 41–45. See also the use of Paul's message about renewal of the mind in Romans 12 as the point of departure for another expression of cognitive-behavior therapy interpreted in a conservative Christian context by Crabb, L. (1975). *Basic principles of biblical counseling.* Grand Rapids, MI: Zondervan Publishing House, p. 80.

27. The Christian theologian, Paul Tillich, lamented the replacement of Paul's letters by John's gospel as a primary source of theology in the post-apostolic period, and by the predominance of the Synoptic Gospels and even Old Testament prophets in modern

Protestantism. I do not agree that the Synoptic Gospels are the predominant sources of either popular Christianity or Christian theology today, and I do not accept Tillich's reliance upon Paul's letters as primary sources (e.g., 2 Corinthians 5:17; Romans 8). See for example, Tillich, P. (1951). *Systematic theology* (Vol. 2). Chicago: University of Chicago Press, pp.17, 23, 47–52; 50, n.13; and (Vol. 3), pp. 144–148. In my view, orthodox Christianity has been shaped more by the theology of Paul who never knew Jesus of Nazareth than by the theology of Jesus whom all Christians claim knew God.

28. A scholarly introduction to the central theme of reconciliation in Pauline theology is Martin, R. (1981). *Reconciliation: A study of Paul's theology.* Atlanta: John Knox Press.

29. The position here is comparable to that expressed by my own denomination in its statement that creeds and confessions are testimonies of faith rather than tests of faith. See *The United Church of Christ. Who we are, what we believe.* Cleveland, Ohio: The United Church Press. A comparable position is expressed by the Presbyterian Church, USA (1967). *Book of order*, #49.042; and (1991) *The book of confessions*, #9.03. New York: Office of the General Assembly.

30. The fourfold authority of scripture, tradition, reason, and experience for both theology and faith has been expressed in the Methodist tradition as the Wesleyan quadrilateral. See Abraham, W. (1985). The Wesleyan quadrilateral. In T. Runyon (Ed.), *Wesleyan theology today: A bicentennial theological consultation* (pp.119–126). Nashville: Kingswood Books. Trust in the authority of reason and experience characterizes liberal religion expressed by Mendelsohn, J. (1964). *Why am I a Unitarian-Universalist?* Boston: Beacon Press, pp. 64, 83, 95. See also Buehrens, J., & Church, F. (1989). *Our chosen faith: An introduction to Unitarian Universalism.* Boston: Beacon Press, pp. xiv, xvii, xxiii, 21, 28, 35–38, 121–123, 163; Mendelsohn, J. (1995). *Being liberal in an illiberal age.* Boston: Skinner House Books, pp. xii, 40–43; and Marshall, G. (1991). *Challenge of a liberal faith* (3rd ed.). Boston: Skinner House, pp. 108, 182. Authority to formulate its own covenants and confessions of faith is granted to the local congregation in the United Church of Christ. See Shinn, R. (1990). Afterword: The United Church of Christ Tomorrow. In D. Johnson & C. Hambrick-Stowe (Eds.), *Theology and identity: Traditions, movements, and the polity of the United Church of Christ* (p. 182). Cleveland, OH: United Church Press.

31. Throckmorton, B. (1992). *Gospel parallels: A comparison of the synoptic gospels.* Nashville: Thomas Nelson Publishers. This edition is based upon the New Revised Standard Version of the Bible and includes noncanonical references such as the gospel of Thomas discovered in 1945. It does not limit the database to the 101 citations of Jesus' teachings considered authentic by the Jesus Seminar. For a listing, see Funk, R. W. (1996). *Honest to Jesus: Jesus for a new millennium.* New York: HarperSanFrancisco, pp. 139, 326–335. See also Funk, R. W., Hoover, R., & The Jesus Seminar. (1993). *The five Gospels: The research for the authentic words of Jesus.* New York: Macmillan.

32. For references to earlier views, see Vande Kemp, H. (1984). *Psychology and theology in western thought (1672–1965): A historical and annotated bibliography.* Mill Wood, NY: Kraus, and Vande Kemp, H. (1996). Historical perspective: Religion and clinical psychology in America. In E. Shafranske (Ed.), *Religion and the clinical practice of psychology* (pp. 71–112). Washington, DC: American Psychological Association. For discussion of more contemporary efforts at integration, see Foster, J. D., Horn, D. A., & Watson, S. (1988). The popularity of integration models, 1980-1985. *Journal of Psychology and Theology, 16,* 3–14. See also Clinton, S. M. (1990). A critique of integration models. *Journal of Psychology and Theology, 18,* 13–20; Fleck, J. R., & Carter, J. D. (Eds.). (1981). *Psychology and theology: Integrative readings.* Nashville, TN: Abingdon; Worthington, E. (1994). A blueprint for intradisciplinary integration. *Journal of Psychol-*

ogy and Theology, 22, 79–86; and Ingram, J. (1995). Contemporary issues and Christian models of integration: Into the modern/postmodern age. *Journal of Psychology and Theology, 23*(1), 3–14; and Narramore, S.B. (1997). Psychology and theology: Twenty-five years of theoretical integration. *Journal of Psychology and Theology, 25*(1), 6–10. For an integrationist's perspective on the use of the Bible in psychology see Johnson, E. (1992). A place for the Bible within psychological science. *Journal of Psychology and Theology, 20*(1), 346–355; Wimberly, E. (1994). *Using scripture in pastoral counseling.* Nashville, TN: Abingdon Press; and Rollins, W. (1997). The bible and psychology: New directions in biblical scholarship. *Pastoral Psychology, 45*(3), 163–177.

33. Herink, R. (Ed.). (1980). *The psychotherapy handbook: The A to Z guide to more than 250 different therapies in use today.* New York: Meridian. For a discussion of typologies of numerous theological systems and Christologies, see Cowdell, S. (1996). *Is Jesus unique? A study of recent Christology.* New York: Paulist Press. In terms of his own typology, the present work is an expression of a liberal Christology.

34. Patterson, C. H. (1980). *Theories of counseling and psychotherapy* (4th ed.). New York: Harper & Row, p. xx. Perhaps the same attitude could be affirmed toward religion.

35. Capps, D. (1981). *Biblical approaches to pastoral counseling.* Philadelphia: Westminster Press.

36. Adams, J. (1977). *Competent to counsel.* Nutley, NJ: Presbyterian and Reformed Publishing Co. More moderate Christian, cognitive theories of therapy are Propst, L. (1988). *Psychotherapy in a religious framework.* New York: Human Sciences Press; and McMinn, M. (1996). *Psychology, theology, and spirituality in Christian counseling.* Wheaton, IL: Tyndale House. These authors present a perspective more conservative than my own.

37. Borg, M. (1994b). *Meeting Jesus again for the first time.* New York: HarperSan-Francisco, pp. 69–95, especially p. 89, n.4.

38. Oglesby, W. (1980). *Biblical themes for pastoral care.* Nashville. TN: Abingdon Press.

39. Capps, D. (1979). *Pastoral care: A thematic approach.* Philadelphia: Westminster Press.

40. Clinebell, H. (1984). *Basic types of pastoral care and counseling.* Nashville, TN: Abingdon Press. A companion volume is by Stone, H., & Clements, W. (Eds.) (1991). *Handbook for basic types of pastoral care and counseling.* Nashville, TN: Abingdon Press. See also Clinebell, H. (1995). *Counseling for spiritually empowered wholeness: A hope-centered approach.* New York: The Haworth Pastoral Press.

41. I am indebted to Dr. Clyde Steckel of United Theological Seminary in New Brighton, Minnesota for this insight expressed in a personal communication March 20, 1997. For references relating reconciliation and liberation, see chapter 4, n.53. The way of reconciliation is the way of peace, but there is no lasting peace without justice. See Rader, W. (1989). Just peace and revolutionary nonviolence. *Prism, 4*(2), 48–61.

42. See Carlson, D. E. (1976). Jesus' style of relating: The search for a biblical view of counseling. *Journal of Psychology and Theology, 4,* 181–192.

43. For a discussion of goals and values in psychotherapy, see Mahrer, A. H. (Ed.). (1967). *The goals of psychotherapy.* New York: Appleton-Century-Crofts; Burton, A. (1972). *Interpersonal psychotherapy.* Englewood Cliffs, NJ: Prentice-Hall; Patterson, C. H. (1985). *The therapeutic relationship: Foundations for an eclectic therapy.* Monterey, CA: Brooks/Cole Publishing Company, pp. 12–28; and Patterson, C. H., & Hidore, S. (1997). *Successful psychotherapy: A caring, loving relationship.* Northvale, NJ: Jason Aronson.

44. For a discussion of some classic Christian theories of personality see Burns. J. P. (Ed.). (1981). *Theological anthropology*. Minneapolis, MN: Fortress Press. Other relevant references include Meehl, P., Klann, R., Schmiedling, A., Breimeier, K., & Schroeder-Slomann. S. (1958). *What then is man? A symposium of theology, psychology, and psychiatry*. St. Louis, MO: Concordia Publishing House; and Lauer, E., & Mlecko, J. (Eds.). (1982). *A Christian understanding of the human person: Basic readings*. New York: Paulist Press. See also n.71.

45. As a type of explanation, teleology is discussed further in chapter six dealing with the conative (intentional) dimension of psychological reconciliation.

46. See for example, Fowler, J. (1981). *Stages of faith: The psychology of human development and the guest for meaning*. San Francisco: Harper & Row; and Fowler, J. (1987). *Faith development and pastoral care*. Minneapolis, MN: Fortress Press; and Joy, D. (Ed.). (1983). *Moral development foundations: Judeo-Christian alternatives to Piaget/Kolberg*. Nashville, TN: Abingdon Press.

47. The efficacy of forgiveness as therapy has been demonstrated in empirical research. See note 5 in chapter two for illustrative references. For theoretical models relating salvation and health see Lapsley, J. (1972). *Salvation and health: The interlocking processes of life*. Philadelphia: Westminster Press, and Campbell, A. (1997). *Health as liberation: Medicine, theology, and the quest for justice*. Cleveland, OH: Pilgrim Press.

48. Kirk Farnsworth (1985) expressed a similar conclusion in his book, *Wholehearted Integration: Harmonizing psychology and Christianity through word and deed*. Grand Rapids, MI: Baker Book House. A related emphasis upon relationship-oriented therapy was expressed by Kirwan, W. (1984). *Biblical concepts for Christian counseling*. Grand Rapids, Michigan: Baker Book House, and by Oglesby, W. (1980). *Biblical themes for pastoral care*. Nashville. TN: Abingdon.

49. A "Spirit-centered therapeutic relationship" includes consciousness of the sacred transpersonal dimensions of life as an essential therapist attribute in addition to empathic understanding, unconditional positive regard, and genuineness experienced by the client. For discussion of the Spirit-consciousness of Jesus, see Borg, M. (1994b). *Meeting Jesus again for the first time*. New York: HarperSanFrancisco, n.26 (p. 42) and n.28 (p. 43).

50. Parsons, T., & Shils, E. (Eds.). (1962). *Toward a general theory of action*. Cambridge, MA: Harvard University Press. Functionalism is a theoretical orientation that treats society as if it were composed of mutually dependent and determinant parts called subsystems (e.g., the polity, economy, education, religion, and family) working together to maintain, enhance, and change the social system as a whole. It is a holistic, systems perspective on society viewed as a dynamic, living organism. Although adherence to functionalism has declined recently in the academic discipline of sociology, it remains influential. Several references are found in Ashley, D., & Orenstein, D. (1990). *Sociological theory: classical statements*. Boston: Allyn and Bacon, pp. 30, 95–96, 119, 128, 131, 173, 296.

51. Human freedom is affirmed in voluntaristic theories of action. From this perspective, human behavior is always an outcome of free will, at least partially, hence not wholly determined. In sociological theory, voluntarism is the view that social behavior involves freedom to choose between alternative forms of social behavior. Voluntaristic action is (a) goal-directed (teleological), (b) takes means into consideration, (c) is normatively regulated with respect to the choice of ends and means, and (d) depends upon reason and choice. In a voluntaristic theory, the human will is one cause and explanation of social behavior. It is a theory espoused more by classical sociologists than by academic psychologists. See Ashley, D., & Orenstein, D. (1990). *Sociological theory: Classical statements*. Boston: Allyn and Bacon, pp. 12, 28, 30–31, 95–96, 119, 128–129, 131–132, 173, 272, 296, 398.

52. Two introductory works are Merton, T. (1957). *The silent life*. New York: Farrar, Straus, & Giroux, and Merton, T. (1961). *New seeds of contemplation*. New York: New Directions Book. A good secondary source is Higgins, J. (Ed.). (1975). *Thomas Merton on prayer*. New York: Image Books.

53. The Quaker emphasis upon religious experience is illustrated by Steere, D. V. (1984). *Quaker spirituality: Selected writings*. Mahwah, NJ: Paulist Press. Recognition by Catholic writers of Douglas Steere's contribution to development of the Ecumenical Institute of Spirituality is found in Hinson, E. G. (Ed.). (1993). *Spirituality in ecumenical perspective*. Louisville, KY: Westminster/John Knox Press.

54. Mowrer emphasized the counselor's own confession as central to a therapeutic outcome of Integrity Therapy. See Mowrer, O. H. (1960). Sin, the lesser of two evils. *American Psychologist, 15,* 303; Mowrer, O. H. (1964). *The new group therapy.* Princeton, NJ: Van Nostrand; and Mowrer, O. H. (1967). Modeling the role is the heart of integrity therapy. *The Dis-Coverer, 4*(4), 5. Mowrer felt such a need to confess himself that he did so publicly in print. See Mowrer, O. H. (1966). *Abnormal reactions or actions.* Dubuque, IA: William C. Brown Co. See also Drakeford, J. W. (1967). *Integrity therapy.* Nashville, TN: Broadman Press; Mowrer, O. H. (Ed.). (1966). *Morality and mental health.* Chicago: Rand McNally Co.; and Mowrer, O. H. (1972). Integrity groups: Basic principles and objective. *The Counseling Psychologist, 3,* 7–32.

55. All knowledge is situated in the writer's social context and is bounded by the interpretive horizons of its procedures as noted by Harding, S. (1991). *Whose science? Whose knowledge?* Ithaca, NY: Cornell University Press. It is critical that we question unarticulated ideological elements that permeate our own theories, both religious and scientific. But recognition of the potential biases need not lead us to succumb to either ethical relativism or cynical skepticism.

56. For elements distinguishing a prophetic from a rationalistic liberal theology, see Stackhouse, M. (Ed.). (1976). *James Luther Adams: On being human religiously*. Boston: Beacon Press, pp. 12–19, 43. For a summary of nineteenth century Protestant, evangelical liberalism see Niebuhr, H. R. (1988). *The kingdom of God in America*. Hanover, NH: Wesleyan University Press, pp. 186–190. Tillich contrasts existential with legalistic liberalism. He favors the former over the latter, but he criticizes both as attempts to establish the historical foundations of the Christian faith in the message or teachings of Jesus. Tillich, P. (1957). *Systematic theology* (Vol. 2). Chicago: University of Chicago Press, pp. 105–106. For a critique of liberal theology, seminaries, and churches, see Oden, T. (1995). *Requiem: A lament in three movements.* Nashville, TN: Abingdon Press.

57. The term "Word" is translated from "Logos." Tillich cites this Logos doctrine about the incarnation of the divine in the human, and the universal in the concrete as the necessary and exclusive foundation for any theology that claims to be Christian. This criterion makes his theological system dependent upon John's Gospel in which this doctrine is presented, though he cites Paul's letters as his primary source. Tillich, P. (1951). *Systematic theology* (Vol. 1). Chicago: University of Chicago Press, p. 17. See his discussion relating a Logos Christology with a Spirit Christology in his *Systematic theology* (Vol. 3), pp. 144–149. Tillich notes that the Synoptic Gospels presented a Spirit Christology.

58. This norm depends primarily upon the theology of Paul (e.g., Romans 3:26–28; 5:1; 10:4, Galatians 2:16, 3:24). In this manner, Luther emphasized Paul's teachings over Jesus' message recorded in the Synoptic Gospels of Matthew, Mark, and Luke.

59. This is a principle expressed in *The United Church of Christ: Who we are, what we believe*. Cleveland, Ohio: The United Church Press. The United Church of Christ is a liberal Christian denomination if we mean by the term "liberal" "a willingness to use

historical-critical tools in the interpretation of scripture, an appreciation of the contributions of the post-Enlightenment natural and social sciences in our anthropological and sociological analyses, a willingness to work ecumenically with other denominations and sympathetically with the world religions, and an inner tendency to be active for peace, human rights, and social justice." Stackhouse, M. (1986). Obedience to Christ and engaged in the world. *Prism, 1*(2), 9. See chapter 3, n.24.

60. This is the full expression of Tillich's theological norm containing both the material element or content ("the New Being in Jesus as the Christ") and the formal element defining faith ("ultimate concern"). Tillich, P. (1951). *Systematic theology* (Vol. 1). Chicago: University of Chicago Press, p. 50.

61. Quoted in Bratton, F. (1968). *The legacy of the liberal spirit.* Gloucester, MA: Peters Smith Publishing, p. vii.

62. Perhaps others will consider this a useful construct for interpreting physical, chemical, and biological phenomena. As an example, a principle of reconciliation avoids the static connotations of the biological principle of homeostasis and may provide a heuristic perspective on the dynamics of life itself. There is also potential value in speculating about the process of reconciliation in terms of the creation, transformation, and conservation of energy. Does the concept of reconciliation help us to understand the dynamics of energy and force fields? It is my own belief that reconciling events are energizing and forceful, or in phenomenal language, they are inspiring and produce change in individuals and societies. As another example, how does one reconcile a belief in a lawful order of cause-effect connections with a theory of the universe as chaos? Could we speak instead of a reconciling universe? A classic Christian affirmation is that God was in Christ reconciling the world (2 Cor. 5:18–19). A better English translation than "world" is "cosmos" based on the Greek word *kosmos.* See Shinn, R. (1990). *Confessing our faith: An interpretation of the statement of faith of the United Church of Christ.* Cleveland, OH: United Church Press, p. 71.

63. A "critical psychological theory" recognizes that theories of psychotherapy assume and provide a basic vision of the nature of the world, the purpose of life, and principles by which life should be lived. Browning advocates creating a variety of interdisciplinary, critical theories pertaining to the various provinces of life. As a basis for a normative theory of psychotherapy he advocates a "limited theism" and "ethic of mutuality." See Browning, D. (1987). *Religious thought and the modern psychologies: A critical conversation in the theology of culture.* Philadelphia: Fortress Press, pp. xi, 5, 238, 242–245. Jones suggests that a defining characteristic of a critical theory is that interpretations are made from an explicitly value-committed framework (Jones, S. L. [1994]. A constructive relationship for religion with the science and profession of psychology: Perhaps the boldest model yet. *American Psychologist, 49*[3], 185). See also Haberman, J. (1983). Interpretive social science vs. hermeneutics. In Bellah et al., *Social science as moral inquiry*, pp. 251–270, cited by Browning, D. (1987), p. 256, n.13.

64. The conative dimension refers to the experience of willing and deciding in favor of an alternative for the sake of which one intentionally acts.

65. I have not found compelling evidence for the superiority of one empirically derived therapeutic orientation over another. Meta-analyses have not supported that conclusion. See for example, Smith, M., & Glass, G. (1977). Meta-analysis of psychotherapy outcome studies. *American Psychologist, 32,* 752–760, and Lipsey, M., & Wilson, D. (1993). The efficacy of psychological, educational, and behavioral treatment: Confirmation from meta-analysis. *American Psychologist, 48,* 1181–1209. For a summary of numerous meta-analytical studies on the efficacy of psychotherapy see Lambert, M., & Bergin, A. (1994). The effectiveness of psychotherapy. In A. Bergin & S. Garfield (Eds.), *Handbook of psychotherapy and behavior change* (pp.143–189). New York: John Wiley & Sons.

66. According to William Frankena, one is taking the moral point of view "if and only if (a) one is making normative judgments about actions, desires, dispositions, intentions, motives, persons, or traits of character; (b) one is willing to universalize one's judgments; (c) one's reasons for judgments consist of facts about what the things judged do to the lives of sentient beings in terms of promoting or distributing nonmoral good and evil; and (d) when the judgment is about oneself or one's own actions, one's reasons include such facts about what one's own actions and dispositions do to the lives of other sentient beings as such, if others are affected." In making value judgments, one seeks to be free, informed, clear-headed, impartial willing to universalize, and open-minded about other alternative candidates or rankings of values and moral obligations. Frankena, W. (1973). *Ethics* (2nd ed.). Englewood Cliffs, NJ: Prentice-Hall, pp. 113, 111.

67. Reconciliation expresses the meaning of Jesus' commandment to love God, neighbor, and self. Reconciliation is also consistent with the norm of "mutuality," and it is preferable to the more egoistic norm of self-actualization. See Browning, D. (1987). *Religious thought and the modern psychologies: A critical conversation.* Philadelphia, PA: Fortress Press, pp. 131– 132, 138–140.

68. Tillich, P. (1951). *Systematic theology* (Vol. l). Chicago: University of Chicago Press, p. 5. Theology is itself a dialogue between the message it presents and the situation it addresses. In its use of both questions and answers, Christian theology may be evaluated based on at least two criteria: (1) Does it ask the right questions? (2) Does it give the Christian answer? Expressed another way, is the theology both apologetic and kerygmatic? (Ibid., p. 8). The word "kerygma" is a term used by New Testament scholars to describe the core declarations of faith expressed in the early preaching of the Christian community. Examples are the sermons of Peter (Acts 2:14–36) and of Stephen (Acts 7:2–53). In my view the preaching of Jesus contains the essential Christian message and the core confession of faith.

69. Ibid., p. 7. I am using Tillich's meaning of "situation" as "the totality of man's creative self-interpretation in a special period." Ibid., p. 4.

70. Reiff, P. (1987). *Triumph of the therapeutic: Uses of faith after Freud.* Chicago: University of Chicago Press.

71. A contemporary expression of Christian theological anthropology is Schnelle, O. (1996). *The human condition: Anthropology in the teachings of Jesus, Paul, and John.* Minneapolis, MN: Fortress Press. See also n.44.

72. A Christian pluralist affirms the truth of the Christian tradition and recognizes that other traditions express truths Christians need to discover. This is an alternative to both a dogmatic exclusivism which claims absolute, final Truth and rejects others' claims to any saving truth, and to religious relativism which denies any criterion of truth and implies it really doesn't matter which religion you believe. Contemporary examples of Christian pluralism are discussed by Hick, J., & Hebblewaite, B. (Eds.). (1980). *Christianity and other religions.* Philadelphia, PA: Fortress Press; and by Cowdell, S. (1996). *Is Jesus unique? A study of recent Christology.* New York: Paulist Press, 237–262.

Chapter Two

Theoretical Reconciliation of Psychology and Theology

Because any theory of counseling grounded in a faith tradition expresses a particular position on the relation between theology and psychology, it is helpful to be aware of some of the alternatives with respect to the latter as a context for development of the former.

Since Freud's rejection of all religion as a collective neurosis with the future of an illusion,[1] there has been a strain between psychology and religion. And as psychology made efforts to become a respectable science by rejecting its roots in either philosophy or religion, along with methods such as introspection, intuition, and meditation, religion has been defined out of its boundaries except as an object of study. Psychology sought to become a natural science modeled after physics. As a result, in some respects, it has become less of a human science.

With the exception of a small number of psychologists, very few in academic psychology have dared to derive an applied psychology from any of the world's magnificent religions, despite the fact that nearly every world religion includes not only a metaphysic and an ethic, but an anthropology as well.[2] It is the latter that appreciates the spiritual dimension of human experience as the realm of meaning and values, wisdom, courage, and compassion, mystery, and reverent wonder. To ignore the spiritual dimension of life is to be less than comprehensive; it is also bad science, for it amounts to a denial of what it means to be fully human. Humans experience life in a spiritual dimension as well as in biopsychosocial dimensions.

The rejection of any religiously based psychology is presumed justified in part because including religious constructs, especially those lacking an operational (measurable) definition, would violate the scientific principles of verifiability or falsifiability. These epistemological principles, derived from a particular philosophy of science called logical positivism,[3] state that only those claims that can be proven true or false according to scientific method are legitimate. In other words, by definition any statement that cannot be either supported or refuted by testing it empirically cannot be considered a scientific statement.

In contrast, I believe it is possible to develop a religious-scientific psychology, though the very combination of words—"religious-scientific"—will seem like an oxymoron to those whose primary allegiance and identity are tied to one discipline versus the other. Nevertheless, in principle it is possible to construct a religious theory of counseling in such a manner that it leads to hypotheses that can be tested empirically.[4]

As an example, consider the general hypothesis that the religious experiences of repentance and forgiveness have therapeutic benefits. Phrased more precisely, such a hypothesis could be stated in the "if-then" language of causal relationships that are in principle verifiable or falsifiable. The hypothetical constructs of "repentance" and "forgiveness" can be given operational definitions, so both independent and dependent variables can be specified in a measurable manner, and the predicted cause-effect relationships evaluated empirically.[5] My own opinion is that this general hypothesis has been verified directly through the personal experiences of many religious individuals, through the documented benefits of both pastoral counseling and the Catholic sacrament of reconciliation, and indirectly through some process research in psychotherapy, particularly those studies showing salutary effects of the counselor's acceptance of the client.[6] The latter studies are relevant to this discussion by virtue of Paul Tillich's interpretation of forgiveness as acceptance.[7]

Having said that, I hasten to add that a review of pastoral counseling journals will lead readily to the conclusion that there is a paucity of controlled outcome research on the efficacy of religiously based counseling.[8] The same may be said about the theory of counseling presented in this book. The research remains to be done. One of the functions of theory is to guide research; hence developing a coherent theory will help us make a decision about what research to do. Hopefully this book will express a theory that leads to testable hypotheses to support its presuppositions, principles, and derivative procedures. If it does not, this theory will remain in the realm of speculation; interesting perhaps, but mere opinion. I am aware of the difference between opinions and facts.[9]

In this chapter I discuss dualistic and reductionistic approaches that advocate continued separation of psychology and religion based upon their points of divergence. After citing two risks of reconciliation between these two disciplines, I note four points of convergence leading to three conclusions and both positive and negative implications.

TWO SEPARATIST APPROACHES: DUALISTIC AND REDUCTIONISTIC

Since my goal is to provide a theologically informed theory of counseling, I have set aside the view that the two disciplines of psychology and theology are totally unrelated, hence they have no basis for any kind of interaction. There are two basic versions of this separatist point of view—dualistic and reductionistic approaches.

The Dualistic Approach

In one version of this point of view, the two disciplines are *separate, but equal.* From this perspective, the content and focus of these two disciplines have nothing in common. Their ways of knowing are so dissimilar that there are no points of contact or comparison. Because their goals, methods, and language are so different, there is no basis for dialogue between them. And since they are totally separated, conflict between them is also unnecessary. At the same time, neither discipline can make any positive contributions to the other. Psychology and theology are viewed as autonomous disciplines, completely independent of each other. A theologian is to be concerned with the logos (theory) of God, whereas a psychologist's concern is limited to the logos of the psyche.

This separation came about historically in part as a result of the desire for some peaceful coexistence between science and religion generally. As evident in the Church's initial reactions to the Copernican, Newtonian, Darwinian, and Freudian revolutions, religion has at times hindered the growth of science ever since the sixteenth century of Western intellectual history. By separating the two, science could proceed without interference, and religion could avoid any potential threats to its worldview and claims to truth, whether about nature, God, or persons.

In the eighteenth century, Immanuel Kant hastened the separation by suggesting that while both science and religion could be logical in their approaches, their spheres of interest and influence were independent of each other. Science applies categories of time, space, and causality, and its experimental method to understand the natural world, whereas religion applies its practical (ethical) reasoning to address human problems of moral choice. Because they occupy two different realms, conflicts between them could be "resolved" by mutual avoidance.[10]

Additional rationales for this separation of science and religion have been provided by Protestant theologians. In the nineteenth century, liberal Christian theology defined the province of religion to be human experience in either its subjective dimension (Schleiermacher's feeling of absolute dependence) or in its moral dimension (the emphasis of Albrecht Ritschl).[11] Neo-Orthodox theologians of the twentieth century such as Karl Barth and Emil Brunner in Europe and Reinhold Niebuhr in America stressed revealed truth in the person of Christ and Holy Scripture as the exclusive province of theology and religion. Their claim was that the uniqueness of divine revelation makes theology totally separate from all other disciplines. Science generally, hence scientific psychology particularly, can contribute nothing to theology. The two disciplines function best where they communicate least, working without interference from each other.

Existentialist theologians such as Søren Kierkegaard, Rudolf Bultmann, and Martin Buber suggested that the proper sphere of theology is I-Thou relationships between persons who are committed to understanding and caring about one another. Science focuses instead upon I-It relations between natural events of a causal, impersonal sort. Science is inquiry about objects in a detached, instrumental manner. Religion addresses human subjects in an existential manner as they make personal decisions and seek to relate meaningfully to one another and to life's deepest questions of meaning and being.

Another basis for the separation of psychology and theology came from a linguistic analysis of the functions of scientific and religious language.[12] Scientific language functions primarily to predict and control natural events, whereas religious language expresses personal commitments and seeks to evoke attitudes of reverence. Alternatively, psychology is viewed as providing only technical knowledge to answer process questions about how events occur, whereas theology provides theoretical knowledge about why they occur in terms of their ultimate meaning and purpose.

A contemporary basis for separating psychology and theology is the view that these two disciplines provide independent and mutually exclusive perspectives. Both can throw light upon human experience, but they contain nonoverlapping spectrums of light. For example, a psychological perspective may provide a phenomenological description and causal analysis of experience, whereas a theological perspective provides a religious, ethical, or teleological analysis. Alternatively, while both address the nature of being, psychology emphasizes the experience of being, philosophy the structure of being, and theology the meaning of being.[13] In these "perspectivalist" approaches it is argued that an exhaustive description of an event at one level of explanation (psychological) does not preclude the validity of description at another level of explanation (theological), hence interaction between them is possible, though not necessary. However, while perspectivalists may argue that multiple views on the truth are required, based on the differences emphasized between theological and scientific descriptions, it is equally possible to maintain their separation,[14] or to relate the two levels hierarchically.

Finally, the resistance to any rapprochement between psychology and religion may be argued on practical grounds. Dualists may point to both the separatist and exclusivist claims made by so many diverse spiritual traditions, denominations, and sects, and secondly, to the lack of a unified science of psychotherapy. The traditional divisions of Protestant, Catholic, and Jew in Western religion have a parallel classification in the major divisions of psychodynamic, behavioral, and humanistic approaches in Western psychotherapy. But these summary categories do not begin to express the enormous diversity within both religion and clinical psychology. Sectarian allegiances among "true believers" seem to be as characteristic of the more than 250 approaches to psychotherapy[15] as denominational differences are among so many different religions. The parochial attitudes of practitioners of both psychotherapy and religion, combined with the enormous range of alternatives in both areas have led some to conclude that fruitful dialogue among them is impossible and efforts in that direction are futile. A history of psychotherapy integration shows that "ever since Myerson's horrified response to French's (1933) presentation of the commonalities between behaviorism and psychoanalysis, staunch supporters of circumscribed orientations have argued that rapprochement is neither possible nor desirable."[16] Better to let psychotherapy and religion remain separate until each one gets its house in order. From this practical point of view, psychology and religion are separate and equal—separate in approaches and equally confusing. In varying degrees, both lack controlled empirical research to support the validity of their respective claims.[17]

The several rationales just presented lead to the continued separation of psychology and theology analogous to the Cartesian split between mind and body. The split here, however, is between psyche and spirit. The result is neither dialogue nor cooperation; it is total separation and independence. The two remain unreconciled. Head and heart remain apart.

A completely autonomous psychology celebrates its own structure and dynamics against any and all imposed religious language and concepts. The shortcoming of such an autonomous psychology is its neglect of the spiritual dimension of life and of religious concepts that inform vital human experiences of courage and hope, meaning and being, alienation and reconciliation. Likewise, a completely autonomous theology grounded solely in scripture and tradition may derive a theological anthropology to the neglect of the knowledge about the psychological dimension informed by scientific psychology, and risk thereby, a sacrifice of scientific truth accorded by human reason and grounded in human experience.

As a result of the separation, there is little recognition of how the positive attitudes toward both nature and reason expressed in the Judeo-Christian doctrine of creation encouraged investigation and observation of a world believed to be intelligible by virtue of its rational and purposeful Creator. Nor is it remembered that many who contributed to the scientific revolution of the seventeenth century (e.g., Galileo and Newton) were religiously motivated individuals, and the later puritan concept of vocation and the Protestant work ethic had similar positive effects upon the advancement of science generally.[18]

From this dualistic perspective, if the two disciplines of psychology and theology are related at all, perhaps they interact dialectically as a thesis and antithesis. Unfortunately, there is no potential for a meaningful synthesis that preserves and integrates both into a transcending unity. There is only the possibility of a peaceful coexistence, provided they ignore each other and stay off each other's turf. It is basically a relationship of mutual indifference expressed practically by clergy and clinicians who avoid one another.

The Reductionistic Approach

This dualistic relationship between psychology and theology has been a tenuous one at best. It is basically as unsatisfactory as "separate but equal" has been in race relations. And comparable to its application in human relations, frequently this position has disguised another view, namely that of being *separate and unequal*. The latter view is evident particularly in reductionistic approaches to relating psychology and religion. From this perspective, the authority of one is presumed to be higher than the authority of the other. Unfortunately, the only relationship possible is competition as each struggles to dominate or defeat the other. If one discipline considers the other seriously, it is primarily as a potential threat. Basically they remain independent of each other, but interacting competitively if not antagonistically.

Whereas the first position is dualistic, this second is a reductionistic approach of a monistic nature. Either religious phenomena are reduced to psychological phenomena (or treated as epiphenomena) or all psychological processes are "reduced" to religious phenomena. Two examples of the former are (a) when psychologists reduce ethical decisions to the selection of instrumental strategies for meeting one's psychological needs, as if there were no moral dimension in decisions whatsoever, and (b) when God becomes a psychological phenomena such as the self archetype, as some have misinterpreted Carl Jung to affirm. An example of theological reductionism is the view that all nonorganic forms of mental illness are expressions of sin and essentially or exclusively religious or ethical problems. In both cases, a phenomenon defined in one domain is redefined in another through some form of reduction.

In this separate but unequal position, psychology and theology are related in a hierarchical manner. The two disciplines are "organized" into levels according to their grade of value. The hierarchy gives to the higher level a higher quality and value.

There is an advantage of this way of seeking some unity among diverse disciplines. Any theory or event that is classified as psychological in nature can be placed within the psychological level. All similar theories are categorized on a common plane with relative equality among them. The same organizing principle applies to theological views.

The disadvantage of a hierarchical principle for relating these two disciplines derives from the intrinsic independence of each from the other. There is no real interaction or dynamic movement between them, nor any mutual enrichment since they have a superior/inferior relation. The higher level is not implicit within the lower level, nor the lower included within the discipline judged to be higher. They remain mutually exclusive. The relationship between them is one of mutual interference, either by control or revolt.

As an example of interference, theology might claim the existence of a "soul" as a separate substance or function exercising a particular (spiritual) causality and consider the psychological concept of "psyche" to be a misrepresentation unless it is spiritualized. Alternatively, psychology may reduce the soul to a self with no spiritual dimension whatsoever. Such theoretical reductions amount to efforts on the part of one discipline either to assert its own independence or to assume ultimate authority and control over the other. The result is conflict, disunity, and disintegration. The two disciplines become increasingly alienated with mutual contempt.

As another example of interference, psychology may assert that any moral philosophy must be grounded in the insights about human nature derived from such empirical fields as experimental, social, and clinical psychology, and particularly from psychopathology and psychotherapy. Aside from the logical error of such attempts to derive values from facts,[19] or "ought" from "is," this position is an exclusivist claim to the ethical domain that has been addressed for centuries by the world's great religions. Furthermore, an ethical analysis of theories of psychotherapy as examples of moral philosophy reveals their implicit values and ethical reasoning to be quite arbitrary and frequently inconsistent.[20] That observation, however, is likely to be seen as interference by psychologists who prefer to claim they are scientists rather than moral philosophers. At best, I think we are both; at worst, we are neither.

The use of the hierarchical metaphor of "levels" for relating psychology and theology has additional methodological problems associated with it. It leads to attempts to describe, define, and understand psychological experiences in exclusively theological language, and/or to use exclusively psychological methods to evaluate theological claims. Depending upon the method and language chosen, phenomena discussed at one level may be excluded from the other.

The view that all phenomena can be explained by either psychological laws or spiritual/moral principles is a form of epistemological reductionism. The view that the only reality that exists or matters is either psychological or spiritual in nature is a form of ontological reductionism.[21] Neither position constitutes a satisfactory way of reconciling psychology and theology. Their mutual goals remain dominance rather than dialogue, or conversion rather than cooperation.

There is an arrogant attitude expressed by advocates of both positions, which lead to imperialist dismissals and struggles for domination characteristic of the interdisciplinary warfare of the past. Are psychological theories the only reliable guides to truths about what it means to be human? I think not. Are religious views the only sources of truth? That too seems doubtful. Truth may be either revealed religiously or discovered scientifically, but regardless of the source, it constitutes verifiable truth relevant to human welfare. It is an illusion, however, to assume that either psychology or theology has captured the whole truth and nothing but the truth.

The reductionistic position is reflected in the historical and hysterical antipathy between theology and psychology, which is symptomatic of the deeper divorce between religion and science.[22] Unfortunately, the divorce between the two disciplines continues for a majority of academics and professionals, and it is sometimes fraught with the acrimony of parents fighting over custody of the kids. At best it amounts to a benign neglect of one discipline by the other. At worst, each strives to establish hegemony over the other akin to a hostile takeover of one corporation by another.

POINTS OF DIVERGENCE

Whether the relationship between clinical psychology[23] and theology is construed as separate and equal, or separate but unequal, the recommendations for their separation are usually grounded in their points of divergence. The three differences drawn by Paul Tillich[24] between theology and philosophy are germane to understanding the differences in cognitive attitudes, their sources, and the content of each discipline. A fourth difference I wish to add is their methodologies.

The *attitude* of the psychologist as scientist is detached, objective, and empirical. The attitude of the theologian who seeks to articulate the meaning of faith is more involved, subjective, and existential.

The *sources* of psychology and theology are also different. Empirical research and clinical experience are the sources of both psychological theory and clinical practice, whereas historical revelation, religious and pastoral experience constitute the primary sources of theology and ministry.

In terms of *content*, psychology focuses on psychological phenomena such as sensation and perception, memory and learning, motivation, psychopathology, and psychotherapy. It deals with natural antecedents and consequences observable in finite time and space. By contrast, the contents of theology are religious phenomena such as the experiences of conversion and forgiveness, unitive consciousness, experiences of the sacred dimension of life, ethical decision-making, and spiritual dimensions of estrangement and reconciliation.

Methods also vary. As scientists, psychologists formulate hypotheses and test them experimentally according to the canons of acceptable research design and statistical analysis. Many clinicians approach psychological assessment and therapy using a similar hypothesis-testing model.[25] In contrast, theologians rely upon the tests of logic; literary, form, and redaction criticism of biblical sources; and hermeneutic principles of interpretation of revealed truth in both human history and in personal and collective religious experience.

The Christian theologian, Paul Tillich advocated an existential ontology by suggesting that the special object of theological reflection consists of matters of ultimate concern. By definition, ultimate concerns affect our being or non-being,[26] that is, the very structure and meaning of being itself, and relate to the nature and aims of existence. It follows from this definition that theology is relatively unconcerned with the results and methods of psychological science because the special objects of psychology are preliminary concerns, such as the nature and measure of intelligence. It also follows that theology has neither the obligation nor the right to determine or prejudice, psychological inquiry. A corollary of this position is that no result of a psychological investigation can be either directly productive or disastrous for theology or faith.

TWO RISKS OF RECONCILIATION

I have been describing some of the points of divergence between psychology and theology that have been used to justify separation of these two disciplines of reflective inquiry and professional practice. If neither a separation nor divorce is acceptable, then efforts must be made to reconcile these two disciplines and professions. That is a task fraught with considerable risk.

One of the risks characterizing efforts to reconcile these two disciplines is the use of one as a criterion for the validity of the other. One could approach "integration" of these fields in a "nothing-but" manner. For example, nothing but those psychological principles consistent with a literal interpretation of infallible scripture are acceptable.[27] Alternatively, nothing but those scriptural principles consistent with both psychological theories and empirical research may be judged as acceptable. Neither approach appreciates the unique contributions and the validity of both fields and their distinct sources and methods. At best this is a position of *integrated, but unequal* disciplines. At worst the insights of one discipline are rejected based on the presuppositions or prejudices of the other.

The Risk of Psychological Dominance

If one considers psychological theory to be the deciding criterion, one of the risks of integration is expressed in the search for biblical justification for a theory of counseling that has been chosen previously on other grounds. For example as Oglesby[28] notes, persons emphasizing insight-oriented therapies might cite as biblical support Romans 12:2, John 4:29, or John 8:32. Those emphasizing behavioral approaches could cite Luke 18:22, Matthew 19:21, Mark 10:21, Luke 10 and 17, and Romans 15:14. Those favoring relationship-oriented therapy might cite Luke 15:11– 32, Romans 3:23–25, or Ephesians 2:14–15. In this approach to integration, psychological theory is dominant. Scripture and theology are used in a secondary role to provide credibility to the secular theory of counseling, especially with Christian audiences.

This approach may result from a conscious decision to give priority to one's psychological presuppositions over theological convictions and scriptural meanings. It may occur due to presuppositions of which an author is unaware. Alternatively, this approach may be occasioned by self-serving motives of counselors who wish to market themselves in religious dress. The latter case would be like receiving counseling from a Pharisee.

Whatever the reasons or motives, in this approach to "integration," psychological theory functions as the prism through which all biblical material is filtered. Like any prism that allows a limited spectrum of light waves through, psychological prisms both filter in and filter out potential enlightenment from spiritual wisdom, including religious concepts and principles relevant to counseling. Theology cannot be reduced to anthropology, but anthropology can be transformed by theology.[29]

The Risk of Theological Dominance

If on the other hand, one looks to scripture and theology for the foundation of a psychological theory of counseling, one runs the risk of rejecting all of psychology that fails to meet religious criteria. In this position of theological dominance, much of psychology is excluded, even if relevant to counseling. In more extreme positions, most of psychological theory and knowledge is rejected.[30] For example, psychological theories about unconscious motives might be rejected on theological grounds as a potential threat to moral responsibility. Another example is the rejection of psychological theories of ego development as incompatible with the religious doctrine of creation of the human spirit. Similarly, the very concept of mental illness as a focus of counseling may be rejected as a threat to a theological view explaining human distress in spiritual and moral terms of human sin.[31] Psychological theories about physiological drives, psychological needs, or environmental contingencies as explanations of human behavior may be rejected as contradicting the theological concepts of the human and divine will. Psychological determinism is rejected, if not censored, as contrary to the theological notion of responsible freedom. In these and other examples, theology dominates psychology as the authority of scripture supersedes the authority of science in conservative theology.

Neither the domination of psychology by theology, nor of theology by psychology is a satisfactory relation. The preferred model of interaction is dialogue. This dialogue between theology and psychology must avoid both an uncritical Christian baptism of psychological theories and a compromise of the Christian gospel of reconciliation. It must also avoid an uncritical endorsement of Christian anthropology and a compromise of psychological science.

Some efforts to "integrate" these two disciplines amount to a veiled form of theological heteronomy, that is, the imposition of theological language and methodology upon the structure and dynamics of psychological experience and psychological science. What is needed is a theonomous psychology[32] in which the structures and dynamics of psychological experience are allowed to be themselves, but as transformed and fulfilled in a religious experience of the unconditional and pervaded by a religious meaning such as reconciliation. We need not only a psychology of reconciliation, but a reconciling psychology. And we need not only a theology of reconciliation; we need a reconciling theology.

A more satisfying reconciliation is to utilize religious wisdom as a source of a psychological theory from which one can deduce hypotheses to be tested using scientific methodologies. I use the plural form of methodologies deliberately here to suggest both the variety available and to be inclusive of both qualitative and quantitative research methods. It is this position that I find most appealing, so long as the methodology selected is appropriate to the theory tested. A Christian theory of counseling that is tested by scientific methods will most likely lead to more credible, efficacious interventions derived from the theory and modified by empirical research. It will also advance the development of both the theory and practice of counseling.

POINTS OF CONVERGENCE

The foundation for a reconciliation between psychology and theology is grounded in their points of convergence. These commonalties are evident in (1) shared attitudes, (2) philosophical foundations, (3) empirical content, and (4) ethical perspectives.

Common Attitudes

In terms of attitudes, both theologians and psychologists manifest a degree of personal involvement with their subject matter. Both disciplines involve subjectivity and intuition in the creative phases of their respective enterprises, whether it appears in the scientist's hunches and formulation of hypotheses; in the clinician's diagnoses, ideas about etiologies, understanding of dynamics, or formulations of treatment plans; or in the theologian's reflections upon religious experiences of revelations recorded in scripture and summarized in church doctrine.

The choice of their respective careers and objects of both scientific and theological inquiry are decisions that reflect basic values and determining commitments. Furthermore, the attitudes of both are conditioned by their concreteness as persons who have a particular psychological makeup or religious orientation, and by their sociological and cultural settings in history.

Both psychology and theology involve nonrational commitments, whether it is belief in the rational unity of nature that can be comprehended by scientific methods as the means for discovering its truth, or the theologian's faith in the same rationality and unity of life that derives from a rational and purposeful Creator known through methods of revealed theology and religious experience. At the same time, both the psychologist and theologian require some degree of objectivity and detachment in their work, and both employ logical reasoning in their efforts to achieve semantic clarity and to reach credible conclusions.

Moreover, as individuals both psychologists and theologians have their own ultimate concerns about life's meaning and the purpose of their own lives, though perhaps with varying levels of awareness and differing degrees to which their ultimate concerns are integrated into their theories and professional practice.[33]

Finally, within the past two decades there have been changes in attitudes among both theologians and psychotherapists toward those within their own disciplines whose allegiances and theories are different, perhaps even contradictory. The ecumenical movement[34] among Protestant denominations, and between Protestant, Catholic, and Jewish theologians and religious leaders finds a parallel in the movement toward eclectic and integrative theories of psychotherapy. Both are expressions of the desire for unity and reconciliation. Though the meaning of "eclectic" is somewhat ambiguous, the majority of mental health professionals identify themselves as eclectic in their approach.[35] There is also a growing interest in theoretical integration based upon common factors that account for a substantial percent of variance in therapy outcomes, including the repeated findings from meta-analyses of research that diverse interventions appear to yield equivalent positive results.[36]

It appears that the perspective of religious pluralism finds a parallel in psychological pluralism, both of which manifest a deeper appreciation for the contributions from those holding alternative points of view. Extending these attitudes of tolerance and openness across traditional disciplinary boundaries will provide encouragement in the direction of a mutually beneficial rapprochement between psychology and theology. Seeing these and other commonalties in attitudes might help members of both disciplines to perceive one another as not so strange after all. Neither must they remain estranged.

Common Philosophical Foundations

In addition to commonalities in attitude, theology and clinical psychology converge in terms of their common philosophical elements. As modes of human inquiry, both disciplines rest upon philosophical assumptions about the nature of reality (ontology), how we know what we know (epistemology), and what we ought to be and do (ethics). Since both disciplines provide answers to these questions, explicitly or implicitly, dialogue between them becomes possible at a philosophical level as a way of describing and understanding both their commonalties and their differences. They can communicate because they share a common language in philosophy.[37]

Ontological Convergence. From a philosophical point of view, neither psychologists nor theologians can escape ontological questions concerning the nature of reality, being, and meaning. Many in both professions consider their disciplines to be legitimate pathways to understanding *reality*, the nature of which is the subject of ontology.[38] Both make claims of a cognitive nature expressed in assertions of fact, whether these facts are the empirical data of research or historical revelations recorded in scripture and disclosed in religioùs experience. Both also make cognitive claims of truth in theoretical propositions expressed either as scientific principles and psychological laws, or as ecclesiastical doctrines and theological interpretations of faith.

Second, ontological questions about the nature and structure of *being* cannot be avoided by either discipline by virtue of the nature of human experience. Knowing, feeling, intending, and doing are all acts that participate in, and presuppose being, and being itself is the proper focus of ontological inquiry.[39] To speak particularly about the experience and process of counseling, for example, or about the growth that occurs through counseling, is to speak in ontological categories of experience, process, and growth. The fact that neither a psychologist nor a theologian may want to explore this ontological depth of their theories does not allow them to escape this common ground and their mutual dependence upon it.[40]

Third, philosophical questions of *meaning* are also addressed by both psychology and theology. The meaning of life and human suffering are shared concerns of both disciplines. Within psychology, it is particularly existentialists such as Viktor Frankl[41] and Rollo May[42] who have addressed the ontological question of what it means to be.

Finally, neither psychology nor theology can escape the ontological questions of being and meaning because every epistemology has ontological implications and consequences, including both the logic of scientific verification and spiritual discernment of divine self-disclosures. Neither the attempt of logical positivism to reduce philosophy to epistemology (particularly to the logic of the scientific method), nor a reduction of philosophy to ethics (practical reasoning) has proven satisfactory.

To summarize, both psychology and theology contain implicit assumptions and assertions about reality, being, and meaning. The writings and texts from both disciplines reveal their authors' views of what reality is truly like, which is evident in their use of ontological categories as a part of their shared vocabulary. Included among these categories are time and space, causality and purpose, subject and object, process and substance, growth and movement, meaning and being, life and experience, freedom and destiny. Thus the two disciplines employ words and concepts as well as syntax and grammar that constitute a common language and shared vocabulary which makes communication between them possible.

Epistemological Convergence. Psychology and theology converge philosophically at a second level. Both fields provide and depend on answers to epistemological questions about how we know what we know. They share in common a *rational epistemology*, that is, a commitment to employ reason and the rules of logic both to determine truth and to guide and interpret their approaches to the phenomena they study. One of the tasks of theology is to develop the rational elements in faith by addressing a variety of theoretical and practical questions, for example, questions about the nature and purpose of God and about human nature and destiny. Through the exercise of both analytical and analogical reasoning, theology develops a reasonable and reasoning faith, though faith is not established by reason alone.[43] Theology adds revelation, but not as the antithesis to reason, for revelation may inform reason without destroying it, as grace builds upon nature.[44] In my view, revelation and reason become synthesized in reconciled reason as a transcendent way of knowing reality and truth. By that phrase I mean that reason is reconciled with revelation as ways of knowing.[45]

Second, both psychology and theology have an *empirical epistemology*. By that I mean both disciplines look to human experience as a medium of knowledge and as the realm in which verification or falsification of both scientific and religious claims to truth may occur.[46] While psychology may consider human experience as the sole medium, if not the exclusive source of knowledge, theology recognizes experience as an ambiguous medium and adds revelation as the ultimate source. But even divine revelation is received and occurs within human experience, hence the two disciplines of psychology and theology meet in the empirical realm of human experience.[47]

Empirical Convergence

The empirical nature of both disciplines is also evident in the focus on human experience as the *content* of their respective inquiries. Reinhold Niebuhr suggested that both psychology and theology focus upon human experience. They differ in the range of experience they address: psychology focuses on discrete, empirical data from controlled experiments, whereas theology addresses a broader network and range of human experience. In this view, theology is the more inclusive discipline, however both disciplines are related to experience and to each other.[48]

While scientific psychology seeks to predict and control behavior in a manner that theology does not, both disciplines share in common the desire to describe and understand human experience.   This commonality is particularly evident in phenomenological and existential theories within psychology (e.g., Rogers, Maslow, Gendlin, Giorgi, Frankl, Satre, Assagioli, van Kamm, Yalom, Bugenthal, and May) and in historical and empirical approaches within theology (Wesley, Coleridge, Schleiermacher, Ritschl, von Harnack, Troeltsch, Hocking, Otto, Bultmann, Buber, Kierkegaard, Tillich, Macintosh, and Wieman).[49]

As examples of their shared empirical content, both disciplines make statements about the experience of the human self. Both address the question of what it means to be a person. Both have implicit, if not explicit theories of personality structure and human motivation. Both fields make assertions about various aspects of human experience, such as the cognitive, affective, behavioral, and conative[50] dimensions. Psychology and theology also provide diagnoses of the human condition and recommendations for solving human problems of a social and psychological nature. The point here is that the empirical orientation of both theology and psychology constitutes a bridge between them by virtue of their shared focus upon the nature and content of human experience in general, and upon psychological and religious experience in particular.[51] Therein lies an empirical foundation for their reconciliation.

Ethical Convergence

There is another realm of inquiry in which psychology and theology may dialogue. That is the specialty within philosophy known as ethics. Both psychology and theology advocate theories about what constitutes the good life, and both espouse human virtues and moral obligations. These are embodied within ethical codes of conduct and quality assurance standards of practice for the delivery of psychological services and pastoral counseling. They are evident in both psychological theories of personality, psychopathology, and psychotherapy as well as writings in the area of theological ethics and pastoral theology. For example, whether construed in the clinical construct of psychopathology or in the theological concept of sin, both appraisals of problems in living involve value judgments.[52] Ethical principles and value judgments concerning desired ends and the acceptable means for achieving them characterize writings in both fields.

The moral philosophies expressed by both disciplines constitute another common ground for dialogue between the two as ethical systems.[53] Both disciplines may be evaluated respectively in terms of their ethical principles and endorsed virtues and their adequacy as moral philosophies. From this perspective, certain counseling procedures may be technically effective, but not applied because they violate an ethical principle. Additionally, particular theories of psychotherapy may be theoretically coherent and empirically supported, but morally dubious, such as those that manifest an underlying egoistic hedonism.

Neither psychology nor theology is a value-free or value-neutral discipline.

The role of values and value judgments is a central concern of both disciplines.[54] In the Kantian tradition of emphasizing the moral foundations of a rational Christian faith, the liberal Protestant theologian, Albrecht Ritschl, emphasized the cognitive truth of value judgments and the indissoluble relation between fact and value. He based his view on the mind's dual functions of making both causal judgments and value judgments.[55] In the field of psychotherapy, survey research suggested that by the 1980s a majority of therapists believed that values are embedded in psychotherapy and that values are involved as a natural part of the change process.[56] A recent expression of this ethical emphasis is found in the area of family therapy. William Doherty[57] places family therapy within a moral context. The therapist's role is described as an ethical consultant, and therapy itself is construed as moral guidance to promote ethical decision-making and moral responsibility. It is a perspective that would be enriched by the understanding of responsibility presented within Christian ethics.[58]

CONCLUSIONS AND IMPLICATIONS

I have been discussing the points of convergence between psychology and theology evident in their ethical reasoning, philosophical foundations, empirical content, and cognitive attitudes. The presence of both convergence and points of divergence in the relation between psychology and theology suggests three conclusions.

First, while some conflict between these two disciplines may be inevitable given human proclivities to pride and self-aggrandizement, in light of shared philosophical foundations and empirical content, complete separation is neither necessary nor possible in principle. Theology highlights the spiritual dimension of experience, and psychology the psychical dimension; both are needed to describe and understand experience that is fully and truly human.

Second, the two cannot and should not become unified into a single discipline. Attempts to synthesize them are likely to violate the independence and integrity of both disciplines and probably end in a hierarchical relationship that may be characterized as integrated, but unequal.

Third, a greater degree of reconciliation between them is both possible and desirable; however that reconciliation must preserve the independence of both disciplines and acknowledge their differences, while seeking their commonalties at philosophical, ethical, and empirical levels, including research and practice.

Reconciliation is a process more like dialogue than a merging of two into one. Two separate identities are required to dialogue, not one, and dialogue is neither domination nor destruction by the absorption of one into the other. The interaction of psychology and theology that I recommend is one of dialogue rather than dominance, cooperation rather than competition, reconciliation rather than either separation or integration.[59] Described figuratively, the two fields interact like partially intersecting circles. The areas of overlap are their common foundation in philosophy, their empirical focus upon human experience, and their shared use of human reason to complement both research and revelation.

From the theological side, the nonintersecting portion of the overlapping circles of psychology and theology is established by the formal criterion of theology as that discipline devoted to ultimate concerns of being and nonbeing, the nature and aims of existence.[60] This formal criterion constitutes a boundary line between the two disciplines.

Ultimate concerns are total, final, absolute, universal, and transcending in nature and scope. All other disciplines, including both the natural and social sciences, focus upon more preliminary, partial, contingent, particular, relative, and finite concerns. This formal principle makes theology the more inclusive discipline, but only with respect to ultimate concerns, as it must be for those within the theological circle of faith.[61]

Negative Implications

This contrast in content between ultimate and preliminary concerns provides a basis for further dialogue between psychology and theology with both negative and positive implications. Negatively it means *first* that theology should not become preoccupied with the preliminary concerns of psychology. Theology has no business in making judgments about the scientific value of psychological theories, nor about the most efficacious methods of psychological (or medical) healing. Selections and applications of counseling strategies and therapeutic procedures are both theoretical and technical decisions that should be empirically grounded in scientific evidence for their efficacy and efficiency with respect to the welfare of clients. Theologians are not psychologists nor should they claim such expertise.

Among the preliminary concerns that belong properly within the province of psychology are those addressed in theories of psychological development and learning, the biopsychosocial and cognitive-affective bases of behavior, the merits of various research methodologies, psychological theories of personality, emotion and motivation, psychopathology and psychotherapy. These are all properly the focus of psychology, not the primary concern of theology. Having said this, however, I wish to add that to the degree any of these psychological topics raise matters of ultimate concern, theology may claim involvement with them, the right to address them and to dialogue about them, but not to control them. For example, insofar as the purpose of psychotherapy is related to the nature and aims of life, and its therapeutic goals are related to an experience of the good life, theology has a significant contribution to make to theories of psychotherapy.

From the point of view of psychology, a *second* negative implication, equally important, is that psychology limit its role to the investigation of psychological concerns and issues. Psychology has no business making judgments about the spiritual value of religious beliefs and practices, nor about the existence and attributes of God. The selection of modes of meditation and worship and formulations of religious doctrine, for example, are properly religious and theological decisions that should be grounded in scripture, church history, religious experience, and theological reasoning. Psychologists are not theologians, nor should they pretend to be.

These negative implications suggest that while the two disciplines intersect, they do so only partially, and there are important areas where they do not overlap. In these nonoverlapping areas, the two disciplines should mind their own business.

From this latter statement the reader might infer that I am counseling a peaceful coexistence based upon mutual indifference. That is neither a necessary inference, nor is it what I wish to imply. I believe the two disciplines can be related positively as well. One constructive way that might occur is illustrated in this book, but preliminary remarks are in order by way of anticipation.

Positive Implications

One of the positive implications is that neither psychology nor theology needs to fear dominance by the other. Quite the contrary, they can look to each other for important corrections of their own theoretical implications and omissions. Theology can correct the tendency of psychology to elevate its preliminary concerns to ultimate levels, and psychology can help theology avoid any tendency to lapse into preliminary concerns. Both errors constitute boundary violations, and historically both disciplines are guilty of such errors, for which mutual repentance and forgiveness are warranted and provide another basis for reconciliation.

At the same time, any preliminary concern can become the positive vehicle and symbol of an ultimate concern. It is sometimes in and through preliminary concerns of a psychological nature that ultimate concerns of a theological nature arise and are actualized. Implicit within the psychological experience of fear, for example, is the universal experience of existential anxiety related to human finitude and freedom, which in turn raises the theological question of the ultimate source of courage.[62]

The point here is that insofar as preliminary psychological concerns raise ultimate concerns, the objects of psychological inquiry become the legitimate objects of theological reflection. But theology deals with them only insofar as they are expressed within psychology as a medium or vehicle, pointing beyond itself to these more ultimate concerns.[63] Theology does not look to psychology for either the source, the norm, or the content of its ultimate concern.

Since the ultimate concerns addressed by theology may be expressed implicitly within the preliminary concerns of psychology, a *second* positive implication is that psychology in turn has the obligation to inform theology of the psychological implications and consequences of theological propositions and religious practices. For example, it is both legitimate and important for psychologists to apply their scientific knowledge and criteria of mental health to evaluate the relative health of religious beliefs and practices.[64] The question of what constitutes a healthy religion is a valid psychological question. There is such a thing, after all, as a neurotic religion, including religious obsessions about ultimate concerns! Religious guilt is not necessarily neurotic, but some of it may be. Spiritual direction with respect to religious scrupulosity is one recognition of psychopathology that occurs within the spiritual realm.[65] Psychology can help theology to appreciate the difference between healthy and neurotic religion, as well as the potential for both spiritual abuse and psychological exploitation within religious communities.

Similarly, psychology can help to evaluate whether a person's religious visions are the hallucinations of a schizophrenic or are an authentic religious experience of a healthy individual. During my pastoral clinical training experience at St. Elizabeth's Hospital in Washington D.C., I learned to do a religious life history. One of the patients I interviewed insisted he had visions of Christ. His evidence for that assertion was his very own existence. He considered himself to be the Christ he envisioned. His claims were not very credible because he suffered from paranoid schizophrenia.

By way of summary, I wish to emphasize that the presence of both points of divergence and convergence make possible the reconciliation of theology and psychology, but not their synthesis or integration into one unified discipline or profession. Their reconciliation may occur through dialogue at both theoretical and methodological levels. In the following chapter, I suggest that the concept of critical correlation is a basis for methodological reconciliation.

NOTES

1. Freud, S. (1961). The future of an illusion. *Standard Edition, 21,* 1–56. For a theological response see Perry, J. (1988). *Tillich's response to Freud: A Christian answer to the Freudian critique of religion.* Lanham, MD: University Press of America. The strain between science and religion generally began before Freud during the period of European history known as the Enlightenment in the late seventeenth and eighteenth centuries.

2. This result should not be surprising in light of the observation that the majority of psychologists are either agnostic or atheistic and consider other religious psychologists as a puzzlement if not pathological. Seymour Sarason made this observation in the August 1992 at the Centennial Address before the American Psychological Association. (Quoted in a book review by Weaver, A. (1995). *The Journal of Pastoral Care, 49*[2], p. 243.) For a survey of psychologists' religious preferences, see Bergin, A., & Jansen, J. (1990). Religiosity of psychotherapists: A national survey. *Psychotherapy, 27*(1), 3–7.

3. For a theological critique of logical positivism, see Foster, J. D., & Ledbetter, M. F. (1987). Christianity and psychology and the scientific method. *Journal of Psychology and Theology, 15,* 10–18. For a counter point, see Vande Kemp, H. (1987). The sorcerer was a straw man—apologetics gone awry: A reaction to Foster and Ledbetter. *Journal of Psychology and Theology, 15,* 19–26. Additional critiques from the perspective of the philosophy of science and psychology are provided by Hillman, J. (1975). *Re-visioning psychology.* New York: Harper & Row; Barbour, I. (1990). Religion in an age of science: The Gifford lectures, 1989–91, (Vol. 1). New York: HarperCollins; Bevin, W. (1991). Contemporary psychology: A tour inside the onion. *American Psychologist, 46,* 475–483; O'Donohue, W. (1989). The (even) bolder model: The clinical psychologist as metaphysician-scientist-practitioner. *American Psychologist, 44,* 1460–1468; Manicas, P., & Secord, P. (1983). Implications for psychology of the new philosophy of science. *American Psychologist, 38,* 399–412; and Jones, E. S. (1994). A constructive relationship for religion with the science and profession of psychology. *American Psychologist, 49*(3), 184–197.

4. H. N. Wieman presented an example of a scientific Christian theology. See Bretall, R. (Ed.). (1963). *The empirical theology of Henry Nelson Wieman.* New York: Macmillan.

5. Illustrations of empirical research on the experience and therapeutic efficacy of forgiveness are provided by Enright, R. (1995). *The psychology of forgiveness.* Paper presented at the National conference on Forgiveness, Madison, WI, March 1995; McCullough, M., & Worthington, E. (1994). Models of interpersonal forgiveness and their applications to counseling: Review and critique. *Counseling and Values, 39*(1), 2–14; McCullough, M., & Worthington, E. (1994). Encouraging clients to forgive people who have hurt them: Review, critique, and research prospectus. *Journal of Psychology and Theology, 22*(1), 3–20; Pingleton, J. (1989). The role and function of forgiveness in the psychotherapeutic process. *Journal of Psychology and Theology, 17*(1), 27–35; Phillips, L., & Osborne, J. (1989). Cancer patients' experiences of forgiveness therapy. *Canadian Journal of Counseling, 23*(3), 236–251; Fitzgibbons, R. (1986). The cognitive and emotive uses of forgiveness in the treatment of anger. *Psychotherapy, 23*(4), 629–633. A number of relevant articles appeared in the Special Issue: Grace and forgiveness. (1992). *Journal of Psychology and Christianity, 11*(2). See also Halling, S., & Rowe, J. (1996). *The implications of a phenomenological understanding of forgiveness for psychotherapy.* Paper presented at the Second National Conference on Forgiveness in Clinical Practice. Baltimore, MD, April 26, 1996.

6. For reviews in this area see Beutler, L., Crago, M., & Arizmendi, T. (1986). Research on therapist variables in psychotherapy. In S. Garfield & A. Bergin (Eds.), *Handbook of psychotherapy and behavior change* (3rd ed., pp. 257–310). New York: John Wiley and Sons; Orlinsky, D., & Howard, K. (1986). Process and outcome in psychotherapy. In S. Garfield & A. Bergin (Eds.), *Handbook of psychotherapy and behavior change* (3rd ed., pp. 311–384). New York: John Wiley and Sons; Beutler, L., Mochado, P., & Neufeldt, S. (1994). Therapist variables. In A. Bergin & S. Garfield (Eds.), *Handbook of psychotherapy and behavior change* (4th ed., pp. 229–269). New York: John Wiley and Sons; and Orlinsky, D., Grawe, K., & Parks, B. (1994). Process and outcome in psychotherapy—Noch einmal. In A. Bergin & S. Garfield (Eds.), *Handbook of psychotherapy and behavior change* (4th ed., pp. 270–378). New York: John Wiley and Sons. The conclusions reached by reviewers in this area of research depend in part upon their own theoretical position and the studies they select for review. For a critique of several reviews, see Patterson, C. H. (1985). *The therapeutic relationship: Foundations for an eclectic psychotherapy.* Monterey, CA: Brooks/Cole Publishing Company, pp.197–244.

7. Tillich, P. (1963). *Systematic theology* (Vol. 3). Chicago: University of Chicago Press, pp. 224–227.

8. Johnson, W. (1993). Outcome research and religious psychotherapies: Where are we and where are we going? *Journal of Psychology and Theology, 3*(2), 297–308. A comprehensive review was provided by Gartner, J., Larson, D., & Vaclar-Mayberry, C. (1990). A systematic review of the quantity and quality of empirical research published in four pastoral counseling journals, 1978-1984. *Journal of Pastoral Care, 44,* 115–123. A helpful, though somewhat dated resource is Hughes-McIntyre, M. F. (Ed.). (1979). *Abstracts of research in pastoral care and counseling.* Richmond, VA: Joint Council on Research in Pastoral Care and Counseling. See also Strunk, O. (1988). Research in the pastoral arts and sciences: A reassessment. *Journal of Pastoral Psychotherapy, 2,* 3-12. The paucity of research on pastoral counseling is in striking contrast to the extensive psychological research on the processes and outcomes of psychotherapy. See Bergin, A., & Garfield, S. (Eds.). (1994). *Handbook of psychotherapy and behavior change.* New York: John Wiley & Sons.

9. To put this in perspective, currently most approaches to integrative psychotherapy lack controlled research to support either their efficacy or the specific constructs and combinations of techniques utilized. See Norcross, J., & Goldfried, M. (1992). *Handbook*

of psychotherapy integration. New York: Basic Books.

10. Barbour, I. (1966). *Issues in science and religion.* New York: Harper Torch-books, pp. 69, 77.

11. Ibid., pp. 36, 107. Two original sources are Schleiermacher, F. (1958). *On religion: Speeches to its cultured despisers.* New York: Harper and Row; and Ritschl, A. B. (1902). *The Christian doctrine of justification and reconciliation: The positive development of the doctrine* (2nd ed.). (H. R. Mackintosh & A. B. Macaulay, Trans.). Edinburgh: T. & T. Clark. Some helpful secondary sources are Barth, K. (1959). *Protestant thought from Rousseau to Ritschl* (B. Cozens, Trans.). New York: Harper; Livingston, J. (1971). *Modern Christian thought from the enlightenment to Vatican II.* New York: Macmillan; Marty, M., & Peerman, D. (1984). *A handbook of Christian theologians.* Nashville, TN: Abingdon; and Macquarrie, J. (1988). *Twentieth Century religious thought.* Philadelphia, PA: Trinity Press International.

12. Ferre, F. (1961). *Language, logic, and God.* New York: Harper and Brothers; Miles, T. R. (1959). *Religion and the scientific outlook.* London: George Allen and Unwin, Ltd.

13. See for example, Tillich, P. (1951). *Systematic theology* (Vol. 1). Chicago: University of Chicago Press, pp. 18–19, 40–44. Tillich sees psychology and theology related through philosophy, and he does not limit a psychological perspective to the experience of being.

14. Bube, R. (1971). *The human quest: A new look at science and the Christian faith.* Waco, TX: Word Books; Jeeves, M. (1971). *The scientific enterprise and Christian faith.* Downers Grove, IL: InterVarsity Press; Myers, D. (1978). *The human puzzle: Psychological research and Christian belief.* New York: Harper & Row . A perspectivalist position about historical events was expressed by H. R. Niebuhr in his contrast between inner and outer history. Neither perspective was pronounced as superior to the other. Both were judged as indispensable and interdependent. Presently, there is not merely two, but a plurality of views of both history and human experience. See Niebuhr, H. R. (1960). *The meaning of revelation.* New York: Macmillan.

15. Herink, R. (Ed.). (1980). *The psychotherapy handbook: The A to Z guide to more than 250 different therapies in use today.* New York: Meridian.

16. Goldfried, M., & Newman, C. (1992). A history of psychotherapy integration. In J. Norcross & M. Goldfried (Eds.), *Handbook of psychotherapy integration* (p. 70). New York: Basic Books.

17. Most of the 250 different therapies have not been tested empirically in controlled outcome research according to Norcross, J., & Goldfried, M. (1992). *Handbook of psychotherapy integration.* New York: Basic Books, p. 99.

18. Barbour, I. (1966). *Issues in science and religion.* New York: Harper Torch-books, pp. 36, 45.

19. Frankena, W. (1973). *Ethics* (2nd ed.). Englewood Cliffs, NJ: Prentice-Hall.

20. London, P. (1964). *The modes and morals of psychotherapy.* New York: Holt, Rinehart, and Winston; Browing, D. (1987). *Religious thought and modern psychologies.* Philadelphia, PA: Fortress Press; Prilleltensky, I. (1994). *The morals and politics of psychology.* New York: State University of New York Press.

21. The classic example of the psychological reduction of religious phenomena is Feuerbach's reduction of Christian theology to anthropology, an approach followed subsequently by Freud. See Feuerbach, L. (1989). *The essence of Christianity.* New York: Prometheus Books.

22. For a thorough discussion of this history and some of the positions taken, see Barbour, I. (1966). *Issues in science and religion.* New York: Harper Torchbooks. More recent discussions are Barbour, I. (1991). *Religion in an age of science: The Gifford*

Lectures, 1989–91 (Vol. l). New York: HarperCollins; and Peacock, A. (1993). *Theology for a scientific age: Being and becoming—natural, divine, and human.* Minneapolis, MN: Fortress Press.

23. Some of the points of comparison drawn between theology and clinical psychology may not be as salient for the traditions of depth psychology, which like theology, strive to address the depth dimension of the human condition.

24. Tillich, P. (1951). *Systematic theology* (Vol. 1). Chicago: University of Chicago Press, p. 25.

25. Two examples are Kelly, G. (1955). *The psychology of personal constructs.* New York: W. W. Norton, and Beck, A., Rush, A., Shaw, B., & Emery, G. (1979). *Cognitive therapy of depression.* New York: Guilford.

26. lbid., pp. 14, 18. In a similar manner, Viktor Frankl defined religious consciousness as the realm of ultimate meaning. Frankl, V. (1975). *The unconscious God: Psychotherapy and theology.* New York: Simon and Schuster, p.13.

27. See for example, Crabb, L. (1981). Biblical authority and Christian psychology. *Journal of Psychology and Theology, 7,* 305–311. Farnsworth characterizes this approach as the convertibility model of interaction between psychology and theology. See Farnsworth, K. (1982). The conduct of integration. *Journal of Psychology and Theology, 10,* 308–319. Separate rebuttals to Crabb were provided by Elens, J. (1979). Biblical authority and Christian psychology. *Journal of Psychology and Theology, 9,* 318–325; and by Breshears, G., & Larzehere, R. (1979). The authority of scripture and unity of revelation: A response to Crabb. *Journal of Psychology and Theology, 9,* 312–317; and by Guy, J. D. (1982). Affirming diversity in the task of integration: A response to 'biblical authority and Christian psychology'. *Journal of Psychology and Theology, 10,* 35–39. See also Bartlett, D. I. (1983). *The shape of scriptural authority.* Philadelphia, PA: Fortress Press.

28. Oglesby, W. (1980). *Biblical themes for pastoral care.* Nashville, TN: Abingdon, chp. l.

29. To quote Tillich, "Theology is not anthropology and when studied as if it were it surrenders itself into the hands of Feuerbach and his psychological and sociological followers. But theology is the solution of the anthropological question, which is the problem of the finiteness of man." Quoted in Taylor, M. K. (1991). *Paul Tillich: Theologian of the boundaries.* Minneapolis, MN: Fortress Press, p.112.

30. Examples include Adams, J. (1973). *Competent to counsel.* Phillipsburg, NJ: Presbyterian and Reformed Publishing Co., and Adams, J. (1979). *More than redemption: A theology of Christian counseling.* Phillipsburg, NJ: Presbyterian and Reformed Publishing Co. A current expression of conservative biblical counseling is MacArthur, J., Mack, W., and the Master's College Faculty. (1994). *Introduction to biblical counseling: A basic guide to the principles and practice of counseling.* Dallas, TX: Word Publishing.

31. Bobgan, M. & Bobgan, D. (1987). *Psychoheresy.* Santa Barbara, CA: East Gate; Hunt, D., & McMahon, T. (1985). *The seduction of Christianity.* Eugene, OR: Harvest House; Rushdoony, R (1977). *Revolt against maturity.* Fairfax, VA: Thoburn. These evangelicals have been described as hyper-orthodox by Johnson, E. (1992). A place for the bible within psychological science. *Journal of Psychology and Theology, 20*(1), 346–355.

32. This is an application of Tillich's discussion of the conflict of autonomy versus heteronomy in actual reason which prompts the quest for a theonomous (reconciling) reason and for revelation. See Tillich, P. (1951). *Systematic theology* (Vol. 1). Chicago: University of Chicago Press, pp. 83–94, 147–155. A theonomous psychology would be one which "expresses in its creations an ultimate concern and a transcending meaning not as something strange but as its own spiritual ground." Quoted from Taylor, M. K. (1991).

Paul Tillich: Theologian of the boundaries. Minneapolis, MN: Fortress Press, p. 121. What qualifies the theory of psychotherapy presented in this book as a theonomous psychology is both the ultimate concern and transcending meaning of reconciliation and the critical correlational method of relating psychology and theology. See also chapter 3, note 7 in this book.

33. "The real question is not whether or not to live by faith, but rather: 'By what kind of faith shall I live?'" Ferre, N. (1953). *The sun and the umbrella.* New York: Harper and Brothers, p. 135.

34. In his history of the United Church of Christ 1957–1987, Gunnemann noted that between 1925 and the mid 1980s more than sixty church unions had been formed world-wide, with at least one third of them between different confessions (e.g., Lutheran and Reformed). By the 1970s *united* churches represented an ever-broadening expression of church unity. The United Church of Christ is itself a merger of other diverse Protestant traditions. It was formed in 1957 by the union of the Evangelical and Reformed Church and the General Council of the Congregational Churches of the United States. Gunnemann, L. (1987). *United and uniting: The meaning of an ecclesial journey.* New York: United Church Press, p. 41.

35. Jensen, J., Bergin, A., & Greaves, D. (1990). The meaning of eclecticism: New survey and analysis of components. *Professional Psychology: Research and Practice, 21,* 124–130.

36. See for example, Grencavage, L., & Norcross, J. (1990). Where are the common-alities among the therapeutic common factors? *Professional Psychotherapy: Research and Practice, 21,* 372–378; and Lambert, M. (1992). Psychotherapy outcome research: Impli-cations for integrative and eclectic therapists. In J. Norcross & M. Goldfried (Eds.), *Handbook of psychotherapy integration* (pp. 94–129). New York: Basic Books.

37. This view of philosophy as something intermediate between science and religion was expressed by Russell, B. (1972). *A history of western philosophy.* New York: Simon & Schuster, p. xiii.

38. Ferre suggested that religion is essentially our relation to reality. Religion includes our presuppositions for thinking and orientation for living, and it involves our continuous choices of what within our experience is both most important and most real. Ferre, N. (1953). *The sun and the umbrella.* New York: Harper and Brothers.

39. Tillich, P. (1951). *Systematic theology* (Vol. l). Chicago: University of Chicago Press, pp. 19, 21.

40. Don Browning's philosophical analysis disclosed the "metaphors of ultimacy" evident in psychological theories of psychotherapy. These metaphors express basic assumptions about reality, the ultimate context of experience, the nature and purpose of life, our origins, destiny, and the basic value of life. Moreover, these ontic metaphors constitute the building blocks of theoretical models and the foundations for the theories of moral obligation implicit in all psychological theories of psychotherapy and necessary to them. See Browning, D. (1987). *Religious thought and the modern psychologies.* Philadelphia, PA: Fortress Press, pp.18–20, 41–44.

41. Frankl, V. (1959). *Man's search for meaning: An introduction to logotherapy.* New York: Washington Square Press.

42. May, R. (1983). *The discovery of being.* New York: W. W. Norton. Another existentialist is Yalom, I. D. (1980). *Existential psychotherapy.* New York: Basic Books. See especially pp. 419–484 for Yalom's discussion of the human problem of mean-inglessness.

43. Niebuhr, H. (1960). *Radical monotheism and Western culture. With supple-mentary essays.* Louisville, KY: Westminster/John Knox Press, pp. 11–16. According to

Niebuhr, theology not only develops reasoning faith; its second task is to criticize faith itself in relation to faith's object (God).

44. The role of reason in religion was expressed in Niebuhr's description of the dual task of theology: (1) to develop reasoning in faith (a constructive role), and (2) to criticize faith (a critical role). Niebuhr, H. R. (1960). *Radical monotheism and Western culture. With supplementary essays.* Louisville, KY: Westminster/John Knox Press, p. 11.

45. Tillich, P. (1951). *Systematic theology* (Vol. l). Chicago: University of Chicago Press, pp. 71–162. Tillich's discussion of the relation between reason and revelation is one example of this kind of reconciliation. Neo-Thomist Catholic theologians have affirmed the role of reason in natural theology as preparation for a revealed theology. See Phillips, R. P. (1964). *Modern Thomistic philosophy* (Vols. 1–2). Westminster, MD: Newman Press.

46. Niebuhr suggests that whereas the role of reason in faith is to organize, reflect, compare, criticize, and even develop hypotheses, the role of experience is to test faith's claims to validate or invalidate them. He suggests further that the relation of sense experience to natural objects is analogous to the relation of faith to the object of faith (God). Both statements reflect an empirical epistemology. See Niebuhr, H. R. (1960). *Radical monotheism and Western culture: With supplementary essays.* Louisville, KY: Westminster/ John Knox Press, pp. 12–13.

47. Within the history of Christian theology, an experiential emphasis was evident in liberal Protestant theologians such as F. Schleiermacher, S. T. Coleridge, D. Macintosh, and among Christian existentialists such as S. Kierkegaard, P. Tillich, and J. Macquarrie. See Livingston, J. C. (1971). *Modern Christian thought from the enlightenment to vatican II.* New York: Macmillan; and Macquarrie, J. (1988). *Twentieth Century religious thought.* Philadelphia, PA.: Trinity Press International, chps. 4, 12, 13, 22. It was also evident in John Wesley's emphasis on religious experience and his definition of faith as neither belief nor trust, but as spiritual experience known through "spiritual senses." See Matthews, R. (1985). With the eyes of faith: Spiritual experience and the knowledge of God in the theology of John Wesley. In T. Runyon (Ed.), *Wesleyan theology today: A bicentennial theological consultation* (pp. 406–415). Nashville, TN: Kingswood Books—An imprint of The United Methodist Publishing House.

48. Cited by Browning, D. (1987). *Religious thought and the modern psychologies: A critical conversation.* Philadelphia, PA: Fortress Press, p. 13.

49. For a summary, see Tillich, P. (1951). *Systematic theology* (Vol. l). Chicago: University of Chicago Press, p. 43.

50. The term "conative" has been used more in philosophy and theology than in psychology. I use it to refer to the human experience of willing and deciding among alternatives upon a particular purpose for the sake of which one intentionally acts. Conative experience is voluntaristic by virtue of the freedom of will it presupposes, and teleological by virtue of the role that purpose and intentions serve in the explanation and motivation of behavior. I believe the experiences of willing and deciding are central in psychotherapy. See chapter 6 for further discussion of this domain of the psychological dimension of human experience.

51. An empirical definition of faith was provided by the eighteenth century Protestant theologian, John Wesley. In his own theological development, he moved from defining faith as belief, then as trust, and finally as the direct experience of God. In other words, faith is spiritual experience. See Matthews, R. (1985). With the eyes of faith: Spiritual experience and the knowledge of God in the theology of John Wesley. In T. Runyon (Ed.), *Wesleyan theology today: A bicentennial theological consultation.* Nashville: Kingswood Books—An Imprint of United Methodist Publishing House, pp. 406–415.

52. Clinicians who lament theological preoccupations with sin fail to appreciate the

negativism of their own obsession with psychopathology.

53. London, P. (1964). *The modes and morals of psychotherapy.* New York: Holt Rinehart, and Winston. Don Browning's analysis of theories of psychotherapy as systems of practical moral philosophy revealed a variety of implicit principles of moral obligation. Examples include the nonhedonistic, ethical egoism of humanistic psychologies (Rogers, Maslow, & Perls), the theory of just consequences implicit in Skinner's radical behaviorism, and the cautious reciprocity in Freud. He evaluates these as unsatisfactory based on an independent criterion of a rational core of morality (the principle of mutuality) and upon Christian ethical principles of mutual love and agape. See Browning, D. (1987). *Religious thought and the modern psychologies.* Philadelphia, PA: Fortress Press, pp. 130–160.

54. Where the social sciences once defensively insisted they were "value-neutral," they now tend to present themselves as unavoidably "value-loaded." Robinson, D. N. (1985). *Philosophy of psychology.* New York: Columbia University Press, p. 142. Similarly, in New Testament studies, "the value-neutral stance is also yielding to the understanding that values guide everything we do including our choice of subject matter to study." Robinson, W. B. (1986). An overview of new testament studies in the last decade with a brief historical review. *Prism, 1*(2), 89.

55. For discussion of Ritschlian theology, see Livingson, J. (1971). *Modern Christian thought: From the enlightenment to vatican II.* New York: Macmillan, pp. 248–251.

56. Reported in Garfield, S., & Bergin, A. (1994). Introduction and historical overview. In A. Bergin & S. Garfield (Eds.), *Handbook of psychotherapy and behavior change* (4th ed., p. 12) New York: John Wiley & Sons.

57. Doherty, W. (1995). *Soul searching: Why psychotherapy must promote moral responsibility.* New York: Basic Books.

58. See for example, Niebuhr, H. R. (1963). *The responsible self: An essay in Christian moral philosophy.* New York: Harper and Row; Gustafson, J. (1983). *Ethics from a theocentric pespective: Theology and ethics* (Vol. 1). Chicago: University of Chicago Press; and Atherton, J. (Ed.). (1994). *Christian social ethics: A reader.* Cleveland, OH: The Pilgrim Press.

59. The reader may prefer the term "rapprochement" when referring to the interaction of disciplines characterized by mutually respectful dialogue. In this context, I am using the term "reconciliation" in a more limited way than the deeper theological meaning relating to an existential reunion of a divided self, the healing of broken relationships, or as the communion of the human with the divine.

60. Tillich, P. (1951). *Systematic theology* (Vol. l). Chicago: University of Chicago Press, p. 12.

61. Tillich suggests three possible relations between preliminary and ultimate concerns. Tillich, P. (1951). *Systematic theology* (Vol. l). Chicago: University of Chicago Press, p. 12.

62. Tillich, P. (1952). *The courage to be.* New Haven, CT: Yale University Press. A similar point about the theological dimensions of psychological guilt was made by Nanamore, B. (1974). Guilt: Where theology and psychology meet. *Journal of Psychology and Theology, 2,* 18–25.

63. Tillich, P. (1951). *Systematic theology* (Vol. 1). Chicago: University of Chicago Press, pp. 1, 13.

64. See discussion of various concepts of mental health in Jahoda, M. (1958). *Current concepts of positive mental health.* New York: Basic Books.

65. A recent book on scrupulosity is Ciarrocchi, J. (1994). *The doubting disease: Help for scrupulosity and religious compulsions.* Mahwah, NJ: Paulist Press. The phenomena of cults and spiritual abuse constitute others areas in which psychopathology is revealed. See for example Johnson, D., & Van Vonderen, J. (1991). *The subtle power of spiritual abuse.* Minneapolis, MN: Bethany House.

Chapter Three

Methodological Reconciliation and Formal Aspects

In the previous chapter, I discussed some of the positive theoretical implications of Tillich's construct of ultimate and preliminary concerns for the reconciliation of psychology and theology. If a meaningful reconciliation is to take place, it must occur at both the theoretical and methodological levels in order to occur at a practical level.

A method is needed to relate psychology and theology that will permit them to preserve their uniqueness and independence, while fostering a mutually constructive dialogue and creative interdependence. With some revisions, the method of correlation that Tillich used as a basis for a dialectical interaction between theology and philosophy[1] provides a heuristic model for relating (but not synthesizing) theology and psychology. I use the adjective "critical" to convey the revision that is needed in Tillich's method of correlation.

Following discussion of method, I introduce three formal aspects of this theory of psychotherapy: the source, norm, and medium of experience. I conclude with endorsement of both an empirical theology and experiential psychotherapy.

CRITICAL CORRELATION AS A METHOD OF RELATING PSYCHOLOGY AND THEOLOGY

As applied by Tillich, correlation refers to the interdependence of two independent factors. The two factors are considered to be both independent and interdependent.[2] They are related dialectically in the form of question and answer. The method of correlation is the unity of dependence and independence.

Tillich utilized existential philosophy to raise questions about the nature of human existence. He applied Christian theology to provide answers to these questions. The answers were not derived from the existential questions (the approach of natural theology), nor were the theological answers presented without concern for their relationship to human questions (the approach of supernatural theology).

Tillich derived theological answers from scripture as the basic source (though not the sole source) of historical revelation under the norm of the "New Being in Jesus as the Christ as our ultimate concern" through the medium of human experience in which this revelation is both received and interpreted.

The theological answers Tillich provided in his three volume *Systematic Theology* [3] were expressed in both the philosophical language of existentialism used to raise relevant questions and in the symbolic language of the Christian faith used to provide theological answers. Thus the existential and ontological concept of being and the threat of nonbeing raise the question of being itself, answered symbolically in the Christian doctrine of God as the ground, power, and meaning of being. Second, the estrangement characterizing human existence revealed from an existential analysis raises the question of reconciliation answered symbolically as the New Being in Jesus as the Christ. Third, the ambiguities of human life revealed from an existential analysis of finite freedom raise the question of the unambiguous life and union with the ground of being answered in the religious symbol of the Spiritual Presence. In a similar manner, the ambiguities of reason raise the question of a truth that is both certain and significant, answered in the doctrine of revelation. Finally, the ambiguities of human history raise the questions of both the unambiguous life and the ultimate destiny of humankind answered theologically in the symbols of the kingdom of God and eternal life.

This method of correlating questions and answers is a helpful approach to dialogue between theology and psychology, but with one important caveat. Both theology and psychology are sources of both relevant questions and meaningful answers.[4] The conclusions expressed in psychological theories that are based on scientific research raise questions of a theological nature. And as expressions of religious experience and convictions, theological answers raise psychological questions. By ensuring that both disciplines perform both functions of raising questions and providing answers, there is greater potential for genuine dialogue between these two discrete disciplines without sacrifice of their unique sources, content, or methodologies. This can be a dialogue based on mutual respect and grounded in a shared desire for reconciliation. It can help avoid the tendency of both disciplines to either ignore or dominate the other. It helps also to clarify their implicit philosophical premises and theories of moral obligation.

As an expression of the mutual benefit of such a dialogue between equals, I believe we can learn a great deal from a psychological understanding of religious experience, just as we can learn much from a theological understanding of psychological experience. Because both disciplines address dimensions of human experience in general, one perspective is needed by the other for a more complete understanding. The result can be mutual enrichment and enlightenment.

In my view, both scientific and religious truths are received through the medium of human experience, and the nature of experience influences the interpretations of these truths. Consequently, both theological and psychological claims to truth can be understood more clearly if both disciplines are applied to understanding human experience as their shared medium and object of study. This is another way of emphasizing the common empirical orientation of both fields.

Both psychology and theology, for example, have much to say about the human experience of alienation in social, psychological, and spiritual realms. Both approaches may be used phenomenologically to describe and understand this experience, whether it is construed in terms of psychological conflict or spiritual estrangement. And both disciplines can be applied to highlight the implicit question in such an existential analysis, namely the question of a reconciled life. Is a reconciled life really possible?[5] If so, what is it like, and what are its causes and consequences? How is it experienced, by whom, when, where, and why?

An estranged life raises the question of a reconciled life in a more ultimate sense; hence it becomes a theological concern, just as psychopathology raises the question of the nature of mental health as a preliminary concern. Furthermore, the psychological answers provided about the nature of mental health raise further questions about theological concepts of spiritual health. And theological answers provided about the nature of spiritual health raise questions about psychological meanings of mental health.

The quest for a mentally healthy and reconciled life is implicit in the descriptions and understandings of human experience noted throughout this book. I find this quest evident in the human desires for social, psychological, and spiritual reconciliation. It is evident in specific ways within the psychological realm of human experience in the cognitive, affective, behavioral, and conative domains illustrated in chapters five and six.

Questions arise within each of these psychological domains. Our cognitive experience of knowing raises the question of wisdom and its sources. The affective experiences of anger, fear, despair, and entitlement raise questions about the nature and sources of compassion, courage, joy, and gratitude. In the behavioral domain, self-destructive actions and unethical conduct raise the question of moral conduct (righteousness) and the ultimate source of all human values. In the conative domain, the volitional experience of making choices and decisions raises questions of freedom and destiny, and the ultimate aim of life: The question of "what do you want?" is not merely a preliminary concern; it implies an ultimate concern. In response to each of these questions, I seek to provide answers derived from the teachings of Jesus of Nazareth recorded in the Synoptic Gospels as their source.

I believe it is important to raise these questions if theological answers are to be received as relevant. We are not likely to receive answers to questions we have not asked, or if we do, we are likely to discount them as frankly irrelevant to our experience. However true Jesus' message, it must be shown to be relevant to life if it is to be both credible and significant. This is a position that endorses the apologetic nature of Christian theology.[6]

The questions I am raising in this book are not merely intellectual in nature. They are not the idle musings of an academic isolated in an ivory tower. They are existential and practical questions that arise from my own struggle for a healthy and reconciled life, and particularly for the reconciliation of psychology and theology in a theory of counseling and psychotherapy that will guide this same existential quest shared by others.

From my perspective, human experience is the medium in which and through which reconciliation occurs. As one form of human experience, the experience of counseling is therefore a potential medium of reconciliation. Insofar as reconciliation is also a religious experience, as Jesus taught, then the experience of counseling itself may be construed as a religious experience, not merely as a psychological or social experience. Therein lies a basis for a theology of counseling and a theonomous psychotherapy that discloses the religious meaning and the spiritual dimension of the therapeutic experience.[7]

The experience of counseling is a religious experience in a second sense, namely, to the degree that it addresses and includes matters of ultimate concern. By ultimate concern, I mean what Paul Tillich[8] described as that which pertains to our being or not-being, and to the ground, power, and meaning of our being. These matters include the reality and structure of human experience, the meaning and aim of one's own existence. These matters concern us ultimately, totally, and unconditionally. By definition, they are matters of faith.

Here I endorse Tillich's formal definition of faith as ultimate concern. The object of faith is that which concerns us ultimately, that which we trust ultimately as the source of meaning and value, and to which we pledge our ultimate loyalty as our chosen cause.[9] The object of our ultimate concern is whatever we believe gives our life meaning and worth, and whatever we live for as the purpose of life. Since we may choose any one of several ultimate concerns, sources of value, and objects of loyalty, it follows that faith takes many forms. When the content of that concern becomes loving the Lord your God with all your heart, soul, mind, and strength, and your neighbor as yourself, that faith takes a Judeo-Christian form.[10]

By suggesting that psychology and theology have a critical correlational relationship through continuous dialogue, I am rejecting both views that conflict between them is necessary and that a synthesis is desirable or even possible. If psychology is not derived from theology, nor theology from psychology, the independence of each is affirmed and protected. But their correlational interaction is also encouraged dialectically in terms of their shared roles of raising questions and providing answers. In both roles, each discipline preserves its unique attitudes, sources, and content, and its distinct methodology. And each approaches the other not to dominate, but to dialogue, not to compete or convert, but to cooperate for the welfare of humankind. Both psychologists and theologians are called to the kingdom of God, and together we can help to advance God's kingdom of healing reconciliation.

FORMAL ASPECTS: THE SOURCE, NORM, AND MEDIUM OF THIS COUNSELING THEORY

I have been discussing the dialectical relation between psychology and theology as the context for development of my theory of counseling. One mode of this dialectical relationship is reflected in the use of a spiritual tradition as the foundation for a critical evaluation of psychology. Another more positive mode of interaction is the constructive use of a spiritual tradition as a source of constructs and hypotheses about psychological phenomena.[11] The following discussion provides the foundations for the construction attempted in the remainder of this book.

The theory of counseling presented in this book is distinguished by its norm, its source, and its medium. Since its theological norm is the kingdom of God expressed in Jesus' gospel of reconciliation as our ultimate concern, its historical-literary source is the Synoptic Gospels in which this message is recorded. This message is received and the reality to which it points is encountered through the medium of human experiences of reconciliation. The experience of reconciliation through counseling is the particular focus of this book. I describe these three formal characteristics of my theory prior to presenting, in subsequent chapters, a definition and a phenomenology of the reconciled life as the purpose of counseling.

The Problem of Sources

Any attempt to derive the purpose and principles of psychotherapy from the teachings of Jesus presumes that we have knowledge of the content of Jesus' message. Unfortunately, access to that knowledge is somewhat problematic because, as New Testament scholars have acknowledged, we have no documents written by Jesus, and the primary sources of our knowledge of Jesus' teachings (the Synoptic Gospels) cannot be read as objective, unvarnished records of what Jesus actually taught.[12] The consensus is that the gospel writers shaped and edited Jesus material. For this reason, methods such as source, form, narrative, and redaction criticism are essential to recover his message.[13]

Moreover, R. Bultmann and M. Dibelius suggested that at best the gospels provide a summary of the message about Jesus preached by the early church; thus it is difficult if not impossible to separate the historical message of Jesus from the theological message about him. I am inclined to agree with Bultmann that we can know relatively little about the personality profile of Jesus, such as his self-concept.[14] However, this does not preclude knowing quite a bit about his beliefs and aims based upon what he said and did, as N. Wright[15] has noted recently. Nor does it preclude our achieving an accurate view of Jesus' vision of life as noted by M. Borg.[16] I agree also with Bultmann that the gospels need to be demythologized of the legendary material and the mythical worldview in which the message was cast, and to some degree confined. However, I agree with other New Testament scholars that the preaching of the early church (kerygma) is found primarily, though not exclusively, in the Book of Acts and the letters of the Apostle Paul. This is not to say the voice of the early Christian community is not heard in the Gospels. I am saying that to hear the voice of Jesus most clearly, we must study the Synoptic Gospels particularly and thoroughly. The Synoptic Gospels are considered the most reliable sources of Jesus' teachings, even by Bultmann.[17]

This does not negate the view that the gospel evangelists presented the Jesus of history as the risen Christ of faith. Nor must we accept the detachment of faith from history implied by Bultmann and Kähler, nor conclude that historical research to determine Jesus' authentic message is pointless, as suggested by Schweitzer and Kähler at the turn of the century.[18] Since the second half of the twentieth century, New Testament scholars such as E. Käsemann and G. Bornkamm[19] have expressed renewed confidence that while Jesus' message was certainly interpreted by persons who received him as the Messiah, this does not mean they could not or did not preserve authentic historical recollections from the oral traditions that served as the sources of their written records of his teachings. After all, these faithful disciples of Jesus were learners who memorized and recited his teachings. As Witherington notes, "this was the way Jewish educational processes worked. In fact it was the staple of all ancient education, including Greco-Roman education."[20]

We can know something about Jesus' message by using historical-critical methods, form and redaction criticism, narrative analysis, and social scientific investigations. Thus, it seems possible to distinguish Jesus' authentic teachings,[21] and this conviction underlies the contemporary resurgence of interest in what has been called the third quest for the historical Jesus of Nazareth beginning in the 1980s.[22] This quest also rests on the view that Jesus' message is not only recoverable, but also relevant to the present. I share both views.[23] I would argue also that in order to take Jesus seriously we must strive to understand what he taught.[24] To say it another way, to be a Christian is to be a disciple of Jesus. In order to be a disciple of Jesus we need to discover his message and discern what he meant. How else can we become his faithful followers?

This discussion emphasizes Jesus' message over his ministry, personality, the biographical details of his life, and the circumstances surrounding his death. This emphasis is consistent with the view of Jesus in the Synoptics, namely, that for Jesus the transforming message was of primary import, not his alleged miracles or exorcisms, not even his inclusive meals with persons of all stations of life.[25] It is also my view that his transforming message was more about the kingdom of God and less about himself, his life, death, or resurrection.[26]

Selection Criteria. How does one decide what are authentic teachings of Jesus and which sources are reliable? New Testament scholars have used a variety of criteria to answer these questions. Two criteria are dissimilarity and embarrassment, that is, the more dissimilar Jesus' teachings are from his Jewish historical background or the more embarrassing to the early Church (e. g., the baptism of Jesus by John, a baptism of repentance, and Jesus' crucifixion), the more likely the sayings and events are authentic. Other scholars have emphasized the more credible criterion of multiple attestation, to wit, that the teachings recorded in more than one source are more likely to be authentic. The criterion of coherence has been applied as well: those teachings that are coherent in content and form with the material already known to be authentic are also likely to be authentic.[27] I would add to this list a thematic criterion, namely, those passages consistent with the meaning of the central theme of reconciliation expressed in Jesus' teachings about the kingdom of God are more likely to be his authentic teachings.

New Testament scholars differ according to which criteria they emphasize, and this difference leads some to favor noncanonical sources such as the gospel of Thomas, the gospel of Peter, an alleged secret gospel of Mark, the Dead Sea Scrolls, writings of the Qumran Community of Jesus' day, or other documents. But the majority of New Testament scholars continue to rely upon the canonical gospels and particularly the Synoptics as the most reliable sources of Jesus' teachings.[28] Of course, the majority of experts could be wrong. What the majority believes to be true is not always so.[29] Nevertheless, the majority of expert opinion provides a preponderance of evidence even if it does not meet the standard of being beyond all reasonable doubt. So long as expert testimony is human testimony, unanimous agreement about all facts and their interpretations remains unlikely. It is also unnecessary to reach such unanimity in order to proceed with scholarly inquiry or to make a decision about the truth and value of Jesus' teachings for one's personal life or for the social good. New Testament scholarship seems to move back and forth like the tides of the sea. That does not prevent one's faith in God from remaining firm like a rock, but it requires us to appreciate the connection between rock and sea, between faith and facts.

The Synoptic Sources

Implicit in this discussion is the notion that the Bible as a whole does not constitute the source for the norm of reconciliation; rather, all biblical material is itself judged by this norm, the source of which is found in the Synoptic Gospels in which Jesus' gospel of reconciliation is recorded in the symbolic and religious language about the kingdom of God. The authenticity and value of revelations within the various books of the Bible are judged by the degree to which they are consistent with this normative message of Jesus' gospel of reconciliation.

The Synoptic Gospels are not the only source of a theory of counseling, but they are the primary source of any theory that claims to be based on the teachings of Jesus of Nazareth. The Gospels of Matthew, Mark, and Luke are generally acknowledged as among the earliest and most reliable records of Jesus' message and ministry as the founder of what has become a religion different from his own.[30] I agree with Sanders that the three Synoptic accounts of Jesus' teachings about the kingdom of God should be judged credible unless there are compelling reasons to think they are not trustworthy.[31]

By selecting the Synoptic Gospels within the New Testament as the primary source for a theory of reconciliation counseling, I am rejecting other religious works (e.g., the Bhagavad Gita, Koran, or Tanakh)[32] and even the discoveries of natural and social sciences as primary sources. The Synoptics are not, however, the only source. The rest of the New Testament and the Tanakh (called the Old Testament in the Christian Bible) are secondary biblical sources for Christian counseling.[33] Within the Tanakh, the Book of Job, the Psalms, Proverbs, and Ecclesiastes seem particularly relevant. So are the narratives of biblical figures such as Abraham, Joseph, Moses, and David. The Pauline corpus in the New

Testament includes explicit references to the theme of reconciliation (e.g., Rom. 3 and 5; 2 Cor. 5; Col. 1).[34] Though not a part of the original canon, the gospel of Thomas discovered in 1945 has been cited by a contemporary panel of biblical scholars as a reliable source of many of Jesus' teachings.[35] Also relevant to counseling are the various psychological theories of psychotherapy and the spiritual wisdom and approaches to healing found within other world religions including Native American traditions.[36] These are all secondary sources for me, but they are important and inspiring sources. Their inspiration, validity, and relevance are judged by the criterion of Jesus' message of reconciliation expressed in the religious symbol of the kingdom of God recorded in the Synoptic Gospels. Those portions of sacred scriptures that disclose the structure and meaning of the experience of reconciliation with God are most inspiring to me as expressions of the message of Jesus of Nazareth.

Although an inspired source, I do not view either the Synoptics, or the Bible as a whole as an infallible source. The Bible is a human creation, not a divine dictation. To transform the Bible itself into an infallible authority as literally, uniquely, exclusively, and absolutely true is a destructive bibliolatry.[37] Jesus called us to worship God, not to idolize the Bible. I consider Scripture as not merely a witness among others, but the witness without parallel to God's work of reconciliation in ancient Israel and in the life of the early Christian community.[38] Nevertheless, it is also the work of human hands[39] and subject to fallible human interpretations and misinterpretations. We need not be bound by biblical interpretations of the past. There is yet more truth and light to break forth from the study of Scripture relevant to our present condition.[40]

I also think it is important at least to attempt to separate Jesus' authentic message from both his disciples' subsequent interpretations of his message and from their own messages about his nature, origin, and destiny. In this process, we shall discover that the degree of confidence that certain sayings of Jesus are authentic may vary from a high degree of probability to being virtually uncertain, with degrees in between such as likely, or possible but unlikely.[41]

The absence of absolute certainties in the quest for the authentic teachings of the historical Jesus is not likely to be either comfortable or agreeable for those who have a low tolerance for ambiguity, nor for those who do not wish to be awakened from the slumber of unreflective religion. Nevertheless, we must be both realistic and honest: the historical-critical methods of biblical exegesis cannot prove absolutely that Jesus actually did say this or that, nor can they prove that Jesus did not say this or that. The most that can be accomplished is to establish a good probability that certain sayings attributed to him were his authentic teachings. This is not a limitation unique to New Testament studies, however, for the historical study of many persons from ancient times has such limitations (e.g., Socrates), and the scientific enterprise itself is based on probable truths. But this does not mean that either historical or scientific research must lead to a dead end of agnostic skepticism.

Insofar as the Christian faith remains a historical religion and not merely a philosophy of life, its foundation rests upon actual events that happened in a particular place and time, and upon the actual teachings of the Jesus of history as its founder. What happened during Jesus' life and what he actually taught are critical to our understanding of the Christian faith as a whole.[42] To be a disciple of Jesus requires one to take seriously his meaningful message and to advance his reconciling mission.

A related point here is that the limitations of exegetical methods for discovering Jesus' message cast doubt about doctrines of inerrancy of Scripture as the indispensable and final revelation. To press the point a bit further, all of us as students of the Bible approach it with unconscious assumptions and limited skills in handling the information. The clarity of evidence available also varies according to the sources that have differing degrees of reliability. But judgments about the written "word of God" are not identical with the view that the Bible contains the written words of God. One can be inspired and guided by biblical teachings without considering them infallible. One may affirm the authority of the Bible for faith and life while recognizing it is the refracted revelation of God. By that I mean the word of God is refracted by human words and concepts, which are themselves products of language and culture, a function of human reasoning and experience, and influenced by historical circumstances including economic and political conditions.

What then is the authority of Scripture? Scripture has authority insofar as it accurately records real human experiences of reconciliation with God. The Bible is particularly authoritative as a record of human interpretations of God's acts of reconciliation within ancient Jewish and early Christian history. Beyond that, the authority and power of the Bible to transform lives inheres in its faithful description and understanding of the experience of reconciliation with God. The actual experiences of reconciliation constitute the warrant for the validity of the written record. These experiences are the primary revelatory events. The Bible itself is revelatory insofar as it discloses the origin, structure, and consequences of this spiritual experience of reconciliation with God.

The recorded experiences of reconciliation constitute the most inspired and inspiring content in Scripture. They are also normative for evaluating Scripture as a whole. In addition, they constitute criteria by which to evaluate my own experiences and other contemporary human experiences both as to their spiritual nature and truth and with regard to their human value. Contemporary experiences that result in reconciliation are religious experiences in which and through which God is acting in the present as God acted in the past according to Scripture. The God we encounter and know in our own experiences of reconciliation is the same God revealed in the experiences of those who were inspired to write the sacred Scriptures. By virtue of their more profound and collective experience of God, I have chosen to interpret my own experience in the categories drawn from Scripture. Reconciliation is one of these central categories. Thus Scripture remains the authoritative source as a record and interpretation of normative religious experience. As a Christian hermeneutic principle, the Bible as a whole is to be interpreted in the light of its witness to God's work of reconciliation in Christ.[43] Those biblical passages that are most inspirational express Jesus' gospel of reconciliation and the religious experiences of reconciliation with God.[44]

Accepting the primary authority of Scripture is not the same as affirming the Reformation principle of *sola Scriptura*. In addition to Scripture, religious truths must be tested by tradition, reason, and human experience. This is the insight of contemporary Wesleyan theologians, which helps to avoid a one-sided emphasis upon Scripture, or upon any of the other three criteria. The truth of any theological proposal cannot be judged without evaluating it by all four standards.[45]

Having addressed some general and methodological issues about sources, I turn now to specific discussion of the particular sources of Jesus' gospel of reconciliation in the kingdom of God. It is generally accepted among New Testament scholars that the Synoptic Gospels were not written until about A.D. 70 to 90, forty to sixty years after the end of Jesus' life.[46] These documents were based on religious oral tradition and passed on by Jesus' early disciples. They are not an objective history of pure facts. They are edited recollections and records of interpreted facts about the message and ministry of Jesus. They were written not by dispassionate observers of human history, but by persons who were influenced profoundly by the life and teachings of Jesus. Nor were the authors divine messengers or angelic hosts; they were devoted human disciples who sought to describe and understand both Jesus' message and his life and death, to live according to his teachings, and to share the good news of great joy as transformed evangelists.

The authors of each gospel provide unique, expressionistic portraits[47] of both Jesus and his message and ministry. These portraits of Jesus in the Synoptics vary in their emphasis. Mark was most intent upon presenting Jesus as the Messiah, whose status was kept a secret during his life. Mark used this theme of the Messianic secret to explain why many did not accept Jesus. Anticipating Jesus' passion, and thinking in apocalyptic terms, Mark wrote to express the early Christian hope for the imminent return of Jesus as the Son of Man.[49] The view that the kingdom of God was the central theme of Jesus' message is rooted particularly in Mark's gospel (e.g., Mk. 1:15; 9:1; 13:24–30).

Matthew and Luke also present Jesus as the Messiah, but they emphasize his role as a teacher and report more of his sayings. In Matthew, Jesus is the teacher of a new ethical law for the Jews, which fulfills both prophecy and the Torah (the Law of Moses).[49] Though Matthew takes over Mark's summary of Jesus' teachings (e.g., Mk. 1:15/Mt. 4:17; Mt. 16:28) the "inaugural address" of the Jesus of Matthew is summarized as the Sermon on the Mount (Mt. 5-7). Luke's summary of Jesus' message is "the Spirit of the Lord is upon me, and has anointed me to preach good news to the poor" (Lk. 4:18).[50] Luke tends to present for Gentiles those teachings of Jesus that stress the universality of God's kingdom of love and justice for humankind in light of a parousia (end of time) postponed to some indefinite future. Luke presents the life of Jesus as the model of what Christians should imitate.[51] Each evangelist has a particular image of Jesus and a unique way of expressing the essence of Jesus' message.

While there are differences in meanings and emphases based on the gospel writers' purposes and context, there is agreement among these Synoptic writers[52] that a central teaching of Jesus was his message about the kingdom of God: "The kingdom of God has come near" (Mk. 1:15). Through the use of analogies and parables (Lk.15: 8–9), metaphors and similes (Mt. 5:13; Lk. 10:3), and even enacted parables (Mk. 11:15–19), Jesus sought to lead people to understand and to experience the kingdom of God and to learn what it means with respect to our relationship with God and with one another. It was an inspiring message of both personal reconciliation with God, like that between a forgiving parent and prodigal child, and a message of social reconciliation among all persons in a reign of righteousness and justice under the sovereign rule of the God of all creation.

Thus although the Synoptic portraits are not identical, they are very similar. In my view they are the most essential portions of Scripture for learning about Jesus' authentic teachings. I invite the reader to study the Gospels of Matthew, Mark, and Luke as companions to this book and as a basis for evaluating the biblical foundation of this theory of counseling.

When I have presented this material to other faithful Christians, I have been asked why I have excluded the *Gospel of John* as a source for my theory of counseling. The answer is that because I am attempting to develop this theory based on Jesus' teachings, I must look to the most reliable sources of his teachings. It appears to me that the Gospel of John is less reliable in this respect. Since the advent of modern biblical criticism, the Gospel of John has been controversial with respect to its authorship, place of origin, theological background and affiliations, and its historical accuracy as a record of the teachings of Jesus.[53]

Concerning its historical accuracy, the Gospel of John appears to be a less reliable account of Jesus' teachings for several reasons. First, there is a wider range of opinion as to the date of origin of John's gospel compared to dates of the Synoptics. Dates of the origin of John have been estimated from as early as A. D. 90 to as late as A.D. 150.[54] This range of dates suggests its origin is less certain, and lies anywhere from sixty to as many as 120 years after Jesus' death. There appears to be little disagreement that it was written later than the Synoptics, which have been dated from about forty to sixty years after Jesus died. The reliability of John's gospel as a historically accurate record of Jesus' teachings can be questioned by virtue of its later date of origin. The later dating of John is not prima facie evidence of a less authentic document, but the earlier Synoptic sources with more firm dating seem relatively more reliable as sources closer to the time of Jesus' actual message and ministry.

Second, the order of events in Jesus' life and ministry recorded in John are different from the order in the other three Synoptics. For example, in John's gospel the cleansing of the temple is placed at the beginning of his ministry along with the anointing at Bethany. The organization and order of John's gospel appears to be determined theologically, rather than chronologically.[55] It is therefore less reliable historically.

Third, John contains several incidents to which the Synoptics have no parallel. For example, the beginning of "signs" at Cana, baptisms by Jesus and his disciples, Jesus' conversations with Nicodemus and the Samaritan woman, his repeated visits to Jerusalem, his preaching and miracles there, and his raising of Lazarus. None of these events are recorded in the other three Synoptics.[56]

Fourth, John's gospel also omits events to which some or all of the other evangelists appear to attach considerable importance. For example, he omits the birth and baptism of Jesus, his temptations during forty days in the wilderness, his exorcisms, his transfiguration, and his blessing and distribution of bread and wine at the Last Supper.[57]

Fifth, John's gospel also has alternative versions of what look like the same events. Examples include the first encounter of Jesus with John the Baptist and with Simon Peter (Jn. 1:29–34 versus Mk. 1:9–11; Jn. 1:42 versus Mk. 1:16–17). Different versions are also evident in John's description of the events of the Last Supper, Jesus' arrest and trial, his crucifixion and resurrection (e.g., Jn. 21:4–8 versus Lk. 5: 1–11).

In addition to these differences in the records of events and their sequence, there are also differences in the form of Jesus' teachings in John's gospel that raise questions about its accuracy as an historical record of what Jesus actually taught. In the Synoptics, Jesus' teachings are given mainly as parables and epigrams, in forms that often resemble those of Hebrew prophecy and rabbinical teachings. In contrast, Jesus' teachings in John's gospel are presented mainly as long, meditative discourses and dialogues.[58] It appears their sermonic form and emphasis are the evangelist's.[59]

Besides differences in form, there are also differences in the content of Jesus' teachings recorded in the gospel of John compared to the Synoptics. Among these differences are the teachings ascribed to Jesus about time and the end of time (eschatology), Jesus' teachings about himself, the Hellenistic influence evident in John's dualism and logos doctrine, John's doctrine of the Holy Spirit, and the way in which Jesus' humanity and inclusive compassion are diminished in the Gospel of John.

Further questions about the accuracy of John's report of what Jesus taught arise when one compares the content of the fourth gospel relative to the other three combined. In fact, the real focal point of the controversy about the Gospel of John is less about its authorship, and more about why it differs in content as much as it does from the Synoptics.[60] Its content is so evolved theologically as to be unsuitable for the historical investigation of Jesus' teachings,[61] and particularly because the central content of Jesus' teachings about the kingdom of God present in the Synoptics is absent in the Gospel of John.[62]

Based on commentaries I have read, my conclusion is that the teachings that the author(s) of the Gospel of John attribute to Jesus do not all appear to have been Jesus' actual message. "It would indeed appear that a considerable amount of material in John represents the results of meditation upon the life and teachings of Jesus by the evangelist, based upon actions and sayings of Jesus, but modifying them considerably in the process."[63] For the reasons given, I consider John's gospel as a less reliable record of Jesus' teachings than the Synoptics.[64]

Nevertheless, all four gospels are theological writings by devout evangelists, and all four have been canonized as a part of the unified witness to Jesus as the Christ.[65] Like the Synoptics, John's gospel appears to express primarily a Jewish Christian theology, though different by virtue of its translation into the language of Gentiles influenced by both Greek philosophy and by Gnostic dualism.[66]

The Norm of the Kingdom of God

Within the three Synoptic Gospels there is unity about Jesus' central message of reconciliation expressed in religious language as the kingdom of God. The kingdom of God as the realm of reconciling relationships is the primary focus of Jesus' message. It is widespread throughout the Synoptic tradition in various forms: parables, proverbs, beatitudes, narratives, and controversial encounters with religious and political figures of his time.[67] It is this message that constitutes the norm for the theory of counseling described in this book.[68]

By "norm" I mean the criterion by which all other sources, criteria, and mediating experiences are judged.[69] More specifically, my theological norm is the *kingdom of God expressed in Jesus' gospel of reconciliation as our ultimate concern.* This theocentric norm refers to the reality of God's healing presence and loving power to reconcile human relationships. Expressed in Jesus' message of reconciliation, this theological norm refers to the present power and reality of reconciliation experienced with God, self, and others. Stated another way, the normative principle is God's healing power of reconciliation experienced in human relationships. This norm emphasizes the sovereignty of God, the therapeutic power of reconciliation, and the central concepts of experience and relationships as media through which this power is revealed, received, and actualized as a present reality.[70]

This theological norm is also an existential message. It addresses the estrangement[71] that characterizes human existence, and it reveals the pathway to reconciliation: Repent and strive first for the kingdom of God and God's righteousness (Mt. 4:17; 6:33; Mk.1:15). This kingdom is a realm of reconciled and reconciling relationships. Where such relationships exist, there the kingdom of God is present.

It is through this experience of reconciliation within the kingdom of God that human knowledge is transformed into wisdom; feelings of anger, fear, despair, and entitlement are transformed into compassion, courage, joy, and thanksgiving; and human conduct is transformed into right living (righteousness). All this occurs through the process and experience of willing the will of God. The result is a more reconciled life experienced as a beatitude (Mt. 5:1–12). Human happiness is experienced as one becomes more reconciled and reconciling.

I have said that the norm of reconciliation is derived not from the Bible as a whole as its source, but from Jesus' message and ministry recorded in the Synoptic Gospels. This biblical norm serves for me as the criterion of truth for evaluating other biblical material and the Bible as a whole. It serves as protection against a biblical literalism (bibliolatry) that considers the Bible in its entirety as an infallible, divine dictation,[72] and it serves also as the criterion by which to judge the spiritual wisdom of other religions and the discoveries in the natural and social sciences relevant to human reconciliation in general and to counseling in particular.[73]

This norm also judges any theoretical transformations of Jesus' message through the medium of human experience, including this particular application as a theory about the experience of counseling. No application constitutes the source of this ultimate concern to seek first the kingdom of God. The source is the Synoptic Gospels, in which the truth about the kingdom of God revealed by Jesus of Nazareth is recorded and interpreted.

Selecting the Synoptic Gospels as the primary source for Jesus' teachings does not mean one should ignore other biblical sources. In fact, to understand Jesus' concept of the kingdom of God, it is both helpful and necessary to trace the development of this normative concept within the Jewish community to which Jesus belonged.[74] This historical development demonstrates that reconciliation is a common theme in both the Jewish and Christian traditions.

The Kingdom of God in the Tanakh. In the preprophetic era, prior to the ninth century B.C.E., Israel's concept of God's kingdom was more limited and anthropomorphic than Jesus taught. "Yahweh" was a territorial God whose sovereignty was limited to the subjects within the nation who worshiped him. God was conceived of as a king of a particular land and people defined by national and geographic boundaries.

Second, Yahweh's sovereignty was limited not only geographically, but functionally. God's functions were (a) to provide help against the nation's enemies, (b) to provide counsel by oracles or soothsayers in matters of national difficulty, and (c) to provide a decision or a sentence of justice when a case was too hard for human decision.

A third limitation of this earlier concept of God's kingdom was evident in the view that God's sovereignty was dependent upon his subjects within the geographic realm of God's rule. A God without a land and people to rule over seemed inconceivable.

This limited view of the kingdom of God was expanded into a more universal conception during the age of the prophets. God's rule was extended beyond geographic and national boundaries, and also beyond the limited function as a divine helper in time of need. In this universalized conception, God became not so much the champion of Israel, but the guardian of righteousness, justice, and mercy. The God of Israel became the God of the world; a national monarchy became a world theocracy. It also became an ethical and spiritual kingdom in contrast to a political reign or military rule.[75]

In the postexilic period, that is, after Israel's liberation from Babylonian domination lasting about fifty years in the sixth century B.C.E., the new conception of God's sovereignty over the whole world had to be reconciled with the reality that God's rule was not universally recognized and obeyed, and that evil and suffering continued to exist. This problem of theodicy, as it is called, was addressed partly through Jewish eschatology expressed in the hope for a golden age of universal peace under the reign of God. This would be a Messianic age, ushered in perhaps by one of the saints of God, or a divine mediator, one like the Son of Man.[76]

In rabbinical teachings of Jesus' time, God's sovereignty was expressed in ethical terms as a divine discipline to be accepted by individuals through obedient submission to God's will. They also viewed themselves as elected by God to restore creation from its aberrant evil. Obedience to God's law and wisdom found in the Torah[77] was central to Jewish faith and remains so. This was expressed in the notion of "taking upon oneself the yoke of the kingdom of God." In this sense, of course, the kingdom of God is thought of as a reality that is present and effective whenever the rule of God is accepted through obedience to the Law.

The place where God's reign is effective and where the kingdom finally comes is earth, not heaven. The Jews expected not an apocalyptic end of the world, but a radical renovation of the present world order. The coming of the kingdom of God was not the end of the present world and an escape into the next, but a transformation of this world by God's reign of love and justice.[78]

Israel's story of God's kingship expresses its basic image of the world as a multidimensional reality that includes a real spiritual dimension as the origin and ground of this material world. Moreover, through its story of the kingship of God, Israel affirmed that this spiritual dimension is actually experienced, not merely believed or hypothesized. The spiritual and existential dimensions were seen as interconnected historically, personally, and culturally: historically through the communal liberation from Egyptian oppression in the Exodus and through Israel's return home from the Babylonian exile; personally through mediators such as Abraham, Moses, and the prophets inspired by God; and culturally through the Torah and Temple.[79] The kingship of God expresses the faith that this world had its origin in the power and sovereignty of God, and that God's reign continues in the present. Accordingly, in Israel's vision of God's kingdom we can see the normative theme of reconciliation as witnessed in the full biblical tradition.

This background provides a context for understanding Jesus' teaching about the kingdom of God. The authors of the Synoptic Gospels tell us that the kingdom of God was the central theme of Jesus' public preaching during his Galilean ministry (Mk. 1:15; Mt. 4:23; 6:33; 9:35; Lk. 4:43–44; 8:1; 9:11).

There are, of course, differing views of what Jesus meant by the kingdom of God. In contrast to an eschatalogical interpretation of the kingdom of God as a proclamation of the imminent end of the world,[80] I am inclined to agree with Borg's noneschatalogical interpretation. Borg views the kingdom of God symbolically as Jesus' reference to the spiritual dimension of life as an element of human experience. More specifically, the kingdom of God is a symbol of the power of God (Mt. 12:28/ Lk.11:20), the presence of God (Lk.17:20), life under the kingship (covenant) of God, an ideal state of affairs, and a spiritual-political reality.[81] The meaning of this concept for counseling will be developed in the remainder of this book. For now it is important to note that the kingdom of God is the symbolic expression of the norm of reconciliation that serves as the criterion for the theory of counseling being presented.[82]

The Variety of Christian Norms. I wish to note that this criterion of the reconciling reign of God is different from the norm chosen by other disciples of Jesus.

It is helpful to know that a variety of norms have been used within the history of the Christian faith in baptismal formulae, ecclesiastical creeds, and theological systems. As summarized by Tillich,[83] for the early Greek church the norm was the incarnation as the source of human *liberation* from both finitude and error. For the Roman church it was *salvation* from guilt and sin through the atonement of the God-man recreated through transubstantiation in the eucharistic sacrifice. For the Lutheran reformation of the sixteenth century, the norm was *justification by grace through faith* based primarily upon the theology of the apostle Paul and Martin Luther.[84]

For Calvinists, predestination of the elect served as a criterion, though for Calvin himself, the *sovereignty of God* was the primary idea, and the concepts of Grace and gratitude were also normative in Calvin's theology according to a recent book by B. A. Gerrish.[85] For Methodists it was *sanctification* by grace through faith grounded in religious experience and expressed through works of love in a life in the Spirit.[86] For liberal Christians of the late nineteenth and early twentieth centuries, the norm was Jesus as the *human ideal* or *ethical teacher*. For more conservative Christians, it has been the confession of Jesus Christ as *Lord and Savior*, and/or the Bible as a whole as the infallible Word of God. For other contemporary Protestant Christians, the norm is the prophetic message of the *kingdom of God* in both the Old and New Testaments taken as a whole.

The theological norm advocated by the Christian historian, Ernst Troeltsch, was *redemption* experienced as union with God. "Anchoring individual souls in God and uniting souls together through God, that is what Christianity is about."[87] This present experience of redemption is not the immersion of the self in God, nor the disappearance of the soul into a sea of infinity. Rather, this personal experience of redemption involves finding oneself through surrender of the soul to God as the highest value and as the final goal of life. The fundamental Christian principle is about a new birth (regeneration) through surrender to the will of God. This is a religion of personal monotheism in contrast to a pantheistic monism. It is a teleological and voluntaristic norm of personal redemption through a union of the human will with the divine will.[88]

As the criterion of his systematic theology, Paul Tillich advocated "the New Being in Jesus as the Christ as our ultimate concern."[89] Tillich's concept of *New Being* refers to the union of existential being with essential being under the human conditions of existential estrangement. In another context he construes this norm in terms of the logos doctrine, namely, as the principle of divine self-revelation manifest in the historical event "Jesus as the Christ." He considers this logos doctrine of incarnation of the divine in the human as the only possible foundation of a Christian theology that claims to be *the* theology. He justifies this notion philosophically as the unity of something that is both absolutely universal and absolutely concrete at the same time.

Tillich's criterion for affirming the New Being and logos doctrine of incarnation is more philosophical than biblical or theological in origin, and even Tillich acknowledged that it is not necessary to label that which is considered to be absolutely universal as the Logos; other words, derived from other traditions could replace it.[90] I have chosen to replace it with the kingdom of God as the universal element and Jesus' gospel of reconciliation as the concrete element. I do not share Tillich's need to establish the absolute truth of the Christian religion as the final revelation compared to all others.[91]

In contrast to the above mentioned alternatives, I have chosen the concept of reconciliation based on Jesus' symbol of the kingdom of God recorded in the Synoptic Gospels as the norm for this theory of counseling.[92] It is a norm that affirms God's reign of reconciliation in the realm of human experience. It is therefore both a religious and empirical criterion with social, psychological, political, and economic implications.

This emphasis upon the normative theme of reconciliation in the teachings of Jesus is not new in the history of Christian theology. In the late nineteenth century, Albrecht Ritschl favored as the norm for theological statements, "the Christian experience of the gospel of Jesus Christ."[93] Jesus' gospel was a message about reconciliation between God and persons, and among persons in the kingdom of God. The experience of this gospel is the medium of reconciliation. Jesus' gospel of reconciliation is about the reality of God's healing power experienced in human relationships characterized by love, justice, and peace.

My selection of Jesus' teaching about the kingdom of God as the norm for interpretation of Scripture and as the foundation for this theory of counseling is closer to Ritschl's historical-experiential norm in this regard than to Schleiermacher's subjective norm (the feeling of absolute dependence) or to Tillich's existential norm (ultimate concern). Like Ritschl, I consider the doctrine of reconciliation to be central to the Christian faith. Like Ritschl, and Kant who influenced him, I also emphasize the moral or ethical dimension of faith in my stress upon the conative dimension found in chapter six.[94]

The Medium of Experience

Regardless of the norm and its source, truth revealed religiously or discovered scientifically is received and grasped through human experience. Experience is the medium through which truth is known. Whatever we define as the source of truth—whether philosophy, religion, or science, whether reason, revelation, or research—all truth is mediated through human experience. As Tillich expressed succinctly, "truth from all sources is mediated truth; it is truth as experienced."[95] Because experience is the medium of knowledge, all truth may be considered as existential truth—fallible, but not fictitious. It is empirically grounded truth that serves as the foundation for an empirical theology.

Influenced by Lockean empiricism, the eighteenth century Protestant theologian, John Wesley, developed an empirical theology by extending the meaning of "senses" beyond the common reference to physical sensations and the perceptions thereof. Rather than limit sensation solely to interactions between a physical organ (the eye) with a material environment (light and color), Wesley used the term to include spiritual sensations and perceptions as a way of understanding the spiritual experience of faith in God. He affirmed that the object of faith (God) was an objectively real phenomenon, just as the objects of physical sensation are presumed to be real.[96] He affirmed also that the revelation of God in human experiences recorded in Scripture is confirmed by our own personal experience of God through the Holy Spirit.[97] In this empirical perspective, faith is neither belief nor trust, but spiritual experience, and spiritual experience is faith.

An empirical emphasis within Christian theology was provided in the nineteenth century by Friedrich Schleiermacher, who defined religion experientially as the "feeling of absolute dependence" (in contrast to a cognitive or behavioral definition of religion as either metaphysics or ethics). By that he did not mean that religious experience was solely affective or emotional, hence non-rational; rather he meant that religious experience is the intuitive consciousness of something unconditional, that is, the consciousness of being in relation with God.[98] This experiential awareness transcends both intellect and will, and subject-object dichotomies. Tillich[99] cited Schleiermacher's "feeling of absolute dependence" as rather near to what he termed ultimate concern about the ground and power and meaning of being, the latter serving as his ontological definition of faith in God.

Like Schleiermacher, I consider the Christian faith to be based upon the historical figure of Jesus of Nazareth. With Schleiermacher I affirm that the uniqueness of the Christian faith as a form of ethical monotheism is that everything in it is related to the redemption accomplished through Jesus of Nazareth. I agree also that God accomplishes human redemption not as the consequence of Jesus' sacrificial death, but through Jesus' communication of his unique and full consciousness of God as the dominant principle of life and its life giving power.[100] My own preference is to emphasize particularly Jesus' conscious experience of reconciliation with God as normative and redemptive. From this perspective, Jesus' message and ministry matter more than theological meanings ascribed to his birth or death as in incarnational and atonement theologies.

This is not to say that our own personal experience of the redeeming power of Jesus' consciousness of God is the source from which all theological contents may be derived. The primary source is Scripture, particularly the Synoptic Gospels, in which Jesus' conscious experience of being reconciled with God is revealed along with others' similar religious experiences of reconciliation. However, our own personal experiences of reconciliation serve as media through which the redeeming message of Jesus' gospel of reconciliation is existentially lived and empirically verified.[101] It is only through the medium of experience that Jesus' reconciling message is given and received. This emphasis upon the medium of experience expresses my preference for an empirical theology.[102] An empirical theology of counseling should produce hypotheses that can be verified or falsified scientifically through controlled research on the experience, process, and outcomes of counseling.

Since the concept of experience is central to my theory of counseling, it is important to explore the meaning of this term. Oakeshott has written that "experience" is "of all the words in the philosophic vocabulary . . . most difficult to manage; and it must be the ambition of every writer reckless enough to use the word to escape the ambiguities it contains."[103] What does experience mean? Standard dictionary definitions provide several denotations associated with the different uses of "experience" as a noun, a verb, and an adjective. As a noun, experience is the knowledge or feeling obtained through direct impression (e.g., the experience of pain); an instance of direct knowledge (e.g., she has had more than one experience of disappointment); the skill or judgment gained by practice (e.g., experience showed in every task she completed); an interesting or remarkable event in a person's life, something suffered by a person, or all that has happened to a person (one's life) or in a particular sphere of activity (e.g., in all his professional experience he had never met such a case).

As a transitive verb, "experiencing" means to have experience of something, to undergo, or to feel something (e.g., to experience a sense of loss). As an adjective, "experienced" means endowed with experience, with the knowledge and skill derived from experience (e.g., an experienced clinician). The adjective "experiential" means concerned with or provided by experience (from the Latin *experientia*, a putting to the test).

The latter meaning suggests an important function of experience—it serves as the test of the validity of ideas. A theory that looks to experience for verification would be called "empirical" because it makes use of, or is based on experience. An empirical generalization is one supported by experience, or in a scientific experiment, by empirical data.

An empirical approach is not the same as "empiricism." The latter is a philosophical position that confines all knowledge to the physical senses and rejects what cannot be verified by these senses. Representatives of empiricism include Locke, Berkeley, and Hume. I do not endorse empiricism as a philosophical position because it tends to exclude the spiritual dimension of human experience. Moreover, empiricism and its related logical positivism reduce meaning to measurement, and limit experience to experiments.

I have chosen "experience" as a central category in my theory of counseling because I believe that Jesus' teachings speak to our experience, and because this concept expresses the nature of reality as an experiential reality. In this respect the concept of "experience" is an ontological category akin to Tillich's use of the concept of "life."

Tillich notes three meanings of the concept of experience: ontological, scientific, and spiritual meanings.[104] Consistent with the emphases of Ritschl, von Harnack, and Troeltsch, I wish to add two meanings of moral and historical experience.

Ontological Experience. The first meaning of experience important to both an experiential theory of counseling and to an empirical theology is its ontic meaning. The word "ontic" is an abbreviation for "ontological." Both terms refer to ontology, which is a branch of philosophy devoted to the study of the nature of reality and the nature of being itself. Ontology addresses these questions: What is the nature of reality? What is real? What is the nature of being itself? What does it mean to be? To suggest that human experience is ontic is to affirm, first, that experience is real, and second, experience has to do with being itself.

There is an additional meaning implied here. The ontological meaning of experience asserts that what really matters for human living is not some objective, impersonal, or external reality, but reality as it is experienced. The effective or determining reality for the individual is an experiential reality. What I experience is what is most real for me, not a report of others' experience. It is also important to keep in mind that experience is both distinct from, and more than observable behavior; nor can it be reduced to any other single domain of psychological experience such as the cognitive, affective, or conative domain. Nor is experience unidimensional (e.g., physical, but not psychological, or social but not spiritual). We must preserve the multidimensional unity of experience.

If human experience is real and involves my very being, then the experience of reconciliation is also an ontological reality, not merely or exclusively a social, psychological, ethical, or spiritual phenomenon. The experience of reconciliation has to do with my very being, which includes, but is not limited to any one of the domains of being such as my knowing, feeling, willing, or doing. As Christians, we believe we are not merely informed by Jesus' teachings (the error of Gnosticism), nor are we merely to be conformed in our actions to his ethical commandments (the error of legalism). The Christian claim is that we are transformed[105] by God through Jesus' message and ministry of reconciliation. To be a Christian is a way of being, not merely a way of believing or behaving. The apostle Paul emphasized this holistic and ontic concept in his idea that in Christ we are a new creation: "Everything old has passed away. See, everything is new!" (2 Cor. 5:17). More specifically, the Christian way of being is being reconciled. Thus, reconciliation is an ontological experience as a way of being and, therefore, it has ontic meaning.

To say reconciliation has ontic meaning is not to say that it is entirely rational. Real human experience is also irrational and unconscious as well as conscious. Nevertheless, through empirical investigation we may discover an a priori rational order,[106] not as something imposed by either experience itself nor by history; rather, there is a rational meaning immanent in all experience, including religious experience. The experience of reconciliation is both rational and empirical, both universal and concrete, absolute and contingent, objective and subjective, transcendent and immanent. To describe reconciliation as an ontological experience is to point to its universal, absolute, objective, and transcendent meanings.

Reconciliation is also a very real experience. It is as substantial as any physical object, as real as anything else we experience through our senses. And since experiences of reconciliation are unique religious experiences, the real occurrences of reconciliation constitute empirical verification of the religious truths taught by Jesus about the power of God's reconciling love. That is not to say such experiences are the source, but they are the media through which such truths are received and verified. Implicit here is a position of experiential realism.

Scientific Experience. I have suggested previously that hypotheses about counseling derived from Jesus' teachings need to be tested scientifically. This view counts scientific experience as a valid medium of empirical verification of truth. I agree with Tillich[107] that scientific experience cannot provide either the source or the criterion (norm) of faith, but I wish to emphasize that controlled research can evaluate empirical claims made by a religious theory of counseling.

For example, I conceptualize the counseling process in part as the "compassionate confrontation of client incongruities." It is a valid, empirical question to ask for operational definitions of these constructs. These must be provided if this theory about therapy is to be empirically verifiable, hence credible.

I have proposed also that both the purpose and process of counseling are construed heuristically as the experience of reconciliation. The meaning and dimensions of reconciliation will be developed theoretically in this book. The next steps will require operational definitions to establish the construct and criterion validity of the dimensions of reconciliation described, and particularly its psychological dimensions in order to develop empirical measures, to derive testable hypotheses for research, and to engage in dialogue with psychological theories and the practice of psychotherapy.

As an example of this approach, if experiences of reconciliation through repentance and forgiveness were postulated as dynamic processes of counseling, these processes could be, and should be investigated empirically.[108] If religiously based counseling, pastoral counseling, or spiritual direction claim efficacious and therapeutic outcomes, these claims should be evaluated as well, using measures of both mental health and spiritual well-being. A goal-oriented outcome appraisal would be an appropriate evaluation procedure.[109] The outcomes achieved by religious counseling should be compared experimentally with no-treatment control groups and with other forms of counseling.[110]

The theory presented in this book suggests that as a result of reconciliation counseling, a client will experience healing and growth by becoming a more reconciled and reconciling person. Measures of such experiential growth are in principle both possible and desirable. They are also necessary if religiously based counseling is to have any credibility whatsoever with psychologists trained in scientific methodology.

A useful model to guide empirical investigation in this area is Carl Rogers' programmatic research[111] used to delineate the characteristics of the fully functioning person, the stages of growth occurring through the process of client-centered therapy, and the conditions deemed necessary and sufficient to produce such growth. Initial measures of the dimensions of reconciliation will be approximations, perhaps more qualitative than quantitative, but their applications will help to achieve greater conceptual clarity and predictability.

The phenomenological descriptions of the dimensions of the reconciled life provided in subsequent chapters of this book constitute sources for qualitative research and for the development of operational definitions to help address the following questions: What are the indicators that a reconciled life is present or absent, and to what degree? What are the necessary and sufficient conditions for a reconciling outcome? What are the antecedents and consequences of the experience of reconciliation? How does this process occur through time? Is there a linear progression through stages, or a circular or spiral movement? Or is it like most learning curves, a steady progression toward the goal punctuated by frequent lapses, gradually decreasing in number and degree? Answers to these questions are most likely to come from multiple sources such as therapists, clients, significant others, and observers' ratings, using multiple methods and measures.[112]

The point I wish to emphasize here is that the scientific study of the experience of reconciliation will advance our understanding of this experience and encourage empirical research as a common ground for meaningful dialogue between Christian theology and clinical psychology. The results from such research would help to evaluate the validity, reliability, and range of application of this theologically informed and biblically based theory of reconciliation counseling.

A prerequisite step, however, is to develop the theory of counseling that defines its nature and from which empirical hypotheses and procedures can be deduced and tested experimentally according to accepted scientific procedures. My goal in this book is to develop such a theory by first defining the purpose of counseling as reconciliation, and second, by describing the experiential dimensions along which change can be expected to occur in the process of becoming a more reconciled person.

Historical Experience. In addition to its ontic and scientific meanings, another meaning of experience is associated with the dimension of time. Human life is experienced in the present with memories of the past and anticipations of the future. Human life is a temporal experience with a beginning and an ending.

While there are differences according to their emphases upon the past, present, or future, most psychotherapists appreciate the role of an individual's past history as a significant factor contributing to understanding their present condition. This is evident at a theoretical level in etiological views that specify predisposing, precipitating, and reinforcing causes of mental disorders. At a practical and clinical level, social histories are obtained to understand dynamic factors salient in the development of psychopathology. A historical perspective is implicit in such clinical syndromes as "adult children of alcoholics."

Classical psychoanalytic therapy in particular has stressed that present symptomatology finds its roots in unresolved childhood conflicts involving sexual and aggressive drives. Psychoanalytically-oriented therapists used to spend years with their clients in archaeological diggings for repressed wishes, blocked emotions, and unacceptable thoughts, all on the assumption (unproven) that such activity was necessary for the client to gain insight into one's unconscious conflicts in order to experience a cure.

But psychoanalysis is not unique in its focus upon past history. Behavioral psychologists presuppose historical experience in their attempts to determine the patterns of faulty learning and to assess their client's failures to learn adaptive coping skills. In either case, it is the learning history that is counted and conceptualized in terms of eliciting, discriminative, and reinforcing stimuli within the client's past and present environment. The central concepts of reinforcement, antecedents, and consequences include the dimension of time in both classical and operant conditioning paradigms.[113]

The current popularity of narrative therapy may be its recognition that everyone has a story to tell, and that telling it is itself an essential phase of psychotherapy and a mechanism of change. Life stories occur through time, just as human development occurs through stages in a life cycle, each stage with its unique challenges and potential positive or negative outcomes, as Erik Erikson outlined. These are some of the ways in which psychotherapists acknowledge that human experience is historical experience.

In a similar manner, theology recognizes that human life is lived in time. Within the liberal Protestant tradition, theologians such as Albrecht Ritschl, Adolf von Harnack, and Ernst Troeltsch developed a historical theology as either an alternative to metaphysical approaches or as a foundation for philosophical theology. From this historical perspective, Scripture, the Church, and Jesus Christ are all affirmed as a part of history. Jesus in particular was not viewed as a supernatural being exempt from a historical life, hence neither is he exempt from historical investigation. He was a man of his time, and his life and teachings were relative to his origin and context. This does not deny that his life and teachings had a universal significance, but it means that the historical Jesus remains indispensable to a vital Christian faith of the present.[114] This latter statement, the historical-critical research on the biblical sources discussed earlier in this chapter, the periodic quests for the historical Jesus among New Testament scholars, and my own emphasis upon his historically authentic gospel of reconciliation all imply a position on how history is relevant to faith. I affirm with Ernst Troeltsch[115] that in Christianity faith and history are inseparable, and faith depends upon history just as faith interprets history. We cannot separate faith from history.[116] Faith is a part of human life, and human life is experienced through time as a finite existence. It follows that the life of faith is a historical experience.

Because experience is the medium through which truths are disclosed and discovered, and in which persons strive for reconciliation, human history—both personal and collective—is also a medium of both truth and reconciliation. Hence we may speak of the history of reconciliation, or of reconciliation history, evident for example in the life of ancient Israel and in the early Christian community, just as we may speak of an individual's religious life history or one's spiritual journey through time.

Perhaps the greatest weakness of both dogmatic theology and psychological theories of counseling is their neglect of the historical context of the human lives they seek to describe and understand, to guide and to heal. It has been feminist theologians and feminist psychologists who have helped us to recover this contextual perspective. We are bound by our times and we are products of our time. We may also transcend time and fill our time with meaning and joy. In any case, time is a determining category of finite existence. Human experience is historical experience.

Spiritual Experience. In addition to looking to historical, scientific, and ontic experience, a transpersonal theory of counseling may utilize spiritual experience as a further medium of knowledge relevant to understanding the experience of reconciliation in counseling and in other human relationships.[117] By spiritual experience I do not mean some kind of esoteric, mystical experience. I mean the kind that yields wisdom and insight into existential questions. Here's a humorous example of an existential question: "If lutefisk is dropped into the forest with no Norwegians within a thousand miles, would it still smell so bad?" The answer, of course, is that it depends on how it was fixed and when: No lye, no smell. Unfortunately, no lye, no lutefisk. It is a Norwegian paradox as profound as the Zen koan: "What is the sound of one hand clapping?"

Existential questions are more serious than either of these, and often less paradoxical or enigmatic. They are questions about the nature of existence and the meaning of being, about determining values and the purpose of life in the face of human suffering and social injustice. These are spiritual questions, for the spiritual dimension of life addresses the realms of both meaning and being.[118]

Christians believe that the Spirit of God is revealed through an encounter with the gospel of Jesus in the experience of love, faith, and hope.[119] Through regular meditation on Scripture, and through sustained worship and prayer, counselors will grow in faith and acquire spiritual discernment and wisdom with regard to life in general, to their own life in particular, and to their clients' lives as well. Our own spiritual growth depends upon continuous communion with our Creator, who is the ultimate source of whatever wisdom, compassion, and courage we can receive, hence share. In our study and meditation on Scripture, through contemplative prayer, and through intercessory prayers for our clients we may gain both insight and motivation to care for those whom God has entrusted to our care as counselors. Contemplative prayer and Christian meditation are media of healing for counselor and client alike. Consultations with a qualified spiritual director are recommended for both.

This is not to say, however, that such spiritual experience is the source of counseling theory and procedures, or for that matter, the source of either ultimate concern or absolute truth. Whatever insights are derived from spiritual experiences must be tested against the norm of Jesus' teachings about the reconciling reign of God revealed in the Synoptic sources.

Nor can such spiritual experience become a substitute source for the religious truth revealed in the Synoptic Gospels. Only if we were fully reconciled (if not united in identity) with the spiritual source of all religious experience could our own spiritual experiences function as an independent and normative source. Our reconciliation with God is one of communion rather than union or identity.[120] Since this involves the shared purpose of the human will with the divine will, the experience of reconciliation may be described as primarily a conative communion. This process of reconciliation is lifelong and never fully actualized in this life because it is inhibited by our estrangement from God resulting from our own pride and error.[121] Moreover, as a result of this ambiguity, which characterizes all human experience, any insights gained from our own spiritual experiences remain fallible at best and must be evaluated relative to the criterion of Jesus' gospel of reconciliation expressed in his concept of the kingdom of God as recorded in the

Synoptic Gospels.

Our separation from God does not, however, preclude God's overcoming this separation. That God does bring about reconciliation is symbolized by the coming of the kingdom of God, the nature of which was the subject of Jesus' message and advancement of which was the purpose of his ministry. Nevertheless, we receive this revealed truth from Jesus about the reconciled life through the medium of our experience. And so did the authors of all the books in the New Testament, who shared their own experiences of religious truth along with their interpretations of their own unique, spiritual and historical experiences of reconciliation. Experiences of reconciliation are spiritual experiences. Authentic religious experiences are reconciling.

Despite these limitations, which are a function of the ambiguities and limitations of existence itself as finite freedom, spiritual experiences are vital media for receiving spiritual wisdom relevant to life, and for actually experiencing the love of God and the healing that results from reconciliation with God through love, faith, and hope. Meditation and prayer are pathways to both truth and personal transformation. They are also media for insights about counseling.

Moral Experience. In addition to its spiritual, historical, scientific, and ontological dimensions, human experience also has a moral dimension. It is particularly the spiritual and moral dimensions of human experience that distinguish life as uniquely and fully human. Human experience is by nature moral experience, and a moral life is a meaningful and good life worthy of living. That being so, a religious theory of counseling may look to moral experience as a further medium of knowledge relevant to understanding the reconciled life and to comprehending the experience of reconciliation that occurs through counseling and other human relationships.

In the history of Christian thought, moral experience was emphasized in eighteenth century Romanticism by Jean Rousseau, in the eighteenth century Enlightenment by Immanuel Kant, in the nineteenth century by Samuel Coleridge and Albrecht Ritschl, and for several centuries in Catholic moral theology. In the nineteenth century Søren Kierkegaard and in the twentieth century Paul Tillich discussed the existential and ontological dimensions of moral experience. An emphasis upon moral experience has also characterized American liberal Protestantism in the twentieth century, reflected for example in the realistic empirical theology of D. C. Macintosh and in the theological naturalism of Henry Wieman, and in the theocentric ethics of H. R. Niebuhr and James Gustafson. Based in part on Kohlberg's theory of moral development, J. Fowler suggested that the moral dimension of experience was an important aspect and stage of faith development.[122] Throughout the twentieth century, many Christian writers have developed approaches to social ethics which address economic and political issues.[123]

Discussion of the social implications of Christian ethics is beyond the scope of this book. Here I wish to note that moral experience is an important medium of knowledge about God's moral purpose of reconciliation. Moral experience also constitutes a medium for insights about counseling guided by this ethical and therapeutic goal of reconciliation. Like ontic, scientific, historical, and spiritual experiences, moral experience is another medium through which knowledge about God is existentially received and empirically verified.

This discussion of moral experience suggests that I am not interested in reconciliation merely as a hypothetical construct. I am interested in reconciliation also as a normative concept. For me it functions as the most general statement of what counseling ought to be about. Reconciliation is both a value and a principle of moral obligation. It expresses the desired outcome of psychotherapy—a reconciling life. This involves a transformation of character as well as conduct, a change in conscience as well as cognitions, a reorientation of values in conformity with the will of God with the help of God's reconciling grace. This moral emphasis suggests a character-conduct therapy in contrast to a cognitive-behavior therapy.

By way of summary, I wish to say that human experience is not the basic source of the revealed truths Jesus taught about the kingdom of God. However, in all of its ontological, scientific, historical, spiritual, and moral dimensions, experience is the medium through which that revealed truth is received. All five forms of experience are valid media, and while none constitutes an exclusive source, each may function as a medium through which confirming or disconfirming evidence for religious truth is found. In this respect, the authority of experience complements the authority of Scripture.

EMPIRICAL THEOLOGY AND EXPERIENTIAL COUNSELING

This discussion expresses my preference for both an experiential theory of counseling and for an empirical theology.[124] Theology is empirical to the extent it is linked to experience. Theological concepts like reconciliation must be relevant to, and realized in human experience, and they must be tested by experience to determine if they are credible.

By advocating an empirical theology I am not proposing an inductive derivation of a theological norm from human experience. Rather, I am attempting to relate the theological concept of reconciliation to human experience as an answer to the question of alienation and estrangement that arises in human experience. Human experience is not the source of the theological norm, and even if it were, one could not avoid selecting some characteristic of experience to serve as the empirical basis of theology. Selection of the characteristic or quality of experience is based on either some personal experience, a value judgment, or personal commitment. Some a priori experience and valuation is implied.

In the present theory, reconciliation functions as the value judgment and a priori experience, or that characteristic of experience that is determinative for the theory. But my selection of reconciliation is on theological grounds, not on empirical grounds. The selection is based on my personal commitment to the teachings of Jesus of Nazareth in which the norm of reconciliation is expressed symbolically as the kingdom of God. This is the symbolic expression of my faith as ultimate concern and the foundation for my empirical theology.

It seems to me that one of the strengths of an empirical theology particularly is to show that religious experience is not so esoteric after all, but a unique quality or dimension of human experience in general. A religious experience is not some metaphysically altered state of consciousness; rather it is an experience of the spiritual dimension of life in ordinary life. My experience of the eternal is a dimension within my ordinary experience of time. My experience of God is not as an object among other objects, nor as a being among other beings, but an experience of Being itself—the ground and power and meaning of my being. This is an experience of the transcendent, sacred, or depth dimension of all ordinary life.[125]

An empirical theology counts human experience, but not to the exclusion of Scripture, tradition, and reason. A satisfactory Christian theology is not only empirical; it is also biblical, reasonable, and conversant with tradition without being bound by it. We need to depend upon the witness of Scripture, the faith traditions of the past, the deliberations of reason, and the content of religious experience at both personal and collective levels. Accordingly, the ultimate test of religious truths is not singular, but multiple. By including multiple criteria we are more likely to avoid a one-sided emphasis evident in biblicism, traditionalism, rationalism, and experientialism.[126] Having said this, I wish to reiterate that among these multiple standards is the test of human experience shared by persons within a particular faith tradition. The experience shared by those in the liberal Protestant tradition serves as the foundation for this book.

While the concept and reality of experience is central to both empirical theology and experiential counseling, it is the theological perspective that defines the depth of experience as its reconciling power, and identifies some experiences as more reconciling (and revelatory) than others. The foundation of this theological perspective and the primary literary source of the theological norm of reconciliation is Scripture in which the reality of God's acts of reconciliation in human life is affirmed and revealed in the history and experience of ancient Israel, in the message and ministry of Jesus, and in the early Christian community. The ultimate source of all experiences of reconciliation is God, who acts to reconcile the world.

For the Christian, Jesus' experience of reconciliation with God constitutes the criterion by which to test our own experiences of reconciliation and the authenticity of revelations of God's love in human life. The literary source for this normative experience of Jesus is the Synoptic Gospels in which Jesus' experience with God is disclosed. Yet this special revelation must be interpreted by tradition, evaluated by reason, and tested by our own experience. The reconciliation with God experienced in the past by Jesus and by the authors of Scripture is confirmed by our own personal experiences of God in the present through reconciling acts, events, persons, and relationships.[127] Thus, a special revelation is accessible to human experience, and therefore, in principle, available to everyone as other empirical theologians have affirmed.

Ordinary human experience becomes religious experience to the degree it is a bearer of reconciliation. It is in and through my human experiences of reconciliation that I experience the divine, albeit through a glass darkly. Accordingly, when a counselor helps a couple on the verge of divorce become reconciled, that is empirical evidence of God acting in human experience. When a lay care support group helps someone become reconciled to divorce or to the loss of a loved one, that too is a religious experience of reconciliation. When an attorney mediates a dispute between two antagonistic parties, that is another expression of a ministry of reconciliation. When a mother brings peace between two fighting siblings, that too is empirical evidence of God acting through persons to reconcile those whom God loves. All of these common experiences of reconciliation constitute a media of revelation of the one spiritual source of all experiences of reconciliation. That source is the God who transcends my experience, though revealed as the One who reconciles within my experience. Thus, experiences of reconciliation are "disclosure situations" or "ciphers of the divine in human life,"[128] and these experiences lend credibility to the truth of Jesus' teachings about God as the One who reconciles.

Wherever reconciliation of alienated persons occurs, there is empirical evidence of the healing power of the Spirit of God.[129] Wherever estrangements are reconciled, separations are reunited, or broken relationships are healed, there we may gain experiential knowledge of the power of divine healing; for alienated persons cannot heal either themselves or their broken relationships. The source of reconciliation is God, but not as an abstract concept or moral ideal. God is experienced as a very real presence and power in our concrete lives. God acts within and through human experiences of reconciliation. As a result, it becomes possible to know God through our experience. In this sense faith is an empirical phenomenon.

To affirm that faith is empirical is not to claim empirical proofs for the existence of God, nor to reason inductively from experiences of reconciliation to a reconciling God as the logically necessary inference. Theological reflection begins with faith in God as its premise. Faith is not an inductive or deductive conclusion based on either reason or experience. One reasons theologically from faith and with faith, not to faith. Faith begins as trust in God, and loyalty to God, expressed as ultimate concern.[130] Ultimate concerns, however, are empirical concerns arising within human experience.

Faith is empirical in another sense: faith makes a difference in our experience. It is through faith that we receive meaning and purpose, courage to take risks, to endure our suffering, and to find the moral will to help others struggle for justice and to alleviate their suffering. It is through faith that God heals us from the anguish of a wounded spirit, from fear, sorrow, bitterness, and discontent.

The empirical nature of faith became real for one of the men in my graduate course on psychotherapy and spiritual direction. He identified himself as a cultural Jew on a spiritual journey expressed in his desire to integrate psychology and spirituality within his clinical practice and personal life. I think of him as a kindred spirit. He wrote a moving, experiential paper, reflecting upon his own life in terms of this concept of experiences of reconciliation as evidence of God acting in human life.

He shared his sad story of the agony he experienced from his divorce and the resulting separation from his son. He recalled the pain he experienced the day he took his son to the airport to board a plane to go to be with his mother who had gone to Europe with her new husband. "After he boarded the plane," he said, "I returned to my car and began to cry, and I couldn't stop . . . for a long time." That was a heart-breaking experience for him, the kind that drops you to your knees, but in his case, it was not kneeling to pray, but to curse God.

That traumatic divorce from his wife and separation from his son resulted in spiritual estrangement from God that lasted for years. After nearly twenty years of separation and loss of contact, he received an excited phone call, "Dad, this is David." They were reunited. And in their experience of reunion this man recognized that God had not abandoned him, but that God's hand was in that concrete experience of reconciliation with his beloved son. What he is also beginning to realize is that God is with us in our experiences of painful separation in addition to our times of healing reunion. God is with us when all others leave.

This man's concrete experience of reunion with his son illustrates the social, psychological, and spiritual dimensions of reconciliation, and the existential nature of the reconciled life. As preparation for an existential-phenomenological analysis of the reconciled life, in the next chapter I shall develop a working definition of reconciliation and several reasons for commending it as the general purpose of counseling and psychotherapy.

NOTES

1. Tillich, P. (1951). *Systematic theology* (Vol. 1). Chicago: University of Chicago Press, pp. 60–64. See also Tillich, P. (1957). *Systematic theology* (Vol. 2). Chicago: University of Chicago Press, pp. 13–16 for his further discussion of correlation as "the interdependence of two independent factors." A dialogical relation between psychology and theology has been advocated by both physical and social scientists as well. See Barbour, I. (1990). *Religion in an age of science: Gifford lectures, 1989-91* (Vol. 1). New York: HarperCollins; Evans, C. S. (1982). *Preserving the person: A look at the human sciences*. Grand Rapids, MI: Baker; and Jones, S. (1994). A constructive relationships for religion with the science and profession of psychology. *American Psychologist, 49*(3),184–197.

2. Tillich, P. (1957). *Systematic theology* (Vol. 2). Chicago: University of Chicago Press, pp. 13–16.

3. Tillich, P. (1951, 1957, 1963). *Systematic theology* (Vols. 1–3). Chicago: University of Chicago Press. There are several good introductions to Tillich's Christian existential theology: McKelway, A. J. (1964). *The systematic theology of Paul Tillich: A review and analysis*. Richmond, VA: John Knox Press; Eisenbeis, W. (1983). *The key ideas of Paul Tillich's systematic theology*. Washington, DC: University Press of America; Church, F. (Ed.) (1967). *The essential Tillich: An anthology of the writings of Paul Tillich*. New York: Macmillan; Rademacher, R. (1968). *A Tillich glossary*. Dubuque: Wartburg Theological Seminary. Critiques are provided by Thomas, J. H. (1961). *Paul Tillich: An appraisal*. Philadelphia, PA: Westminster Press; Hamilton, K. (1963). *The system and the gospel: A critique of Paul Tillich*. New York: Macmillan; Kegley, C., & Bretall, R. (1964). *The theology of Paul Tillich*. New York: Macmillan; Miller, A., & Arthur, D. C. (Eds.). (1975). *Paul Tillich's systematic theology: A philosophical analysis of being human and an apologetic theology of the divine life*. St. Louis, MO: Eden Publishing; and Taylor, M.

(1991). *Paul Tillich: Theologian of the boundaries.* Minneapolis, MN: Fortress Press. A relevant chapter by Tillich is included in Lefevre, P. (Ed.). (1984). *The meaning of health. Essays in existentialism, psychoanalysis, and religion.* Chicago: Exploration Press.

    4. This modification of Tillich's correlational method is compatible with the "revised critical correlational approach" advocated by Tracy, D. (1975). *Blessed rage for order.* New York: Seabury Press, and with the "mutually critical correlation" advocated by Browning, D. (1987). *Religious thought and the modern psychologies.* Philadelphia, PA: Fortress Press, pp. 15–17, 140.

    5. A related question was raised by Patton, J. (1985). *Is human forgiveness possible: A pastoral care perspective.* Nashville, TN: Abingdon Press.

    6. The apologetic nature of theology was emphasized by Tillich, P. (1951). *Systematic theology* (Vol. 1). Chicago: University of Chicago Press, pp. 6–8. An alternative view emphasizing the confessional nature of theology was expressed by Niebuhr, H. R. (1960). *The meaning of revelation.* New York: Macmillan, p. 42. It seems to me that both approaches are valid and the two can be combined.

    7. A theonomous psychotherapy applies an existential-phenomenological method to describe the ultimate concerns implicit in the client's concrete concerns without controlling either the content of therapeutic conversation or its methods. Hence to describe psychotherapy as theonomous does not mean the acceptance of theology as a higher authority imposed upon psychology; rather it refers to an autonomous psychology united with its own transcendent dimension of being and meaning. The form of theonomous psychotherapy presented here attempts to disclose the spiritual dimension of therapy as the experience of reconciliation. In this manner, therapeutic insight is complemented by spiritual insight, but not replaced by it. Moreover, in this form, ontological reasoning and receiving knowledge complement technical reasoning and controlling knowledge to disclose the transcending meanings of the therapeutic experience not as something strange or supernatural, but as its own ground and structure in the experience of the sacred and unconditional. Tillich, P. (1951). *Systematic theology* (Vol. 1). Chicago: University of Chicago Press, pp. 72–73, 85, 95–96, 110, 121–123, 147. See also chapter 2 of this book, n.32.

    8. Tillich, P. (1951). *Systematic theology* (Vol.1). Chicago: University of Chicago Press, pp.14–15. See also chapter two, n.26 of this book.

    9. Here I am adding Niebuhr's concepts of faith as confidence and fidelity to Tillich's formal definition of faith as ultimate concern. See Niebuhr, H. R. (1960). *Radical monotheism and Western culture. With supplementary essays.* Louisville, KY: Westminister/John Knox Press, pp.16–23.

    10. Mark 12:19 records these two sacred commandments taught by Jesus. For elaboration, see Tillich, P. (1951). *Systematic theology* (Vol. l). Chicago: University of Chicago Press, p. 11, and Tillich, P. (1957). *The dynamics of faith.* New York: Harper and Brothers Publishers. Tillich's view of faith is existential and experiential in contrast to intellectualistic, voluntaristic, and emotional views of faith as merely belief, an act of will, or a feeling. Tillich's definition of faith as ultimate concern is compatible with H. R. Niebuhr's view of faith as confidence and loyalty to that which one considers an ultimate value center and the unconditional cause for the sake of which one lives. See Niebuhr, H. R. (1960). *Radical monotheism and Western culture. With supplementary essays.* Louisville, KY: Westminister/John Knox Press, pp. 16–23.

    11. Jones noted the relative absence of constructive models of psychological theory based upon spiritual traditions. See Jones, S. (1994). A constructive relationship for religion with the science and profession of psychology. *American Psychologist, 49*(3), 184-197. Subsequent responses to his article suggest continued debate over this type of interaction between psychology and religion. See the Comments section in the *American*

Psychologist, July, 1995, pp. 540–545. Don Browning called for the development of a critical psychological theory of psychotherapy as a practical discipline that "tries self consciously and critically to ground itself in an ethic and a metaphysic. . . ." See Browning, D. (1987). *Religious thought and the modern psychologies: A critical conversation.* Philadelphia, PA: Fortress Press, pp. xi, 124, 161, 238.

12. Scripture is the revelation and reception of what concerns us ultimately. It also records the preparation for both revelation and reception, hence it is neither a scientific record nor objective history. Taylor, M. K. (1991). *Paul Tillich: Theologian of the boundaries.* Minneapolis, MN: Fortress Press, p. 132.

13. Witherington, B. (1995). *The Jesus quest: The third search for the Jew of Nazareth.* Downers Grove, IL: InterVarsity Press, p. 200. As Ernst Käseman noted, we can recover the message and ministry of Jesus through, and thanks to the faith-testimony of Jesus' interpreters, not just behind and in spite of their testimony as von Harnack implied. See Cowdell, S. (1996). *Is Jesus unique?* New York: Paulist Press, p. 9.

14. Bultmann, R. (1958). *Jesus and the word.* New York: Scribner's, p. 14.

15. Wright, N.T. (1997). *Jesus and the victory of God: Christian origins and the question of God* (Vol. 2). Minneapolis, MN: Fortress Press.

16. Borg contrasts Jesus' vision of a compassionate life with the conventional wisdom of his day and our own time in Borg, M. (1994b). *Meeting Jesus again for the first time: The historical Jesus and the heart of contemporary faith.* New York: HarperSanFrancisco. Sanders concurs that we can know quite a bit about what Jesus thought and taught, and what others thought about him. Sanders, E. P. (1994). *The historical figure of Jesus.* New York: Penguin Books, pp. 4–5, 54, 75–76.

17. See Witherington, B. (1995). *The Jesus quest: The third search for the Jew of Nazareth.* Downers Grove, IL: InterVarsity Press, pp. 79, 143–144, 264, n.23. Witherington cites other New Testament scholars who support the reliability of the canonical gospels as sources of Jesus' teachings, including himself, P. Meier, N. Wright, P. Stuhlmacher, J. Dunn, M. DeJonge, and M. Bockmuehl. Another scholar who agrees with the view that the Synoptic Gospels are the most reliable sources is Sanders, E. P. (1994). *The historical figure of Jesus.* New York: Penguin Books, pp. 75–76. Biblical scholars associated with the Jesus Seminar accept portions of the Synoptic Gospels as authentic records of Jesus' teaching, but add other sources such as the Sayings Gospel of Q and the coptic Gospel of Thomas. See Funk, R. W. (1996). *Honest to Jesus: Jesus for a new millennium.* New York: HarperSanFrancisco, pp. 20, 121–139.

18. Cited in Witherington, B. (1995). *The Jesus quest: The third search for the Jew of Nazareth.* Downers Grove, IL: InterVarsity Press, p. 9–10.

19. Cited in Witherington, B. (1995). *The Jesus quest: The third search for the Jew of Nazareth.* Downers Grove, IL: InterVarsity Press, p. 11.

20. Ibid., p. 80.

21. Ibid., p. 281, n.3. There are, of course, those who consider efforts to recover Jesus' authentic teachings as neither possible nor relevant. It is essential, however, to a theology of counseling which claims to be based upon the teachings of Jesus. See n.42 of this chapter.

22. Ibid., p. 10. New Testament scholars have chronicled three phases in the history of the search for Jesus' authentic message. The first quest of the nineteenth century ended with Schweitzer's and Kähler's critiques. The second quest of the 1950s and 1960s was summarized by Robinson, M. (1951). *A new quest of the historical Jesus.* The third quest beginning in the 1980s has been summarized by Witherington, B. (1995). *The Jesus quest.*

Three annotated bibliographies helpful to historical Jesus research are Evans, C. (1992). *Jesus.* Grand Rapids, MI: Baker Books, and Evans, C. (1989). *Life of Jesus research: An annotated bibliography.* Leiden: Brill, both cited by Witherington, B. (1995), p. 254, n.4 and n.5; and Harrington, D. (1988). Second testament exegesis and the social sciences: A bibliography. *Biblical Theology Bulletin, 18,* 77-85.

Seven recent reviews of the quests for the historical Jesus are (1) Brown, C. (1992). "Historical Jesus, quest of" in J. Green, S. McKnight, and I. Marshall. *Dictionary of Jesus and the gospels.* Downers Grove, IL: InterVarsity Press, pp. 326–341; (2) Borg, M. (1994a). *Jesus in contemporary scholarship.* Valley Forge, PA: Trinity Press; (3) Witherington, B. (1995). *The Jesus quest: The third search for the Jew of Nazareth.* Downers Grove, IL: InterVarsity Press; and (4) Shanks, H. (Ed.). (1994). *The search for Jesus: Modern scholarship looks at the gospels.* Washington DC: Biblical Archeology Review; (5) Eckardt, A. (1992). *Reclaiming the Jesus of history: Christology today.* Minneapolis, MN: Fortress Press; (6) Charlesworth, J. (1986). From barren mazes to gentle rappings: The emergence of Jesus research. *Princeton Seminary Bulletin, 7,* 221–230; and (7) Borg, M. (Ed.). (1996). *Jesus at 2000.* New York: HarperCollins.

23. Witherington, B. (1995). *The Jesus quest: The third search for the Jew of Nazareth.* Downers Grove, IL: InterVarsity Press, p. 247. He notes three common threads in the works of the third quest for the historical Jesus: (1) "the search for a common object, knowledge about an ancient historical person, using all the available historical and critical tools; (2) placing Jesus more firmly in his social and economic setting leads to a focus on the social aspects of his life, ministry, and teaching as a distinguishing feature; and (3) the desire to say something new and fresh characterizes almost all of the works examined in this study, sometimes to the extreme of preferring the new over the probable." Borg adds two other elements: (4) an increased appreciation for the non-eschatological message of Jesus; and (5) a new understanding of Jesus as a teacher of a spiritual wisdom contrary to the conventional wisdom of his day characterized as the politics of purity. See Borg, M. (1994a). *Jesus in contemporary scholarship.* Valley Forge, PA: Trinity Press International, pp. 7–12.

24. I find it curious that some conservative Christians who affirm Jesus Christ as their Lord and Savior seem to deemphasize his teachings in favor of the teachings of Paul, the gospel of John, or other contemporary orthodox theologians. A liberal interpretation is like the following: "To confess Jesus Christ as Lord and Savior is to affirm that as the nature and purpose of God can be discerned in a human, it is most clearly to be found in the New Testament account of Jesus, as understood by personal insight and scholarly inquiry." Wagoner, W. (1994). To the editors. *Prism, 9*(2), 3. See chapter 1, n.59.

25. I have adopted here the view presented by the New Testament scholar, Witherington, B. (1995). *The Jesus quest,* p. 74. Borg notes as well that the popular view that Jesus' self-conscious purpose was to die for the sins of the world has been largely discredited by modern New Testament scholarship. See Borg, M. (1994a). *Jesus in contemporary scholarship.* Valley Forge, PA.: Trinity Press International, pp. 144–45, 193–94.

26. Borg, M. (1994a). *Jesus in contemporary scholarship.* Valley Forge, PA.: Trinity Press International, p. 145. This point is compatible with, but not identical to the position of liberal Protestant theology illustrated by Adolph von Harnack. See chapter 1, n.16. The theological error of orthodox Christianity has been to substitute Jesus as King for his teachings about God's kingdom.

27. See Witherington, B . (1995). *The Jesus quest* for discussion of these and other selection criteria, pp, 46, 58, 202. Additional criteria include consistency between what Jesus said and did, context-bound speech, and the absence of witnesses who could have heard what Jesus said. See Funk, R. W. (1996). *Honest to Jesus: Jesus for a new millennium.* New York: HarperSanFrancisco, pp. 138–139.

28. Ibid., pp. 201; 254, n.5; 264, n.53. For a review of how the Gospels and other New

Testament writings have been interpreted by scholars see Neill, S., & Wright, T. (1988). *The interpretation of the New Testament, 1861–1986* (rev. ed.). Oxford: Oxford University Press, cited by Witherington, B. (1955), p. 253, n.1.

29. This is Witherington's (1995) criticism of the method of voting used by members of the Jesus Seminar to determine the authentic teachings of Jesus. See p. 260, n.13.

30. Introductions to the Synoptic gospels include: Perrin, N., & Dulling, D. (1982). *The new testament: An introduction* (2nd ed.). New York: Harcourt Brace Jovanovich; Lee, H. C. (1983). *Understanding the new testament* (4th ed.). Englewood Cliffs, NJ: Prentice-Hall; Nickle, K. (1988). *The synoptic gospels: An introduction*. Atlanta: John Knox Press; Bultmann, R. (1958). *Jesus and the word*. New York: Charles Scribner's Sons; Vermes, G. (1993). *The religion of Jesus the Jew*. Minneapolis, MN: Fortress Press.

31. Sanders, E. P. (1985). *Jesus and Judaism*. Philadelphia, PA: Fortress Press, cited by Witherington, B. (1995). *The Jesus quest: The third search for the Jew of Nazareth*. Downers Grove, IL: InterVarsity Press, p. 270, n.7. Witherington agrees that "while the canonical Gospels are not our only sources for learning about Jesus, they are our primary sources, and in fact we learn very little of importance about the historical Jesus from anywhere else." (p. 200).

32. These are sacred Scriptures of Hindus, Moslems, and Jews respectively.

33. The religious writings contained within the Bible tell us how two ancient communities—Israel and the early Christian community—experienced God, thought about God, and worshiped God, as well as how they thought they should live in response to God, both as individuals and as a community. The Bible's specific ethical prescriptions were directly relevant to their lives in their time, not divine laws given by God for all time. Nevertheless, their experiences of reconciliation with God commend the Bible as a collection of documents with which Christians are to be in a continuing conversation and dialogue. Borg, M. (1994a). *Jesus in contemporary scholarship*. Valley Forge, PA: Trinity Press International, p. 178.

34. The theme of reconciliation is more central to Paul's theology than the theme of justification according to Martin, R. (1981). *Reconciliation: A study of Paul's theology*. Atlanta, GA: John Knox Press. Secondary sources are cited in chapter 4, n.22.

35. Funk, R. W., Hoover, R. W., & The Jesus Seminar. (1993). *The five gospels: The search for the authentic words of Jesus*. New York: Macmillan, p. 15. The gospel of Thomas and other noncanonical sources have been included in Throckmorton, B. (1992). *Gospel parallels: A comparison of the synoptic gospels* (5th ed.). Nashville, TN: Thomas Nelson Publishers. Apart from the members of the Jesus Seminar, the majority of New Testament scholars consider the gospel of Thomas as a document written later than the Synoptics, hence a less reliable source of Jesus' teachings, according to Witherington, B. (1995). *The Jesus quest*. Downers Grove, IL: InterVarsity Press.

36. See Sheikh, A., & Sheikh, K. (Eds.). (1989). *Eastern and western approaches to healing: Ancient wisdom and modern knowledge*. New York: John Wiley and Sons. See also McGaa, E. (1990). *Mother Earth spirituality: Native American paths to healing ourselves and our world*. New York: HarperSanFrancisco; Swinomish Tribal Mental Health Project. (1991). *A gathering of wisdoms. Tribal mental health: A cultural perspective*. LaConner, WA: Swinomish Tribal Community; and Neihardt, J. (1979). *Black Elk speaks: Being the story of a holy man of the Oglala Sioux*. Lincoln, NE: University of Nebraska Press.

37. As one illustration, taking literally the Scriptural admonition to forgive seventy-seven times is both unreasonable and inhumane in the experience of battered women and abused children. A common observation in the United Church of Christ is to say that we take the Bible too seriously to take it literally. The phrase is a way of affirming the biblical

witness as authoritative without adhering to a view of verbal inspiration of every word. See Wehrli, E. (1993). Biblical interpretation in the United Church of Christ. *Prism, 8*(2), 97–103, especially p. 100.

38. It follows that sacred Scriptures of other religions may be considered inspirational and true insofar as they reflect God's realm of reconciliation in human life. Consequently, the Christian may view other religious works as potential disclosures of the divine and as sacred sources of wisdom about the nature and purpose of life, about who God is, who we are, and how we ought to live. This is an expression of Christian pluralism, distinct from religious relativism.

39. My position is similar to that endorsed by the Presbyterian Church, USA. (1991). *Book of confessions*. New York: The Office of the General Assembly of the United Presbyterian Church in the United States of America, #9.27 and #9.28. Based upon modern biblical scholarship, the Bible has authority not as an infallible, divine dictation, but as the records of how Israel and the early Christian movement experienced God, thought about God, as well as how they thought they should live. See Borg, M. (1994a). *Jesus in contemporary scholarship*. Valley Forge, PA: Trinity Press International, p. 178. The Synoptics in particular are the essential sources of Jesus' vision of life as the experience of a transforming relationship with God.

40. This is a basic principle of my own denomination, expressed succinctly in *The United Church of Christ: Who we are, what we believe*. Cleveland, Ohio: The United Church Press. As D. Horton noted, the UCC constitution refers to God's Word as being spoken in the Scriptures; it does not equate the Scriptures with the Word of God. Horton, D. (1962). *The United Church of Christ: The origins, organization, and role in the world today*. New York: Thomas Nelson & Sons, p. 48.

41. These are the four categories used by members of the Jesus Seminar to select authentic sayings. For a critique of their methodology and their conclusion that only 18 percent of the Gospel sayings attributed to Jesus were actually spoken by him, see Witherington (1995). *The Jesus quest: The third search for the Jew of Nazareth*. Downers Grove, IL: InterVarsity Press, pp. 42–57.

42. Here I agree with Witherington's emphasis upon historical research as a method for obtaining truths with acceptable probability. Witherington, B. (1995). *The Jesus quest*, p. 12. Several barriers to the search for the historically authentic teachings of Jesus include dominant popular images of Jesus, the view of the Gospels as inerrant and infallible, monolithic literalisms, limitations of biblical scholarship, and others discussed by Funk, R. W. (1996). *Honest to Jesus: Jesus for a new millennium*. New York: HarperSanFrancisco, pp. 47–56.

43. This is the stated position of the Presbyterian Church, USA. (1991). *Book of confessions* #9.29. Louisville, KY: The Office of the General Assembly. This criterion is closest perhaps to the criterion of coherence for determining the authentic teachings of Jesus, and to my own thematic or content criterion. The Book of confessions expresses a similar attitude toward church Tradition: "Confessions and declarations are the subordinate standards in the church, subject to the authority of Jesus Christ, the Word of God, as the Scripture bears witness to him. No one type of confession is exclusively valid, no one statement is irreformable." (The Confession of 1967 #9.03). Creeds and confessions are aids or guides, but they are not normative as Tillich noted. (Taylor, M. K. [1991]. *Paul Tillich: Theologian of the boundaries*. Minneapolis, MN: Fortress Press, p. 133). Furthermore, theological traditions exist apart from "official" doctrine.

44. A shortcoming of modern biblical scholarship has been its attempt to understand Scripture without reference to this spiritual dimension of experience—the experience of reconciliation with God. A purely historical perspective on Scripture without reference to

the Spirit who inspired it is reductionistic as noted by Borg, M. (1994a). *Jesus in contemporary scholarship.* Valley Forge, PA: Trinity Press International, pp. 134–135.

45. See Abraham, W. (1985). The Wesleyan quadrilateral. In T. Runyon (Ed.), *Wesleyan theology today: A bicentennial theological consultation* (pp. 119–126). Nashville, TN: Kingswood Books—an imprint of The United Methodist Publishing House. The quadrilateral was first presented by Albert Outler in the 1972 theological statement prepared for the Book of Discipline of the United Methodist Church. For a more recent and succinct discussion, see Langford, T. (1991). The United Methodist Quadrilateral: A theological task. In T. Langford (Ed.), *Doctrine and theology in the United Methodist Church* (pp. 232–244). Nashville, TN: Kingswood Books—An imprint of Abingdon Press. Langford adds practice as a fifth consideration. The same four sources have been endorsed in the field of Christian ethics by Wogaman, J. (1993). *Christian ethics: A historical introduction.* Louisville, KY: Westminster/John Knox Press, p. 278.

46. Nickel, K. (1980). *The synoptic gospels: An introduction.* Atlanta, GA: John Knox Press, pp. 56, 144; Peril, N., & Dulling, D. (1982). *The new testament: An introduction.* New York: Harcourt Brace Jovanovich, pp. 43, 257, 264, 294; Key, H. (1983). *Understanding the new testament* (4th ed.). Englewood Cliffs, NJ: Prentice Hall, pp. 98, 128; Borg, M. (1994b). *Meeting Jesus again for the first time.* New York: HarperSanFrancisco, p. 18, n.6.

47. An expressionistic portrait is different from either a photograph, phonograph, or even a personality profile (a psychograph). Tillich, P. (1957). *Systematic theology* (Vol. 2). Chicago: University of Chicago Press, pp. 115, 124. In this view, the biblical witness is neither science nor objective history, but more like a work of art. The expressionistic portraits of Jesus convey both the historical narrative of his life and the existential meanings and concerns relevant to present life. In this book I affirm both the historical fact of Jesus of Nazareth and the meaning of his message for the field of psychotherapy.

48. Perrin, N., & Dulling, D. (1982). *The new testament: An introduction.* New York: Harcourt Brace Jovanovich, pp. 238, 255.

49. Ibid., p. 267. The Torah summarizes the sacred Jewish law. It consists of the first five books of the Jewish Bible called the Tanakh. These books are incorporated into the Christian Bible as part of the collection called the Old Testament, a label to which some Jews take umbrage.

50. Borg, M. (1994a). *Jesus in contemporary scholarship.* Valley Forge, PA: Trinity Press International, p. 96, n.66.

51. Ibid., pp. 298, 326. Those who prefer to describe the uniqueness of Jesus as the archetypal example of what it means to be fully human by being reconciled with God may favor Luke's gospel. Luke is also the gospel which contains the greatest number of references to Jesus' teachings about the kingdom of God.

52. There is also a consensus among New Testament theologians that the "kingdom of God" or "reign of God" was the central theme of Jesus' teachings: Bultmann, R. (1951). *Theology of the new testament* (Vol. 1). New York: Charles Scribner's Sons, p. 4; Bultmann, R. (1958). *Jesus and the word.* New York: Charles Scribner's Sons, p. 27; Bornkamm, G. (1960). *Jesus of Nazareth.* New York: Harper and Row, p. 64; Perrin, N. (1967). *Rediscovering the teaching of Jesus.* London: SCM Press, p. 54; Jeremias, J. (1971). *New testament theology: The proclamation of Jesus.* New York: Charles Scribner's Sons, p. 96; Sanders, E. P. (1993). *The historical figure of Jesus.* New York: Penguin Books, pp. 70, 169; Vermes, G. (1993). *The religion of Jesus the Jew.* Minneapolis, MN: Fortress Press, p. 119. As Vermes notes, questions about the what, when, and how of God's reign have led to different interpretations. A critical survey of relevant, but somewhat dated literature is found in Perrin, N. (1963). *The kingdom of God in the teachings of Jesus.*

Philadelphia, PA: Westminster Press. Funk concluded, "Scholars are universally agreed that the theme of Jesus' discourse was something he called 'the kingdom of God'." Funk, R. W. (1996). *Honest to Jesus: Jesus for a new millennium.* New York: HarperSanFrancisco, p. 149. As a counterpoint, Borg notes that some New Testament scholars consider the kingdom of God as a central theme of Jesus' teaching, but not *the* central theme. See Borg, M. (1994a). *Jesus in contemporary scholarship.* Valley Forge, PA: Trinity Press International, p. 8; p. 38, n.24; p. 63, n.23.

53. *The interpreter's dictionary of the Bible* (vol. 2). (1962). New York: Abingdon Press, p. 932. More recent expressions of skepticism about the historical accuracy of John's gospel as a record of Jesus' teachings are Borg, M. (1994b). *Meeting Jesus again for the first time.* New York: HarperSanFrancisco, pp. 11, 22; Sanders, E. P. (1994). *The historical figure of Jesus.* New York: Penguin Books, pp. 6, 57, 63, 66–73; and Funk, R. W. (1996). *Honest to Jesus: Jesus for a new millennium.* New York: HarperSanFrancisco, pp. 125–127. The current quest for the historical Jesus makes little use of the Gospel of John as a source.

54. Bartlett, C. K. (1978). *The gospel of John* (2nd ed.). Philadelphia, PA: Westminster Press. Bartlett dates John between 90 A.D. and 140 A.D. A recent panel of independent biblical scholars has confirmed these approximate dates: Mark (70 A.D.), Matthew (85 A.D.), Luke (90 A.D.), and John (90 A.D. to 150 A.D.). See Funk, R. W., Hoover, R. W., & The Jesus Seminar. (1993). *The five gospels: The search for the authentic words of Jesus.* New York: Macmillan, p. 128.

55. *The interpreter's dictionary of the Bible* (Vol. 2). (1962). p. 946.

56. Ibid., p. 946.

57. Ibid., p. 936.

58. Ibid., p. 936.

59. Ibid., p. 946.

60. Ibid., p. 932. Tillich draws three contrasts between the Synoptic portraits and John's gospel: (a) the participation of New Being in existence (Synoptics) versus the victory of New Being over the condition of existence (John); (b) the kingdom-centered sayings of Jesus in the Synoptics versus the Christ-centered sayings in John; (c) the Synoptic's future eschatology versus John's more realized eschatology. See Tillich, P. (1957). *Systematic theology* (Vol. 2). Chicago: University of Chicago Press, pp. 136–138.

61. Bultmann, R. (1958). *Jesus and the word.* New York: Scribners' Sons, p. 12; Vermes, G. (1993). *The religion of Jesus the Jew.* Minneapolis, MN: Fortress Press, p. 4. Marcus Borg notes that the Christ of faith presented in John's gospel is very different from the Jesus of history presented by the Synoptics. "The contrast between the Synoptic and Johannine images of Jesus is so great that one of them must be nonhistorical. Both cannot be accurate characterizations of Jesus." Quoted in Witherington, B. (1995). *The Jesus quest: The third search for the Jew of Nazareth.* Downers Grove, IL: InterVarsity Press, pp. 102–103. A counter point is expressed by Kee, H. (1983). *Understanding the new testament* (4th ed.). Englewood Cliffs, NJ: Prentice-Hall, pp. 157–158.

62. Perrin, N., & Dulling, D. (1982). *The new testament: An introduction* (2nd ed.). New York: Harcourt Brace Jovanovich, p. 332.

63. Ibid., p. 941. A similar conclusion has been reached by contemporary biblical scholars. See Funk, R. W., Hoover, R. W., & The Jesus Seminar. (1993). *The five gospels*, pp. 10, 23.

64. This is the conclusion of Bultmann, R. (1951). *Theology of the new testament.* New York: Charles Scribner's Sons, p. 13; Bultmann, R. (1958). *Jesus and the word.* New York: Charles Scribner's Sons, p. 12; and Borg, M. (1994b). *Meeting Jesus again for the first time.* New York: HarperSanFrancisco, p. 11. A counterpoint is advocated by Barman,

B. (1994). *John the believable gospel.* Quaker Home Service. Available through Friends General Conference of the Religious Society of Friends, 1216 Arch Street, 2B, Philadelphia, PA 19107.

65. Tillich finds unified witness among all biblical writers and by the entire Christian tradition in affirming Jesus as the Christ. He rejects the emphasis on the three Synoptics as sources of the message given *by* Jesus in contrast to the fourth gospel and Epistles as the message about Jesus. See Taylor, M. K. (1991). *Paul Tillich: Theologian of the boundaries.* Minneapolis, MN: Fortress Press, pp. 134, 220–221, 231–232.

66. *The interpreters dictionary of the Bible* (Vol. 2). (1962). p. 944.

67. Borg, M. (1994a). *Jesus in contemporary scholarship.* Valley Forge, PA: Trinity Press International, p. 53. The Greek word *basileia* has been translated as kingdom, empire, sovereignty, rule, reign, realm, dominion, or domain of God. All translations affirm a real sphere of influence under God. See for example, Patterson, S. (1996). Shall we teach what Jesus taught? *Prism, 11*(1), 40–57; and Throckmorton, B.H. (1987). Evangelism and mission in the new testament. *Prism, 2*(1), 30–41.

68. Jesus' teachings about the kingdom of God served as the regulating principle of the liberal Protestant theologies of Albrecht Ritschl and Adolph von Harnack. Both affirmed this as a central theme of the gospel of Jesus, and both claimed this as the essence of Christianity in contrast to metaphysical doctrines about Jesus' person. This is a theological position with which I concur. For an introduction to their historical theology, see Livingston, J. (1971). *Modern Christian thought from the enlightenment to vatican II.* New York: Macmillan, pp. 245–270. Two recent works are Jodock, D. (Ed.). (1995). *Ritschl in retrospect: History, community and science.* Minneapolis, MN: Fortress Press, and Von Harnack, A. (1986). *What is Christianity?* (T. B. Saunders, trans.). Minneapolis, MN: Fortress Press. See also n.93 in this chapter.

69. Tillich, P. (1951). *Systematic theology* (Vol. 1). Chicago: University of Chicago Press, p. 47. As a norm, Jesus' gospel of reconciliation serves as the criterion for evaluating the validity of all other truths derived from Scripture, tradition, reason, and experience. This is the manner in which Tillich applied his norm of "the New Being in Jesus as the Christ as our ultimate concern." Taylor, M. K. (1991). *Paul Tillich: Theologian of the boundaries.* Minneapolis, MN: Fortress Press, pp. 35–38, 132–134.

70. In Jesus' teachings, the kingdom of God was not exclusively nor primarily a soon-to-come future reality, but a present reality experienced here and now. See Borg, M. (1994b). *Meeting Jesus again for the first time.* New York: HarperSanFrancisco, p. 92, n.34. According to R. W. Funk, Jesus' message and vision of reality was the inclusive domain of God's rule already present. See Funk, R. W. (1996). *Honest to Jesus: Jesus for a millennium.* New York: HarperSanFrancisco, pp. 41, 166–169, 211.

71. What Tillich wrote more than thirty years ago still seems relevant: "It is not an exaggeration to say that today man experiences his present situation in terms of disruption, conflict, self-destruction, meaninglessness, and despair in all realms of life." Taylor, M. (1991). *Paul Tillich: Theologian of the boundaries.* Minneapolis, MN: Fortress Press, p. 49.

72. As noted in the Confession of 1967, the Bible itself "is to be interpreted in the light of the witness to God's work of reconciliation in Christ." The Presbyterian Church of the USA. (1991). *The book of confessions,* #9.29.

73. Tillich, P. (1951). *Systematic theology* (Vol. 1). Chicago: University of Chicago Press, pp. 47–52. The Synoptic gospels constitute corrections of the creedal transformations of the Jesus of history into the Christ of faith. See Funk, R. W., Hoover, R. W., & The Jesus Seminar. (1993). *The five gospels,* p. 7. Marcus Borg noted that the Christ of faith and the Jesus of history are by and large very different, "if by the Christ of faith one means the Son

of God who came and died for our sins on the cross and rose again from the dead." Cited by Witherington, B. (1995). *The Jesus quest*, p. 102.

74. See "the kingdom of God" in *The interpreter's dictionary of the Bible* (Vol. 3), pp. 17–26. Witherington notes: "It is necessary not only to understand Jesus in his Jewish context, but also to understand the handing on of his teachings in the context for at least the period leading up to 70 AD." (Witherington, B. [1995]. *The Jesus quest*, p. 260, n.23.) One of Witherington's critiques of Crossan's portrait of Jesus is that he over emphasized the inclusive (egalitarian) side of Jesus' teachings at the expense of the more Jewish and sectarian side (Ibid., p. 263, n.4).

75. The fundamental structures of the Jewish world view were the concepts of monotheism and covenant. Witherington, B. (1995). *The Jesus quest*, pp. 222–223. These continue as central ideas in contemporary Judaism. God is one, not none, not two, not three or more. See Steinberg, M. (1975). *Basic Judaism*. New York: Harcourt, Brace, pp. 42–45. In the liberal Protestant tradition, covenental theology affirms reconciliation as its aim, expressed as unity of heart and spirit, a just peace church, and a church united and uniting. See Fackre, G. (1990). Christian doctrine in the United Church of Christ. In D. Johnson & C. Hambrick-Stowe (Eds.), *Theology and identity: Traditions, movements, and polity in the United Church of Christ* (p. 142). Cleveland, OH: United Church Press; and Shinn, R. (1990). *Confessing our faith: An interpretation of the statement of faith of the United Church of Christ*. Cleveland, OH: United Church Press, pp. xi, 3, 82, 85.

76. The Jews believed they had the wrong rulers, hence suffered, because of their collective sin. Repentance and sacrifice were considered as necessary to restore their nation. See Witherington, B. (1995). *The Jesus quest*, p. 220. For a discussion of the relation of the Son of Man to the kingdom of God, see Beastly-Murray, G. R. (1986). *Jesus and the kingdom of God*. Grand Rapids, MI: Wm. B. Eerdmans.

77. Witherington, B. (1995). *The Jesus quest*, pp. 221–223. The central symbols of Jewish identity and religion in Jesus' day included not only Temple and Torah, but also Territory. The Jews believed they were the chosen people of God in the Holy Land, but under the wrong (Roman) rulers. The perceived solution was a new rule or ruler under God (Ibid., p. 219, 221).

78. Witherington, B. (1995). *The Jesus quest*, pp. 225, 230. Sanders concurs with this view that Jesus believed God would intervene in history to bring about a change in the world, though his more complete statement is that "Jesus thought that the kingdom was in heaven, that people would enter it in the future and that it was also present in some sense in his [Jesus'] own work." See Sanders, E. P. (1994). *The historical figure of Jesus*. New York: Penguin Books, pp. 95, 178, 183–189.

79. Borg, M. (1994a). *Jesus in contemporary scholarship*. Valley Forge, PA: Trinity Press International, p. 56.

80. A recent example is Reiser, M. (1997). *Jesus and judgment: The eschatological proclamation in its Jewish context*. Minneapolis, MN: Fortress Press.

81. Borg, M. (1994a). *Jesus in contemporary scholarship*. Valley Forge, PA: Trinity Press International, pp. 8; 38, n.24; 63, n.23; 96, n.66; 87–88. Borg's interpretation is consistent with the multidimensional ontology presumed in my theory.

82. Numerous books and articles have been written about this central concept of Jesus' teaching. See for example, Dodd, C. H. (1935). *The parables of the kingdom*. London: Nisbet and Co; "the Kingdom of God" in *The interpreter's dictionary of the Bible* (Vol. 3), pp. 20–26; Weiss, J. (1985). *Jesus' proclamation of the kingdom of God*. Chico, CA.: Scholars Press; Beasley-Murray, G. R. (1986). *Jesus and the kingdom of God*. Grand Rapids, MI: Wm. B. Eerdmans; Kaylor, R. D. (1994). *Jesus the prophet: His vision of the kingdom on earth*. Louisville, KY: Westminster/John Knox Press. For a survey of contem-

porary interpretations see Willis, W. (Ed.). (1987). *The kingdom of God in 20th century interpretation.* Peabody, MA: Henrickson Publishers. A more current cross-cultural theology of the kingdom of God is provided by Song, C. S. (1993). *Jesus and the reign of God.* Minneapolis, MN: Fortress Press. See also Chilton, B. (1996). *Pure kingdom: Jesus' vision of God.* Grand Rapids, MI: Wm. B. Eerdmans.

    83. Tillich, P. (1951). *Systematic theology* (Vol. l), pp. 47–48.

    84. Recent works by Lutheran theologians include Braaten, E. E. (1990). Justification: The article by which the church stands or falls. Minneapolis, MN: Fortress Press; Anderson, G., Murphy, T., & Burgess, J. (Eds.). (1985). *Justification by faith: Lutherans and Catholics in dialogue VII.* Minneapolis, MN: Fortress Press. The revelation of God's Grace in human conscience is discussed by Zachman, R. (1993). *The assurance of faith: Conscience in the theology of Martin Luther and John Calvin.* Minneapolis, MN: Fortress Press.

    85. Gerrish, B. A. (1992). *Grace and gratitude: The eucharistic theology of John Calvin.* Minneapolis, MN: Augsburg Fortress Press.

    86. In Wesleyan theology, sanctification is a transforming experience whereby we are freed from our past to live more fully in the present and future in the image of God. By the power of the Holy Spirit through faith we are enabled to love God and our neighbors as ourselves. Sanctification is one of the two aspects of reconciliation, the second one being the experience of justification (forgiveness or acceptance). See Sano, R. (1985). A theology of evangelism. In T. Runyon (Ed.), *Wesleyan theology today: A bicentennial theological consultation* (pp. 240–250). Nashville, TN: Kingswood Books—An imprint of The United Methodist Publishing House. As the critical principle of his Spirit-centered theology, the Unitarian theologian, James Luther Adams, emphasized the Holy Spirit as the power of life bringing new meaning and wholeness. The Holy Spirit is present in Christ, but also appears among peoples and in groups not consciously Christian. See Stackhouse, M. (Ed.). (1976). *James Luther Adams: On being human religiously.* Boston: Beacon Press, p. xxiii. This is a position consistent with my own Christian pluralism, which avoids the extremes of both exclusivism and relativism.

    87. Troeltsch, E. (1991). *The Christian faith.* (Garrett E. Paul, trans.). Minneapolis, MN: Fortress Press, p. 66. A balanced view of strengths and limitations of Troeltsch's historical theology is given by P. Garrett, pp. xxxv-xxxvii.

    88. Ibid., pp. xxx, 66, 90, 261, 267–268, 271, 279, 283.

    89. Tillich, P. (1951). *Systematic theology* (Vol. l), pp. 40, 50. Tillich defined the "New Being" as "a reality of reconciliation" (Ibid., p. 49). I prefer the concept of reconciliation over New Being because the former is less metaphysical and more empirical. For similar reasons I favor reconciliation over other material norms such as the Apostle's Creed or confessions of faith as "Jesus Christ is my Lord and Savior."

    90. Tillich, P. (1951). *Systematic theology* (Vol. l), p. 17. Tillich described his material norm ("The New Being in Jesus as the Christ") as grounded in Paul's doctrine of the Spirit and in his constructive doctrine of the new creation in Christ, rather than relying upon Paul's protective doctrine of justification through faith, as Karl Barth did in his critique of liberal theology. (Ibid., p. 50, n.13).

    91. Ibid., pp. 16–18. See also his discussion of final revelation (pp. 132–147), his Logos Christology (pp. 157–159), and his Spirit Christology in Tillich, P. (1963). *Systematic theology* (Vol. 3). Chicago: University of Chicago Press, pp. 144–149.

    92. What has been written of the Spirit of God can be applied to God's realm of reconciliation: "It inspires and transforms, it invites and guides, it propels and grasps, and it calls all under its influence into new associational communities of liberation, righteousness, and inner depth." Stackhouse, M. (Ed.). (1976). *James Luther Adams: On being human relig-*

iously. Boston: Beacon Press, p. xxiii.

93. Cited in McKelway, A. (1964). *The systematic theology of Paul Tillich.* Richmond, VA: John Knox Press, p. 23. Ritschl's emphasis upon the concept of the kingdom of God as a realm of reconciliation was particularly evident in his more practical book. See Ritschl, A. (1901). Instruction in the Christian religion. In A. T. Swing (Ed.), *The theology of Albrecht Ritschl* (pp. 171–286). (A. M. Swing, Trans.) New York: Longman's, Green, & Co. A more contemporary secondary source with an excellent biblography is Hefner, P. (1966). *Faith and the vitalities of history: A theological study based on the work of Albrecht Ritschl.* New York: Harper.

94. McKelway suggested that Ritschl identified the divine process with natural history, the law of God with human value, and the holiness of God with human goodness. He suggests further that Ritschl interpreted Jesus' person idealistically as the highest human expression of "religious values" and his work as "exemplary." McKelway, A. (1964). *The systematic theology of Paul Tillich,* p. 22. Further study is warranted to evaluate the validity of these critical interpretations of Ritschlian theology.

95. Tillich, P. (1951). *Systematic theology* (Vol. 1), p. 40. Experience may be viewed as natural, historical, and religious, just as there are three media of revelation: nature, history, and scripture. Ibid., pp. 118–120.

96. See Lovin, R. (1985). The physics of true virtue. In T. Runyon (Ed.), *Wesleyan theology today: A bicentennial theological consultation* (pp. 264–274). Nashville: Kingswood Books—an imprint of The United Methodist Publishing House. We do not literally see God, but neither do we literally see the air the breathe.

97. Birch, B. (1985). Biblical theology: Issues in authority and hermeneutics. In T. Runyon (Ed.), *Wesleyan theology today: A bicentennial theological consultation* (pp. 127–136). Nashville: Kingswood Books—an imprint of The United Methodist Publishing House.

98. Schleiermacher spoke of "the consciousness of being absolutely dependent" as the same thing as "being in relation with God." Schleiermacher, F. (1989). *The Christian faith.* Edinburgh: T. & T. Clark, p. 12.

99. Ibid., p. 42.

100. Ibid., p. 52. See also Niebuhr, R. (1964). *Schleiermacher on Christ and religion.* New York: Charles Scribner's Sons, p. 226. Schleiermacher's view could be characterized as an experiential theory of redemptive inspiration in contrast to an objective theory of substitutionary atonement. The latter focuses on the efficacy of Christ's sacrificial death to pay the sin debt of the world or to satisfy the wrath and/or justice of God. The former affirms that Christ's death was neither the necessary nor the sufficient condition for the reconciliation of humanity. Nevertheless, the Christian experience of being in relation with God as Jesus taught and lived is one medium through which reconciliation occurs.

101. This is Tillich's distinction and his critique of Schleiermacher's attempt to derive all contents of the Christian faith from the Christian's religious consciousness of redemption through Jesus Christ. Tillich, P. (1951). *Systematic theology* (Vol. 1). Chicago: University of Chicago Press, p. 42.

102. Ibid., pp. 42–46. In addition to Schleiermacher's experiential method in theology, Tillich distinguishes three types of empirical theology: ontological, scientific, and mystical. John Wesley's theology is an example of one form of Christian empirical theology. Though initially he defined faith in terms of belief and subsequently as trust, ultimately he defined faith empirically as spiritual experience and used the analogy of "spiritual senses." See Matthews, R. (1985). With the eyes of faith: Spiritual experience and the knowledge of God in the theology of John Wesley. In T. Runyon (Ed.), *Wesleyan theology today: A bicentennial theological consultation* (pp. 406–415). Nashville, TN: Kingswood

Books—An imprint of The United Methodist Publishing House.

103. Quoted in Langford, T. (1991). The United Methodist quadrilateral: A theological task. In T. Langford (Ed.), *Doctrine and theology in the United Methodist Church* (p. 237). Nashville, TN: Kingswood Books—An imprint of Abingdon Press.

104. Tillich, P. (1951). *Systematic theology* (Vol. 1). Chicago: University of Chicago Press, pp. 40, 91. Tillich actually uses the term "mystical" for "spiritual" meanings.

105. I concur with Borg's view that a significant element of Jesus' unique vision of life was his emphasis upon personal transformation. This occurs through the religious experience of God within a compassionate community of Jesus' disciples. Borg, M. (1994a). *Jesus in contemporary scholarship*. Valley Forge, PA: Trinity Press International; pp. 151–155.

106. For a discussion of this point, see Troeltsch, E. (1991). *The Christian faith.* (Garrett E. Paul, trans.). Minneapolis, MN: Fortress Press, p. xviii.

107. Ibid., p. 44.

108. Illustrations of empirical research on forgiveness are cited in n.4 in chapter two.

109. Kiresuk, T., Smith, A., & Cardillo, J. (Eds.). (1994). *Goal attainment scaling: Applications theory, and measurement.* Hillsdale, NJ: Lawrence Erlbaum Associates.

110. One example of this type of research is Propst, R., Ostrom, R., Watkins, P., Dean, T., & Mashburn, D. (1992). Comparative efficacy of religious and nonreligious cognitive-behavioral therapy for the treatment of clinical depression in religious individuals. *Journal of Consulting and Clinical Psychology, 60,* 94–103. Another illustration is Johnson, W., Devries, R., Ridley, C., Pettorini, D., & Peterson, D. R. (1994). The comparative efficacy of Christian and secular rational-emotive therapy with Christian clients. *Journal of Psychology and Theology, 22*(2), 130–140. Note that both studies used cognitive behavioral approaches, not an experiential approach to counseling with religious clients.

111. Rogers, C. (1961). *On becoming a person: A therapist's view of psychotherapy.* Boston: Houghton Mifflin Co.

112. Due to the lack of agreement among various raters on the outcomes of psychotherapy, current research in this area is summarized according to therapist, client, and other raters. See Orlinsky, D., Grawe, K., & Parks, B. (1994). Process and outcome in psychotherapy—noch einmal. In A. Bergin & S. Garfield (Eds.), *Handbook of psychotherapy and behavior change* (pp. 270–378). New York: John Wiley & Sons.

113. Both stimulus-response theories and mediational theories view learning as quantitative changes occurring across time. By contrast, Gestalt-phenomenological theories emphasize qualitative change as the direct result of patterns occurring *within* time. It is a contrast between theories based on efficient causes versus formal causes. See Rychlak, J. (1981). *Introduction to personality and psychotherapy: A theory construction approach* (2nd ed.). Boston: Houghton Mifflin Company, pp. 768–773.

114. See for example, Troeltsch, E. (1991). *The Christian faith.* (Garrett E. Paul, trans.). Minneapolis, MN: Fortress Press, p. xvii. A counter point has been expressed recently by Johnson, L. T. (1996). *The real Jesus: The misguided quest for the historical Jesus and the truth of the traditional gospels.* Scranton, PA: Harper Collins.

115. Troeltsch, E. (1992). *The Christian faith.* (Garrett E. Paul, trans.). Minneapolis, MN: Fortress Press, p. xxviii.

116. Troeltsch addressed to my satisfaction several objections to making faith dependent on history. None of these objections would justify either a metaphysical or mystical approach which is ahistorical and discounts historical investigations and findings. Christianity is a historical religion. Ibid., pp. xxviii, 73–84.

117. For discussion of scientific versus mystical experience, and the "open experience" of liberal American theology, see Tillich, P. (1951). *Systematic theology* (Vol. 1). Chicago: University of Chicago Press, pp. 42–46.

118. Jesus was unique as a Spirit-person by virtue of his own religious experiences and practices within the tradition of Jewish mysticism. He was believable because he spoke with an authority that flowed from his own spiritual experiences, as noted by Borg, M. (1994b). *Meeting Jesus again for the first time.* New York: HarperSanFrancisco, pp. 35–36.

119. Borg noted that one need not make an ontological assertion about the objective reality of the spiritual dimension in order to appreciate it's definitive influence upon Jesus' message. Instead we may bracket the ontic question to provide a phenomenological description. Nevertheless, one cannot comprehend Scripture without reference to the spiritual dimension. See Borg, M. (1994a). *Jesus in contemporary scholarship.* Valley Forge, PA: Trinity Press International, pp. 133, 137, 145, 152–153, 173.

120. Tillich defines "religious experience" as a relationship, namely, the relation between God and persons. Tillich, P. (1951). *Systematic theology* (Vol. 1). Chicago: University of Chicago Press, p. 60. This is distinct from monistic religions which affirm the absorption of the ego into the One ultimate reality.

121. In contrast to Hegelian essentialism, Christian existentialism affirms that the essential goodness of human nature (affirmed in the concept of *Imago Dei*) is not fully actualized in human existence. Existence is neither the logical, necessary, nor progressive expression of essence, but a fall away from it. Creation itself is the transition from essence to existence made possible by the finite freedom which characterizes human life. This transition (and separation) is symbolized by the Christian myth of Adam's Fall. Thus human existence is fundamentally the estrangement from our essential nature (an estranged existence), though it is not a total separation. Nevertheless, reconciliation in human life, both in an individual and in society, is at most partial and fragmentary, hence life itself and all human actions and experiences remain ambiguous. See Tillich, P. (1957). *Systematic theology* (Vol. 2), pp.169, 174; and (Vol. 3), p. 30.

122. See Fowler, J. (1981). *Stages of faith: The psychology of human development and the quest for meaning.* New York: HarperSanFrancisco; Fowler, J. (1984). *Becoming adult, becoming Christian.* New York: Harper and Row. Other applications of a developmental model are Keen, S. (1983). *The passionate life.* San Francisco: Harper; and Liebert, E. (1992). *Changing life patterns: Adult development in spiritual direction.* New York: Paulist Press. For a discussion of these Christian writings about moral experience, see Livingston, J. (1971). *Modern Christian thought from the enlightenment to vatican II.* New York: Macmillan.

123. An excellent and current summary is Atherton, J. (Ed.). (1994). *Christian social ethics: A reader.* Cleveland, OH: The Pilgrim Press. Some discussion of social ethics is also found in Wogaman, J. (1993). *Christian ethics: A historical introduction.* Louisville, KY: Westminster/John Knox Press, and Cahill, L., & Childress, J. (Eds.). (1996). *Christian ethics: Problems and prospects.* Cleveland, OH: The Pilgrim Press.

124. Examples of empirical theology in the liberal Protestant tradition are Ogden, S. (1969). Present prospects for empirical theology. In B. Meland (Ed.), *The future of empirical theology* (pp. 65–88). Chicago: University of Chicago Press. See also Ogden, S. (1976). Sources of religious authority in liberal Protestantism. *Journal of the American Academy of religion, 44*(3), 403–416. H. R. Niebuhr claims an empirical methodology was applied by such noteworthy Protestant thinkers as Luther, Calvin, Edwards, Schleiermacher, Kierkegaard, and Kant. He adopts a similar method to understand how faith in God is possible. Niebuhr, H. R. (1960). *Radical monotheism and Western culture. With supplementary essays.* Louisville, KY: Westminster/John Knox Press, pp. 16–23, 116. For a critical discussion of four types of empirical theology, see Tillich, P. (1951). *Systematic theology* (Vol. 1). Chicago: University of Chicago Press, pp. 40–44.

125. Marcus Borg emphasizes this spiritual dimension of life and views Jesus as essentially a Spirit filled person, or a man of the Spirit. See Borg, M. (1987). *Jesus: A new*

vision. San Francisco: Harper and Row. "At the heart of Borg's affirmation is the experience of the sacred in nature, human and nonhuman. This, in his view, seems to be the essence of having a relationship with God." (Witherington, B. [1995]. *The Jesus quest*, p. 106). Borg's proposal places Jesus in the more transcultural category of a person in close touch with the sacred dimension of life (Ibid., p. 267, n.1). See also Borg, M. (1994b). *Meeting Jesus again for the first time.* New York: HarperSanFrancisco, pp. 30–36; p. 42, n.26; p. 43, n.28. It seems compatible with, but not identical with Schleiermacher's earlier emphasis upon Jesus' complete consciousness of God. It is an experiential emphasis that I find both congenial and inspiring.

126. Foster, D. (1985). Wesleyan theology: Heritage and task. In T. Runyon (Ed.), *Wesleyan theology today: A bicentennial theological consultation* (p. 31). Nashville, TN: Kingswood Books—an imprint of The United Methodist Publishing House.

127. It is one thing to read and understand the Scriptures; it is another to have personal experiences of the truths taught by Scripture. H. R. Niebuhr expressed the relation of Scripture and experience as follows: "Scripture without experience is empty, but experience without Scripture is blind." Niebuhr, H. R. (1988). *The kingdom of God in America.* Hanover, New Hampshire: Wesleyan University Press, p. 109.

128. Revelatory experiences have been described as "ciphers" by the psychiatrist-philosopher Karl Jaspers and as "disclosure situations" by Ian Ramsey. See Macquarrie, J. (1988). *Twentieth century religious thought.* Philadelphia: Trinity Press International, pp. 313, 357.

129. Some implications of a doctrine of the Holy Spirit for counseling have been explored by Gilbert, M., & Brock, R. (Eds.). (1985). *The Holy Spirit and counseling. Vol. 1: Theology and theory.* Peabody, MA: Hendrickson Publishers, and especially in Gilbert, M., & Brock, R. (Eds.). (1988). *The Holy Spirit and counseling. Vol. II: Principles and practices.* Peabody, MA: Hendrickson Publishers.

130. Niebuhr, H. R. (1960). *Radical monotheism and Western culture. With supplementary essays.* Louisville, KY: Westminster/John Knox Press, p. 14. Niebuhr applied an empirical, inductive method of approaching the existence and nature of God from the universal experience of faith as trust in something or someone as the source of one's meaning, purpose. and worth, and faith as the cause to which one is ultimately loyal. (Ibid., pp. 116–119). The mnemonic phrase, "faith involves t.l.c.," expresses the three basic elements of trust, loyalty, and concern.

Chapter Four

The Meaning of Reconciliation as the Purpose of Counseling

The purpose of this chapter is to develop a working definition of reconciliation as the central construct of this theory and to provide reasons for commending reconciliation as the purpose of counseling. I begin by stating several conclusions drawn from an analysis of how reconciliation is used in both popular and theological contexts.

CONCLUSIONS FROM A LINGUISTIC ANALYSIS

I explored several common and theological denotations and connotations of the cognates of the word "reconciliation," including its use as a noun (reconciliation), personal noun (reconciler, reconciliator), as a transitive and intransitive verb (to reconcile or to be reconciled), and as an adverb or adjective (reconciling, reconciled). There are seven conclusions I draw from this functional analysis of the various uses and meanings of the word reconciliation.

The first is that reconciliation is a construct with multiple meanings. The range of its connotations commend it as a comprehensive concept, hence useful as a building block for both a theory of counseling and a Christian theology. It has both personal and interpersonal dimensions. Reconciliation is a fruitful concept for understanding human experience, a term rich with meaning.

Second, by definition reconciliation is both a process or act and also a state or condition. It is the process or act of reconciling and the state or condition of being reconciled. The former denotations suggest a process perspective: Reconciliation is an active, dynamic process.

Third, reconciliation has existential and ontological meanings. Reconciliation denotes a state of being or a way of being, a mode of existence or a way of living. It may be used as an ontological category for comprehending human experience. Accordingly, in addition to such categories as time, space, and causality, being and becoming, constructs such as alienation and reconciliation may be used to describe and understand the basic dialectics of reality and the dynamics of human life.

Fourth, reconciliation is also an empirical construct. As both a process and a state of being it refers to an experience, not merely to an abstract idea or value. Experiences of reconciliation can be seen and heard, touched and felt. As an empirical phenomenon, it can be investigated phenomenologically and scientifically.

Fifth, while the term has been applied in social, political, economic and religious realms, reconciliation has not been applied extensively in the psychological realm. One may search in vain for an explicit psychology of reconciliation,[1] though there is a very extensive Judeo-Christian theology of reconciliation. Nevertheless, some articles have appeared in psychological literature on the related concept of forgiveness, and three national conferences have been held recently on the role of forgiveness in psychotherapy.[2] Viewing alienation and reconciliation as bipolar anchors on a continuum suggests these terms may be used psychologically to describe individual differences, to inform a theory of human development, and to build theories of personality, psychopathology, and psychotherapy.

Sixth, on the theological side, the concept of reconciliation highlights the crucial importance of relationships. This is compatible with Martin Buber's emphasis upon the I-Thou relation in the Jewish tradition and with the views expressed by Protestant Christian theologians such as Karl Barth, Paul Tillich, Paul Sponheim, and some feminist theologians.[3] Both the explicit and implicit meanings of reconciliation are necessarily relational. This is evident in the frequent connection of reconciliation to the preposition "with." Thus, one speaks of being at one with, coming to terms with, being at peace with, in harmony with, or reconciled with, and so forth. There is usually some interpersonal reference signified; a relationship is implied. The concept of reconciliation has the advantage of affirming "relation" as a fundamental reality and category of thought, as Martin Buber emphasized.[4]

Finally, the concept of reconciliation provides a bridge for relating psychology and theology. As opposed to alternative models of either separation or integration, we may speak of reconciliation as a way of relating these two independent disciplines. In a reconciled relation, neither discipline would be absorbed or dominated by the other, nor would their independence be compromised. Areas of agreement and disagreement are clarified through dialogue, and territorial disputes are mediated. A rapprochement is achieved that resolves conflicts and reestablishes respectful communications based on mutual understanding and a shared commitment to advance the welfare of humankind. Whether that commitment is motivated by pragmatic considerations, by a naturalistic and humanistic ethic, or by religious gratitude for redeeming grace, psychologists and theologians can find common ground in their shared values and goals to achieve a reconciliation of their worldviews, methodologies, and professional ethics and practices. Of course, this presumes they have the will to reconcile. There's the rub.

A DEFINITION OF RECONCILIATION

Definitions of basic terms sometimes employ the category of "substance" to indicate their fundamental or essential "nature." These categories of thought seem less useful than terms that emphasize the process or the purpose of the phenomenon defined. A more fruitful type of definition combines both of the latter elements and adds the experiential dimension. Reconciliation is, after all, a human experience, not merely an abstract concept. What follows is a working definition that incorporates some of the insights obtained from the linguistic analysis of reconciliation.

Reconciliation is a multidimensional, unifying experience of resolving conflicts within and among alienated persons, whose being and relations are transformed through the power of forgiveness and the process of compassionate confrontation into a healing reunion of love, justice, and peace for the sake of which one decides to intentionally act.

By this definition I wish to suggest several meanings and implications of reconciliation:

(a) Reconciliation is simultaneously an experience and a way of being, a relation, a power, a process, a state, and an act. Reconciliation cannot be reduced to any one of these elements, all of which are included in this phenomenological definition.

(b) Reconciliation is a multidimensional phenomenon—it occurs in social, psychological, and spiritual dimensions of life; it occurs interpersonally, intrapsychically, and spiritually. One may speak of biological and environmental dimensions as well.

(c) As a multidimensional phenomenon, reconciliation cannot be reduced to any particular dimension, nor to a specific domain within an individual (cognitive, behavioral, affective, or conative); reconciliation is a holistic and comprehensive construct.

(d) Reconciliation is an ontological construct; it refers to a way of being and a mode of existing in a self-world structure. It may serve as an ontological principle and a fundamental category of thought for the development of a philosophy of life.

(e) Reconciliation is a realistic and empirical notion; it acknowledges the conflict and alienation that actually exist both within and between persons, and it refers to empirical realities such as experience and observable behaviors. It acknowledges also that there are varying degrees of reconciliation, and that persons exist and move in a continuum between alienation and reconciliation.

(f) Reconciliation is a relational concept: whether the relation is with self, others, or God, a relation is essential to the meaning of reconciliation. Interpersonal relations as well as personal being are transformed through experiences of reconciliation.

(g) This definition gives priority to establishing a healing reunion as the purpose of reconciliation, for the sake of which behavior is intended. The elements of purpose and intention make this a teleological definition, which presupposes human agency and determining acts of will. It presumes that like most human behaviors, acts of reconciliation are intended, not merely caused. Human behavior is goal-oriented, and cannot be explained without reference to final causes and future strivings. Phrased another way, all human behavior has meaning, and its meaning lies in its purpose.[5]

(h) This is also a voluntaristic definition because it presupposes the roles of finite freedom, conscious deliberations about alternative ends and various means to achieve them, and intentional decisions and acts. Reconciliation is not limited to conscious experiences, aims, or decisions; we may speak of unconscious reconciliations both within and between individuals. However, this definition of reconciliation implies that human choices and conscious decisions are effective causes of human behavior. A transformation of the human will is integral to the experience of reconciliation and antecedent to acts of reconciliation.[6] The immediate cause of human behavior is a behavioral intention.[7]

(i) The reunion achieved is healing because it is characterized by all three elements of love, justice, and peace. By affirming all three elements, reconciliation cannot be reduced either to appeasement or to a sentimental relationship. Including all three values makes reconciliation an ethical construct upon which to build a theory of moral value and a theory of moral obligation for both personal and social ethics. By implication, reconciliation requires liberation of marginalized people through a continuous struggle for social justice.

(j) This definition points to the therapeutic and practical benefits of reconciliation by specifying it as both a unifying experience and a healing reunion. Through reconciling experiences an individual becomes personally integrated and relationships are restored to genuine mutuality. Both intrapsychic and interpersonal conflicts are resolved through experiences and acts of reconciliation, and through psychotherapy guided by the purpose of reconciliation.

(k) The process of compassionate confrontation suggests that reconciliation is an alternative to both passive acceptance and aggressive domination. The one who has wounded or wronged another is confronted and held accountable, but the motivation for doing so is not revenge but justice and compassion, not retribution but restitution and restoration. A therapist who confronts compassionately is neither directive nor nondirective, but indirective.[8]

(l) Experiences of reconciliation are transforming. Individuals change both in who they are and how they relate to others as they become more reconciled and reconciling individuals. Effecting change is an essential purpose of psychotherapy and counseling, hence reconciliation is relevant to both.

(m) The power of forgiveness is the transforming dynamic and central mechanism of reconciliation. Accordingly, this is a biblical definition consistent with the teachings of Jesus of Nazareth. It recognizes that the power of forgiveness is human, but ultimately it refers to the power of God's reconciling love manifest decisively in the message and ministry of Jesus, and in human acts and experiences of reconciliation in the past, present, and future. Reconciliation is a central construct upon which to build a Judeo-Christian theology and a theology of counseling. Theologically, I use reconciliation to subsume both phases of the Christian life understood as justification and sanctification.[9] It suggests also the concept of a reconciling vocation.

(n) This definition highlights the existential meanings of reconciliation relevant to human existence as it is lived concretely and uniquely by each person in the present, yet it avoids the individualistic focus that has plagued both evangelical Christianity and theories of psychotherapy. An emphasis upon reconciliation is an antidote both to a spiritual narcissism stressing personal salvation and to a psychological egoism focused upon self-actualization.

(o) This generic definition may function as a hypothetical construct from which operational definitions can be derived to guide both phenomenological research on the essential structure and meaning of reconciliation as it is experienced and causal research on the antecedents and consequences of reconciliation.

The definition of reconciliation is central to this theory because the stated *purpose of counseling* is to experience reconciliation in social, psychological, and spiritual dimensions through the process of compassionate confrontation of client incongruities in a Spirit-centered, therapeutic relationship. What does it mean to say that the purpose of counseling is reconciliation? In common usage, to be reconciled means to come to agreement, as when two persons reconcile their differences. To be reconciled also means to be reunited, to bring together that which has been separated. The Christian counselor seeks to help persons overcome such separations and to work through their differences by becoming reconciled with others, with themselves, and with God. Stated in another way, reconciliation has social, psychological, and spiritual dimensions, all of which need to be addressed if counseling is to be both faithful and effective.[10]

WHY CHOOSE RECONCILIATION AS THE PURPOSE OF COUNSELING?

I have selected reconciliation to express the general purpose of counseling for several reasons: It affirms that change is multidimensional and healing is holistic; that brokenness is real, but relationships heal; it affirms hope and the developmental nature of holiness; it serves as a norm for counseling decisions; it expresses the church's ministry and guides its pastoral functions; it is consistent with the church's confessions of faith and is supported by a Christian theology of reconciliation; and it provides an even broader context for unification in ecumenical discussions as well as guidance on social issues.

Change Is Multidimensional

Reconciliation has been selected to express the general purpose of counseling first because it appreciates the multidimensional nature of constructive personality change. Through counseling people change the way they think, how they feel, and what they want and do. Their relationships change along with their experiences of themselves, others, and God. Reconciliation expresses these multidimensional changes in a way that other purposes of counseling do not. For this reason, I prefer this term over the numerous other purposes of counseling that have been proposed.

There have been so many purposes advocated, their names seem to be legion. Included among them are improved mental health, personal security, ego strength and autonomy; positive changes in self-concept or self-esteem; self-actualization or interpersonal competence; symptom management, stress management, or behavior modification; rational problem solving, cognitive restructuring, or conflict resolution; moral guidance and values clarification; development of social interest and spiritual well-being; insight, catharsis, growth, and meaning; wellness, wholeness, liberation, or healing.

While thoughtful persons in the fields of both psychological and pastoral counseling have favored these other purposes, these terms do not denote or connote for me the breadth and depth of the purpose of counseling nor help me comprehend its process and practice. Fortunately, we do not have to construe reality in the same ways, nor claim that our way is the only way. Diversity at the level of theory is as enriching as it is interpersonally. My first reason for choosing reconciliation as the purpose of counseling is because it expresses the multidimensional nature of change that occurs through counseling.

Healing Is Holistic

I choose reconciliation as the purpose of counseling secondly because it is a term that expresses the holistic nature of healing that occurs through counseling. Equally important, Jesus taught that reconciliation is a holistic experience in social, psychological, and spiritual dimensions. The integral relationship between the spiritual and social dimensions of reconciliation was described by Jesus in his connection between worship and fellowship. If alienated from another, he said, leave your gift at the altar and go, first be reconciled with that person and then come and offer your gift of thanksgiving (Mt. 5:21-26). The holistic nature of reconciliation is evident also in his teaching that in order to be forgiven by God for our own sins, we must forgive others (Mt. 6:14-15/Mk.11:25-26). Forgive and you will be forgiven (Lk. 6:37). And the numerous healings Jesus performed and ascribed to faith suggest the intimate connections between the spiritual, psychological, and physical dimensions of health (e.g., Mk. 1:40-42). In a similar way, persons in counseling experience holistic healing among psychological domains of knowing, feeling, wanting, and doing, and particularly in their relationships.

Relationships Are Central

Third, I choose reconciliation as the purpose of counseling because this term expresses the focus upon human relationships evident in the teachings of Jesus. Individuals are nurtured, hurt, and healed in their relationships with others. The concept of reconciliation accentuates this interpersonal dimension in a way that other terms, such as self-actualization, personal wholeness, or spiritual well-being, do not for me, though perhaps for others.

Like reconciliation, the concept of "wholeness" can be construed as including relational dimensions.[11] Nevertheless, I favor the concept of reconciliation as the general purpose of counseling because it is an explicitly relational construct; it denotes that both human and divine healing occur in and through relationships. Reconciliation is about restored relationships expressed symbolically and theologically as atonement (at-one-ment).[12]

A Realistic Concept

As the purpose of counseling, I prefer reconciliation fourthly because it expresses a theological anthropology and a realistic appraisal of human nature. What I mean is that the term reconciliation recognizes the reality of human alienation[13] which characterizes our lives of finite freedom. To speak of reconciliation as the goal of counseling implies that persons are not reconciled—not with themselves, with others, or with God. In traditional theological language, this is our shared condition of sin that makes all human acts ambiguous at best and destructive at worst. It is also our common estrangement from self, others, and God that serves as a unifying theory of human distress and an explanation for much of the needless human tragedy.

A Promise and Hope

But human destiny is not necessarily tragic. There is good news of great joy (Mt. 13:44; Lk. 2:10). It is the gospel of reconciliation in the kingdom of God taught by Jesus of Nazareth (Mt. 4:23). Jesus taught that we have the potential of becoming reconciled, and that is what God has been seeking and achieving with humankind throughout human history and decisively through the message and ministry of Jesus. Reconciliation is the *telos* of human history and our final destiny symbolized in Christian concepts of the kingdom of God and eternal life. The fifth reason for selecting reconciliation as the general purpose of counseling is that it expresses this promise and hope.[14]

A Developmental and Dynamic Construct

Sixth, like counseling, reconciliation is a dynamic, developmental process. As both a process and experience, reconciliation involves the dynamics of conversion and repentance, confession and penance, forgiveness and healing.[15] As a concept, reconciliation expresses the developmental nature of the Christian life as one of spiritual growth in holiness and communion with our Creator. Moreover, it subsumes the conditions and stages leading to its fulfillment. These conditions are the religious experiences of justification, sanctification, and glorification, the traditional terms used to describe the redemptive dynamics of the Christian life. It is in justification by Grace through faith and love[16] that reconciliation begins, through sanctification in a life in the Spirit that it continues, and in eternal glory that we are finally and fully reconciled with God. Reconciliation is the unifying motif of the Christian life.

A Norm for Counseling Decisions

Seventh, psychotherapy is neither a value-free nor a value-neutral experience. It is essentially a decision-making process in which individuals deliberate about alternative ways of being, behaving, and relating, and through which they eventually make a decision in favor of a particular alternative for the sake of which they subsequently and intentionally act. From this teleological perspective, therapy progresses logically from unconscious desires through conscious deliberations to intentional decisions and enacted deeds.[17] One might summarize this as a 4-D theory of action involving desires, deliberations, decisions, and deeds. The values implicit in all four phases are revealed in one's emotions and relationships as well as one's thoughts, decisions, and actions.

Both clients and counselors need to include in their deliberations the values that define their goals, the standards by which they choose one alternative among those available, and the ethical principles by which they decide what they should do. Psychotherapy is a moral relationship, not merely a psychosocial or therapeutic relationship. Indeed, it could be argued, and I would do so, that for human beings to become self-determining, autonomous agents of their actions, therapy must involve moral considerations and provide guidance for ethical decision-making.

Since value judgments and decisions about what one ought to do cannot be avoided in therapeutic practice, by clients and counselors alike, it is critical to make explicit the values and principles of moral obligation according to which such judgments and decisions are made. In the theory presented here, reconciliation functions as the purpose of psychotherapy. In this role, reconciliation serves as an intrinsic value defining the goal or end of psychotherapy. To the degree that the process of psychotherapy brings about the experience of reconciliation, psychotherapy is ethically justifiable as an instrumental value. It is instrumentally good as a means to accomplishing the intrinsic good of reconciliation. In this respect, both reconciliation and psychotherapy constitute "nonmoral values" in a theory of moral obligation.[18]

Reconciliation may be construed also as a trait of character. Both the trait of being a reconciling individual and the intention to act as an agent of reconciliation function as moral values in a normative theory of virtue. To speak of virtues is to develop an ethic of being or character. To be reconciling is a virtue that may be considered with other virtues such as faith, hope, and love, wisdom, courage, and integrity. In my view, both the reconciling individual and the one who strives to be an agent of reconciliation are being virtuous and responsible, praiseworthy and admirable, and in many instances even heroic and holy.

Human virtues are actualized in behavior. Character is expressed partly in conduct. Being of good character means at the very least that one intends to act in an ethically responsible manner. Since psychotherapy generally includes behavioral change as one of its goals, one needs principles by which to decide what to do, and to determine what one is obligated to do. Thus a theory of psychotherapy needs an ethical theory of moral obligation. "Do what reconciliation requires" qualifies as an ethical principle of moral obligation to guide the practice of psychotherapy.

One need not choose between an ethic of doing versus an ethic of being, or limit the use of a concept such as reconciliation to either an ethic of moral virtue or to an ethic of moral duty. A morality of character and a morality of conduct are complementary aspects of a normative theory. To speak colloquially, being and doing go together like love and marriage; virtue and duty belong together like a horse and carriage.[19] We need both a morality of principles to guide our conduct and an ethic of virtue to know what moral traits to cultivate in order to enable and to motivate ourselves and others to do willingly what we ought to do.

The main point of this section is that reconciliation is not merely a metaphor upon which to build a model of psychotherapy, although it is that to be sure.[20] Reconciliation functions also as an ethical norm for counseling decisions. Reconciliation is an explicit value and the foundation for both an ethic of virtue and a theory of moral obligation. Both are needed in a normative theory of psychotherapy. An ethic of reconciliation undergirds and informs a reconciling therapy.

A Ministry of Reconciliation

Eighth, by choosing reconciliation as the purpose of counseling I am placing counseling within the context of the ministry of reconciliation that belongs to the Christian Church as a whole. It is to this general ministry of reconciliation that all disciples are called by Christ.[21] Regardless of our particular occupations, our common vocation is to be reconciling friends of God with one another in a shared ministry of healing (Mt.10:5–13/Mk. 6:7–11/Lk. 9:1–6; Mt. 9:35; Lk. 8:1; Lk. 10:1– 12).

This same emphasis upon reconciliation as a shared ministry is also found in the writings of the apostle Paul.[22] It suggests both biblical and theological grounds as well as the practical value of providing counseling as a ministry of the Church. Christian counseling is one specialized form of this shared ministry of reconciliation.

Reconciling Pastoral Functions

The ninth reason for selecting reconciliation as the general purpose of counseling is that it has the advantage of subsuming the traditional functions of pastoral care as their ultimate purpose. Summarized by Howard Clinebell,[23] these additional functions are the healing, sustaining, guiding, and nurturing of persons in need.

A Creedal Affirmation

Tenth, the concept of reconciliation is the unifying theme of the Christian faith expressed in various creeds and confessions. One example devoted to this theme is the Confession of 1967 of the Presbyterian Church, USA. This statement of faith may help other denominations to formulate a mission and vision of reconciliation. In the Preface to that Confession of Faith is the following statement: "God's reconciling work in Jesus Christ and the mission of reconciliation to which he has called his church are the heart of the gospel in any age. Our generation stands in peculiar need of reconciliation in Christ. Accordingly, this Confession of 1967 is built upon that theme."[24]

This confession is elaborated in a three-part discussion: First, an affirmation of God's work of reconciliation through Jesus Christ in the communion of the Holy Spirit; second, the ministry of reconciliation given to the church; and third, the fulfillment of reconciliation in the eternal kingdom of God.

In the ten-page exposition of this Confession of faith,[25] the concept of reconciliation occurs thirty-four times as "reconciliation" (nineteen times), "reconciling" (eleven), and "reconciled" (four). The Lord's Supper is described as "a celebration of the reconciliation of persons with God and with one another."[26] Jesus' message itself is described as "the gospel of reconciliation."[27] Furthermore, the criterion by which Presbyterians are to select, maintain, and modify their polity (that is, their form of government, officers, finances, and administrative rules) ought to be in terms of the church's mission of reconciliation: "Every church order must be open to such reformation as may be required to make it a more effective instrument of the mission of reconciliation."[28]

Presbyterians consider such confessions of faith as subordinate standards in the Church, subject to the authority of Jesus Christ as the Scriptures bear witness to him, hence "no one confession is exclusively valid, no one statement is irreformable."[29] Nevertheless, confessions of faith aid our understanding of the wisdom of Jesus' message about the wonder of a reconciled life. The 1967 Confession of faith provides a theological vision of the reconciled life. It warrants careful study by other Christian denominations as well as revisions to include more gender-neutral language.[30]

A Theology of Reconciliation

Finally, the concept of reconciliation has a firm foundation in the history of both Judaic and Christian theologies.[31] It has been enlightening to discover how extensively this concept has been studied. Reconciliation has been interpreted as the content and criterion of prophecy, the central theme of the biblical witness and the essence of Christianity.[32] It has been interpreted as the meaning of the call to discipleship, equated with salvation, contrasted with atonement theology,[33] and grounded in both incarnational theology and Christology.[34] Whether one emphasizes the objective role of Christ's sacrifice as a substitutionary atonement, an incarnational perspective, or a more subjective interpretation emphasizing the inspiration of Jesus' consciousness of God (Schleiermacher) or the moral influence of his godly life (Ritschl), Christians have been united in affirming as a cardinal belief that reconciliation occurs through Christ.[35] In the history of Protestant theology, reconciliation has been linked with the central doctrine of justification in both the early Church confessions and Reformation theology.[36]

As a human experience, reconciliation is viewed as the answer to problems of human estrangement.[37] It is a healing process of forgiveness leading to renewal and liberation,[38] considered by some authors to be the meaning of Jesus' vision of the reign of God, and a summary of both the message and mission of the Church.[39] This reconciliation motif informs Christian worship and guides Christian education.[40]

Within the Catholic tradition, reconciliation has been elevated to the status of a sacrament, specifically the sacrament of confession and penance.[41] Official pronouncements have been made to define the purpose and practice of this sacrament.[42] There is a solid foundation in a theology of reconciliation evident within contemporary Catholicism,[43] including efforts to renew the sacrament of reconciliation, and the publication of an international bibliography.[44]

Along with the anointing of the sick, Catholics describe reconciliation as one of the two sacraments of healing. It is described simultaneously as the sacrament of conversion, penance, confession, forgiveness, and reconciliation because all of these phases are involved in this religious and therapeutic experience. The term reconciliation refers particularly to the effects of this sacrament, namely, that it imparts to persons the love of God who reconciles. The sacrament of reconciliation restores persons to God's grace and to reunion with God in intimate friendship. The healing effects are experienced as peace and serenity of conscience with spiritual consolation and an increase in spiritual strength. As the Church is considered the instrument of reconciliation, Catholics consider reconciliation with the Church to be inseparable from reconciliation with God.[45]

Within twentieth century Protestant theology, the concept of reconciliation has been emphasized by both the kerygmatic theologian Karl Barth[46] and the Christian existentialist Paul Tillich.[47] Karl Barth devoted a considerable portion of his dogmatic theology to the doctrine of reconciliation. He viewed justification, sanctification, and vocation as expressions of, and subsumed by reconciliation, which in turn, is experienced in the gathering, developing, and sending of disciples who are characterized by the Christian virtues of faith, hope, and love. Paul Tillich presented reconciliation as the Christian answer to the existential problem of estrangement. He described the reconciled life as participation in New Being (regeneration), acceptance of New Being (justification), and transformation by New Being (sanctification) manifested as content in faith and love, and experienced ultimately in the unambiguous life symbolized by the kingdom of God and eternal life.[48]

In Church teachings on social issues, reconciliation is viewed as the Christian way of accepting and dealing with differences, including differences both within the Church and between groups within society.[49] Reconciliation is both the goal and approach to resolving conflicts among races, sexes, generations,[50] and even nations.[51] Reconciliation is a way of achieving peace,[52] justice, and liberation.[53] The model of reconciliation has served as a foundation for a political agenda for the church.[54]

Reconciliation is also an approach to resolving personal conflicts, and a general conflict management strategy both in counseling and in spiritual direction.[55] In effect, it is a pathway to restored relationships[56] at both an interpersonal and community level.

Reconciliation has become a recurring theme in discussions guiding the ecumenical movement toward Christian unity,[57] in dialogue with other faiths,[58] and with both philosophy and science.[59] Contemporary authors also appreciate the connection between reconciliation, righteousness, and the law, the preparation needed for reconciliation, and an awareness that reconciliation is less of a state or trait than a process or journey.[60] Among the consequences of reconciliation are both peace and joy.[61] Christians pray for the reconciliation of the world and with the earth itself.[62]

This brief introduction to some of the biblical and theological literature on reconciliation shows both its depth and breadth as a unifying theme. It is a meaningful concept that subsumes justification, sanctification, and vocation; liberation and healing from alienation, estrangement, conflict, strife, and bitterness. It informs our understanding of discipleship and ministry; confession, forgiveness, and penance; sacramental healing, renewal, peace, and joy. In light of the extensive literature on this concept, including numerous articles not mentioned here, it is frankly distressing that reconciliation is a theme heard so infrequently in contemporary preaching. Reconciliation is the heart of Jesus' message and the central mission of the Church.[63]

By way of summary, I favor reconciliation as the general purpose of counseling because it expresses (1) the multidimensional nature of constructive personality change; (2) the holistic nature of healing that occurs through counseling; (3) the centrality of interpersonal relationships; (4) the reality of human alienation; and (5) the promise and hope of healing. Furthermore, (6) it expresses the dynamic and developmental nature of the redemptive life, subsuming the conditions and stages of salvation; (7) it constitutes a norm for counseling decisions; and (8) it places counseling within the context of the ministry of reconciliation that belongs to the Church as a whole. Moreover, (9) it includes and guides the other traditional functions of pastoral care; (10) it expresses the Church's confession of God's reconciling work in Jesus Christ and the mission of reconciliation to which he has called his Church, and (11) it rests upon a firm foundation of theological reflection unifying various dimensions of the Christian life, and especially the sacramental dimension. Reconciliation is a sacred experience, and an experience of the Holy. To be reconciled is to know that life is sacrosanct and that life with God is good. It is a truly awesome experience of healing and renewal.

I have said that the purpose of counseling is reconciliation. The expected outcome of counseling so defined is a more reconciled life. And that is what this book is really about. What does it mean to live a reconciled life, to be a reconciled person? What does it mean to be reconciled and reconciling with others, with oneself, and with God? It is to these questions that the following chapters are addressed.

In the remaining pages, I will attempt to describe what the experience of reconciliation is like in order to understand it. By doing so, I am providing a phenomenological and existential interpretation of Jesus' message of reconciliation. While the experience of reconciliation is multidimensional and occurs in social, psychological, and spiritual realms, the focus of this book as related to psychotherapy is the psychological dimension of reconciliation. Descriptions of the experience of reconciliation constitute an elaboration of this purpose of counseling and provide principles for both therapeutic objectives and counseling procedures. Moreover, implicit within each dimension[64] are hypotheses to be tested empirically.

NOTES

1. There have been occasional articles applying the concept of reconciliation to specific clinical conditions. See for example Hunter, M. (1996). Ritual of reconciliation– another way. *The ISTI Sun,* 2(2), 3. Published by The Interfaith Sexual Trauma Institute at Saint John's University and Abbey in Collegeville, MN, 56321-2000.

2. See n.5 in chapter two. The second national conference on forgiveness in psychotherapy was coordinated by Dr. Frederick DiBlasio of the Social Work Department of the University of Maryland at Baltimore on April 25, 1996. The third national conference on this topic was held September 25–28, 1997 in Kansas City, MO coordinated by Mack Harnden.

3. Sponheim, P. (1993). *Faith and the other: A relational theology.* Minneapolis, MN: Fortress Press. A relational theology is particularly evident among feminist theologians. Examples are Johnson, E. (1992). *She who is: The mystery of God in feminist theological discourse.* New York: Crossroads Publishing Company; and LaCugna, C. (1991). *God for us: The trinity and Christian life.* New York: HarperSanFrancisco. Transformational and experiential themes are also evident in two other Christian feminist authors: Brock, R. (1988). *Journey by heart: A Christology of erotic power.* New York: Crossroad; and Heyward, I. (1982). *The redemption of God.* Washington: University Press of America.

4. Buber, M. (1958). *I and Thou.* New York: Macmillan Publishing Company. Buber preferred the concept of "relation" over both "substance" and "experience" as a basic category of thought.

5. The teleological nature of human behavior is expressed in the concept of the "telosponse" in phenomenological theory as an alternative to simply "response" in learning theory and behavioral psychology. See Rychlak, J. (1981). *Introduction to personality and psychotherapy.* Boston: Houghton Mifflin Company, p. 793. See chapter 6, n.55.

6. See chapter 1, n.51.

7. An emphasis upon intentional behavior in the social psychology of attitude change is Fishbein, M. (1980). A theory of reasoned action: Some applications and implications. In H. E. Howe, Jr., & M. M. Page (Eds.), *Nebraska symposium on motivation, 1979* (Vol. 27, pp. 65–116). Lincoln: University of Nebraska Press. Additional factors such as motivation to comply and one's attitude toward performing an act of reconciliation are both mediated through behavioral intentions.

8. The term "indirective" was used by Capps, D. (1979). *Pastoral care: A thematic approach.* Philadelphia: The Westminster Press. The emphasis is upon changing one's perceptions through counseling based upon Jesus' parables, a theme which is extended in Capps, D. (1990). *Reframing: A new method in pastoral care.* Minneapolis, MN: Fortress Press.

9. Precedents for this comprehensive theological meaning include Karl Barth's use of reconciliation to subsume justification, sanctification, and vocation (see n.46 this chapter), and Sano, R. (1985). A theology of evangelism. In T. Runyon (Ed.), *Wesleyan theology today: A bicentennial theological consultation* (pp. 240–247). Nashville: Kingswood Books—An Imprint of the United Methodist Publishing House. Sanyo adds the concept of redemption to reconciliation. He includes the two elements of justification and sanctifcation in the concept of reconciliation.

10. Full discussion of the social and spiritual dimensions of reconciliation is beyond the scope of this book. Here the focus is upon the psychological dimension and its role as the purpose of psychotherapy.

11. See Clinebell, H. (1984). *Basic types of pastoral care and counseling.* Nashville, TN: Abingdon Press, chp. 2, for an emphasis upon Spirit-centered wholeness as the goal of Christian counseling. A further development of this model is Malony, H. N. (Ed.). (1983). *Wholeness and holiness: Readings in the psychology/theology of mental health.* Grand Rapids, MI: Baker Book House; and Malony, H. N., Papen-Daniels, M., & Clinebell, H. (Eds.). (1988). *Spirit centered wholeness: Beyond the psychology of self.* Lewiston, New York: Edwin Mellen Press.

12. For a contemporary theology that emphasizes relationships see Buber, M. (1970). *I and Thou.* New York: Scribner's; Buber, M. (1985). *Between man and man.* New York: Collier Books; Sponheim, P. R. (1993). *Faith and the other: A relational theology.* Minneapolis, MN: Fortress Press; Kirwan, W. (1984). *Biblical concepts for Christian counseling: A case for integrating psychology and theology.* Grand Rapids, MI: Baker Book House. See also Crabtree, A. (1963). *The restored relationship: A study of justification and reconciliation.* Valley Forge, PA: Judson Press; and Walker, W. (1909). *The gospel of reconciliation: Or at-one-ment.* Edinburgh: T. & T. Clark; Workman, G. (1911). *At-onement, or reconciliation with God.* New York: Fleming H. Revell.

13. For an expression of the theme of alienation in literature see Scott, N. (1952). *Rehearsals of discomposure: Alienation and reconciliation in modern literature: Franz Kafka, Ignanzio Silone, D. H. Lawrence, and T. S. Eliot.* New York: King's Crown Publishers.

14. DeYoung, C. (1997). *Reconciliation: Our greatest challenge—our only hope.* Valley Forge, PA: Judson Press; Banks, R. (Ed.). (1974). *Reconciliation and hope: New testament essays on atonement and eschatology presented to L. L. Morris on his 60th birthday.* Grand Rapids, MI: Wm. B. Eerdmans. The universality of this hope extended to all persons was expressed by Ballou, H. (1853). *A treatise on atonement.* Boston: A. Tompkins. Current books on the role of hope in counseling are Capps, D. (1995). *Hope: A pastoral psychology.* Minneapolis, MN: Fortress Press; and Lester, A. (1995). *Hope in pastoral care and counseling.* Louisville, KY: Westminster/John Knox Press.

15. Helling, M. (1982). *Sign of reconciliation and conversion: The sacrament of*

penance for our times. Wilmington, DE: M. Glazier; Henchal, M. (Ed.). (1987). *Repentance and reconciliation in the church: Major presentations given at the 1986 national meeting of the Federation of Diocesan Liturgical Commissions.* Collegeville, MN: Liturgical Press; Buzzard, L., Buzzard, J., & Eck, L. (1992). *Readiness for reconciliation: A biblical guide.* Annandale, VA: Christian Legal Society; Stott, J. (1965). *Confess your sins: The way of reconciliation.* Philadelphia, PA: Westminster Press; Brennan, P. (1986). *Penance and reconciliation.* Chicago, IL: Thomas More Press; Doran, K. (1988). *More joy in heaven: Confession, the sacrament of reconciliation.* Collegeville, MN: Liturgical Press. Books emphasizing forgiveness in the sacrament of reconciliation include Taylor, V. (1952). *Forgiveness and reconciliation: A study in new testament theology.* London: Macmillan; Hiltner, S. (1969). *Psychological understanding of reconciliation and forgiveness* (sound recording). Princeton, NJ: Princeton Theological Seminary; Aridas, C. (1987). *Reconciliation: Celebration of God's healing forgiveness.* Garden City, NY: Image Books; Fernandez Garcia, D. (1992). *The father's forgiveness: Rethinking the sacrament of reconciliation* (Palmo Olmedo, trans.). Collegeville, MN: Liturgical Press. Recent books within the Protestant tradition that emphasize forgiveness include Augsburger, D. (1996). *Helping people forgive.* Louisville, KY: Westminster/John Knox Press; Meninger, W. (1996). *The process of forgiveness.* New York: Continuum; Smedes, L. (1984, 1996). *Forgive and forget: Healing the hurts we don't deserve.* New York: HaperSanFrancisco; and Smedes, L. (1996). *The art of forgiving: When you need to forgive and don't know how.* Nashville, TN: Moorings.

16. Here I favor Catholic teaching that while neither faith nor love constitute merit for justification, justification is experienced through both faith and love. Both are necessary; neither one alone is sufficient. See United States Catholic Conference. (1994). *Catechism of the Catholic Church.* Mahwah, NJ: Paulist Press, pp. 483, 487. Perhaps the two could be combined as in the phrase "justification by Grace through faithful love."

17. Rychlak calls the resulting behavior "telosponsive action" or a "telosponse" to emphasize the teleological and voluntary nature of human behavior. A telosponse is the integrated, triphasic act of consciously reasoning about various options, and choosing one of the alternatives as one's purpose for the sake of which behavior is intended. A telosponse may involve cognitive, affective, volitional, and behavioral elements as well as relationships. Rychlak advocates this construct to integrate the insights about human nature found in psychodynamic, phenomenological, and behavioral theories of psychotherapy. I think this construct also serves to integrate psychological and ethical perspectives since the alternatives considered and selected as goals or purposes constitute values, and provide answers to such questions as "what should I do?" See Rychlak, J. (1981). *Introduction to personality and psychotherapy* (2nd ed.). Boston: Houghton Mifflin Company, pp. 788–798.

18. Frankena, W. (1973). *Ethics* (2nd ed.). Englewood Cliffs, NJ: Prentice-Hall, p. 82.

19. Frankena's paraphrase of Kant expresses this idea: "principles without traits are impotent and traits without principles are blind." Ibid., p. 65.

20. For a definition of metaphors and models, see Browning, D. (1987). *Religious thought and the modern psychologies: A critical conversation.* Philadelphia: Fortress Press, pp. 18–20, 32–35.

21. Curtis DeYoung views Christian disciples as ambassadors of reconciliation. See DeYoung, C. (1997). *Reconciliation: Our greatest challenge—our only hope.* Valley Forge, PA: Judson Press, pp. 58–59.

22. For secondary and technical resources on Paul's theology of reconciliation see Martin, R. (1981). *Reconciliation: A study of Paul's theology.* Atlanta, GA: John Knox Press; Lloyd-Jones, D. (1972). *God's way of reconciliation (studies of Ephesians, chp. 2).*

Grand Rapids, MI: Baker Books; Hedquist, P.M. (1979). *The Pauline understanding of reconciliation in Romans 5 and II Corinthians 5: An exegetical and religio-historical study* (microform). Ann Arbor, MI: University Microfilms International; Arrington, F. (1980). *The ministry of reconciliation: A study of II Corinthians.* Grand Rapids, MI: Baker Book House; Mitchell, M. (1991). *Paul and the rhetoric of reconciliation: An exegetical investigation of the language and composition of I Corinthians.* Tubigan, Germany: J.C.C. Mohr. A more practical exposition of Paul's central concept of reconciliation is DeYoung, C. (1997). *Reconciliation: Our greatest challenge—our only hope.* Valley Forge, PA: Judson Press.

23. Clinebell, H. (1984). *Basic types of pastoral care and counseling.* Nashville, TN: Abingdon Press (p. 42; cf. pp.10, 17, 25–34). Clinebell lists reconciliation as one of the functions of pastoral care rather than using it to subsume the rest as I have done. He prefers the unifying construct of Spirit-centered wholeness as a basis for a holistic model of liberation and growth.

24. The Presbyterian Church, USA. (1991). *The book of confessions,* #9.06. The concept of reconciliation appears in another denomination's statement of faith to express God's redemptive act in Jesus Christ. See the 1981 revision of the "Statement of Faith" in The United Church of Christ. (1991). *History and Program of the United Church of Christ).* Cleveland, OH: The United Church Press, p. 4.

25. The Presbyterian Church, U.S.A. (1991). *The book of confessions,* #9.01–9.56.

26. Ibid., #9.20.

27. Ibid., #9.20.

28. Ibid., #9.40. The degree to which this Confession actually inspires and guides local churches toward an effective ministry of reconciliation is a relevant, but unanswered question.

29. Ibid., #9.03.

30. "In 1982, in connection with a symposium at Princeton Seminary on 'the Confession of 1967: Contemporary Implications', the Rev. Cynthia A. Jarvis and Professor Freda A. Gardner prepared an inclusive language text of the Confession of 1967 which has been used unofficially." Quoted from Rogers, J. (1985). *Presbyterian creeds: A guide to the book of confessions.* Philadelphia: The Westminster Press, p. 229.

31. Denner, J. (1985). *The biblical doctrine of reconciliation.* Minneapolis, MN: Klock & Klock Christian Publishers; Jones, J. E., & Boneck, J. D. (1984). *Reconciliation.* Minneapolis, MN: Bethany House Publishers; Rutenber, C. (1960). *The reconciling gospel.* Philadelphia: Judson Press.

32. Taylor, V. (1952). *Forgiveness and reconciliation: A study in new testament theology.* London: Macmillan; Wood, F. (1975). *Hosea: Prophet of reconciliation.* Nashville, TN: Convention Press; Watson, D. (Ed.). (1991). *Persuasive artistry: Studies in new testament rhetoric in honor of George A. Kennedy.* Sheffield, England: JSOT Press; Hennelly, A. (Ed.). (1993). *Signs of the times: Theological reflections of Juan Luis Segundo.* Maryville, NY: Orbis Books. Two books depicting reconciliation as the essence of Christianity are Pieper, F. (1953). *What is Christianity? And other essays* (J. T. Mueller, trans.), St. Louis, MO: Concordia Press; and Farmer, H. (1966). *The Word of reconciliation.* Nashville, TN: Abingdon Press.

33. Come, A. (1960). *Agents of reconciliation.* Philadelphia: Westminster Press; and Stuhlmueller, C. (1975). *Reconciliation: A biblical call.* Chicago: Franciscan Herald Press; and DeYoung, C. (1997). *Reconciliation: Our greatest challenge–our only hope.* Valley Forge, PA: Judson Press. An early book expressing the view of reconciliation as the meaning of salvation is by Taylor, W. (1875). *Reconciliation: Or how to be saved.* London: S. W. Partridge; Hagstrom, J. (n.d.). *Reconciliation or atonement.* Chicago: Covenant Book

Concern; Banks, R. (Ed.). (1974). *Reconciliation and hope: New testament essays on atonement and eschatology presented to L. L. Morris on his 60th birthday.* Grand Rapids, MI: Wm. B. Eerdmans.

34. Simon, D. (1898). *Reconciliation by incarnation: The reconciliation of God and man by the incarnation of the divine word.* Edinburgh: T. & T. Clark; Song, C. S. (1993). *Jesus and the reign of God.* Minneapolis, MN: Fortress press.

35. Van Buren, P. (1957). *Christ in our place: The substitutionary character of Calvin's doctrine of reconciliation.* Grand Rapids, MI: Eerdmans; Hicks, F. (1959). *The fullness of sacrifice: An essay on reconciliation.* London: SPCK; Simon, D. (1898). *Reconciliation by incarnation: The reconciliation of God and man by the incarnation of the divine Word.* Edinburgh: T. & T. Clark; Lampe, G. (1956). *Reconciliation in Christ.* New York: Longmans, Green, & Company; and Clark, T. (1959). *Saved by his life: A study of the new testament doctrine of reconciliation and salvation.* New York: Macmillan. One may claim Jesus as the Christ (Messiah) solely on the grounds that he served as a unique and definitive medium of reconciliation by virtue of his own experience of a transforming relationship with God.

36. Ritschl, A. (1872). *A critical history of the Christian doctrine of justification and reconciliation.* (J. S. Black, Trans.). Edinburgh: Edmonston and Douglas; Ritschl, A. B. (1902). *The Christian doctrine of justification and reconciliation: The positive development of the doctrine.* (English translation, edited by H. R. Mackintosh and A. B. Macaulay.) (2nd ed.). Edinburgh: T. & T. Clark; Dierks, T. (1938). *Reconciliation and justification as taught by Christ and the apostles and as it was confessed in the Christian church in the first century after the apostles.* St. Louis, MO: Concordia Publishing House. Catholic theology has also connected these two central doctrines. See for example Osborne, K. (1990). *Reconciliation and justification: The sacrament and its theology.* New York: Paulist Press.

37. Morrison, C. (1968). *Estrangement from God* (sound recording). Princeton, NJ: Princeton Theological Seminary; Tillich, P. (1957). *Systematic theology* (Vol. 2). Chicago: University of Chicago Press; Hansen, O. (1956). *The problem of alienation and reconciliation: A comparative study of Marx and Kierkegaard in the light of Hegel's formulation of the problem.* Princeton, NJ: Olaf Hansen.

38. Aridas, C. (1987). *Reconciliation: Celebrating God's healing forgiveness* (1st ed.). Garden City, NY: Image Books; Garrooto, A. J. (1982). *Christians reconciling: A process of renewal.* Minneapolis, MN: Winston Press; Loehman, J. M. (1980). *Reconciliation and liberation: Challenging a one dimensional view of salvation.* (D. Lewis, Trans.). Philadelphia: Fortress Press. Morrison, M. C. (1974). *Reconciliation: The hidden hyphen.* Wallingford, PA: Pendle Hill. The liberating power of confession and absolution is grounded in divine grace that makes reconciliation possible. See United Church of Christ. (1986). Order for reconciliation of a penitent person, and order for corporate reconciliation. *Book of worship United Church of Christ.* New York: Office for Church Life and Leadership, pp. 268–288.

39. Song, C. S. (1993). *Jesus and the reign of God.* Minneapolis, MN: Fortress Press (pp. xi, 2, 283); Perrin, N. (1967). *Rediscovering the teaching of Jesus.* New York: Harper and Row, p. 54. Authors emphasizing reconciliation as the central message and mission of the Church include Ricker, B. (1988). *The message of the church* (sound recording). San Diego, CA.: Bethel Theological Seminary, West Campus; Harkness, G. (1917). *The ministry of reconciliation.* Nashville, TN: Abingdon Press; Schreiter, R. J. (1992). *Reconciliation: Mission and ministry in a changing social order.* Maryknoll, NY: Orbis Books; Rutenber, C. G. (1965). *Reconciling agents of a reconciling Lord.* Oakland, CA: Color Art Press; Bianchi, E. (1969). *Reconciliation: The function of the church.* New York: Sheed and Ward; Tibbetts, O. L. (1969). *The reconciling community.* Valley Forge, PA:

Judson Press; Barry, D. (1975). *Ministry of reconciliation: Modern lessons from Scripture and sacrament.* New York: Alba House; Cooks, B. (1986). *Reconciled sinners: Healing human brokenness* (forward by D. Donnelly). Mystic, CT: Twenty-Third Publications; Song, C. S. (1993). *Jesus and the reign of God.* Minneapolis, MN: Fortress Press (pp. 283–284). See n.41–n.50 for Catholic views on the ministry of reconciliation.

40. Talley, T. (1990). *Worship: Reforming tradition.* Washington, DC: Pastoral Press; Habermas, R., & Issler, K. (1992). *Teaching for reconciliation: Foundations and practice of Christian educational ministry.* Grand Rapids, MI: Baker Book House.

41. Schillebeeck, E. (1971). *Sacramental reconciliation.* New York: Herder & Herder; Crichton, J. (1974). *The ministry of reconciliation: A commentary on the order of penance. Ordo paenittentiae.* (G. Webb, Trans.). London: Chapman; Gula, R. M. (1984). *To walk together again: The sacrament of reconciliation.* New York: Paulist Press; Brennan, P. J. (1986). *Penance and reconciliation.* Chicago, IL: Thomas More Press; Dallen, J. (1986). *The reconciling community: The rite of penance.* New York: Pueblo Publishing Co.; Pastva, M. L., Romancik, M. R., & Stanko, M. D. (1983). *Growing up to God: A guide for teenagers on the sacrament of reconciliation.* New York: Alba House.

42. United States Catholic Conference (1984). *Reconciliation and penance: Post-synodal apostolic exhortation, reconciliatio et paenitentia of John Paul II to the bishops, clergy, and faithful on reconciliation and penance in the mission of the church today.* Washington, DC: Office of Publishing and Promotion Services; Catholic Church Synod of Bishops. (1984). *Penance and reconciliation in the mission of the church: Synod of Bishops, Rome, 1983.* Washington, DC: National Conference of Catholic Bishops; Cuschieri, A. (1992). *The sacrament of reconciliation: A theological and canonical treatise.* Lanham, MD: University Press of America; U. S. Catholic Conference. (1986). *Penance and reconciliation in the church.* Washington, DC: Office of Publications and Promotion Services. Along with the anointing of the sick, the sacrament of penance and reconciliation is discussed as one of the sacraments of healing in the new *Catechism of the Catholic Church.* (1994). Mahwah, New Jersey: Paulist Press, pp. 357–375.

43. Halligan, F. (1973). *The sacraments of reconciliation.* New York: Alba House; Kelly, G. (1975). *The sacrament of penance and reconciliation: Sociological and histori-cal perspective of the exigencies of various ages for the discipline of penance.* Chicago: Franciscan Herald Press; Hamelin, L. (1980). *Reconciliation in the church: A theological and pastoral essay on the sacrament of penance.* (M. J. O'Connell, Trans.). Collegeville, MN: Liturgical Press; Buckley, F. (1981). *Reconciling.* Notre Dame, IN: Ave Maria Press; Osborne, K. B. (1990). *Reconciliation and justification: The sacrament and its theology.* New York: Paulist Press; Cuschieri, A. (1992). *The sacrament of reconciliation: A theo-logical and canonical treatise.* Lanham, MD: University Press of America.

44. De Gidio, S. (1985). *Reconciliation: Sacrament with a future.* Cincinnati, OH: St. Anthony Messenger Press; Kenned, R. (Ed.). (1987). *Reconciliation: The continuing agenda.* Collegeville, MN: Liturgical Press; Fernandez, D. (1991). *The Father's forgive-ness: Rethinking the sacrament of reconciliation.* (Palmo Olmedo, Trans.). Collegeville, MN: Liturgical Press; Schlicket, J., Zimmermann, M., Hari, A., & Messner, F. (Eds.). (1984). *Penance and reconciliation: International bibliography, 1975–1983.* Strasbourg, France: Cerdic Publications.

45. United States Catholic Conference. (1994). *Catechism of the Catholic Church.* Mahwah, New Jersey: Paulist Press, pp. 358, 362, 369, 374

46. Bromiley, G., & Torrance, T. (Eds.). *Church dogmatics by Karl Barth (1936–1969).* New York: Scribner; Barth, K. (1981). *The Christian life: Church dogmatics. (Vol. IV. 4): Lecture fragments.* (G. W. Bromiley, Trans.). Grand Rapids, MI: Wm. B. Eerdmans; Barth, K. (1956). *The doctrine of reconciliation.* (G. W. Bromiley, Trans.).

New York: Scribner; Barth, K. (1958). *Church dogmatics* (Vol. 4: Parts 1, 2, 3a, 3b). Edinburgh: T. & T. Clark. For appraisals, see Klooster, F. (1961). *The significance of Barth's theology: An appraisal with special reference to election and reconciliation.* Grand Rapids, MI: Baker House; and Mueller, D. L. (1991). *Foundation of Karl Barth's doctrine of reconciliation: Jesus Christ crucified and risen.* New York: E. Mellen Press.

47. Tillich, P. (1957, 1963). *Systematic theology* (Vols. 2, 3). Chicago: University of Chicago Press.

48. Tillich, P. (1957). *Systematic theology* (Vol. 2), pp.176–180 and (Vol. 3), pp. 129–138, 362–423. Tillich wrote that the question arising out of the human condition of estrangement is "the question of a reality in which the self estrangement of our existence is overcome, a reality of reconciliation and reunion, of creativity, meaning, and hope. We shall call such a reality the 'New Being'. . . . It is based on what Paul calls the 'new creation'" (*Systematic theology* [Vol. 1], p. 49). Since Tillich describes the Christian message as "the message of the 'New Being', and he equates this with a power and reality of reconciliation, his own interpretation can be characterized as an existential theology of reconciliation.

49. Talley, J., & Stobbe, L. (1985). *Reconciling differences.* Nashville, TN: T. Nelson; Pote, L. (1977). *Acceptance: Balancing our differences in grace.* Kalamazoo, MI: Master's Publishing. As a solution for conflicts within the Church, see Hessel, D. (1969). *Reconciliation and conflict: Church controversy over social involvement.* Philadelphia: Westminster Press; and Graham, S. A., & Graham, M. W. (1994). *First the kingdom: A call to the conservative pentecostal/charismatics and the liberal social justice advocates for repentance and reunification.* Lanham, MD: University Press of America. Applications of reconciliation to the wider community are illustrated by Schaller, L. (1966). *Community organization: Conflict and reconciliation.* Nashville, TN: Abingdon Press; Dallen, J., & Favazza, J. (1991). *Removing the barriers: The practice of reconciliation.* Chicago: Liturgy Training Publications; and McCullough, C., & Sherry, P. (1991). *Resolving conflict with justice and peace.* Cleveland, OH: The Pilgrim Press.

50. Pannell, W. (1993). *The coming race wars: A cry for reconciliation.* Grand Rapids, MI: Zondervan; Washington, R. (1993). *Breaking down walls: A model for reconciliation in an age of racial strife.* Chicago: Moody Press; Shearer, J. (1994). *Enter the river: Healing steps from white privilege toward racial reconciliation.* Scottdale, PA: Herald Press; Battle, M. (1997). *Reconciliation: The Ubuntu theology of Desmond Tutu.* Cleveland, OH: Pilgrim Press; Van Leeuwen, M. S. (1993). *After Eden: Facing the challenge of gender reconciliation.* Grand Rapids, MI: Wm. B. Eerdmans; Pew, W. L. (Ed.). (n.d.). *The war between the generations: An attempt at reconciliation.* Minneapolis: (s.n.).

51. Dodd, C. (1952). *Christianity and the reconciliation of nations.* London: SCM; DeYoung, C. (1997). *Reconciliation: Our greatest challenge–our only hope.* Minneapolis, MN: Judson Press. The latter book addresses separations based on race, gender, culture, and class, as well as nationalism.

52. Page, K. (1939). *How to keep America out of war.* Philadelphia: American Friends Service Committee, Peace Section. New York: Fellowship of Reconciliation; International Fellowship of Reconciliation (1961). *Therefore choose life: Essays on the nuclear crisis.* Nyack, NY: Fellowship of Reconciliation; Pratt, C. et al., (1979). *Peace, justice, and reconciliation in the Arab-Israeli conflict: A Christian perspective.* New York: Friendship Press; Chacour, E. (1990). *We belong to the land: The story of a Palestinian Israeli who lives for peace and reconciliation.* New York: HarperSanFrancisco; Polner, M., & Goodman, N. (1994). *The challenge of Shalom: The Jewish tradition of peace and justice.* Philadelphia: New Society Publishers; Haring, B. (1968). *Shalom: Peace—the sacrament of reconciliation.* New York: Farrar, Strauss, & Giroux; Lachmund, M. (1979). *With thine adversary in the way: A Quaker witness for reconciliation.* (F. Likite, Trans.).

Wallingford, PA: Pendle Hill Publishing; Donaghy, J. (1983). *Peacemaking and the community of faith: A handbook for congregations.* (Prepared by the Covenant Peacemaking Program, Fellowship of Reconciliation). Ramsey, NJ: Paulist Press.

53. Sterba, J. (1985). *How to make people just: A practical reconciliation of alternative conceptions of justice.* Totowar, NJ: Rowman & Littlefield; Umbreit, M. (1985). *Crime and reconciliation: Creative options for victims and offenders.* Nashville, TN: Abingdon Press; Roberts, J. (1971). *Liberation and reconciliation: A Black theology.* Philadelphia: Westminster Press; Lochman, J. (1980). *Reconciliation and liberation: Challenging a one-dimensional view of salvation.* (D. Lewis, Trans.). Philadelphia: Fortress Press; Rusolondraibe, P. (1984). *Liberation and reconciliation: An African ethical reflection on the dialectical interaction between liberation and reconciliation in African political economy: Nyerere's praxis as a case study.* (publisher unknown).

54. Stith, C. (1995). *Political religion: A liberal answers the question: "Should politics and religion mix?"* Nashville, TN: Abingdon Press. The United Church of Christ views itself as a just peace church. See Rader, W. (1989). Just peace and revolutionary nonviolence. *Prism, 4*(2), 48–61.

55. Sande, K. (1991). *The peacemaker: A biblical guide to resolving personal conflict.* Grand Rapids, MI: Baker Book House; Falconer, A. D. (Ed.). (1988). *Reconciling memories* (1st ed.). Blackrock, CO: Columbia Press; Stierlin, H. (1969). *Conflict and reconciliation: A study in human relations and schizophrenia.* Garden City, NY: Anchor Books; Powell, P. W. (1992). *Basic bible sermons on handling conflict.* Nashville, TN: Broadman Press; Lowry, L. R., & Meyers, R. W. (1991). *Conflict management and counseling.* Dallas, TX: Word Publications. Applications in spiritual direction include Hassel, D. J. (1990). *Healing the ache of alienation: Praying through and beyond bitterness.* New York: Paulist Press; Brother Roger of Taize. (1987). *Awakened from within: Meditations on the Christian life* (1st ed.). New York: Doubleday.

56. Wilson, K. (1982). *How to repair the wrong you've done: Steps to restoring relationships.* Ann Arbor, MD: Servant Books; Kraybill, R. S. (1981). *Repairing the breach: Ministering in community conflict.* Scottdale, PA.: Herald Press; Nelson, J. O. (1969). *Dare to reconcile: Seven settings for creating community.* New York: Friendship.

57. Jessop, T. (1969). *Not this way: A Methodist examination of the final 1968 Anglican-Methodist union scheme, with special reference to the Service of Reconciliation and the theology which lies behind it, and a plea for theological integrity.* Appleford, Berkshire, England: Marchan Manor Publications; Miller, A. (1969). *Reconciliation in today's world: Six study papers introducing the theme of the uniting general council of the World Alliance of Reformed and Presbyterian Churches and the International Congregational Council.* Nairobi, Kenya: August, 1970. Grand Rapids, MI: Wm. B. Eerdmans; Torrance, T. (1976). *Theology in reconciliation: Essays towards Evangelical and Catholic Unity in East and West.* Grand Rapids, MI: Wm. B. Eerdmans; Stauffer, R. (1986). *The quest for church unity: From John Calvin to Isaac d'Huisseau.* Allison Park, PA: Pickwick Publications; Presbyterian Church of the USA. (1964). *Christian foundations* (Vol. 1). Philadelphia: The Westminster Press. Along with the theme of liberation, reconciliation defines the purpose of ministry in the ecumenical Consultation on Church Union. See Laurie, W. (1989). The nature of ministry in the COCU consensus. *Prism, 4*(2), 16–22.

58. Basetti-Sani, G. (1974). *Louis Massignon (1883–1962): Christian ecumenist prophet of interreligious reconciliation.* (A. H. Cutler, Trans.). Chicago: Franciscan Herald Press.

59. Clark, R. (1960). *Christian belief and science: A reconciliation and a partnership.* London: English Universities Press; Lund, N. (1980). *A common call to care for the whole person: An argument for the reconciliation of the Christian faith and medical science*

in a holistic approach to health care. St. Paul, MN: (s.n.); Clift, W. (1982). *Jung and Christianity: the challenge of reconciliation.* New York: Crossroad; Morris, T. (1994). *God and the philosophers: The reconciliation of faith and reason.* New York: Oxford University Press.

60. Stuhlmacher, P. (1986). *Reconciliation, law, and righteousness: Essays in biblical theology.* (E. R. Kalin, Trans.). Philadelphia: Fortress Press; Buzzard, L, Buzzard, J., & Eck, L. (1992). *Readiness for reconciliation: A biblical guide.* Annandalte, VA: Christian Legal Society; Herman, H. J. (1993). *Faith and order: The reconciliation of law and religion.* Atlanta, GA: Scholars Press. The view of reconciliation as a journey is found in Friedlander, A. H. (1990). *A thread of gold: Journeys towards reconciliation.* (John Bowden, Trans.). Philadelphia: Trinity Press International; Garrotto, A. (1982). *Christians reconciling: A process for renewal.* Minneapolis, MN: Winston Press.

61. Lozoff, B., & Braswell, M. (1989). *Inner corrections: Finding peace and peacemaking.* Cincinnati, OH: Anderson Publications; Doran, K. (1988). *More joy in heaven: Confession, the sacrament of reconciliation.* Collegeville, MN: Liturgical Press..

62. Dunn, S., & Longergan, A. (Eds.). (1991). *Befriending the earth: A theology of reconciliation between humans and the earth.* Mystic, CT: Twenty-Third Publications; Clinebell, H. (1996). *Ecotherapy: Healing ourselves, healing the earth.* Minneapolis, MN: Fortress Press; Cloud, F. (1970). *Prayers for reconciliation.* Nashville, TN: Upper Room; United States Catholic Conference. (1975). *Eucharistic prayers for masses of reconciliation: Arranged for celebration.* Washington, DC: Publications Office.

63. Song, C. S. (1993). *Jesus and the Reign of God*, p. 28.

64. In relating twentieth century physics with Christian existentialism, Karl Heim used the spatial metaphor of "dimension" to reconcile the scientific and spiritual attitudes toward the world. He suggested that what is inconceivable in one kind of space (physical) may become possible in another space (interpersonal and archetypal) by disclosing new dimensions of phenomena. (Heim, K. [1953]. *The Christian faith and natural science.* New York: Harper and Brothers, pp. 126–174.) In addition, Viktor Frankl applied and modified the dimensional ontology of Nicolai Hartmann and Max Scheler's anthropology to develop a dimensional psychology of personality with somatic, psychic, and spiritual dimensions as a foundation of logotherapy. Frankl, V. (1988). *The will to meaning: Foundations and applications of logotherapy.* New York: Meridian, pp. 21–30.

Chapter Five

Cognitive and Affective Reconciliation

In the preceding chapters I provided a theoretical and methodological foundation for the development of this theory of counseling. This discussion led to the definition given in chapter four along with several reasons for favoring reconciliation as the general purpose of counseling. The tone of my discussion so far has been objective and discursive, and many of the ideas presented have been theoretical and general in nature.

In this chapter and the next I provide a phenomenological description of the essence of reconciliation disclosed in the concrete experience and particular teachings of Jesus of Nazareth. As a Christian psychologist, I turn to Jesus' teachings in the Synoptic Gospels as the source of the norm for understanding the structure and content of reconciliation as he experienced it. My tone becomes more existential and confessional as I seek to express the implications of Jesus' message in terms of the process and dimensions of change occurring as one becomes a more reconciling individual.

Some readers may experience the following two chapters as homiletical or even parochial. I encourage my readers to see the universal dimensions of reconciliation reflected in the concrete experience described in the teachings of Jesus, and to select additional dimensions of reconciliation from other religious and non-religious resources which they may find equally relevant, and perhaps more congenial. These other perspectives, which may be contradictory to my own, will enrich our understanding of this healing experience so crucial in our present age of alienation and violence. Since my own perspective is shaped by my commitment as a disciple of Jesus, I shall present his teachings about reconciliation. In chapter seven I will return to a more theoretical discussion relevant to the future development of this theory after providing a summary of its major themes.

THE NATURE OF PSYCHOLOGICAL RECONCILIATION

In this section and the next I will suggest that psychological reconciliation is a relational, holistic experience with varying degrees of awareness. It is essentially a way of being a person who is wise, compassionate, courageous, joyful, and thankful.

Jesus stressed that reconciliation was primarily a matter of relationships. Reconciliation occurs between persons, both human and divine. His teachings focus more upon these relationships than upon reconciling conflicts within the individual. He addressed more interpersonal than intrapsychic conflicts. He spoke more about social than psychological reconciliation, but especially about spiritual reconciliation with God. In all cases, he spoke of reconciliation with someone—with other persons, with oneself, or with a personal God.

A second point to emphasize in this section is that Jesus spoke of persons *holistically*. He did not suggest a personality theory with multiple parts such as an Id-Ego-Superego, nor a mind separate from body and soul. Jesus spoke of the whole person as the basic unit of reconciliation. A further reduction into subparts seems both unnecessary and contrary to experience.[1]

Consistent with his holistic view of the person, he spoke of unreconciled persons as lost individuals. The prodigal son was a lost son, lost as a person, not just physically absent from his father nor merely misbehaving (Lk. 15:11-32). When Jesus said that he came to seek and to save the lost, he was speaking of saving persons, not merely their lost souls or confused minds (Lk. 19:1-10). When he called sinners to repentance, it was an invitation for individuals to change who they were in order to become who they truly are; it was not merely a call to relieve their feelings of guilt or to modify their behavior. It is not just a part of myself that I lose when, instead of seeking first the kingdom of God, I seek the world. I lose myself (Lk. 9:25).

This holistic understanding of persons is important because contemporary theories of personality generally postulate a variety of internal subsystems, such as biological drives or psychological needs, multiple traits or ego states, values or goals, defense mechanisms and various levels of consciousness. These parts are considered to exist in either a state of tension or homeostasis depending upon the degree of internal conflict or cooperation believed to exist among them.

Postulating these various subparts of personality is presumed necessary in order to develop a satisfactory theory of personality and to achieve the scientific objectives to describe, understand, predict, and modify human behavior. The result is literally hundreds of complex theories of personality and psychotherapy, each of which is advocated as the most scientific theory, most comprehensive, most empirical, practical, and true.[2]

Jesus' teachings suggest that such theoretical complexity is probably unnecessary. Nor are such complex theories necessary to achieve scientific objectives. In fact, such complexities may lead to inaccurate descriptions and misunderstandings of human experience, to incorrect predictions, and to inappropriate efforts to control human behavior.

One way of expressing Jesus' holistic view of the individual is to speak of *experience* as a central unifying concept. I experience life as an individual. My experience is not identical to yours. And what I wish to describe and really understand is my own unique experience, not merely my behavior. It is also I who experience my life, not some homunculus within me such as my "ego" or my "adult ego state."

Jesus addressed his teachings to human experience. His numerous parables grounded his extraordinary teachings about the kingdom of God in ordinary human experience, thereby showing that the sacred is revealed within the natural, and the natural is a bridge to the sacred. He taught especially about the importance of experiencing the forgiveness and favor of God (Lk. 2:40) and experiencing the fruits of repentance, not merely about changing the way we think or behave (Mt. 3:8/Lk. 3:8). In this manner, his teachings about life were experiential in addition to being holistic.

Jesus also invited those who doubted his teachings to observe the evidence directly: What do you see and hear? (Mt. 11:2-6/Lk. 7:18-23). That being true, his teachings can be tested empirically. I believe them to be true because they are supported by the authority of my own experience in addition to the authority of Jesus' experience of God and the collective experience of the Christian community throughout the ages.

While Jesus emphasized the unitary nature of human experience and addressed the person as a whole, it is also true that he recognized that persons experience life in a variety of dimensions. The *multidimensional unity of human experience* is its essential structure, as Paul Tillich suggested of human life.[3] Human experience is unitary, but it is also multidimensional. I experience my life as one person in several dimensions.

As an embodied being, I experience life in a material and physical dimension. Biological drives such as hunger, thirst, sex, and pain-avoidance are very real aspects of my human experience. There are also social, psychological, and spiritual dimensions of my experience. To be a reconciled person is to experience congruence among these major dimensions of my total life.

Within the individual person, there are both physical and psychological dimenions of experience that Jesus addressed at varying times in his teachings and ministry of healing (e.g., Mt. 9:1-8; Lk. 8:26-39). Psychologically, human experience includes cognitive, affective, conative, and behavioral domains. Psychological change, growth, and healing occur in all these domains. So do repentance and reconciliation.

These psychological domains of experience and reconciliation that Jesus addressed appear to be appropriate based on my own experience. I am aware that I think. I know that I feel. I want certain things and I intend particular outcomes. I also act in a variety of ways. It is because he addressed all of these domains that I find Jesus' teachings to be relevant and true to human experience. They are for similar reasons relevant to the experience of counseling.

Jesus' teachings also suggest that to be reconciled with myself means that these diverse domains of my experience are unified rather than divided, integrated rather than separated, congruent rather than conflicting (Lk. 11:33–36; Mk. 8:36/ Lk. 9:25; Mt. 12:33–34; Mt. 5:21–26; Mt. 6:14–15/Mk. 11:25–26; Mt. 7:1–5/Lk. 6:37–42). To be reconciled with myself is to experience life holistically in an integrated manner. To be reconciled with myself is to be at peace with myself. It is a kind of personal at-one-ment, a psychological atonement, if you will, in which the parts are subordinated to the whole, though none are sacrificed to it.

Human experience is neither exclusively cognitive nor merely affective. I experience various events as meaningful, but these meanings have emotional dimensions as well. They are not merely meanings I know; they are meanings I also feel. They are felt-meanings. Similarly, the feelings I experience have cognitive content. They are feelings filled with meaning, or meaningful feelings. A poignant example is the experience of grieving following the loss of a loved one.

Moreover, both meanings and feelings can be motivating. My strivings are not divorced from my beliefs and feelings. My intentions are emotionally tinged and give my life meaning. Thus my intentions are both meaningful and emotional phenomena. And so is my behavior.

The main point here is to emphasize the interrelatedness of all of these domains of human experience. The concept of experience functions to subsume all these domains into a unified whole. It is within my experience as a whole person that the dialectic occurs among the various domains of my experience.

Another relevant dimension of experience is expressed by the concept of *degrees of consciousness*. All of the psychological domains of human experience exist within varying levels of consciousness from totally unconscious to fully conscious. Consequently, I may be unaware, dimly aware, or fully aware of my thoughts, feelings, intentions, or actions. Similarly I am aware in varying degrees at different times of the movement of God in my life—the ways in which the kingdom of God has come near to me (Lk. 10:11; 12:32; 17:21; Mt. 10:7–8; Mk. 12:28–34/Mt. 22:34–40/Lk. 10:25– 28).

I wish to underscore here that Jesus did not suggest that the mind is the part that thinks, the heart the part that feels, the will that intends, or the body that acts. It is the one whole person who thinks, feels, wills, and acts. This teaching is also consistent with my personal experience. I am aware that I am the agent of my thinking, feeling, willing, and acting, not some multiple or diverse parts of my personality. I am the one person who lives in the many dimensions of my experience. I am the unity of being in the diversity of my experiences. I have a sense of continuity through the changing flow of events that occur in my life through time. To be reconciled with myself means that I experience myself as one person in these many dimensions of life, as the unity and continuity in the diversity of my changing human experience. To be reconciled is to live as a multidimensional unity, and to be wholly one by following the Holy One.

So far I have said that being reconciled with myself is both a holistic and multidimensional experience. I wish to add now that psychological reconciliation is both a way of being and a process of becoming. It is a way of being fully human through the process of becoming more like Jesus of Nazareth. In this chapter and the next I shall focus upon reconciliation as a psychological way of being.[4]

RECONCILIATION IS A WAY OF BEING

Being reconciled is a way of being. It is a way of being a whole, integrated, healthy person. The various dimensions of my experience are united and organized in a coherent pattern or structure. To be reconciled with myself is a way of living by the power and mercy of God.

In this Christian way of being, each of the domains in the psychological dimension of life is transformed by the Spirit of God through love, faith, and hope. In the cognitive domain of my life, knowledge is transformed into wisdom. In the affective domain, feelings of anger, anxiety, despair and entitlement are transformed into compassion and courage, joy and thanksgiving. In the behavioral domain, unethical conduct is transformed into a righteous lifestyle of doing the will of God. In the conative domain, selfish desires are transformed into sanctified strivings as I learn to will the will of God. In this way, to be reconciled means to be wise, compassionate and courageous, joyful and thankful, righteous and sanctified. It is also a way of being psychologically healthy.[5]

In the discussion that follows in this chapter and the next, each of these domains of psychological experience is presented separately and highlighted temporarily to the exclusion of others. This is done solely to elaborate each domain based on my conviction that each involves a unique aspect of human experience in the psychological dimension and warrants attention to enhance our understanding of it. It seems that in order to understand our experience we must separate it into elements, which in reality are all interrelated and interdependent. In this way our conscious mind may become aware of the multidimensionality of our experience. But the separation is literary, not literal or psychological. Each of the domains must be understood as only one facet of the whole of human experience and integral to the whole. In the process of analysis, we must not lose the unity of our experience, the synthesis, the whole, the oneness of it all. Accordingly, within the personality these domains are not really separate, but rather intimately connected and coexisting. As a person experiences life at a particular time more in one domain than another, that domain emerges as a figure within the ground of all other domains. It is important to keep in mind that ground throughout the discussion of each figure if we are to preserve the sense of unity Jesus attributed to the human personality and to human experience. The first figure to emerge from the ground of human experience is the cognitive domain.

THE COGNITIVE DOMAIN OF RECONCILIATION

To become a qualified counselor licensed to practice independently, applicants in most states must have advanced education and supervised practical experience.

In their professional education, candidates are expected to learn theories about human development, the signs and causes of maladjustment, and theories of personality and psychotherapy. Knowledge of individual differences, and the biological, cognitive, affective, and social bases of behavior are deemed prerequisite to competent clinical practice. Knowledge of statistics and research methodologies, testing and measurement, cross-cultural perspectives, professional ethics, and standards of practice are all presumed to be the necessary foundation for professional practice.

There is recognition among those of us who educate counselors that while such technical knowledge may be necessary, it is not sufficient to prepare one for professional practice. What seems to characterize the most effective counselors is their clinical judgment. This is a more abstract, global trait or meta-skill in contrast to technical knowledge or more specific skills. It is the ability to make good decisions, decisions that lead to efficacious outcomes for the welfare of the client. The most effective counselors provide wise counsel.

We are inclined to think of someone whom we judge to be wise as one who is also experienced, hence wise.[6] It has been claimed, for example, that wisdom as a counselor comes primarily through clinical experience. That is a partial truth. On the one hand, as a result of contacts with numerous distressed persons over several years, the seasoned clinician develops norms and expectations that serve as guiding principles which inform the selection and application of clinical interventions. On the other hand, the counsel offered by some seasoned clinicians is more aptly described as prudence rather than wisdom.

Much of secular psychotherapy focuses appropriately upon the client's welfare, but inappropriately defines that to mean the pursuit of personal satisfaction of an individual's needs. Much of psychotherapy theory and practice is an expression of egoistic hedonism as a philosophy of life. The goal of personal happiness based on satisfaction of one's own needs or desires seems implicit if not paramount in the counsel provided. It is the kind of counsel that reminds one of the blind guides of Jesus time (Mk. 7:14).

There is another source of wisdom for the Christian counselor besides either psychological theory or clinical practice. It is a wisdom both profound and healing. This is the spiritual wisdom taught and lived by Jesus of Nazareth. This wisdom involves (a) knowing the truth of God, (b) accepting the reality of human suffering, (c) being truthful with self and others, (d) being realistic about oneself, (e) being practical, (f) being faithful, and (g) being spiritually discerning.

Knowing the Truth of God

Jesus taught that true wisdom comes as a consequence of our knowledge of the truth of God (Mt. 11:25–27/Lk. 10:21–22). This truth of God that Jesus revealed provides the foundation upon which to build the most secure, ethical, healthy, and happy life. Those who are wise build their lives upon this stable rock in contrast to the shifting sands of so many psychological theories, most of which are washed away like fads by the floods of time (Mt. 7:24-27/Lk. 6:47-49).

As a source of wisdom, Jesus' teachings make cognitive claims. They were not merely addressed to how we feel, or to what we want or do. His pronouncements about the kingdom of God were descriptions of a spiritual reality. His many parables about the kingdom of God portrayed what life with God is truly like. The verity of his portrayal of the good life in these terms can be tested empirically. It has worn the tests of time by generations of disciples. It warrants further study through psychological research.[7]

The wisdom of Jesus' teachings is evident in their realism. Jesus was neither an optimist nor a pessimist. He was a realist. He had a realistic understanding of both the nature of life and the nature of persons.

Accepting the Reality of Human Suffering

Concerning the nature of life, Jesus understood the reality of human suffering. His teachings about life's beatitudes for those who love God were grounded in his understanding of the suffering persons experience in a life without God (Mt. 5:1–12/ Lk. 6:17–23). Nor did he tell his disciples that by following him they would escape suffering. Quite the contrary, he cautioned them that discipleship would expose them to additional trials and tribulations (Mt. 24:9–13/Mk. 13:9–13/ Lk. 21:12-17, 19; Mt. 10:16–23; Mt.10:34–36/Lk.12:51–53). The way is hard that leads to life, he said, and those who find it are few (Mt. 7:13–14/Lk.13:23–24).[8]

Jesus' teachings about the reality of human suffering are paralleled by the teachings of another religious genius. When Gautama Buddha experienced enlightenment, he is said to have awakened to four noble truths. The first truth is that life is *dukkha*, usually translated as suffering.[9] Like Jesus, Buddha saw clearly that life as typically lived is unfulfilling and filled with insecurity. *Dukkha* names the pain that colors all existence for persons who live like wheels whose axles are off center, or whose bones are dislocated from their sockets.[10] Life is out of joint, lived with excessive friction that blocks movement. Life hurts.

This hurt is evident in the natural pain of childbirth, in the pathology of sickness and injuries, in the physical decline and disability associated with natural aging, in our fear of death, and of being separated from what we love or being tied to what we loathe. Life is suffering—especially a dislocated life lived off center. To live is to suffer. Consequently, the life of a Christian is not a light-hearted trip from one mountain top experience to another. Everyone has valley experiences of hardship and heartache, times of trouble and tribulation. Everyone has. Everyone will. To understand that and to accept that is wisdom.

Like Jesus, Buddha also taught that a major cause of much suffering is an egocentric life, expressed in the desire for separateness, for personal fulfillment, for the satisfaction of one's own needs. It is sometimes by the self that we suffer sorrow. It is sometimes our own attachments that cause us agony, and our selfish strivings that cause us such unnecessary misery. Misplaced values make us vulnerable, and it is often what we want that wounds us.

Buddha taught an eightfold path as the way to escape the sorrows caused by such egoism. These pathways were not identical to Jesus' counsel, but the spiritual wisdom taught by both Jesus of Nazareth and Gautama Buddha expresses a common view concerning the central problem of human suffering and a primary cause of selfish strivings.

This is the kind of spiritual wisdom upon which to ground effective counseling. It suggests that as a goal of counseling, achievement of total happiness is unrealistic, hence inappropriate. Nor should the goals of counseling be merely to reduce symptoms or pain, or to escape suffering; rather, the goals of counseling are to help persons gain the courage to embrace the suffering that is an inescapable part of living, and second, to help alleviate some of the unnecessary suffering associated with earthly attachments and finite cares and limitations.

Being Truthful with Others and with Ourselves

Related to the realism of his teachings about suffering was Jesus' wise counsel about being truthful. Jesus was not very patient with those who lived a lie. He confronted repeatedly the hypocrisy of pharisaical religion and those who professed a righteousness without justice (Lk. 11:42; Mt. 23:23; 12:18–20).

Another expression of such hypocrisy is the quest for moral perfection. That quest is as grandiose as it is legalistic. A God-centered righteousness works; works-righteousness does not. It is enough to strive to be like Jesus, and both unnecessary and unrealistic to strive to be Jesus or to be above him (Mt. 10:24–25; Lk. 6:39– 40). The latter is a symptom of human pride and grandiosity.

Dishonest dealings with other persons destroys their confidence and trust. Whether one lies by deliberately stating untruths, by withholding material information, or by hiding one's true intentions, the consequences are mutual cynicism and contempt. Persons are alienated by the lack or loss of integrity in their relationships. Experiences of being manipulated and exploited lead to hardening of hearts evident in negative expectations about others and defensive actions to avoid being taken advantage of in the future. Dishonesty betrays trust.

Being Realistic About Ourselves

An antidote to the human proclivity toward dishonesty, hypocrisy, and pride is a realistic self-appraisal. In the cognitive domain of my experience, to be reconciled with myself means to gain a more realistic self-appraisal. It means that I change the way I think about myself. Psychological reconciliation in the cognitive domain of my life involves a change in my self-concept, my sense of identity, my view of who I am and the person I am destined to become by the mercy of God's providential calling and redeeming grace.

Consistent with his realism about life's suffering, Jesus taught a realistic psychology. Persons are neither devils nor angels, neither animals nor gods. We are human beings, and human nature is dialectical, characterized by dual capacities for both good and evil, because we are both finite and free. It was Reinhold Niebuhr who noted that our awareness of our finitude is the basic source of anxiety, which in turn is the occasion, though not the primary cause of human sin.[11] To accept these teachings is to affirm a more realistic self-concept and a spiritual self-theory. We are persons who need to repent of our sin.

The theological concept of sin has been rejected by many persons, including counselors, as leading to a negative, pessimistic, cynical, and demoralizing view of humanity. Disappearance of the concept of sin among mental health professionals was acknowledged by the psychiatrist, Karl Menninger.[12] Admittedly, in the history of Christian thought, the concept of sin has been distorted into a "worm theology," and even misused to manipulate persons by creating neurotic guilt and extracting indulgences as penance. It has been misused to inflict a form of spiritual abuse as real as any physical or sexual abuse, if not more destructive.[13]

Such distortions are aberrations of the realistic self-evaluation Jesus taught when he called us to repentance. Repentance is not a shame-based form of self-condemnation. It reflects a realistic and honest self-appraisal, absent the customary illusions we hold about ourselves. It is the mark of authentic self-acceptance grounded in God's acceptance of us. That is what repentance is.

Jesus knew we are inclined to live a dislocated life separated from God, estranged from others, and alienated from ourselves. He knew that most of us are very resistant to giving up our illusions about ourselves, and more likely to judge ourselves relative to others we consider beneath us than to strive to live by the divine standards Jesus disclosed. But by describing our human condition realistically in terms of the concept of sin, Jesus also called us to become the persons we are capable of becoming, to become the persons we potentially are. You see, Jesus knew that with God's help, we have the capacity to change. Otherwise, there was no purpose in calling us to repentance.

Being Practical

The wisdom of Jesus' teachings is evident in his realistic appraisal of both life's suffering and human nature. His teachings were also very practical. The practical implications of this spiritual wisdom can be found in a variety of areas of life.

To be wise means being able to get our priorities straight and to stick to them. It means that we know which battles to enter and when and how to engage our opponents. To be wise is to know how to negotiate conflicts to a mutually satisfying resolution. It means making friends quickly with your accuser to avoid going to court—making an effort to settle on the way in order to avoid prison (Lk. 12:57–59/ Mt. 5:25–26). Being wise means having realistic expectations about what can be accomplished relative to the risks required. It means also knowing the difference between what I can and cannot change.

To be wise means that I am able to become detached from my desperate strivings, my urgent objectives, and preferred strategies for achieving them. It means separating my ego from my opinions and my worth from my work. Being wise means I recognize that I am other than the roles I occupy and the functions I perform. For as a depressed middle manager once told me as he was facing the loss of his job: "If all that I am is what I do, then what am I when I stop doing it?" Being wise means that ultimately we trust neither princes nor powers but place our trust in God just as Jesus encouraged us to do.

A person reconciled with oneself does think differently about one's self. Personal transformation occurs through the renewal of one's mind as the apostle Paul wrote in Romans 12. This is a truth emphasized by cognitively-oriented Christian counselors who suggest that efficacious outcomes from counseling occur because clients change the way they think—from unbiblical to biblical thinking. Counselors using this approach are likely to emphasize the book of Proverbs of the Old Testament or other wisdom literature such as Ecclesiastes, the Book of Job, the Letter of James, or the parables of Jesus as sources of wise counsel about changing both thinking and behavior.[14]

Implicit within such cognitive approaches is the risk of construing faith as belief, implying that recovery is a function of a change from misbelief to belief in God or in other particular religious truths.[15] By virtue of this cognitive emphasis, an easy inference is that disorders of thinking are the primary cause of human distress, and that human alienation is primarily a cognitive disorder due to a learning deficit (ignorance) or due to faulty learning (error), the cure of which is an educational process. Counseling becomes a form of special education to teach a new way of thinking—a Christian way of thinking. The fundamental error of this approach is assuming that knowing the good produces the good.

Disorders of thinking, such as obsessions and delusions, are recognized by mental health professionals as characteristic of the mentally ill. In fact, some forms of psychosis such as schizophrenia have been described as primarily a thought disorder. Reducing our irrational ideas and obsessive worries will have salutary effects upon our psychological well-being.

It is also important to note that what we believe about ourselves, others, and God really does matter. How we define the good life and our own life's purpose influences what we do and how we feel doing it. Our self-concept is probably the set of beliefs and evaluations most central to our psychological health and growth—knowing who we really are. To affirm that we have been created by God is to know that we were meant to be, and that we have the right to be. To believe we have been created in the image of God is to know also that we have the potential to become who we are essentially.

Being Faithful

Jesus taught that it is very important that we think, and what we think. It was persons who believed God could heal them who experienced healing: For according to your faith, it shall be done to you (Mt. 9:27–31/Mk.10:46–52/Lk. 18:35–43). But faith is not merely belief. Faith is not theoretical knowledge, nor merely belief with a low degree of evidence. Faith is not what we leap to in order to fill the holes in our knowledge with a God of the gaps. Nor is faith merely a reasonable hypothesis. While it has cognitive content, faith is neither produced by belief nor identical with belief. Faith is a response elicited by the living God. Faith involves trust and commitment, intentions and feelings. Faith is the ultimate concern of the whole person as Paul Tillich described so well.[16]

Furthermore, what a person believes is not the paramount factor in understanding him or her anymore than what a person does. It is who the person is, and what they are striving for that really matters. Beliefs are not the same as intentions, and many of the former are irrelevant to the latter. Nor is changing my thinking the key that opens the gate to the kingdom of God. That key, said Jesus, is repentance (Mk. 1:15; 2:15,17; 6:12; 13:10; Lk. 5:32; Mt. 21:28–32). Repentance is not merely a matter of changing my beliefs or eliminating either my unbiblical or "stinking thinking." Jesus said that it is out of the heart that evil thoughts come (Mt. 15:18–20; Mk. 7:21–22). Being is primary—who we are. And being involves our feelings and intentions, our values and commitments, our choices and decisions, as well as our thoughts and beliefs. Thus, to be reconciled by the power of the living God through love, faith, and hope is to be not only wise, but also compassionate and courageous as we strive to will the will of God in a life of grateful service and in our struggles for social justice.

The point of this discussion, however, is that to be reconciled psychologically in the cognitive domain of my life means to be wise, not merely knowledgeable or intelligent, sophisticated or cultured. Neither culture nor knowledge is the same as wisdom, and smart people can act foolishly, and sometimes do. Nor does knowing the good lead automatically to doing the good, contrary to classical Greek philosophy.

Some persons experience this cognitive domain of life more than others. Some think more than they feel. Some think so much they don't act in a timely manner. Those who emphasize this cognitive domain of psychological experience might be characterized as children of the Enlightenment. In Western intellectual history this was the late seventeenth and early eighteenth centuries described by cultural historians as the Age of Reason. One of the results of the rationalistic emphasis of that age was that God became the remote watchmaker of Deism and humankind became the object of adoration by virtue of the human power of reason. Reason replaced revelation as the pathway to knowledge of God, but ended in Hume's skepticism and a natural religion without God.[17]

Cognitively-oriented Christian psychologists are closer to the philosophy of Descartes who developed a mind/matter dualism. Mechanical laws with material and efficient causes account for most natural events from this perspective. Yet belief in God is allowed. It is through the participation of one's mind in the realm of ideas that God is known. From this perspective, religion itself is not primarily a way of life, but a worldview, a metaphysic or philosophy of life; religion is less a matter of living experience than of intellectual assertions and demonstrations. Within the Hindu faith, this intellectual pathway to God is called *jana yoga*.

As Tillich[18] has shown, we think in ontological categories of being, time, space substance, and causality. The central ontological category is being, and for finite existence it is the category of time. "Thought must start with being; it cannot get behind it. . . .Thought is based on being, and it cannot leave this basis."[19] William Oglesby[20] reached a similar conclusion about the primacy of being over both knowing and doing within the biblical witness. I agree with this interpretation.

Furthermore, knowledge gained through reason alone, including the reasonable methods of psychological science, is finite knowledge with limited certitude and significance due in part to the conflicts within reason itself. Consequently, every method based on reasoning is also limited. Tillich[21] provided a phenomenological description of these existential conflicts within reason. These are the conflicts of (a) autonomy versus heteronomy, (b) absolutism versus relativism, and (c) formalism versus emotionalism. The questions arising from these conflicts of reason are answered by revelation. In my view, when reason is transformed by revelation, it becomes reconciled reason. And as reason receives revelation, it becomes reconciling reason, that is, reason helps to further God's grand goal of reconciliation. For the Christian, the source of revelation is found within Holy Scripture as the interpreted record of the life and teachings of Jesus.

Cognitively oriented persons are likely to view Scripture as a source of knowledge or information. The Bible for them is considered a set of propositions. For some persons, the information the Bible provides is inerrant. In this view, the Bible contains infallible knowledge in propositional form verbally imparted by God in a divine dictation reproduced without error or human interpretation. Those holding this view may see the Bible as a source of answers to even scientific questions, not merely spiritual knowledge about one's personal salvation and social justice.

What prevents Jesus' message about the kingdom of God from being reduced to mere information, or merely knowledge, is that the kingdom of God symbolizes the very real acts of God in human experience. God acts within human history and within our personal lives. The religious symbol of the kingdom of God was Jesus' way of describing this very real presence of God acting in human life. Both God and people live within the dynamic realm called the kingdom of God.[22] This is an experienced reality, experienced here and now, not in some distant place in the clouds nor some time in the future, nor is it merely a state of mind or a figment of human imagination: "the kingdom of God has come near" (Mt. 4:17/Mk. 1:15). This kingdom is the presence of real, reconciling relationships, not merely a body of knowledge or a repository of revealed truths.

Being Spiritually Discerning

Spiritual wisdom is not the same as intellectual knowledge, and certainly not an assent to a set of propositions, biblical or otherwise. It is not agreement with certain claims to truth codified in ecclesiastical creeds, nor merely belief in particular facts or ideas. Spiritual wisdom is more akin to the truth known intuitively rather than logically. This truth is known experientially. Wisdom is found ultimately within the spiritual dimension of human experience and it comes as a spiritual gift from God. It is known through spiritual discernment in such media as study and worship, service and prayer, meditation and spiritual direction. God gives us wise counsel through prayer just as the psalmist said (Psalms 5:10; 16:7), and as Jesus received through his own life of prayer (Lk. 5:16; 22:40–46; Mt.14:23; Mk.14:32).

By way of summary, wisdom involves knowing the truth of God, accepting the reality of human suffering, being truthful with others and realistic about ourselves, being practical, faithful, and spiritually discerning.

THE AFFECTIVE DOMAIN OF RECONCILIATION

Psychological reconciliation effected by the living God through love, faith, and hope occurs not only in the cognitive domain of experience manifest as wisdom; it occurs also in the affective domain, in the realm of feelings and emotions. The reconciled person experiences predominantly (though not exclusively) the feelings of compassion and courage, joy and thanksgiving.

Being Compassionate

The dictionary definition of compassion is the feeling of pity aroused by the distress of others, along with the desire to help them. Pity is defined as the feeling of sympathy for the sufferings or privations of others. It is the combination of both compassion and wisdom that constitutes therapeutic empathy. Empathy is compassionate wisdom. It is not merely accurate listening, but listening wisely with care.

When we consult Jesus rather than Webster for an understanding of compassion, the feelings that come to mind are love, mercy and kindness, forgiveness and healing. Love is certainly more than a feeling, but can you imagine love without feeling? Jesus taught that the two greatest commandments were to love God with all our hearts, souls, minds, and strength, and our neighbors as ourselves (Mt. 22:34–40/Mk. 12:28–34/Lk. 10:25–28; Mk. 4:10). While he repeatedly called his disciples to demonstrate their love through acts of kindness and justice, reconciliation and healing, Jesus was also very aware that good deeds, like good thoughts, proceed from the heart, hence they involve emotional and volitional dimensions (Lk. 6:45; Mt. 15:18–20; Mk. 7:21–22). It is often our feelings that motivate us to act and provide the energy to act.

Be Merciful. As a way of being, to be compassionate is to be merciful as God is merciful (Lk. 6:36). This means that a reconciled person is kind and generous even to the selfish and ungrateful; for as Jesus taught, even sinners love those who love them (Mt. 5:46–48/Lk. 6:32–36). To be merciful means more than generosity; it is to be merciful as God is merciful.

Loving Unconditionally. There is an unconditional quality of this kind of compassion distinct from ordinary human kindness. It is expressed when we bless those who curse us, pray for those who abuse us, and give without expecting anything in return (Mt. 5:38–48/Lk. 6:27–36). Jesus' understanding of his own mission was to preach good news to the poor, to proclaim release to the captives, to give sight to the blind, and to set at liberty those who were oppressed (Lk. 4:18–19). None of these persons would be in a position to repay him, nor did he require reciprocity. Jesus responded with compassion to the harassed and helpless solely because he loved them (Mt.14:14; Mt. 15:32–39/Mk. 8:1–10).

According to Jesus' teaching, the compassionate person is nondiscriminatory in caring for others, whose only claim to such care is their need. Such a person is like the Good Samaritan, who stopped to help a stranger who had been hurt, thereby answering the questions of who is my neighbor and what it means to be religious (Lk. 10:29–37; Mt. 22:34–40/Mk. 12:28–34). This quality is also evident in the friend who forgoes sleep to respond at midnight to someone in need (Lk. 11:5–8). The unconditional quality of this love was manifest notably in the father's forgiveness of the prodigal son (Lk. 15:11–32), and most poignantly and powerfully in Jesus' words on the cross: "Father forgive them for they know not what they do" (Lk. 23:34).

To be compassionate is to emulate and actualize the compassion of God in human life, particularly this quality of unconditional love.[23] This is the grace the apostle Paul found so amazing. And so it is, whenever you experience it. And once you have experienced it, life is never the same.

The experience of unconditional love is a healing experience. Years of research by psychologist Carl Rogers and other person-centered theorists has documented the therapeutic benefit of unconditional positive regard expressed through genuine caring and empathic understanding in a therapeutic relationship.[24] The latter is a human approximation of the ultimate acceptance one can experience in the unconditional love of God.

This unconditional quality is evident in another meaning Jesus gave to compassion, and that is forgiveness. To be compassionate is not merely to be sympathetic; it is to be genuinely forgiving. Clearly a defining characteristic of reconciling relationships that characterize the kingdom of God is the healing power of the experience of divine forgiveness to transform human lives. Jesus began his ministry with the invitation for persons to receive God's forgiveness: "Repent for the Kingdom of Heaven has come near" (Mt. 4:17/Mk. 1:15). This was and is the good news of great joy that John the Baptist had anticipated (Lk. 3:16).

Jesus' caring for those neglected or abandoned by others was one of his most notable and noble characteristics. He came to seek and to save the lost (Lk. 19:10/Mt. 18:11; Mt.15:24; Lk. 15:4–9). The lost included social outcasts and sinners (Lk. 5:32). Just as the physically ill need a physician, Jesus knew that sick souls need God's forgiveness (Mt. 9:9–13/Mk. 2:13–17/Lk. 5:27–32).

Antonyms of being forgiving include being judgmental, angry, and blaming. Jesus counseled us to judge not and condemn not, for with the judgment you pronounce you will be judged. In contrast, forgive and you will be forgiven (Mt. 7:1–5/ Lk. 6:37–38). This compassionate forgiveness the Christian experiences is what enables one to love and forgive others (Lk. 7:36–50). The more you feel forgiven, the more you are able to love. Merely believing it isn't as transforming as experiencing it, truly being and feeling forgiven. To emphasize this, Jesus counseled his disciples to forgive as many as seven times a day those who repent (Lk. 17:3–4/Mt. 18:21–22). That's really a lot of forgiving. Of course, this is not to be taken literally, but it expresses that forgiveness was very important to Jesus, perhaps even the essence of his teachings—the reconciling power of this experience of both human and divine forgiveness.

Compassion Through Healings. Compassion is evident in forgiveness. It is also manifest in healings. Clearly Jesus intended to reveal divine compassion through healing of the sick. There are numerous examples in the Synoptics documenting God's loving purpose to bring human healing.[25] Jesus taught that the power to heal comes from God (Lk. 6:19). Indeed, Jesus considered his own healings and those by his disciples to be signs of the presence and power of God (Mt. 4:23). Forgiveness itself is healing, between persons and within individuals as their guilt is relieved, and consequently their psychosomatic symptoms that guilt has caused (Mt. 7:1–5/Lk. 6: 37–42; Mt. 9:1–8/Mk. 2:1–12/Lk. 5:17–26; Mt. 4:23–25). Jesus gave his disciples the charge, authority, and power to heal the sick. He expected them and us to continue in this ministry of healing.[26]

Because so many healings recorded in the New Testament seem to have occurred as a result of the person's faith, the healing ministry has been caricatured as faith healing and exploited by some faith healers.[27] But there were a number of healings reported in the Synoptics that occurred without any reference to the faith of the person healed, nor to the faith of their family or friends. These healings are frequently ascribed to Jesus' compassion for people.[28]

Jesus' compassion was manifested also in his attention to basic human needs such as food for persons he did not even know (Mt. 15:32–39/Mk. 8:1–10). We express that kind of compassion by our contributions to food shelves and shelter for the homeless. Physicians and nurses express the same compassion in their medical ministries of healing, and so do counselors and others in lay-care ministries, and volunteer organizations like the American Red Cross and the Salvation Army who help to bring healing and relief to those who suffer pain and disasters.

The compassion of Jesus portrayed in the Synoptics is summarized in his teaching recorded in Mt. 11:28–30: "Come unto me all you who are weary and are carrying heavy burdens, and I will give you rest. Take my yoke upon you, and learn from me; for I am gentle and humble in heart, and you will find rest for your souls. For my yoke is easy, and my burden is light." To experience compassion, that is, to receive it and truly feel it, is to unload a burden. It means to lighten your load, to rest easy, to experience the peace of God.

Accepting Myself. The healing forgiveness and unconditional love that Jesus encouraged us to share with others were meant also for ourselves. We are among those whom he called to repentance and for whom divine compassion is intended. Herein lies the spiritual foundation for a genuine self-acceptance—accepting God's acceptance of us just as we are. Knowing that God loves me just as I am enables me and inspires me to become the person God calls me to be.

To be reconciled with myself does not mean merely that I think differently about myself; it means also that I feel differently about myself. It is not merely that I gain insight or understanding about myself. I become more genuinely accepting of myself, and more forgiving, more gentle and patient with myself, more caring and kind.

Like Jesus we can experience these feelings of genuine acceptance particularly in our life of prayer in communion with our loving Creator (Mt. 6:5–13). Prayer is a medium through which God enhances our compassion for ourselves in addition to our caring for others. Esteemed by God, we experience a self-esteem that enables us to genuinely esteem all others.

Being Courageous

I have said that a person feels differently when reconciled by the power of the living God through love, faith, and hope. Instead of feeling mostly angry and being judgmental toward both others and oneself, the reconciled person is primarily compassionate. A second indicator of psychological reconciliation in the affective domain is courage. The reconciled person is courageous.

In popular usage, courage is the capacity to meet danger without giving way to fear. Common synonyms are fortitude and resoluteness, boldness and bravery. These virtues are claimed by nations as badges of honor. America prides itself for being not only the land of the free, but also the home of the brave. Every Memorial Day we remember those who died bravely that freedom might live. It is right and proper that we do, though we risk glorifying war by doing so.

To be courageous is to confront danger, to stand up against threat and intimidation. To be courageous is to "take the bull by the horns" or "to face the music." A courageous person has backbone or nerve, pluck, guts, or grit. They are stout-hearted, intrepid, audacious, even heroic. They are willing to bear defeat without losing heart. They are dauntless, daring, unflinching, and valiant. Those who are courageous are game to the end.

It is considered manly to be courageous, though it is sexist to restrict it to either gender. Courageous persons of both genders are confident, assured, and self-reliant, even adventurous and enterprising. To be courageous is to be unalarmed, unabashed, and fearless. These are some of the popular meanings of courage in our culture.

Of course, each of us has our own view of courage. My idea of living daringly is to press the "Clear All" command on my computer without being positive I first saved my document. Or to live on the cutting edge of courage, so to speak, is to drink milk from a carton two days past the expiration date. That's how courageous I am. I've always thought that eating lutefisk was a sign of real courage.

The antonyms of courage include fear, anxiety, and cowardice. A person lacking courage is apprehensive, frightened, or scared. In more extreme degrees, this fear becomes panic, trepidation becomes terror, worry becomes horror, dis–

quietude becomes dread. When the fear becomes so intense as to paralyze action required for the sake of self and the welfare of others, it is common to speak of cowardice. Such persons are sometimes referred to as fainthearted or "chicken." In our culture, there is not much understanding or acceptance of those incapacitated by fear. In wartime, when cowardice leads to desertion, it is considered just cause for severe punishment, even death.

When persons lose their courage, they are most aptly described as discouraged. It is a common characteristic among those who seek counseling. They have usually tried a variety of things to solve their problems, and none has worked. Their discouragement hinders them from persevering or even hoping for any improvement whatsoever. "What's the use?" is a typical response to proposed solutions.

It is during such times of discouragement that we will discover courage. The prefix of discouragement is "dis"; the suffix is "ment"; however, the center of discouragement is the word "courage." Yet we aren't likely to find courage through an analysis of syntax. Nor are we likely to find it alone.

In order to regain their courage, most persons need others to provide encouragement. We are people who need people, as the popular song goes. God created us that way. Encouragement from others who care about us gives us hope and the strength to take action. The experience of encouragement is one of heartening renewal. It restores and strengthens our resolve to go on, to keep on trying, not to give up despite so many reasons for giving up or giving in. Encouragement inspires courage. Effective counseling is an encouraging experience. So is Christian fellowship and so is communion with God in prayer.[29]

The Courage of Jesus. Jesus of Nazareth was a very encouraging teacher and the exemplar of a courageous life. And because he is the model for a Christian life, it is important to look to him for an understanding of courage. Jesus lived a very courageous life. He had the courage to challenge the religious orthodoxy of his time. He dared to expose the hypocrisy of the controlling religious elites (Pharisees and Sadducees) who wielded both political and economic power as well as religious authority in those ancient days in Judea (Mt. 12:38–39/Lk. 12:54–56; Mt.16:1–12/Mk. 8:11–21/Lk.12:1; Mt. 23:12/Lk. 18:9–14; Mt. 23:1–36/Mk. 12: 37–40/Lk. 20:45–47).

Jesus had the courage to be frank and direct with people. He didn't mince words. He called a spade a spade, and some he called vipers (Mt. 3:7; 12:34; 23:23; Lk. 3:7). And he went about Galilee preaching and healing despite all the doubts and criticisms of his detractors (Mt. 16:1–4/Mk. 8:11–13/Lk. 11:16). His style of effecting change might be characterized as courageous and compassionate confrontation.

Jesus was no wimp. Some portraits of him as a meek and mild milquetoast do him a grave injustice. From his first confrontation with evil in his wilderness experience of temptation (Mt. 4:1–11/Mk. 1:12-13/Lk. 4:1-13) to his final martyrdom in Jerusalem (Mt. 27:24-37/Mk. 15:15-26/Lk. 23:24-34), Jesus proved to be a man of courage. He revealed how inspiring and transforming one can be who has the courage of his convictions in the power and love of God. It is this kind of courage that comes from faith in God, which Jesus renewed regularly though his own life of prayer.

Prayer is our lifeline to God. It's like a spiritual intravenous tube. Through prayer the Spirit of God breathes courage into our being. Jesus withdrew repeatedly to pray during his ministry, not only because of his faith and obedience, but because he needed to pray just as we do (e.g., Lk. 6:12). And he assured us that God answers our prayers according to God's will. But we must have the courage to ask for God's answers rather than our own (Mt. 6:9–13). It is in and through prayer that we ask. Seek encouragement from God through prayer. Seek and you shall find it (Mt. 7:7– 11/Lk. 11:9–13).

The Courage of Discipleship. Jesus' first disciples were also courageous individuals, despite their many fears. To become the fishers of men Jesus called them to be, they had to drop their nets to follow him. They had to give up the security of their livelihoods and the comfort of their routines (Mt. 4:18–20/Mk. 1:16–20). And like Simon Peter, they needed courage to believe Jesus when he spoke to them about the kingdom of God, and about God's forgiving love and healing compassion (Lk. 5:8). Dare they believe that Jesus could help them experience what they so desperately needed? Could they risk believing this son of a carpenter from Nazareth? What he taught seemed too good to be true. So many were amazed at what he said and did, including his own incredulous disciples (Mt. 12:23; Mk. 1:27, 2:12; 10:24; Lk. 2:47; 5:9).

Jesus' disciples needed courage to risk persons taking offense at them as followers of the one who was causing such conflict by preaching this good news to the poor, release to the captives, and liberty to those who were oppressed (Lk. 4:18–19). It does take courage to challenge the existing power structures (Lk. 11:37–54/Mt. 23:23–36; Lk. 20:45–47/Mk. 12:38–39; Mt. 26:57–58/Mk. 14:53–56/Lk. 22:54–55; Lk. 22:37). Justice does not come without a struggle and sacrifice. But then if the world were just, there probably would be less need for courage. Jesus' disciples risked dishonor, suffering, and death just as Jesus encountered in his own country (Mt. 13:57–58; Mt. 26:51–58). Jesus elicited very strong reactions from people. They were either for him or against him, adored him or scorned him and finally destroyed him or mourned him (Mt. 27:33–54/Mk. 15:22–39/Lk. 23:33–48).

Jesus told his disciples they could expect to experience all forms of suffering—to be reviled, hated, excluded, and persecuted on his account (Mt. 10:16–23; Mt. 24:9–13/Mk. 13:9–13/Lk. 21:12-19; Mt. 5/Lk. 6). In commissioning the seventy disciples, Jesus cautioned them that they would be going out like lambs in the midst of wolves (Mt.10:16). They needed courage in order to confront the world of unclean spirits (Mk. 1:23/Lk. 4:33; Lk. 10:17–20; Mk. 3:22– 30). So do we. It does take courage to confront evil intelligently, forthrightly, and effectively.

It also takes courage to cope with the realities of life. Recall that one of the elements of the spiritual wisdom Jesus taught was about the reality of human suffering. Insofar as human life is an estranged existence, it is thereby an anxious existence. Thus the courage required of disciples is the courage to affirm life in the face of the existential anxieties that are intrinsic to it.[30] This is what faith is—the courage to be.[31]

Christian courage is not a kind of reckless abandon. Nor is a Christian a courageous fool like Don Quixote. Only a fool tilts at windmills or puts his head in a lion's mouth. Even the king who expects to be overwhelmed in battle will seek peace (Lk. 14:31–32). It takes courage to accept a defeat without being defeated. We must know when to cut our losses. Courage tempered by wisdom is as important as compassion that is wise.

What are the sources of Christian courage? They are the teachings and life of Jesus, our faith in God, and the power of God's Spirit. One important element of Jesus' teachings was his repeated counsel, "Be not afraid" (Lk. 5:10; Mt. 6:25–34/Lk. 12:22–31; Mt. 8:23–27). Be of good courage for God is with you. He also taught that it is the power and authority of God that gives us courage (Lk. 2:10). Hearing and sharing this encouraging good news enables us not to be afraid. We become strong in the Spirit and empowered to serve God without fear, in holiness and righteousness (Lk.1:73–75, 80).

Repeatedly Jesus described his own disciples as fearful. Why were they so afraid? Because they were at times, like us, people of little faith (Mt. 6:25–34/Lk. 12:22–31; Mt. 8:23–26). Thus the antidote to fear and the medium of Christian courage is faith— faith as trust in the mercy and power of God.

Physical death is surely one of the most profound of human fears. Faith is the courage to be in the face of such nonbeing. "Faith in God is the answer to the quest for a courage which is sufficient to conquer the anxiety of finitude."[32] Jesus counseled us not to fear those who can kill the body, for they cannot kill the soul (Mt. 10:28; Lk. 12:5). Perhaps this message is relevant as well to our present fears of illness or injury that can kill the body, but not the soul. But the first disciples of Jesus did not abide by his counsel. They were frequently very frightened, scared to death. And at the end, the shame of his trial and the horror of his execution paralyzed them, and they deserted him in his final hour. The terror of a violent death makes cowards of many. We must not be too harsh of such human frailty. It is easy to be brave away from the battlefield, from a safe distance. Jesus' last words of forgiveness covered even his disciples' acts of cowardice and desertion: "Father forgive them, for they know not what they do."

One of the functions of courage is to enable us to resolve our own fears about being a disciple of Jesus. This is the courage to make the decision that moves us from being a lukewarm "yes-but" disciple to being a courageous, committed Christian and dedicated servant of God. Jesus confronts us with a decision. We are either for him or against him. We cannot serve two masters, for we shall love one and hate the other (Mt. 6:24–25; Mt. 23:9–10). When we make this decision to follow Jesus, and continually renew and strengthen it in our life of worship, study, service, and prayer, we gain even greater courage. This is the courage that comes from commitment, from the encouragement of Christian friends, and ultimately from the power of the living God through love, faith, and hope.

Contemporary Christians need to be courageous, as surely as we need to be compassionate and wise. Courage is required to be a Christian in our age because Jesus did not come to bring us peace of mind, nor guaranteed health and happiness through positive thinking, not even through "possibility thinking."

We must have the courage to confront our own sin, and others who sin against God's holy laws of love. Courage combined with compassion yields tough love. Tough love is what allows us to confront our own sin and others who sin against us (Lk. 17:3–4/Mt. 18:15; Mt. 18:21–22). It is courage that makes love tough. And it was tough love that Jesus lived and called us to give through compassionate confrontations.[33]

We need courage to cope with life's conflicts, to change that which we can, and to endure what we must. We also need courage to bring about reconciliation nonviolently just as Jesus did (Lk. 9:51–56; Mt. 26:52; Lk. 22:35–38), and Buddha, Gandhi, and Martin Luther King, Jr.

Acts of reconciliation always involve risk. The obvious one is that despite one's sincere efforts and actions to reconcile, it does not happen. Thus to be an agent of reconciliation requires courage, the courage of faith even in the face of discouraging outcomes.

It takes courage also to seek first the kingdom of God and God's righteousness, for that calls into question all of our worldly goals and earthly strivings. Courage is needed to conform to the teachings of Christ because that entails resisting the pressures to conform to the ways of the world (Lk. 6:46; Mt. 7:15–21; Mt. 12:33– 35/Lk. 6:43–46). And so many pressures there are, and so persuasive and powerful, as seductive as they are ubiquitous. Christians need courage to resist the overwhelming temptations to live life in pursuit of personal happiness and selfish success at the expense of others, or in the pursuit of pleasure, power, and privilege. We need courage to struggle for justice, to fight for what is fair, and to do the right thing, however unpopular and however strong the opposition or cruel their contempt.

It takes courage to endure our own suffering and the loneliness from the loss of our loved ones. And courage is needed to explore the unknown, to take the leap of faith, and to accept doubt as a dynamic part of faith. We need courage to be a true servant, and to be a servant leader rather than a controlling lord over others. And courage is required to swallow our pride and repent our sin. Therein lies our hope for happiness and the source of life's greatest joy, the joy of reconciliation with God. "The kingdom of God has come near; repent, and believe in the good news" (Mk. 1:15). God's own goodness will lead us to experience God's love. For this gift of reconciliation we may be truly thankful and happy. The reconciled person is not only courageous, but also joyful and thankful.

The Experience of Joy

The Spirit of God acts through love, faith, and hope to transform human feelings. Anger is transformed into compassion, and fear into courage. In addition, despair is transformed into joy. To understand the meaning of Christian joy, it is helpful to begin by first discussing some of the more common terms used to express such positive feelings. The more common term is happiness. Thereafter, I will cite common meanings of joy contrasted with despair. I will end this section with discussion of Jesus' teachings about the good life as a blessed life of joy.

The Nature of Happiness. Happiness is defined as feelings of joy or pleasure experienced in varying degrees, from a quiet happiness to intense happiness. A second meaning of happiness is the satisfaction of desires. To be happy is to experience pleasurable feelings and to express such feelings. We speak of feeling happy or even of "putting on a happy face." In this sense, we speak of happy persons as cheerful, merry, or light-hearted. Both gaiety and laughter characterize a happy state. When they are experiencing even more pleasure, it is common to describe persons as being very pleased or even *delighted*.

Of course, if someone is delighted all the time we begin to wonder, don't we? Is this the pseudo-happiness of an hysterical Pollyanna? Or the constant euphoria of a manic psychosis? The questions suggest what many persons know—most of us are sometimes happy and sometimes sad, and often in between. Life is not a bowl of cherries, and if one has any empathy at all, sadness will be experienced. The capacity to feel sadness is itself a sign of mental health. To attempt to avoid it is to risk feeling nothing at all.

I have been discussing the meaning of happiness as pleasure. The absence of pleasure is displeasure. A more persistent absence of pleasure has been described as a condition of *anhedonia*. This is usually defined as the loss of the capacity to experience pleasure or happiness. It is a symptom of some forms of mental disorder, such as a psychotic depression of a melancholic type or a depressive type of schizo-affective disorder.

Pleasure is often associated with the *satisfaction* of one's desires. This is the second general meaning of happiness which links it to the conative dimension, as when we speak of one's search for happiness. It also suggests that happiness is a by-product of getting what we want—a dubious notion at best.

Satisfaction is the state or quality of being satisfied. To be satisfied means to be free from some desire or need by supplying what it requires. This may be the satisfaction of a specific drive, such as the food that satisfies one's hunger drive, or it may be construed as satisfying a psychological need, such as one's need for security satisfied by employment. Alternatively, it may mean the satisfaction of one's desires, or getting what one wants. At times we even equate freedom from want with the concept of well-being. The degree of well-being and happiness are presumed to be associated with the degree of pleasure, which in turn is associated with the degree to which desires are satisfied or gratified. In heightened degrees of well-being, we speak of elation or euphoria.

There are several other connotations of happiness such as gratification, good fortune or luck, being free of worry, content, or serene, being consoled or at peace. These are only a few of the general meanings. Each individual seems to have a specific definition of what will make them happy. If you asked people what they want in life, you are likely to hear a significant variety of answers. The saying that "one person's meat is another's poison" reflects not only the variety of objects of happiness that people choose, but that their very definitions of happiness may be contradictory. All of them share in common, however, the view of the good life as a happy life. Among all human wants, being happy is high on the list of favorites. "Don't Worry, Be Happy" is a popular theme song for many individuals. For those who have difficulty feeling happy, there is even a popular happy book entitled, *14,000 Things To Be Happy About*.[34] There seems to be no end to what we can choose to be happy about.

Many persons expect to be happy by being religious. Happiness is presumed to be one of the benefits of being a good Christian. Isn't that right? Many are disappointed when they learn that the very term "happy" or "happiness" appears only twice in the entire New Testament (Rom. 14:22 and Jas. 5:11), and not at all in the Synoptic records of Jesus' teachings. For those who are disappointed about this information, there is some consolation in knowing that the term "unhappiness" doesn't occur anywhere in the New Testament.

The absence of these terms is significant. It means that the good life Jesus taught about was not the popular view of a happy life. In contrast to our cultural definitions of happiness, Jesus taught about a joyful and blessed life. The term "joy" appears seventeen times in the Synoptics and a total of fifty-six times in the entire New Testament. Even more striking is the appearance of the term "blessing" and its derivatives. These occur fifty-two times in the Synoptics (eighteen times in Matthew, seven in Mark, and twenty-seven in Luke), and a total of eighty-eight times in the entire New Testament. For Jesus, the good life is a blessed life and a life of joy.

Common Meanings of Joy. To begin to understand the meaning of these terms, it is helpful to note first some common meanings of joy, and eventually, its contrast of despair.[35] Joy reflects a higher degree of satisfaction than the term happiness. Joy is defined as intense happiness or great delight. It refers sometimes to that which gives rise to this emotion, or on that which the emotion centers as in the phrase, "You are my pride and joy." It also refers to the outward expression of this emotion.

To be joyful connotes a greater degree and depth (or height) of feeling than simply being happy or merely merry. Real joy is not simply a matter of light-hearted laughter. To be joyous is to be jubilant, exultant, to rejoice and to celebrate. It means to be truly glad about something.

It means even more. When filled with joy, one is elated, not merely happy. An even more intense state of joy is called rapture. It expresses a full experience of satisfaction, perhaps to the exclusion of all other emotions. Rapture has romantic connotations as the woman who said that when she found the love of her life she just sank into his arms. Then they got married, and she spent the rest of her life with her arms in the sink! Not a very romantic ending do you think?

In its most extreme form, joy becomes ecstatic. Ecstasy is the state in which reason yields to intense joy. It is often used to describe the spiritual experience of contemplative union with God. It differs from the mania associated with a manic-depressive psychosis.

Just as joy connotes a greater degree of happiness, so its antonyms connote more intense negative emotions. The opposite of joy is not just disappointment or discontent. The opposite is sorrow and sadness. When an element of regret or guilt is included, we speak of remorse. One who is joyless is described as afflicted, grieving, or depressed. The opposite of joy is ultimately despair.

The Nature of Despair. Despair is a state of profound sadness and utter hopelessness. One who is despairing is disconsolate—beyond consolation. Such people have "lost heart," perhaps even the will to live, and may wish to die. They are both despondent and desperate.

There is a kind of wretchedness associated with despair. Not in the sense of evil, but as an awful state of dread. This is the "sickness unto death" Søren Kierkegaard experienced and described so poignantly.[36] It is also in the depths of such despair that the psalmists prayed their desperate laments and pleas for relief from their afflictions in the face of which they felt consumed and overwhelmed.[37]

The color of despair is neither blue nor gray; it is black. Despair is felt deeply, down to the core of your being, hence it is sometimes expressed as the pit of despair. It is an emotional hell. One feels utterly lost, as if abandoned in a black hole, and there is no way out. It is a darkness into which no light seems to be able to penetrate. It seems like an interminable, irreversible, and incurable condition, beyond all hope. It is a condition of futility experienced as a state of ruin. Hopes are shattered, dreams destroyed. One has hit bottom and given up. Life holds no meaning or purpose in times of despair. As written in Ecclesiastes 1:2: "Vanity of vanities says the Teacher, vanity of vanities! All is vanity." Our very lives are like a puff of smoke, a passing cloud.

Despair is like a woeful melancholy that grips those experiencing it. It is odious and dreadful, filled with dread. It is a wariness without end, a "slough of despond" as John Bunyan described it. Despair is an awful, unbearable agony. It is life experienced as a veil of tears. Not even meditating upon 14,000 things to be happy about will touch this depth of anguish. In such a state of despair one feels totally lost. It is not merely that one no longer seems to have fun in life; life has become utterly joyless.

Moreover, there is bitterness associated with despair, the bitterness of one disillusioned with life. One feels betrayed, or perhaps even fundamentally wrong for life, as if one was not meant to be. Those in despair are heartbroken. Even their physical countenance is downcast. They feel deeply wounded and do not know why they are so terribly unhappy. They feel oppressed, broken, and tormented. It is a deplorable state of misery and agonizing suffering of unbearable pain analogous to the searing pain experienced by persons suffering with "hot spots" from cancer. It is, as one cancer patient described it, "like a hot iron held to your back; you'll do anything, take anything to escape this hell." Such is the pain of despair. It is like a cancer of the soul.

The intolerable pain of despair drives one to distractions, with the hope that these distractions might help us to cope with it. Perhaps they do, but only palliatively and temporarily. Then the feelings return with a vengeance. Despair is a lamentable, pitiable condition. It feels like a precursor to death, or that one has already died and is now just going through meaningless motions. It is existing without living. This is worse than living like a "vegetable" because the individual is conscious of one's empty, hollow, wooden existence. Despair is like the sting of death. It is construed at times as a form of torture. One craves for an emotional equivalent to morphine. Such is the pain and cruelty of despair.

Who can rescue us from such black despair? Who can liberate us from this emotional hell? Not any human. Not even the wonders of modern medicine. Though anti-depressants may help to numb the pain like morphine numbs the pain of cancer, drugs will not cure despair. Despair is not a biological problem. Nor is it merely an emotional condition. Despair is an existential problem affecting one's total existence as a person. It is a spiritual problem of meaning and being in the face of meaninglessness and the threat of nonbeing.

Not all persons have experienced this depth of despair, but many have, and suffer in silence. When they have spoken of their experience, they have described it with the words and poignancy I have expressed. A religion that fails to appreciate this depth of human suffering is simply irrelevant to human life and to human healing. Even worse, it is a cruel hoax of false promises made to those who are desperate. Jesus taught that by the power and mercy of God through love, faith, and hope, despair is transformed into joy.

Jesus' Vision of the Good Life

I have noted that in contrast to happiness, Jesus' view of the good life is a blessed life of joy. The sources of joy he taught about were (a) joy in the kingdom, (b) the joy of redeeming truth, (c) the joy of participation and belonging, (d) the joy of being healed, (e) the joy of repentance and reconciliation, (f) the joy of being fruitful, (g) the joy of security and peace, (h) the joy of abundant living, (i) the joy of eternal life, and (j) the blessed life.

Joy in the Kingdom. The joy of which Jesus spoke was anticipated by John the Baptist, who saw as his own mission to give light to those who sit in darkness (despair) (Lk.1:79) and "to share the good news of great joy which will come to all people" (Lk. 2:10). It is the joy of the kingdom of God coming near to us.

Jesus also came to bring light into our darkness of despair (Mt. 4:16). He believed that God had anointed him "to preach good news to the poor, release to the captives, recovering of sight to the blind, to set at liberty those who are oppressed" (Lk. 4:18–19). Can you even begin to imagine the profound joy experienced by those prisoners, the poor and blind, the oppressed and despairing, when they heard this good news of great joy? Many who listened were greatly pleased and frankly amazed (Mk. 1:27; 2:12). Many others wanted him to stay with them, but Jesus said, "I must proclaim the good news of the kingdom of God to the other cities also; for I was sent for this purpose" (Lk. 4:43). To bring good news. To bring joy. That was both his mission and his intention (Mk. 1:38–39; 4:2; 4:14), and this mission he gave to his disciples (Mk. 3:14; Mt. 10:5–7).

The teachings of Jesus came as really good news. It was the best news ever. It is the good news of the kingdom of God come near (Lk. 8:1–3). This kingdom of God, he said, is among you (Lk. 17:20–21). Furthermore, there is joy in knowing that this kingdom of God is growing, even though we do not know exactly how it grows (Mk. 4:26–29). This is in part the joy of knowing we do not have to know it all. It is the joy of trusting God's beneficence. God's goodness will lead us to experience the divine joy only God can give. In that promise we may hope.[38]

The Joy of Redeeming Truth. To be a disciple of Jesus is to be blessed with a redeeming knowledge. What Jesus taught was relevant to our salvation from despair and from all other trials and tribulations. Jesus taught transforming truths. And he told his disciples they were fortunate they received the truths he taught, to see what they saw, to hear what they heard from Jesus (Lk. 10:23–24/Mt. 13:16–17). Hearing it we are prompted to respond like Mary: "My soul magnifies the Lord, and my spirit rejoices in God my Savior" (Lk. 1:46-47). This is not merely the joy of knowing about God; this is the joy of experiencing God through Christ, the one who revealed God most unambiguously (Mt. 11:27/Lk. 10:22).

The Joy of Participation and Belonging. The Christian knows another joy, the joy of participation and belonging. One participates in advancing the kingdom of God with the power and authority to teach and to heal (Mt. 10:1–4/ Mk. 6:7–19/Lk. 9:1–16; Mt. 10:5–13/Mk. 6:8–11/Lk. 9:2–5; Lk. 10:8–9). It is our privilege to speak of God to all who are seeking redemption (Lk. 2:38).

If you are looking for a meaning and purpose in life, here it is. If you want the satisfaction and self-esteem that comes with contributing to a great cause, here it is. If you want the opportunity to do some creative, exciting work, consider this calling. Work to the glory of God, helping to advance God's kingdom on earth as it is in heaven; for by loving others we are also healed.

By participating in this holy work we also fulfill our deep desires for belonging. Are you feeling the despair of loneliness? Jesus said that whoever does the will of God is my brother and sister, and belongs to the family of God (Mt. 12: 46–50/Mk. 3:31/Lk. 8:19–21).

The Joy of Being Healed. Another joy experienced by the Christian is the joy of being healed. This may include physical healings from all kinds of diseases as well as healings of mental disorders and spiritual estrangements. There are numerous examples of Jesus and his disciples engaging in a healing ministry.[39] There is profound joy felt in knowing God can heal me, even when I feel I am losing my mind and acting like a maniac (Mt. 8:28–34/Mk. 5:1–20/Lk. 8:26–39). It is not merely that I believe God can and wants to heal me. I do not believe that. I know it, because I have experienced it. That kind of experiential knowledge provides greater certitude than any other kind. My response to such healings will be comparable to others who are healed—to rejoice and glorify God (Mt. 15:29–31/Mk. 7:31–37).

The Joy of Repentance and Reconciliation. Jesus taught his disciples that the purpose of their preaching and their healing ministry was that all should repent and experience forgiveness (Mk. 3:14; Mt. 10:5–15; 18:21–35; Lk. 17:1–4; Mk. 6:6–

13/ Lk. 9:1–6). Accordingly, another joy the Christian experiences is the joy of repentance. In the parables of the lost sheep, the lost coin, and the prodigal son Jesus taught that "there will be more joy in heaven over one sinner who repents than over ninety-nine righteous persons who need no repentance" (Lk. 15:1–10/Mt. 18:10–14; Lk. 15:11–32). The prodigal son's father consoled his other distraught son: "we had to celebrate and rejoice, because this brother of yours was dead and has come back to life; he was lost and has been found." This is a joy of reconciliation as great and greater as that experienced at any happy wedding feast (Lk. 14:15–24/Mt. 22:1–10).

Jesus taught us that, with the exception of blasphemy against the Holy Spirit (i.e., linking God with evil), all sins are forgiven (Mk. 3:28–30). That does not mean we can engage in reckless talk, for we shall have to render an account of every careless word we utter because our words can either hurt or heal another (Mt. 12:36–37). What it does mean is that forgiveness is not merely a possibility; forgiveness is a sacred promise. That is one thing in life we can count on—divine forgiveness. More than that, it is also a duty that obligates us to forgive one another seven times a day, hence there is joy in the hope of reconciliation between us (Lk. 17:4; Mt. 5:23–24).

Furthermore, it is by forgiving our brother or sister from the heart that we are freed from the chains of our own anger that imprisons us like the unforgiving servant (Mt. 18:23–35). Jesus did not say forgive and you might be forgiven. He said, "forgive and you will be forgiven" (Lk. 6:37). In being forgiven, you will experience both gratitude and joy (Lk. 7:36–50).

The Joy of Being Fruitful. Christians experience yet another joy. This is joy in the promise that if I am receptive to God's Word, it will bear fruit in my life. To be receptive I need to accept God's Word and hold fast to it with an honest and good heart. I must not let the cares of this world nor my delight in riches choke the Word of God, lest that divine seed be sown in poor soil and perish (Mt. 13:1–9/Mk. 4:1–9/ Lk. 8:4–8). By receiving God's truth in faith and holding fast to it, I will prosper in that which really matters–in the life of the Spirit. There is joy in receiving the gifts of the Spirit and in bearing the fruits of the Spirit.

The Joy of Security and Peace. The Christian also experiences joy in the security of God's providential care. In some instances, this may include protection of life from natural disasters such as floods or storms at sea (Mt. 7:24–27/Lk. 6:47–49; Mt. 8:23–27). Consequently, we need not hide from life's storms. A ship in a harbor is safe, but that is not what ships are for. We may venture forth in the joy of knowing God cares about our physical safety (Mt. 14:22–27/Mk. 6:45–52; Lk. 8:22–25; Mk. 4:35–41).

A recent personal experience illustrates this theme. When the terrible floods of 1997 occurred in Minnesota, many of us were moved to help our neighbors. On a cold Sunday morning three of us drove together for about three hours to Montevideo to help them raise the twenty foot dike to protect their town's business district. Already, nearly 150 homes had been lost to the ravaging river and about 500 people displaced. They were struggling desperately to avoid further damage. After several hours working in a very cold wind and blowing snow, we departed for our return trip to Minneapolis. We encountered a dangerous storm. For more than an hour—it seemed like an eternity—we drove in intermittent, blowing and blinding snow. We could see only a few feet ahead of us, and at times, not at all in the white-out conditions. At one point our driver lost sight of the road and veered into the left lane of oncoming traffic. Fortunately, the passenger in the front seat grabbed the wheel and brought us back on track. Seconds thereafter another car came out of the cloud of snow and passed safely by as slowly as we moved forward in the other direction. We were lucky to get through that dangerous situation. We were fortunate, for we could have been hurt and hurt others in either an accident or by being stranded in the ditch for hours out of anyone's sight in a freezing wind chill. On the other hand, perhaps we were not merely lucky or fortunate. Perhaps God guided us and protected us because of the help we had given to a drowning town. The town's businesses were saved, by the way, as the result of hundreds of volunteers—each one reaching one more sandbag atop the dike. In the midst of suffering, there is mercy, and a cause for great joy.

One cannot conclude from such an experience that if we take risks to help others that both they and we shall always be protected. There is simply no guarantee of protection from harm, nor a promise to escape all suffering; but neither must we fear that whenever we place ourselves at risk in order to help others that we shall surely experience harm. Instead we may experience God's providential care and sustaining grace, or the joy of being able to endure whatever suffering may bring (Mt. 10:17–23; Mt. 24:9–13/Mk. 13:9–13/Lk. 21:12–17). Knowing God is with us consoles us in the midst of our suffering.

The most profound joy in God's providential care is a joy found paradoxically in the midst of crises and hardship, during our times of greatest distress or loss. It is precisely when life is not going smoothly that we are prompted to search for deeper meanings, and that is exactly what we need to do in order to find God. It is when God is all that I have left that I know that God is all that I need. It is for this reason that I can thank God for my struggles and my hard times as well as the good times.

Regardless of the circumstances, there is the joy of peace the Christian experiences. By seeking first the kingdom of God we will be less anxious about tomorrow, for tomorrow will be anxious for itself. Today's trouble is enough for today (Mt. 6:33–34/Lk. 12:31). The woman who was known to be a sinner was forgiven by Jesus, who said to her, "Your sins are forgiven . . . your faith has saved you; go in peace" (Lk. 7:36–50).

We can learn to let go of our tendencies to be like Martha, anxious and troubled about so many things or distracted with much serving or working (Lk. 10:38–42). We can learn to be like Mary who sits quietly to listen to her Lord. Jesus said that is the one thing needed. Peace. Be still. There is joy to be found in such peaceful stillness with our Lord, in silence and solitude in the presence of God.

The Joy of Abundant Living. The joy of Christian discipleship has been described as the abundant life. But this is not the abundance as the world views it. A person's happiness does not consist in the abundance of material possessions (Lk. 12:13-21). We are foolish to think we will be able to enjoy all the goods we store up to amass personal wealth in order to have a merry and easy retirement. The parable of the rich young fool suggests we may well die before we can enjoy our earthly estates and treasures.

Most of us know persons struck down in the prime of life. None of us know the time or place or manner of our own life's ending. Nor will our destiny change because of our dollars earned and saved. However, we can look forward to rest from our labors and burdens (Mt.11:28–30).

The abundant life Jesus described is not primarily a material life. It is a spiritual blessing. Abundant living is a matter affecting the whole person: "For what will it profit them if they gain the whole world, but forfeit their life?" (Mt. 16:26). The term "life" suggests that I experience God's gift of abundant living as a whole person. The Christian experience of the abundant life is a reconciled life with God. With God one also finds one's true self. Jesus taught that one who loses one's life for his sake shall find it (Mt. 16:24–26/Mk. 8:34–35/Lk. 9:23–24). This is the promise of finding my life, finding myself, finding my very soul as the essence of my being. No longer must I despair over not becoming that self I truly am. I become in Christ my own true self. In union with God I find my own true being. This occurs paradoxically by denying myself in order to follow Jesus (Mt. 10:37–39/Lk. 14:26–27; Mt. 16:24–25/Mk. 8:34– 35/Lk. 9:23–24).

The Joy of Eternal Life. The joy of a fulfilled life, including authentic self-actualization, is not the ultimate joy for the Christian. Most of us are like the lawyer who asked Jesus, "Teacher, what shall I do to inherit eternal life?" Jesus gave us the answer: Follow the first two sacred commandments (Lk. 10:25–28/Mt. 22: 34–40/Mk. 12:28–31). We need not search for another Holy Grail or fountain of youth, nor strive to prolong our earthly lives through all kinds of fantastic fads or compulsive rituals. Jesus pointed to the way: Love God with all your heart and soul and mind and strength, and your neighbor as yourself. It is important to note here that Jesus did not respond to this question about how we gain eternal life by saying, "Accept me as your Lord and Savior, the Son of God, the Christ, the Messiah." Instead of linking eternal life to a confession of faith in his divinity, Jesus related it to loving relationships with God and other persons.

There is joy in knowing the answer to this existential question about our final destiny. Jesus affirmed a spiritual resurrection (Mt. 22:23–33/Mk. 12:18–27/Lk. 20: 27–40). There is no greater joy than the eternal life Jesus promised to his disciples (Mt. 19:16–30/Mk. 10:17–31/Lk. 18:18–30). We may rejoice that our names are written in heaven (Lk. 10:20). We may be joyful unto eternity (Mt. 10:39). To those who have faith even more is given. The abundant life is a spiritual life with God that lasts beyond the limits of finite time.

Out of gratitude and joy for this great gift of abundant living we contribute to the welfare of others (Lk. 21:4). We serve one another out of the abundance of a joyful heart (Lk. 6:45). We have been blessed to be a blessing to others. And by blessing others we become even more blessed as members of the family of God through the joy of loving one another as God loves us.

The Blessed Life. The abundant life of joy that disciples of Christ experience is a blessed life. The terms "blessing" and "blessings" appear only twice in the

Synoptics and twenty-two times throughout the entire New Testament. However, as a verb or adjective, the terms "to bless" or "blessed" appear fifty-two times in Matthew, Mark, and Luke alone, and a total of eighty-eight times in the entire New Testament. Jesus described the joy experienced by his disciples as a blessing. *The good life is a blessed life.* Blessed are those who hear the word of God and obey it (Lk.11:28). Jesus' teachings constitute the Word of God for his disciples.

Blessings are ascribed to God, to Jesus, and to his disciples. God is described as the Blessed One (Mk. 14:61). Blessed is the Lord God of Israel (Lk. 1:68). The kingdom of God is also blessed (Mk.11:10).

Upon his entry into Jerusalem, Jesus was hailed by the crowds as "Blessed is he that comes in the name of the Lord" (Mt. 21:9, 23, 39; Mk.11:9). In lamenting Jerusalem's rejections of her prophets, Jesus said you will not see me until you say, "Blessed is the one who comes in the name of the Lord" (Lk.13:35). In this context it seems to function as a confession of faith.[40] If so, it was a joyous confession. At the Mount of Olives the multitudes of disciples began to rejoice and praise God for all the mighty works that they had seen, saying, "Blessed is the King who comes in the name of the Lord" (Lk.19:38).

When Jesus was asked by two of the disciples of John the Baptist if he (Jesus) was the one to come, Jesus performed more healings and told them to tell John what they had seen and heard. He added, "Blessed is anyone who takes no offense at me" (Lk. 7:23/ Mt. 11:6). And blessed also are those who confess Jesus as the Christ, the Son of the Living God, as Peter confessed, and to whom Jesus responded, "Blessed are you, Simon son of Jona!" (Mt. 16:17).

Jesus' *parents* were blessed by Simeon when they brought him as a boy to the temple (Lk. 2:34). As the mother of Jesus, Mary was blessed among women and blessed was the fruit of her womb (Lk. 1:42). Mary felt herself blessed: "all nations will call me blessed" (Lk. 1:48). She was blessed also because she believed that there would be fulfillment of what was spoken to her from the Lord (Lk. 1:45). She was blessed because she believed.

Similarly *disciples* were blessed by virtue of their faith: "Blessed are your eyes, for they see, and your ears, for they hear" (Lk. 10:23; Mt. 13:16). What they saw in Jesus was an authentic humanity reconciled with God. What they heard was the word of God. Jesus said, "blessed are those who hear the Word of God and obey it" (Lk. 11:27–28).

On numerous occasions Jesus gives a blessing prior to meals (Mt.14:19; Mt. 26:26; Mk. 6:41; 8:7; 14:22; Lk. 9:16, 24–30). Even the ordinary act of eating was placed within a spiritual dimension: "Blessed is anyone who will eat bread in the kingdom of God" (Lk. 14:15). Those who inherit this eternal kingdom are considered to be blessed by God (Mt. 25:34, 46).

Servants who are found worthy by their master are also blessed (Mt. 24:46/Lk. 12:43). And blessed are those servants whom the master finds ready when he comes unexpectedly (Lk. 12:37–38). To experience God's favor upon us and to grow in wisdom and stature and in favor with God like Jesus did is also to be blessed (Lk. 2: 40, 52).

Being blessed we become a blessing to others by doing good works. Why? Because good works are good to do, and because they need to be done. Jesus said that if you give a feast (that is, throw a party), invite not family and friends who may return the favor, but the poor, maimed, lame, and blind, and you will be blessed because they cannot repay you (Lk.14:14). Jesus' message stands in stark contrast to a culture in which everything can be bought for a price, and persons give in order to get.

Jesus blessed children and took them in his arms (Mk. 10:16), but his greatest teachings on the blessed life were meant for children of all ages. In his Sermon on the Mount those whom he described as the blessed ones include the pure in heart, those who hunger and thirst for righteousness, the meek and merciful, those who mourn, who are persecuted and reviled as peacemakers and disciples of Jesus (Mt. 5:3–11). In Luke's version (Lk. 6:20–22), those who are blessed are the poor, you that hunger and weep now, and even you whom others may hate.

The blessings such persons receive include inheriting the earth and the kingdom of heaven, being comforted and satisfied, obtaining mercy, being called the children of God, and seeing God. These blessings are causes for great joy: "Rejoice and be glad for your reward is great in heaven" (Mt. 5:12); "rejoice in that day and leap for joy, for surely, your reward is great in heaven" (Lk. 6:23). The Christian life is a rewarding life and a rewarded life, though not lived for the sake of a reward.

The Sermon on the Mount (Mt. 5–7) and Jesus' other teachings all suggest that the ordinary life lived apart from God is not a blessed life filled with joy. Apart from God there are only fleeting moments of happiness, but ultimately disillusionment and despair. Only those who experience God's blessing know life's greatest joy—the joy of communion with God.

The Bible is a sacred book of the truth of God. *Scripture* is a blessing to us. By meditating upon Scripture we learn of the blessed life of joy that is possible with God. And by praying the Scriptures we experience the blessing of being with God.

The Christian experiences the good life, this blessed life of joy, by the power of the living God through faith. *Faith* is the medium through which the good news of great joy is received—the kingdom of God is near to you. For this reason, faith is itself a blessing, a faith that is lived (Lk.11:28). Faith provides the good soil in which the seeds of this kingdom of heaven will grow. Consequently, we must cultivate our faith through study, worship, and prayer, and by meditating upon Holy Scripture inspired by the living God to make us more holy and to fill us with joy. To live a life inspired by God, we need to pray. We must be devout like Simeon looking for the consolation of Israel, for the Holy Spirit was upon him (Lk. 2:25).

Prayer is another Christian blessing. Prayer is to the human spirit what food is to the body. It is essential, necessary, and vital in order to survive and thrive, in order to live spiritually, which is to truly live. As a reconciled relationship with

God is the medium through which we experience the blessed life of joy, we must keep our focus upon God and spend time alone with God in contemplative silence just as Jesus did throughout his life.

Jesus' life and ministry were sustained by his communion with God through his life of prayer. All wisdom that he learned and taught, all his healings and teachings occurred within the parentheses of prayer. Jesus prayed in the morning (Mk.1:35), during the day (Mt. 26:39), in the evening (Mt. 14:23), and at times throughout the night (Lk. 6:12). Jesus was a man of wisdom, courage, compassion and joy because Jesus was a man of prayer. He withdrew repeatedly to be alone with God in prayer and meditation (Lk. 4:42; Lk. 6:12; Mt. 14:23/Mk. 6:46). It was his life of prayer that was the sacred source of the Lord's Prayer that he shared with all his disciples (Lk. 11:1–4/Mt. 6:9–13).

Jesus taught the Lord's Prayer in order that we too might experience the blessing he enjoyed in a life sustained by prayer. We have the joy of assurance that whatever we ask for in prayer we will receive according to God's will if we have faith, even if we have as little faith as a tiny grain of mustard seed (Lk. 17:6; Mt. 21:22). Such is the mercy of God that our prayers are answered: "Ask, and it will be given you; search and you will find, knock and the door will be opened for you." What God grants us is the joy of the Holy Spirit, if only we ask (Lk.11:9–13/ Mt. 7:7–11). It is a truth so simple, yet a joy so profound.

Based upon both Jesus' teachings and his exemplary life, I can say with confidence that if you want to experience the blessed life, then learn to pray. If you want the life of joy with God, then pray. If you want forgiveness and peace, pray. Pray regularly. Pray faithfully. Pray with confidence. Pray gladly and gratefully. Praise God and God will bless you. And sometimes what we discover in prayer is that God has already blessed us.

Pray also to discern the will of God in your life. Your life and mine are filled with choices and decisions. Let your decisions be based upon the spiritual wisdom Jesus revealed. Pray to discern the will of God in all the situations life brings, and you will bring something more to those situations, probably what is really needed. Ask of every circumstance, of every conflict or opportunity, "What is your will, O God?" And be prepared to also pray, "Not my will, Lord, but Thine be done." This is the prayer and experience of Gesthsemane (Mk. 14:32–36).

It is because the human will is the primary domain of experience that prayer to will the will of God is so essential and vital. The greatest joy in life is found by willing the will of God and doing the will of God. In this sense we may speak of a joyous will.[41] This joy is eternal, unlike so many fleeting pleasures of this world and earthly pathways to human happiness. It is a joy that elicits a response of gratitude as natural and effortless as breathing.[42]

I have been discussing the experience of joy as one of the marks of the reconciled life. Despair is transformed into joy, as anger is transformed into compassion, and fear into courage. Another indicator of the reconciled personality in the affective domain of experience is the transformation of feelings of entitlement into gratitude.[43]

Entitlement Is Transformed into Gratitude

I will begin discussion of this element of the affective domain by exploring the nature of ingratitude and the sources of entitlement that underlie it and contribute to it. Thereafter, I will contrast popular meanings of gratitude with Jesus' teachings about thanksgiving.

The Nature of Ingratitude. Were we to remember our blessings and experience regularly the life of joy in communion with God, we would be more inclined to be thankful. Gratitude does not seem to be one of those feelings that comes naturally or automatically. If it did, there would be much less complaining than all of us voice and hear. It is all too easy to forget how truly blessed we are. More often than we like to admit, we are not mindful of all the benefits we enjoy in life. We attend instead to how much we do not enjoy or have, especially compared to others. And, of course, those others with whom we compare ourselves usually enjoy more, or so we prefer to think, because if we did not think so, we would be less justified feeling so ungrateful.

There does seem to be an inordinate degree of discontent expressed in our times. The daily news is filled with it. So are many daily conversations. Sometimes it seems we are a culture of discontent, fueled by continuous advertising designed to persuade us that what we have is inadequate, and that to be happy we must buy more, bigger and better things. And most of us have also encountered people who seem to be chronically malcontent. For these persons, nothing is satisfying or satisfactory. If they express any gratitude at all it is usually in the phrase, "thanks for nothing."

Chronic carping seems to be a very human characteristic. We moan about this and groan about that. We grumble about what we have not gotten that we think we should have received, about the economy, our demanding boss, controlling parents, inconsiderate kids, the latest insult we have suffered from one whom we used to consider a friend. And of course, there's always the weather to complain about (especially long winters in Minnesota). The list seems endless. We don't need a book on 14,000 things to complain about. Each of us seems to have a ready list. Complaining seems to be such a common and easy way to start a conversation.

Ungrateful people have a high misery index, but not merely as an index of their economic discomfort related to the rate of inflation or their state of unemployment or under-employment. They are unhappy with life itself. Life has become burdensome, a heavy load and a thankless road. There is more pain than gain, more bad luck than good.

This kind of dissatisfaction would hardly function to elicit feelings of gratitude. Ungrateful people tend to be disgruntled and resentful, if not depressed and bitter. They feel not only unhappy, but ill-treated and cheated, and so they feel sorry for themselves. People who experience life as mostly troublesome are also likely to be troublemakers rather than troubleshooters. The trouble they make is due in part to the fact that ingratitude is a contagious attitude.

Sometimes people complain to be the center of attention, to elicit sympathy, or to be excused from responsibility. If they are rewarded for their moaning and groaning, others learn vicariously that griping has a pay off, a secondary gain. Since the squeaky wheels do seem to get the grease, sometimes at least, they might as well squeak up to get their share.

Worse than that, however, is that through imitation negative complaining escalates, as each person attempts to out do the other: "You think you've got it bad! Let me tell you what bad is! When I was a kid I had to walk to school . . . barefoot . . . five miles . . . and it was uphill . . . both ways!" Perhaps by seeing the humor in such brokers in self-pity we can transcend it, but chronic complainers are usually ill-humored people and demoralizing to be with. They drag you down.

Persons who engage in self-pity include those who believe they are suffering as the innocent victims of circumstances. Some of them are victims. The innocent really do suffer, just as Job and Jesus did. But self-pity is neither the necessary nor inevitable response to human hardship or even to tragedy. We always have a choice about how we respond to any and all of life's circumstances.[44] Some bewail their lamentable plight, but others do not. Sympathy from others only reinforces their self-pity. What they need is compassionate confrontation, not merely compassion.

Ingrates tend to be spoiled and pampered people. Being accustomed to getting their own way and whatever they want, they are very quick to express anger when they don't. They are likely to feel something has been taken from them, or something is missing that they should have gotten, something they were entitled to receive.

Beneath this feeling of ingratitude there seems to lie this notion that I have a right to whatever it is I want or think I need. I have earned it, if not even more. This is a reward I am due—what I have coming to me. I am worthy of it. I deserve it. It is your obligation to provide it for me and grant it to me. That is your duty. It is my right to assert my claim to it, and even to demand it. Your obligation is to serve me. You owe me! It is a deeply held feeling of entitlement.

Sources of Entitlement. Where does this sense of entitlement come from? Surely it has social roots and even political reinforcements. Politicians win elections by promising more pork for their electorate's barrel. Isn't that what it takes to get reelected? Maintaining their privileged position by catering to special interests sometimes supersedes the motive of public service and concern for the best interests of society as a whole. A variety of forms of governmental aid are actually called entitlement programs: Social Security, health, education, and welfare benefits. Citizens who have paid taxes for so many years believe they deserve such benefits.

Persons do have legitimate claims upon their government, but it is also true that the increasing demands for more governmental services and expanded benefits both express and reinforce our sense of entitlement. Our insatiable demands and assertions of our rights have driven America into a four trillion dollar debt. We seem to be riding on a runaway train.

The deepest roots of entitlement are not, however, social or political, but philo-

sophical, psychological, and religious. The philosophies of materialism and egoistic hedonism are foundations for this sense of entitlement. Popular psychology
and professional counselors emphasize the satisfaction of personal needs as
necessary for healthy functioning and for a self-actualized life. Both philosophical
and psychological roots support the view that the pursuit of happiness is not merely
a constitutional right; it is a promise, fulfillment of which is due. It is the "something for nothing" philosophy. It is the notion of rights without responsibilities.

The deeper source of this sense of entitlement, hence ingratitude, is human
pride and concupiscence, the latter meaning insatiable desires. It is our egocentric
view of life that leads to the attitude of ingratitude. It is because we see ourselves
rather than God at the center of life that we are prone to make such pretentious
claims upon life.

This is a very jaded view of life, as arrogant as it is narcissistic.[45] The ingrate
is a misanthrope—totally self-absorbed. The orientation toward life is primarily
one of grabbing rather than giving. "What's in it for me?" is the primary concern.
After all, I'm just looking out for Number One like everybody else does. So, you
see, I have to be assertive. No one else is going to look after my best interests, and
it is my interests that matter. We are brazen in our expectations and brash in our
demands because we are so incredibly self-centered. First, last, and always it is me,
myself, and I. My needs, my rights, my demands. Such is the presumptuousness
of persons preoccupied with their own needs and desires.

There is another root of ingratitude and chronic complaining. That is the experience of frustration and with it the sense of helplessness or lack of control over
one's life. Being frustrated repeatedly will elicit complaining behaviors. The
causes of the frustration need to be addressed and the problems solved if we are to
expect a reduction in such negative behavior. When people feel they have neither
the resources nor the control to solve their problems, they are likely to feel even
more frustrated, because they feel helpless to bring about change.

There is a kind of resentful protest expressed by thankless persons. Since they
feel cheated or ill-treated, they obviously believe they deserve otherwise. Telling
them that "life just isn't fair" will yield the angry response, "Well, damnit, it oughta
be!" This is the neurotic protest that reality must be other than it is. This is also
what distinguishes the psychotic from the neurotic: The psychotic thinks two plus
two is five; a neurotic knows that two plus two equals four, but hates it. It reflects
a lack of acceptance of what is real in favor of an ideal image of the way it ought
to be. It is typical of the maladjusted individual who refuses to accept reality because it doesn't meet one's needs, because it frustrates one's wants, or because it
fails to conform to the world created in one's own image—the Walter Mitty syn-
drome.

In the religious life, ingratitude is expressed in angry protests against God for
God's failure to reward both the faith and good works of the self-proclaimed
righteous. It betrays a legalistic view that God's covenant with people is a contract
with mutual obligations. Believing God's part in this bargain has not been
fulfilled, the ungrateful believer expresses grievances to God in lengthy laments as

exemplified in some of the Psalms. Persons are not likely to praise or bless God when God is no longer perceived to be the one from whom blessings flow. Instead they express anger because they expected God to grant them victory in battle, vengeance upon their enemies, or protection from suffering. But God failed to come through for them. Consequently, God is cursed for a perceived betrayal. Blasphemy is a consequence of ingratitude. If there were a higher court of appeal, I suspect many suits would have been filed against God out of anger and a sense of entitlement, the sense that God owes us a happy life.

I have drawn a caricature of the ingrate as an extended complaint to help the reader appreciate how aversive complaining is to hear, and to highlight the contrast of this jaded orientation to life with its opposite of genuine gratitude. Most persons do not live at such extremes. Yet within this portrait there are feelings and thoughts that most of us have had at least occasionally. Who among us has not felt at times like everyone else that we too are unappreciated, overworked, and underpaid, worth so much more than we get, deserving of much greater recognition than we have ever received?

Popular Meanings of Gratitude. It is time now to stop complaining about all the complaining, and to begin to explore positively the meaning of gratitude. What is gratitude? Gratitude is primarily a feeling. "I feel grateful" is an expression of this affective meaning. We do not usually say, "I think grateful," though it does help to "think gratitude." The latter suggests that this feeling has cognitive content. Like other feelings it is a meaningful feeling. It is related to our beliefs and expectations. It also suggests that gratitude is an attitude that I may consciously strive to develop.

A first step is to become more conscious of this attitude by doing such things as noting how many of our conversations are punctuated by expressions of thanks. It might help also to observe how grateful people become for life after they have almost lost it. It is common to hear the bereft express that they wish they could have said thank you to their loved one before he or she died. Part of the grieving process is realizing how many ways they did express such gratitude throughout their lives of caring for their loved ones. It is a normal part of grieving to experience some regrets, but eventually to let them go, and to be reconciled with one's loss.

The experience of loss suggests that gratitude has a behavioral dimension as well. We express gratitude in verbal behavior, as when we say "thank you," and in overt acts of kindness and appreciation. In addition to this behavioral dimension, gratitude has a conative dimension: it is related to our desires. I am more likely to be grateful when I get what I want than when I get what I do not want. It is all a matter of what I want or will. Thus, gratitude is partly a function of our intentionality, an expression of will and a consequence of our choices. Being a matter of choice means that I can decide to be grateful even when I do not get what I want. Our feelings are influenced by our decisions and by what we want and will.

Gratitude has motivational consequences as well; it functions like other feelings as a motive. It energizes me to act in a certain direction or manner. If I feel grateful, I am more likely to give thanks—to express it in words and deeds, including worship and prayer, study and service. It is also true that by giving God thanks and praise I can learn to feel more grateful more regularly. Consciously striving to be grateful will influence my feeling, thinking, and behavior.

The element of control might be one of the important dimensions to the meaning of gratitude. Sometimes we are grateful for fortunate events that occur without any action on our own part. It is because they occurred as a result of others' actions, or some natural or supernatural cause external to us that we think of it as gratuitous. We are grateful when something positive happens, but perhaps less so than when we ourselves have made it happen. It is a kind of external locus of control that seems implicit within this feeling of gratitude. We attribute its source or cause to something external to us, to someone else, or to luck.

It is a constructive exercise to recognize that which we can be thankful for. It is not so trite after all to count our blessings. How about life itself? Or the basics in life—food, shelter, and clothing? A clean and safe environment? How about our health, education, and employment, our democratic government with civil liberties guaranteed by the Constitution and Bill of Rights?

And what about our natural surroundings? I am grateful for the majestic Norway pines and beautiful white birch in northern Wisconsin where we can retreat to a sanctuary provided by Mother Earth. I appreciate that I have good hearing to listen to the sounds of the wind whispering through the tops of the tall pine trees, and that I am blessed with vision to see the ripples on the lake that sparkle like dancing diamonds in the reflection of the sun. I am grateful for the cool, crisp air and the bright colors of fall, for the clean winter snows, the smell of the spring rains, and the feel of the warmth of the sun. And above all, for the times with family and friends in addition to times of solitude and silence that help me to remember how truly blessed I am, and what really matters in life.

The meanings of gratitude in popular usage in American culture are numerous and could be explored further. I turn now, however, to the answers Jesus gave to the questions of what gratitude means, what causes it, and what are its consequences.

Jesus' Teachings about Thanksgiving

What did Jesus mean by gratitude? The first answer to that question may be somewhat of a surprise. Nowhere in the whole New Testament have the Greek words been translated in the New Revised Standard Version of the Bible as equivalent to the terms gratitude or grateful with the exception of Hebrews 12:28 and Acts 24:3. Apparently Jesus never even mentioned the word.

There were several other words he did use with related meanings. In order of decreasing frequency, these terms are presented in Table 1 for both the Synoptics and the New Testament as a whole (including the Synoptics).

In our English language, the words "thanks" and "thankfulness" seem closest to the meaning of gratitude. Jesus taught that being thankful was a virtue. When

Table 1
Frequency of Words Related to Gratitude

Related Words	Synoptics	New Testament
Bless/es/ed/ing	52	88
Glorify/ies/ing/ed/glory	27	191
Honor/s/ed/ing	15	65
Thank/s/ful/ness	12	67
Praise/s/d/ing	8	31
Favor/s/ed/ing	4	15

he referred the ten lepers to the temple priests, all ten had been healed, but only one of the ten returned to give thanks and to praise God for the mercy he received (Lk. 17:11–19). The story suggests that Jesus believed we ought not to take for granted the blessings we receive; rather, we should acknowledge the source with both thanksgiving and praise. The very term "thanksgiving" connotes this obligation of giving thanks. To be thankful is to praise and glorify God for all we have heard and seen (Lk. 2:20). Hence, to say in the Lord's Prayer, "hallowed be Thy name" is an expression of gratitude (Lk. 11:1–4/Mt. 6:9–13). To be grateful is both to feel and to express *appreciation* to the one who favors us. To appreciate someone is to value them. To appreciate something means we perceive the nature and quality of something, whether it be the nature of another's point of view, the quality of a work of art, the beauty of nature, or the love of God.

To appreciate something is also to raise its value by prizing and praising it. It involves a critical estimate and intelligent judgment of the positive value of some-thing. To be grateful is to value both the gift and the giver. It follows that by not being thankful, I depreciate and diminish the value of both, or belittle both. To appreciate something also means that I enjoy it. To be appreciative is to show my enjoyment with what I have received and experienced.

Gratitude involves not only appreciation, but also *recognition*. It expresses an awareness of the meaning and source of the beatitude. Expressions of gratitude to God include remembering God's holy covenant and saving acts in human history (Lk. 1:72). Human history is personal history. This recognition includes the awareness that God has blessed me and granted me favors. We may be thankful for the experience of God's favor upon us (Lk. 2:40) and for living with God's favor (Lk. 2:52). We are among those whom God counts.

In addition to recognition, there is a feeling of *obligation* implicit in gratitude. I am obliged to the person who has shown me goodwill. By feeling grateful I am expressing my feeling of being under obligation, or being indebted to my benefactor. This meaning is expressed in the phrase, "much obliged," which serves sometimes as a substitute for "thank you." One fulfills this obligation in part by the expression of gratitude, but also by emulating the giver through our own good deeds.

This connotation of gratitude is the opposite of the sense of entitlement. In the latter, the attitude is that God owes me something; in the former, I recognize that it is I who owe God. Perhaps this is one of the dynamics of ingratitude. Being ungrateful frees me from an obligation I do not want to assume.

The sense of obligation expressed in gratitude relates to the conative and behavioral dimensions of this feeling. Jesus taught that we were to be not merely hearers of the word, but doers of the word (Mt. 12:46–50/Mk. 3:31–35/Lk. 8:19–21; Mt. 7:24–27/Lk. 6:47–49). We show our gratitude through our obedience to the will of God, thereby expressing both our obligation and indebtedness to God. We express our gratitude to God when we "walk the talk."

This connotation suggests that ingratitude occurs as a result of one's loss of a sense of duty or a lack of obedience. Ingratitude betrays a lack of loyalty and concern, a lack of faithfulness. It suggests that my own lack of faith and the assertion of my own will are roots of ingratitude. Ingratitude is an expression of disobedience. Perhaps it serves as a psychological sign of a state of spiritual rebellion.

In contrast, the grateful person accepts one's duty to honor, praise, glorify, and to serve God, to follow the sacred laws of love, to be faithful in both little and much (Lk.16:10; Mt. 25:21–23). To be thankful to God is to be concerned about God. We express our gratitude by choosing God's will as our ultimate concern, loving God above all else, worshiping God only, serving God with gladness and thanksgiving.

Whom Do We Thank? An important part of Jesus' teachings about gratitude is how he answered the question, "Whom do we thank?" Jesus taught that we ought to thank God first, foremost, and always. He also taught us to be thankful for our parents, spouses, and our children.

Like John the Baptist before him, Jesus' mission of preaching the kingdom of God was an expression of thanksgiving and was motivated by gratitude. Their mission was an expression of their desire to give thanks to God (Lk. 2:38).

By being thankful to people we honor them. Jesus taught us to honor our *fathers and mothers* (Mt. 15:4). We honor them by recognizing and appreciating them. We express our thanks to them by living up to the Christian standards and sacred values they have taught us, and hopefully modeled for us. We express our indebtedness to them by carrying forth their deepest commitments to love God and to serve others in the name of Christ and in the power of the Holy Sprit through faith and love. We give thanks by recognizing them as persons whose company we enjoy, whose wisdom we value, whose love we cherish, and whose life we want to share. It is through our parents' examples, their guidance, counsel, and discipline that we can experience the kind of compassionate confrontation Jesus exemplified in his relationships with people, provided of course, our parents are reconciled with God and with each other.

Just as gratitude involves an expression of faithfulness and loyalty, so we are to be thankful for our *spouses*. We express gratitude by our fidelity to them, by striving to protect and nurture our marriage, thereby avoiding the destructive consequences of both adultery and divorce (Mt. 5:32; Lk. 16:18). It is this feeling of thanksgiving for our loved one that constitutes an antidote to our very human proclivity to take each other for granted.

It is true for many of us that God's greatest blessing is the one whom we call my wife, or my husband, my best friend, my lover, all the same one. How very fortunate, how richly blessed we are to be able to love and to be loved so deeply, and to love as long as we both shall live. Just ask those who have experienced it compared with those who have not, and note how many long for it.

My wife, Mary, is the most compelling cause for me to thank God for living. She has been a beatitude for me, a medium of God's grace, loving me despite my selfish preoccupation with my occupation and avocations, showing me that selfless giving is the secret to living, that compassion and forgiveness are healing, and love is tough. Mary has helped me appreciate that the Spirit of God that dwelt fully in Jesus is the same Spirit that dwells in us as his disciples. It is God's Spirit that makes our matrimony holy and enduring. We have grown together because we have both grown in the Spirit of God. It has not been easy, but it has been good—deep down good.

One of life's important lessons to learn is how to find and preserve unity with diversity. Marriage between a man and a woman is the best medium for that experiential learning. There is no better human laboratory or field training experience, though sustained friendships and membership in a religious community follow close behind.

Fortunately, Mary and I are different in many ways. In terms of psychological types, I appear more like an INTJ and she like an ISTJ. According to the Myers-Briggs inventory, our particular differences have to do with the sources of information we look to for our guidance and decisions. Whereas I trust my intuitive grasp of relationships among ideas, Mary utilizes her more sensory grasp of facts. The difference seems consistent with our respective chosen occupations of teaching and accounting.

The point here is not that we are compatible or unified because we are similar on three of the four dimensions of a Jungian typology. Such typologies are merely descriptive, not explanatory. The point is that union in love is not based on identity nor the conformity of one personality style to another. Christian communion in marriage celebrates our differences, those attributes that make each of us unique, fulfillment of which is essential to becoming fully human as individuals. These differences also make marriages complementary and contribute to the spice of life.

Of course, there are many things a couple can do to spice up their marriage. Early in their marriage Ole and Lena made an agreement that every week they would go out for a nice dinner—a little candlelight, a shot of aquavit. He goes out on Tuesdays and she goes on Thursdays. Such is the nature of Norwegian romance.

The reasons for being thankful for our *children* are numerous and varied. They provide us with the opportunity to experience first hand the miracles of birth and human growth. We are privileged to be able to nurture their development. Caring for our children provides us with a sense of meaning and purpose, significance and fun. To experience the world as an adult through the eyes of a child, to see once again its newness and wonder truly is a blessing. Children help us remember life is filled with mystery and wonderful surprises. They help us to laugh and play.

Jesus suggested spiritual reasons to be thankful for our children. He referred to their role as teachers of the good life. Jesus was thankful to God for revealing divine truths and the Holy Spirit to babes, hiding it from the learned (Lk. 10:21–22/Mt. 11: 25–28). Many truths have been spoken "out of the mouth of babes." Perhaps the most important truth that we can learn from children is as Jesus said, that the way to enter the kingdom of God is with the trust of a child in the beneficence of parents, and with humility and gratitude rather than a sense of entitlement (Mt. 18:1–5/Mk. 9:33– 37/Lk. 9:46–48). When is the last time we thanked our kids for enlightening us, for showing us the value of the simple things in life, including a healthy and simplified lifestyle? Even more, when is the last time we thanked them for being who they are? I have been blessed with two daughters whom I love, Andrea and Kari. They too are different from each other. Their uniqueness is a cause of both joy and wonder.

What Are We Thankful For? Part of the meaning of gratitude for Jesus is found by answering not only the question of whom to thank, but what to thank them for. As disciples of Jesus, we are thankful for the knowledge of forgiveness and salvation God granted us through the prophets (Lk. 1:77). We are thankful for the light shared by both John the Baptist and Jesus to those who sit in the darkness of ignorance and despair (Lk. 1:79; Mt. 4:16). And we give thanks for Jesus' gospel of reconciliation.

Christians are especially thankful for who Jesus was, and that he lived. Whether we affirm with the crowds that he was the one who came in the name of the Lord (Mt. 21:9/Mk. 11:9/Lk. 21:38; Mt. 23:37–39/Lk. 13:34–35; Lk. 19:39–44), or with Peter that Jesus was the Christ (Mt. 16:16/Mk. 8:29/Lk. 9:20), Christians have claimed for centuries the uniqueness of this man from Nazareth. His special status as a medium of divine truth and love has been expressed in portraits of him as a religious genius, a charismatic holy man, an inspired prophet, an ethical teacher and moral example, a religious reformer, a social revolutionary, a person fully human and fully divine, the Messiah and Son of God.

We trust Jesus' teachings because of the spiritual wisdom they reveal. That wisdom was expressed particularly in his teachings about the kingdom of God and the will of God. Christians are grateful that Jesus shared the good news of great joy that the kingdom of God has come near to us (Mt. 11:12/Lk. 16:16; Lk. 2:10; 4:43; 8:1–3). We are thankful that he described for us in so many parables what this kingdom is like, and the way to this life with God by following the sacred commandments (Mt. 22:34–40/Mk. 12:28–34/Lk. 10:25–28). We are thankful for the promise and hope that by doing the will of God we enter the kingdom of heaven (Mt. 7:21). And we are thankful that God's kingdom grows from the smallest beginnings (Mt. 13:31–32/Mk. 4:30–32/Lk. 13:18–19) and despite its enemies (Mt. 13:24–30).

Christians can rejoice that Jesus linked entry into the kingdom of God with repentance, for by doing so he indicated what we need to do in order to experience the good life reconciled with God (Mt. 4:17/Mk.1:15). We are thankful for the baptism of repentance for the forgiveness of our sins (Mk. 1:4/Lk. 3:3; Mt. 4:17/ Mk. 1:15). We give thanks for the unconditional acceptance God shows us even before we repent, like the father showed the prodigal son (Lk. 15:11–32). We are thankful that having been lost like him, we too have been found.

In an age when there are so many competing philosophies of life and diverse lifestyles, Christians are thankful that Jesus showed us the way to true personal fulfillment and authentic self-actualization: "Whoever loses his life for my sake will find it" (Mt. 16:24–25/Mk. 8:34–35/Lk. 9:23–24).

Many Christians are grateful too that Jesus' teachings were not of a pietistic nature with an exclusive emphasis upon individual salvation. Jesus taught us the importance of community and a social ethic of love and justice. He preached good news to the poor, release to the captives, liberty for the oppressed, and recovery of sight to the blind as ways of proclaiming the acceptable year of the Lord (Lk. 4: 18–19).

Jesus taught that the second commandment of loving our neighbor as ourselves is not fulfilled in acts of philanthropy (Mt. 12:28–34/Mt. 22:34–40/Lk. 10:25–28; Mt. 4:10). It is hypocrisy to tithe faithfully while neglecting justice (Mt. 23:1–36/ Mk. 12: 37–40/Lk. 20:45–47). Contributions out of our abundance, which involve relatively little sacrifice, are less commendable than smaller amounts of greater sacrifice given by the poor (Mk. 12:41–44/Lk. 21:1–4).

We may give thanks for the poor among us who give us the opportunity to express the righteousness of God through advances in economic and social justice by our own acts of love and nonviolent reforms to help redress the wrongs afflicting so many. We may thank the poor mostly, however, for showing us how much of what we think we need is really unnecessary to the good life, and frequently a barrier to it (Mk. 10:25; Lk. 6:24, 18:23).

We thank Jesus for inspiring so may social reformers to use nonviolent means to accomplish humanitarian ends, and for showing us that even a violent end can be faced and overcome nonviolently as evident in Jesus' crucifixion and resurrection celebrated in our joyous Easter faith. We are thankful that we too are saved from our enemies and from the hands of those who hate us (Lk.1:71).

Christians are grateful to Jesus for showing us the very direct relationship between spiritual and social reconciliation. A part of the Lord's Prayer is the phrase, "Forgive us our debts as we also have forgiven our debtors" (Mt. 6:12). Forgive and you will be forgiven (Lk. 6:37). Leave your gift at the altar, and go, first be reconciled with those from whom you are alienated (Mt. 5:24).

Christians are thankful also for Jesus' *ethical teachings* (a) on the sanctity of marriage (Mt. 19:1–12/Mk. 10:1–12); (b) for his ethical guidelines concerning work and compensation that allow us to be grateful for our wages (Lk. 3:14; Mt. 20:1–16); (c) for his wise counsel concerning financial planning and investment (Lk. 14:28–30; Mt. 25:14–30/Lk. 19:11–27) so that our money does not manage us, and we are able to resist the temptation of being greedy for gain; (d) for his teaching and modeling an ethic of service to others as a moral path more commendable than the pursuit of wealth or pleasure, power or success for oneself (Mt. 20:20–28/Mk. 10:35–45/Lk. 22:24–27).

Christians are also thankful for the *healing ministry* Jesus conducted and delegated to his disciples with knowledge, skill, and authority and the power needed to bring healing in all dimensions of life for all types of human ailments through spiritual, social-psychological, and medical means. It was through his healing ministry that Jesus enacted the compassion of God that he taught about (Mt. 8:16–17/Mk. 1:32–34/ Lk. 4:40–41; Mt. 8:1–4; 9:1–8; Lk. 6:17–19).

As further means of our sanctification into spiritual maturity like Jesus, Christians appreciate *Scripture* as the sacred witness to God's acts in human history (Mt. 4:4/Lk. 4:4). Scripture constitutes the inspiring testimony to God's self-disclosure in human life, particulary in the life of ancient Israel, in the ministry and message of Jesus, and in the early Christian community. It is the holy and authoritative witness to the reconciling truth against which truths from other sources can be judged. We are thankful that by keeping the word of God within our hearts we shall be blessed (Lk. 11:28). It is through Scripture that the good news of great joy is shared with all peoples across generations so that all may "be not afraid" (Lk. 2:10). It is a wonderful story about the human search for God and God's acts of reconciliation with humanity.

We are grateful that as a result of the *power of the Spirit* through love, faith, and hope, that we have a chance to grow like John the Baptist and Jesus to become strong in the Spirit (Lk. 1:80). Christians are also thankful that we can be inspired by the Holy Spirit as Simeon was (Lk. 2:27), and that we are able to discern what the Holy Spirit reveals to us here and now (Lk. 2:26). We praise God that we have this constant companion and wonderful counselor in the Holy Spirit who guides and counsels us (Lk. 12:12). Hence we rejoice in the Holy Spirit (Lk. 10:21–22/ Mt. 11:25–28) as we are born anew into a spiritual awakening and personal transformation of our being into a new being in Christ (Mt. 18:3) and thereby receive daily the new wine from God (Lk. 5:37–39/Mt. 9:17/Mk. 2:22). We praise God for enabling us to bear the fruits that befit repentance (Mt. 3:8/Lk. 3:8; Mt. 3:10; 7:15–20; 12:33; 21:43).

Christians are thankful for their *faith*, for faith is the medium of salvation and healing, though not its source (Mt. 9:1–8; Mt. 14:22–33/Mk. 6:45–52; Mt. 13:58).

It is through faith that we are made well and sustained during our times of illness, loss, and distress. And we praise God for those who despite their suffering, do not despair of their faith in both God's power and goodness, showing thereby that it is possible to love God unconditionally just as Job and Jesus did. What courageous, inspiring witnesses.

Christians are thankful for the power of faith to effect change (Mt. 21:21–22) even faith as little as a grain of mustard seed (Mt. 17:20/Lk.17:6). We appreciate that with faith comes the spiritual gift of courage so that we need not be so anxious and worried about our life (Lk.12:22–28/Mt. 6:25–33; Mt. 13 :12; Lk. 21:14–19; Mt. 6:19–21). We are blessed with the experiences of faith, hope, and love in our lives.

We are grateful that Jesus shared his teaching about *prayer* and modeled that throughout his life. In solitude and silence he communed with God in prayer, before, during, and after work (e.g., Mk. 1:35/Lk. 4:42; Mt. 12:15; Lk. 5:16; 6:12; Mk. 6:46, 14:32–36). Christians are thankful for the assurance from Jesus that if we ask, seek, and knock, God will answer our prayers according to God's will (Mt. 7:7–11/Lk. 11: 9–13). God's will may not be the same as ours expressed in our prayer of petition or intercession, but we are thankful we can pray with confidence and trust that God will grant us the consolation of the Spirit regardless of our circumstances, whether we are healed or not from our infirmities (Lk. 11:9–13/Mt. 7:7–11). When we are conscious of God's beatitudes, we can thank God in prayer, and receive the additional benefit of family and friends' prayers of intercessions to help us experience healing and growth (e.g., Mt. 15:21–28/Mk. 7:24–30; Mk. 8:22–26; Mt. 9:1–8/Mk. 2:1–12/Lk. 5:17–26).

Christians are especially grateful to have received an invitation to the kingdom of God, for the opportunity to follow Jesus like his first disciples (Mt. 4:19/Mk. 1:17; Mt. 8:22; 9:9; 10:38; 16:24–26). We consider it a privilege and a blessing to be given the power and authority to heal the sick as Jesus' disciples did using prayer, laying on of hands and anointing with oil (Lk. 10:4–8; Mt. 10:1–4/Mk. 3: 13–19/Lk. 6:12–16; Mk. 6:7; Lk. 9:1–2). We are thankful too that our scientific discoveries have advanced beyond the use of oil, which was the medicine of Jesus' time. We appreciate Jesus' revelations of the power of God to heal withered hands and broken hearts through both spiritual and medical means (Mk. 1:34; Lk. 4:41; Mt. 4:23–24; 14:35; Mk. 6:55; Lk. 16:19).

We are blessed with the ability and privilege to work in order to serve others to the glory of God. And we are thankful that Jesus appreciated our human need for rest. He said his yoke was easy if we just learn from him, and he will give us rest (Mt. 11: 28–30).

Christians are thankful for Jesus' demonstration of the power of God to overcome evil, and that the despair of Good Friday is transformed into Easter joy (Mt. 27:32– 28:10; Mk. 1:39; Lk. 23:26–56; Lk. 24:1–12; Mk. 15:33–16:8; Mk. 1:27/Lk. 4:36). We are thankful for the gift of eternal life as the final blessing of Christian discipleship (Mt. 10:39; Mt. 5:3–12/Lk. 6:20–23; Lk. 6:23; 10:20; 18:22; Mt. 5:12; 13:24–52; 18: 18; 19:21).

The Consequences of Gratitude. Besides his discussion of both what to be grateful for and to whom we are to be grateful, Jesus also taught about the consequences of gratitude. One of these consequences is that we become more giving. The term "thanksgiving" expresses this meaning—giving motivated by gratitude. We become more like the grateful giver who expects nothing in return (Mt. 6:1–4; Lk. 16:35). Moreover, when beatitudes come, we have even more reason to be thankful. And come they will. Jesus taught that the measure we give will be the measure we get, yet still more will be given to us than we have given (Mt. 13:12/ Mk. 4:24/Lk. 8:18). Our orientation toward life becomes one of more selfless giving in a world filled with selfish grabbing. Being less selfish, we discover the truth that we need not be afraid in God's kingdom (Lk. 5:10). We can let the day's own trouble be sufficient for the day (Mt. 6:33–34/Lk. 12:31).

Being grateful has the healing consequences of reducing our worry and discontent, and our destructive sense of entitlement. Improvement occurs in our interpersonal relationships because we have stopped griping so much. Being grateful, serving others more, doing the will of God, we become members of the family of God (Mt. 12:46–50/Mk. 3:31–35/Lk. 8:19–21). These are further positive consequences.

Concluding Comments about Reconciled Feelings

I have been discussing the transformation of the feeling of entitlement into the feeling of thanksgiving that occurs by the power of the living God through love, faith, and hope. I noted previously some of the other feelings that change in a more reconciled life: anger changes into compassion, fear becomes courage, despair becomes joy. I wish to conclude this section with a few general comments about the affective dimension of human experience as it is transformed through faith and love.

Some people experience this affective dimension more than others. Those who emphasize this dimension can be characterized as Romantics. In Western culture, Romanticism was a period in the late eighteenth and early nineteenth centuries in which the sterility of reason gave way to the vitality of emotion. Subsequent developments included the emphasis upon personal religious experiences of an emotional nature as the pathway to God. From this perspective, more important than knowledge about God is a personal relationship with God or with Jesus.[46]

In this Romantic view, religion is less a matter of cognitive claims or theological reasoning and more a matter of the "heart." Feelings of forgiveness, of being loved and accepted, feeling inspired, feeling dependence and trust, hope and courage, joy and thankfulness, are all emphasized in this affective type of religious orientation.

Affectively-oriented persons are likely to view Scripture as devotional material that elicits feelings of faith, hope, and love. Scripture is more of a source of inspiration to create and sustain feelings of reverence, worship, and wonder.

In the Hindu faith, the affective pathway to liberation through loving devotion is called *bhakti yoga*. By virtue of its emphasis upon love, the Christian faith is viewed by Hindus as a prime example of this affective path. This is a characterization that misses the cognitive, behavioral, and volitional aspects of the Christian faith.

What Tillich said about the primacy of being is related to feeling as well as to knowing. Feeling is not without content. Feelings are perceived and expressed in cognitive and ontological categories such as time and space, breadth and depth, substance and process. Feeling must start with being; it cannot get behind it. Feeling is based on being, and it cannot leave this basis.

Furthermore, knowledge gained through feelings alone, including the affective experiences of religious ecstasy in meditative states or through spiritual intuitions, is finite knowledge with limited certitude, though perhaps of ultimate significance. And the same existential conflicts limiting reason also affect the cognitive elements of feelings.

What prevents Jesus' gospel of reconciliation from becoming a gospel of feeling good is the cognitive content in his symbol of the kingdom of God as a reference to the objective acts of God manifest in historical events in addition to subjective religious experience. While this is an experienced reality, it has cognitive, factual, and ontological dimensions and claims to truth, not merely to altered feelings.

As noted earlier, feelings are meaningful. To speak of the meaning of one's feelings is to suggest further its cognitive content. Religious feelings are meaningful feelings—feelings filled with meaning. Equally important to understanding the meaning of our feelings is the recognition that our feelings change. In this discussion on the affective dimensions of a reconciled life, I have suggested that by the grace of the living God through love, faith, and hope, our anger is transformed into compassion, fear into courage, despair into joy, and entitlement into thanksgiving.

There are, of course, individual differences in terms of the positions persons occupy on the continuum of each of these affective dimensions. Therein lies a basis for a religious typology of personality and a direction for future research. There are also differences among persons according to which of these general dimensions are salient in their approach to life—cognitive, affective, behavioral, or volitional. Moreover, a given individual can be expected to vary to some degree over time and in different situations on these various dimensions. Herein lies a foundation for a Christian psychology of individual differences. Differences also are evident in behavior and strivings, the topics of the next chapter.

NOTES

1. Contrary to Jesus' teachings, subsequent Christian anthropology has fragmented the person by elevating the importance of spirit over matter, and by an emphasis upon saving the soul as the essential part of the person.
2. The proliferation of more than 200 approaches to psychotherapy, each with its own

concepts and jargon, led Messer to characterize the field as a Tower of Babel. Messer, S. B. (1987). Can the tower of Babel be completed? A critique of the common language proposal. *Journal of Integrative and Eclectic Psychotherapy, 6,* 195-199.

3. Tillich, P. (1963). *Systematic theology* (Vol. 3), pp. 11–29.

4. The social, moral, and spiritual dimensions of reconciliation warrant further discussion, but lie beyond the scope of this book's focus upon the psychological dimensions.

5. One would predict that a psychometric measure of the reconciled personality would correlate positively, but not perfectly with psychological measures of mental health. The construct of reconciliation has meanings not subsumed by mental health or psychological adjustment. On the other hand, a reconciled personality is not maladjusted nor mentally ill. Nor does this mean that a mentally ill person can never be reconciled.

6. The empirical evidence linking therapists' experience with therapeutic outcomes is equivocal. See Stein, D., & Lambert, M. (1984). On the relationship between therapist experience and psychotherapy outcome. *Clinical Psychology Review, 4,* 1–16. Paraprofessionals trained in basic interpersonal skills obtain therapeutic outcomes. See Lambert, M., & Bergin, A. (1994). The effectiveness of psychotherapy. In A. Bergin & S. Garfield (Eds.), Handbook of psychotherapy and behavior change (4th ed., pp. 169–172). New York: John Wiley & Sons.

7. For a discussion of the cognitive claims of faith, see Barbour, I. (1966). Issues in science and religion. New York: Harper and Row, pp. 247–270.

8. For contemporary reflections on the meaning of suffering by Christian theologians, see Soelle, D. (1975). *Suffering.* Minneapolis, MN: Fortress Press; and Milazzo, G. T. (1991). *The protest and the silence: suffering, death, and biblical theology.* Minneapolis, MN: Fortress Press.

9. Smith, H. (1991). *The world's religions.* New York: HarperSanFrancisco, pp. 98–103. Buddhism appeals to some psychologists because it is not only realistic, but also experiential, pragmatic, therapeutic, psychological, and egalitarian. A Buddhist perspective on wisdom and the will warrants further exploration. A therapeutic application is Brazier, D. (1995). *Zen therapy: Transcending the sorrows of the human mind.* New York: John Wiley & Sons.

10. For these metaphors I am indebted to Smith, H. (1991). *The world's religions.* New York: HarperSanFrancisco, p. 101.

11. Niebuhr's oft quoted paradox is that sin is not necessary but inevitable. See Niebuhr, R. (1949). *The nature and destiny of man: A Christian interpretation.* New York: Charles Scribner's Sons.

12. Menninger, K. (1973). *Whatever became of sin?* New York: Hawthorn Books, Inc.; see also Surgerman, S. (1976). *Sin and madness: Studies in narcissism.* Philadelphia: The Westminster Press; and Capps, D. (1993). *The depleted self: Sin in a narcissistic age.* Minneapolis, MN: Fortress Press.

13. Concerns about spiritual manipulation within the church was expressed by Johnson, D., & VanVonderen, J. (1991). *The subtle power of spiritual abuse.* Minneapolis, MN: Bethany House Publishers.

14. See for example, Adams, J. (1977). *Competent to counsel.* Nutley, N. J.: Presbyterian and Reformed Publishing Co.

15. See for example Backus, W. (1985). *Telling the truth to troubled people.* Minneapolis, MN: Bethany House Publishers; Crabb, L. (1977). *Effective biblical counseling.* Grand Rapids, MI: Zondervan Publishing House; and Propost, L. (1988). *Psychotherapy in a religious framework.* New York: Human Sciences Press, Inc.

16. Tillich, P. (1957). *The dynamics of faith.* New York: Harper and Brothers Publishers.

17. Barbour, I. (1966). *Issues in science and religion*, p. 62.

18. Tillich, P. (1951). *Systematic theology* (Vol. 1). Chicago: University of Chicago Press, p. 193.

19. Ibid., p. 163.

20. Oglesby, W. (1980). *Biblical themes for pastoral care*. Nashville, TN: Abingdon.

21. Tillich, P. (1951). *Systematic theology* (Vol. 1). Chicago: University of Chicago Press, pp. 147–155.

22. Ibid., p. 156. The Statement of Faith of the United Church of Christ accents the view of God as the One who acts. Following a brief confession of belief, seven declarations attest to the God who creates, seeks, judges, has come and shared, bestows, calls, and promises. See Shinn, R. (1990). *Confessing our faith: An interpretation of the statement of faith of the United Church of Christ*. Cleveland, OH: United Church Press, pp. xi, 13–18.

23. Consistent with Jesus' central teaching about a Spirit-centered compassion, Borg suggests that the admonition to perfection (Lk. 6:36) is more accurately translated as, "Be compassionate as God is compassionate." See Borg, M. (1994b). *Meeting Jesus again for the first time*. New York: HarperSanFrancisco, p. 46.

24. For a review of other reviews of the role of the therapeutic relationships see Patterson, C. H. (1985). *The therapeutic relationship: Foundations for an eclectic psychotherapy*. Monterey, CA.: Brooks/Cole Publishing Co., chps.11–13. For a more recent extension of this theme and the role of agape in therapy, see Patterson, C. H., & Hidore, S. (1997). *Successful psychotherapy: A caring, loving relationship*. Northvale, NJ: Jason Aronson.

25. Synoptic references to Jesus' healings include Mt. 8:14–16; 9:1–8; 9:18–26; 14:35– 36; Lk. 4:41; Mk. 6:55; Mt. 4:24/Lk. 6:18; Mt. 8:1–3/Mk. 1:40–43/Lk. 5:12–13; Mt. 8:16– 17/Mk. 1:32–34/Lk. 4:40–41; Mt. 12:15–21/Mk. 3:7–12/Lk. 6:17–19.

26. References to the ministry of healing include Mt. 10:1–4/Mk. 6:7–19/Lk. 9:1–16; Lk. 10:19; Mt. 10:5–13/Mk. 6:8–11/Lk. 9:2–5; Lk. 10:4–8; Mk. 6:7; Lk. 9:1–2; Mt. 10:1–4/ Mk. 3:13–19; Lk. 6:12–16. For a discussion of the healing ministry and theology of healing, see Kelsey, M. (1973). *Healing and Christianity*. New York: Harper & Row; Maddock, M. (1990). *The Christian healing ministry*. London: SPCK; MacNutt, F. (1974). *Healing*. Notre Dame, IN: Ave Maria Press; and Bonthius, R. (1948). *Christian paths to self-acceptance*. New York: King's Crown Press.

27. Two objective discussions of faith healers are found in Simson, E. (1977). *The faith healers*. St. Louis, MO: Concordia Publishing House; and Nolen, W. (1974). *Healing: A doctor in search of a miracle*. Greenwich, CT: Fawcett Publications.

28. Lk. 7:11–17, 21; 8:1; 14:16; Lk. 8:28–34/Mk. 5:1–20; Lk. 7:18/Mt. 11:2; Mt. 15:29– 31/Mk. 7:31; Mt. 8:16–17/Mk. 1:32; Mt. 4:23; 9:32–35; Mk. 1:5.

29. For a Christian perspective on encouragement and how to develop it, see Crabb, L., & Allender, D. (1984). *Encouragement: The key to caring*. Winona Lake, IN: Zondervan Publishing House.

30. Tillich identified three forms of existential anxiety grounded in the basic dialectics of individualization and participation, dynamics and form, freedom and destiny. All forms of existential anxiety are rooted ontologically in the tension of these polar elements to separate and to move in opposite directions within finite existence. Thus, existence is estrangement and not reconciliation. The mental disorders are testimony to the variety of ways in which estrangement is manifest both psychologically and socially. Tillich, P. (1951). *Systematic theology* (Vol. 1). Chicago: University of Chicago Press, pp. 159–160, 174–187.

31. Tillich, P. (1952). *The courage to be*. New Haven, CT: Yale University Press,

p. 9.

32. Tillich, P. (1951). *Systematic theology* (Vol. 1). Chicago: University of Chicago Press, p. 273.

33. Tillich noted that courage is needed because human freedom is both finite and anxious freedom, which becomes an "aroused freedom" expressed in the desire to sin. Taylor, M. (1991). *Paul Tillich: Theologian of the boundaries.* Minneapolis, MN: Fortress Press, pp. 194, 207.

34. Kipfer, B. (1990). *14,000 Things to be happy about.* New York, New York: Workman Publication.

35. In his book, *Fallible Man,* the French Christian philosopher of phenomenology, Paul Ricoeur suggested that joy provides a better clue to the human condition than either anxiety or despair. Cited by Macquarrie, J. (1988). *Twentieth Century religious thought.* Philadelphia: Trinity Press International, p. 389.

36. Kierkegaard, S. (1954). *Fear and trembling, and sickness unto death.* Garden City, NY: Doubleday & Co.

37. Examples of Psalms of Lament include Psalms 13, 23, 31, 71, 102, 139, and 146.

38. Don Capps describes authentic Christians as agents of hope and includes a description of the experiencing of hoping. See Capps, D. (1995). *Agents of hope: A pastoral psychology.* Minneapolis, MN: Fortress Press. See also Andrew Lester's discussion of hope disclosed in narrative analyses of persons' future stories. Lester, A. (1995). *Hope in pastoral care and counseling.* Louisville, KY: Westminster/John Knox Press.

39. Lk. 4:39; Mk.1:31–34; 1:39; 6:55–56; Mt. 4:23–24; 8:15; 14:36; Mt. 14:35; Lk. 6:19; Mt. 8:16–17/Mk. 1:32–34/Lk. 4:40–41; Mt. 12:15–21/Mk. 3:7–12/Lk. 6:17–19.

40. If this was a confession of faith for early disciples, perhaps it is a sufficient declaration of faith for contemporary disciples to affirm that Jesus came in the name of the Lord.

41. The joyous will is central in the psychology of joy presented by Assagioli, R. (1973). *The act of will.* New York: Penguin Books, pp. 199–202.

42. In the phenomenological-existentialist tradition, the French Protestant philosopher, Paul Ricoeur suggested that it is joy, not anxiety, which has a better claim to be considered the ontological affect, that is, the mood or state of mind that affords the clue to the human condition and that directs us to an affirmative relation to being rather than alienation. Cited in Macquarrie, J. (1988). *Twentieth Century religious thought.* Philadelphia: Trinity Press International, p. 390.

43. Implicit in the changes occurring in all dimensions and domains is a growing congruence between God's will and one's own will. This point is emphasized in discussion of the conative dimension in chapter six.

44. V. Frankl affirmed that the final freedom is to give meaning to our suffering. Frankl, V. (1984). *Man's search for meaning: An introduction to logotherapy* (3rd ed.). New York: A Touchstone Book.

45. See Lasch, C. (1978). *The culture of narcissism.* New York: W. W. Norton.

46. For discussions of Romanticism, see Barbour, I. (1966). *Issues in science and religion.* New York: Harper Torchbooks, pp. 65–69; and Livingston, J. (1971). *Modern Christian thought from the enlightenment to vatican II.* New York: Macmillan, pp. 40–46, 80–114.

Chapter Six

Behavioral and Conative Reconciliation

In the previous chapter I noted that psychological reconciliation initiated by the living God through love, faith, and hope changes us. It changes what we think, and it changes how we feel. In the affective domain of life, the experience of reconciliation transforms anger into compassion, fear into courage, despair into joy, and entitlement into thanksgiving. In the cognitive dimension, knowledge is transformed into wisdom. Psychological reconciliation also involves behavioral and conative domains. God changes both what we want and what we do. The consequences are a redeemed will and ethical conduct.

THE BEHAVIORAL DOMAIN OF RECONCILIATION

The Nature of Behavior

The behavioral domain of human experience generally refers to our overt actions. To behave is to act, to do something, to engage in some activity, to perform some task or function. Synonyms of behavior include conduct, deportment, practice (in contrast to theory), procedures, implementations, and applications.

Behavior in any situation is our attempt to deal with that situation, to cope with it, or adapt to it. We are behaving when we take measures to bring about change, when we implement a plan, execute a course of action, or carry out a strategy to accomplish an objective, to steer a course.

Behavior is not, however, merely overt physical action. To make a decision is also an action. Within academic psychology, even thoughts and feelings are considered behavior. They are labeled *covert behavior* because they are internal and not directly observable. Both internal and external behaviors are considered learned responses and reactions to environmental contingencies or to internal stimuli.

The first thing that students learn in most introductory psychology courses is that psychology is defined as the science of behavior. It is the study of how human behavior is acquired, maintained, and modified. There is even an entire school of therapy called behavior modification and behavior therapy. Its focus is behavioral change based on principles of learning theory derived mostly from experimental psychology.

Unfortunately, much of behavioral psychology is also grounded not merely in principles of learning, but in a philosophy of naturalism and materialism. The only world that counts is this sensate, empirical world, because that is all there is. What is real are those natural events that can be both observed and measured quantitatively. Only those activities or events that meet these criteria are deemed to fall within the purview of scientific psychology. This is the thrust of the empiricism and "logical" positivism that undergirds and misdirects much contemporary psychological research and practice. Human experience and consciousness are sacrificed on its procrustean bed. Behavior has replaced being as the object of psychological inquiry. In the process, the subject who behaves has been lost. When it stopped studying human consciousness, psychology lost its mind. When it stopped studying being and the self, psychology lost its soul.[1]

But psychology as a science need not be bound by a positivist philosophy. A minority of psychologists informed by phenomenological and existentialist philosophy have reclaimed the person and the centrality of human experience and consciousness, thereby providing a viable alternative. A Christian anthropology is yet another foundation for a genuinely human science, a science of human persons.

While I have serious reservations about the philosophical assumptions underlying behavioral psychology, I wish to emphasize that the Christian faith and Christian counseling are also forms of behavior modification and behavior therapy. Christian counseling is therapeutic in part because it changes the way people behave. This is the insight emphasized by Jay Adams in his book, *Competent to Counsel*.[2] Christian counseling includes behavior modification as one of its objectives. That is not its only or primary objective, but a very important one.[3]

Because it shares this objective with other secular approaches to counseling, they can be compared empirically in terms of their efficacy and efficiency in yielding constructive behavior change. That comparative research needs to be done. To date there is no compelling evidence of the superiority of religiously based counseling relative to secular counseling with religiously committed clients.[4]

Righteous Behavior and Ethical Conduct

Jesus counted among his disciples persons who not only heard his message, but those who lived it. It is those who *do* the will of God who are true disciples of Christ (Mt. 12:46–50/Mk. 3:31–35/Lk. 8:19–21; Mt. 7:24–27/Lk. 6:47–49). But what is the will of God? The will of God is expressed in the sacred commandments of the Old Testament Law and prophets (Mt. 5:17–20). These were summarized by Jesus in the two great commandments upon which all the law and prophets depend. When asked, "What shall I do to inherit eternal life?", Jesus replied that we are to love God with all our hearts and souls and minds and strength, and our neighbor as ourselves. Do this and you shall live (Mt. 22:34–40/Mk. 12:28–34/Lk. 10:25–28). Do this. Don't just think about it. Do it.

Jesus said that knowing the will of God obligates us to do the will of God (Lk. 6:46–49). The message heard must be carried out in a ministry lived. He also taught that the test of goodness was its fruit (Mt. 7:15–20; Mt. 12:33–35/Lk. 6:43–46; Mt. 13:1–9/Mk. 4:1–9/Lk. 8:4–8; Mt. 21:33–41). Thus while goodness comes from the heart (Lk. 6:45), it is expressed in what we do (Lk. 6:46; Mt. 7:21). We must be doers of the Word, not merely hearers of the Word (Mt. 7:24–27/Lk. 6:47–49). We are to bear the fruits that befit repentance (Mt. 3:8/Lk. 3:8). Even wisdom is justified by her deeds (Mt. 11:19).

Based on these passages it would appear that Jesus taught that the real test of true disciples was their loving deeds rather than their faithful convictions, and manifested more in ethical behavior than in correct beliefs (Mt. 5–7). Faith without works is the pious pretense of pharisaical religion (Mt. 6:5–5; 23:1–39). Faith is authentic only when actualized in acts of love. The two are interdependent and both are essential to the reconciled life. "Reconciliation through faithful love" seems a more accurate summary of the Christian kerygma than the Pauline principle of justification by faith alone.

Jesus had a great deal to say about how godly persons are transformed behaviorally. To live a righteous and holy life is to live a *life of service*. All service is not holy; but neither is faith fulfilled without good works. A Christian serves others as Jesus did (Mt. 20:20–28/Mk. 10:35–45/Lk. 22:24–27). As a result, one of the empirical indicators of Christian discipleship is a life of service that enhances human welfare.

Jesus said that whoever might be great among you must be your servant (Mt. 20:25–28/Mk. 10:42–45/Lk. 22:24–30). The question is, whom do we serve? Ourselves? Our family? Our clients? Our employers? Our profession? Our nation? God? Whom do we serve? (Mt. 6:24/Lk.16:13).

A life of service requires some degree of *self-denial*. In a culture in which self-actualization and doing your own thing are considered not only the definitions of the good life, but an entitlement, a call for self-denial is not likely to be popular. But to be truly ethical we must behave in ways that subordinate our own personal wishes and demands for the sake of others. With rights come responsibilities. Jesus said, "If any want to become my followers, let them deny themselves and take up their cross and follow me." He also said that "those who lose their life for my sake will find it" (Mt. 16:24–26/Mk. 18:34–35/Lk. 9:23–24; Mt. 10:38/Lk. 14:27).

To follow the golden rule and second sacred commandment of loving others as ourselves requires a degree of self-sacrifice (Mt. 22:34–40; Mt. 7:12/Lk. 6:31). The ethical life is one that involves sacrifice for the sake of something or someone greater than oneself. Altruism is more honorable than egoism.[5] It provides a more noble purpose for living. The wisdom of Jesus' teaching was his attention to both self and others: Love your neighbor as yourself. This is an ethic of equality and justice.

Many persons manifest both self-denial and sacrifice in their vocation and *work.* Work is a major activity for most persons. It is another area in which our behavior is transformed by our relationship with God through love, faith, and hope. The change effected in our work may mean for some a change in job. For others the change may not be so evident immediately or externally. One could continue in the same job, fulfilling the responsibilities defined by the very same job description. Upon closer observation, however, it becomes evident that the reconciled person works differently.

On a practical level, one learns to work smarter, not harder, in contrast to the following story. Ole was walking down the road when he spotted two friends, Elvis Engebretson and Torvald Bjornson, working with shovels on the edge of the city park. Ole noted that Elvis would dig a hole and Torvald would follow behind and fill in the hole. Even Ole was puzzled by this operation, so he asked them to explain. "Well," said Torvald, "we're really a three man crew, but the guy who plants the trees is sick today."

We need to apply common sense on our jobs and to learn to work smarter. Reconciled persons also learn to work with greater ease, with less anxiety. They cope better with the ups and downs, successes and failures, the wins and losses. In short, one works with a sense of detachment. The Christian works with a kind of holy detachment, doing what one used to do, but now for a different reason, in service to God's glory, as a servant in God's kingdom, and as an agent of reconciliation.

Most persons become very attached to their work, in part because they spend so many of their waking hours doing it. There is an old saying that in order to be happy in our work, we must be suited to it, interested in it, and we must not do too much of it. But that is easier said than done. After all, our work is the means to our survival and economic security, the source of important benefits related to our health and to a secure retirement. Work is a necessity because food, shelter, and clothing don't come free. It's really that simple isn't it? Well, not quite. For many persons, relationships at work constitute significant sources of satisfaction of social and psychological needs, like the needs for esteem and belonging. These needs have become more salient in the work place with the increasing number of single, divorced, and widowed workers.

The psychological and social rewards just mentioned tend to be extrinsic to work. For other persons, the work itself is intrinsically satisfying. They are doing what they love and love what they are doing. Their job allows them to express their most basic vocational interests and personal values. Their work contributes to their sense of purpose, meaning, and worth. By working they are not merely doing what they have to do; they are doing what they want to do.

Whether the rewards and motives for work are intrinsic or extrinsic, both types lead to considerable ego involvement. It is the latter that accounts for coveted promotions based on increased productivity and feared demotions due to reduced efficiency. We become anxious about potential reprisals for perceived disloyalty, and worried about being fired for failure to achieve the goals set by management as the key results that determine performance appraisals, tenure, and promotions.

It is our own ego that demands more pay relative to others, like the workers in the vineyard (Mt. 20:1–16). It is our ego that jealously guards our perks, which so quickly become defined as entitlements. It is Brother Ego that asserts our territorial prerogatives, locks us into disputes over turf, and mires us down into demoralizing office politics, a euphemism for destructive back-biting, petty gossip, and manipulative maneuvering.

Aggressive competition among divisions within the same company for limited resources, corporate power struggles for economic domination in the market place, and hostile take overs are further assertions of Lord Ego. So are acts of corporate espionage and employee sabotage. The many signs of status and prestige in an organization, including corner offices on top floors, salary differentials and bonuses, and the privileges granted by seniority all serve like glue to cement our egos to our jobs and to the outcomes of our work. And in hard times when many are laid off due to "down-sizing," which seems to be the American way of increasing profits by sacrificing employees, we work even harder for fear we'll lose our jobs. Gripped by such fears and the enticements of occupational success, as well as increasing work loads under the guise of "total quality management," Americans are vulnerable to becoming addicted to work.

Addiction to work is addiction.[6] It is both neurotic behavior and a form of enslavement. We become prisoners of our paychecks and perks, which function like golden chains. The imprisonment occurs because we are working for the wrong reasons. The way to freedom is not to quit work, for laziness is but another form of selfishness. The key to liberation from this addiction is to detach our worth from our work and our ego from the outcomes. The secret is to do with less attachment the work we have to do.

Ole Olson learned this secret. He had been having trouble grasping his job, in part because he kept fussing over the minor details—lost in the forest for the trees, as the saying goes. As a result of his obsessive attention to details, he didn't get much work done. Finally, his boss said, "Ole, stop sweating the details. You've got to look at the Big Picture." So Ole took the afternoon off and went to the movies. The picture he saw was entitled, *Weeds*. This is the Norwegian version of another famous ethnic picture, *Roots*. *Weeds* is an adventure story that begins in Oslo, where Mrs. Kunta Olson is preparing to emigrate to Duluth, Minnesota. The picture also ends in Oslo, because while baking lefse, Mrs. Olson misses the boat.

Humor is one way of gaining a kind of detachment from our jobs. But a more effective way is by working for other than selfish reasons. The Christian way of working is to work to the glory of God. As Brother Lawrence wrote: "Our sanctification does not depend upon changing the way we do things; but doing for God what we normally do for ourselves."[7] Loving God is what it's all about. Do whatever you do for the love of God.

As a response to God's love the Christian works as both a privilege and sacred duty, born of gratitude for the beatitudes God has bestowed upon us. Work becomes a way to serve God and to express the love of God through service. We no longer work to build our own little empires or to secure our personal estates, but to advance the kingdom of God on the job, in and through our work, hence into, and unto this world.

For the Christian, the greatest joy in life and its ultimate meaning are found by doing the will of God. It follows that doing God's will through my work does much more than make a virtue out of necessity; work becomes a medium through which I experience God. Work is a pathway to God. Service is sacramental. Work done to the glory of God becomes a liberating, reconciling, fulfilling, and exciting experience.

This pathway to God through work and service is called *karma yoga* in the Hindu faith. It is known as servanthood and vocation in the Christian faith. Regardless of its name, the point is that if I seek God in my job, I will find God there; for God is everywhere and near to all who call upon God, wherever they may be, whatever they are doing, regardless of their occupation or the level of their position on an organizational chart. In everything we do, God is always with us, working in and through us expressing love to reconcile the world. Simply remember God in all that you do. God is always here and always now. Trust in God's steadfast love in your work, and your work will become a labor of love.

Christians who work for the glory of God, doing God's will as both a privilege and a duty, are more likely to be freed from obsessive worries about work and compulsive workaholism. They begin to trust God with the results of their work and make fewer selfish claims to its fruits. As a consequence, they learn to be more calm in the midst of much activity and more steady like the centered axle of a moving wheel.

Life lived at the center is much less hectic and frantic than spinning around in circles, and much more relaxed and free, when that center is God. Being less distressed as a result of detachment, one becomes more able to concentrate upon the task at hand. You learn to take one thing at a time, instead of spinning so many plates on precarious poles so that several fall and break. It is when we care but not too much that we become most efficient, effective, and free.

The secret to making everything easier is to pray for God's grace to do your assigned work, and to do it to God's glory. Fervently ask for God's help in all that you do. Refer all that you do to God. "Lord, I cannot do this unless you help me." God never fails to provide the help we need, though that help may be different from what we asked for and expected.

With God's help one becomes free from the periodic exhaustion and irritation that plague those with such a sense of urgency to get more and more accomplished in less and less time and with fewer co-workers to help get it all done. It is possible to be highly productive without becoming a prisoner of our productivity, provided we do our work according to the will of God. "Not my will, O God, but Thine be done." Can we pray that about our jobs? God help us if we can't. And

God help the emotionally neglected children who suffer because of their parents' addiction to work.

The transforming power of our relationship with God experienced through love, faith, and hope does produce behavioral changes. We do things differently and we do different things. The result is *a changed life style*. Jesus described these behavioral changes in ethical terms. All manner of wickedness is substituted by righteous actions. Murder, theft, adultery, slander, and insults are not the actions of disciples of Christ (Mt. 5:21–48; Mt. 6:14–15/Mk. 11:25). Ethical behaviors are observable and measurable indicators of a transformed person. Ethical conduct becomes an empirical test of a reconciled life. So are the behaviors Jesus taught about social reconciliation. We know a good tree by its fruits.

Our personal, family, and financial lives are important areas in which behavior change can be expected. Honest business dealings and fidelity in marriage are further examples. There is a Christian way to manage money. In the first place, we do not allow money to manage us. Contrary to the message in a popular contemporary film, greed is not good. The lover of money is an abomination in the sight of God (Lk. 16:14–15). Jesus taught that we cannot serve both God and Mammon. We must choose the god we will surrender to (Mt. 6:24/Lk.16:13) and be wary of such idols of destruction as wealth and success.

In managing our resources, we are called to exercise Christian stewardship. Good stewardship of both our personal and environmental resources is characterized by prudent planning. The parable of the talents is counsel to make wise investments (Mt. 25:14–30). But stewardship also involves sharing our wealth with others less fortunate (Lk. 12:22–34/Mt. 6:25–33).

Fidelity in marriage is another example of righteous behavior. Adultery and fornication, that is, both extramarital and premarital sexual relations are not. Except on grounds of infidelity, divorce in order to marry another is contrary to Jesus' teachings (Lk. 16:18/Mt. 5:31–32/Mk. 10:11–12; Mt. 15:1–9; 9:18; Mk. 7:20–23; 10:11–12). And to be holy means we do not tempt others to sin (Lk. 17:1–2/Mt. 18:6–7/Mk. 9:42). Instead we are to confront one another about our sin in a manner described previously as compassionate confrontation. We are to speak the truth in love.

Telling the truth is another example of righteous behavior. Integrity and honesty are Christian virtues (Mt. 15:18–20; 19:18; Mk. 7:20–23). Jesus was very critical of hypocrisy in all areas of life, but especially in the religious life (Mt. 12:9–14/Mk. 3:1–6/Lk. 6:6–11). The problem of hypocrisy is precisely the inconsistency between one's professed beliefs and actual behavior, the contrast between public piety and private immorality.

Developing Habits of Holiness

In addition to counseling ethical conduct, Jesus also taught us to develop and nurture holy habits to cooperate with the work of the living God to transform our lives through love, faith, and hope into a more reconciled life. These habits include study and service, worship and prayer. Whether or not they are performed regularly is an additional empirical indicator of Christian discipleship and reconciliation with God.

We need such holy habits in part because Jesus warned us that when an "evil spirit" leaves us for a while, that does not mean it is gone forever; indeed, it may return with seven more spirits more evil than itself, and they enter and dwell within the man; and the last state of that man becomes worse than the first (Lk. 11:24–26/ Mt. 12: 43–65). If we translate "evil spirits" as bad attitudes or negative emotions, irrational ideas, destructive habits, evil intentions, or neurotic complexes, this passage makes much sense psychologically. There is such a thing as symptom substitution.[8] We need constant spiritual encouragement. We need to confess our sins regularly and forgive one another repeatedly.

By definition, a habit is a settled disposition or tendency, a customary practice, or long-continued practice. It is performed routinely and frequently, if not daily. To be in the habit of doing something is to do it regularly and commonly, if not invariably. A habit is a behavior, the performance of which becomes second nature to us precisely because it is so well practiced.

Prayer is such a habit. Prayer is more than an activity, but to pray is to act. Prayer is a learned behavior, hence potentially also a habit. Since human holiness and righteous conduct are both dependent upon God and granted to those who pray, habitual prayer is essential to one who is serious about changing (Lk. 11:9–13/Mt. 7:7–11). We need to pray to know what to change and for the strength to change it. Jesus taught that practicing our piety in public in order to be praised, or praying by heaping up empty phrases in order to be heard by others were hypocritical habits (Mt. 6:1–8). He counseled us to pray in private the prayer he taught (Mt. 6:9–13/Lk. 11:2– 4; Mt. 6:16–18). He also practiced what he preached. Many times in his ministry Jesus withdrew not only from the crowds, but from his own co-workers, his closest friends and his family to be alone with God in prayer (e.g., Lk. 4:42; 6:12; 9:18; 22:41).

Prayer is a holy habit and a pathway to holiness. It is also one of the most fruitful media we have for apprehending the divine, for in prayer we experience that which is holy.[9] And as Tillich noted, "only that which is holy can give man ultimate concern, and only that which gives man ultimate concern has the quality of holiness."[10] Experiences of reconciliation are also experiences of the holy. Prayer is a medium of reconciliation. Perhaps this is one reason why Jesus left his followers a prayer rather than a creed. It is also noteworthy that this Lord's Prayer was addressed to God, not to Jesus.

I have said that through love, faith, and hope our relationship with God changes our behavior. God changes our behavior by first changing our being. God transforms us from the inside out. It is important to end this section on behavioral changes with a reemphasis on the primacy of being over doing. Behavior is a function of being. Just as ethics presupposes ontology in philosophical inquiry, similarly what we do is a function of who we are. This is a fundamental principle of Taoism as well as the way of Jesus. Action follows being. Stronger, wiser, and new action will follow stronger, wiser, and new being. The way to do is to be.[11]

Surely we are more than what we do. Our behavior is only one aspect of our being and our experience. A good tree is known by its fruits, but its fruits are not the tree; they are outgrowths of it. Another important part of our being is our strivings.

We think about what we want. We usually do what we want, unconsciously if not consciously. We may feel good or bad about doing it. It all comes down to what we want and will. It is to this conative domain of experience that the next section of this chapter is addressed.

THE CONATIVE DOMAIN OF RECONCILIATION

The conative domain of life refers to our experience as moral and volitional beings. I will defer discussion of the moral dimension to chapter seven. Here I will discuss the volitional dimension of reconciliation in terms of motivation and the experience of willing. Thereafter I will suggest that decisional conflicts are moral and volitional experiences of an estranged will that becomes reconciled by seeking first the kingdom of God.

The Nature of Motivation

The conative dimension of life refers to my experience as a volitional being. As a volitional being, I am aware that I intend certain things to happen. I want certain things and I strive to achieve them. I commit myself to a mission or purpose that embodies and expresses important values that I endorse. I choose particular objectives over others. I set goals, make plans for achieving them, and pursue their attainment. I select strategies based on their costs and benefits all relative to the desired end, the end that I have chosen.

All these phrases just noted are some of the common ways of talking about human motivation in teleological terms. From a teleological perspective all behavior has meaning, and its meaning lies in its purpose. Human behavior is less a function of past history or present circumstances than the product of one's future anticipations and goals. One of the propositions of client-centered therapy is that human behavior is the organism's goal-directed attempt to satisfy its needs as perceived.[12] That is probably one of the better psychological expressions of the theological concept of sin by virtue of the implicit egoism involved. For now, the point is that being human means to be a willing creature oriented toward the future. As a potential or capacity to effect outcomes, I have a will, and I will certain things to occur.

The concept of the human will is one way of understanding human motivation. Defined more generically, a *motive* is an impulse to act in a particular way. It is an inducement to do something, or a reason for doing it, and an answer to the question of why it was done. A motive functions theoretically as an antecedent of behavior.

A motive is a stimulus that elicits a response, a cause that produces an effect. It is a force that produces a change.

Used as a verb, to motivate someone is to induce them to act, to propel their movement, though not to compel them to do it. To be motivated is to be moved, influenced, persuaded or encouraged, urged or goaded, aroused, incited, or inspired to act. A motivated person is one who did what she wanted to do. She willed the outcome that occurred, consciously or unconsciously. A motivated act is deliberate or intentional rather than determined or accidental.

Motives matter. They enter into important decisions and actions that we take. Our legal system seeks justice by administering punishment to fit the crime. Determinations of sentences are based on judgments about the accused's motives and presumed intent. Courts distinguish manslaughter from homicide based in part on a judgment of intentionality, or the degree to which the accused was free and intended to commit the crime. Sometimes we do not do what we want or will to do, as in the case of harming someone in an auto accident.

In the history of psychology, numerous motivational terms have been proposed. Instincts or physiological drives of hunger and thirst, sex and aggression, and pain avoidance describe basic biological urges. Numerous psychological needs have been postulated to explain behavior including such needs as security, belonging, or self-esteem, and the needs for growth and meaning. Behaviorists prefer the term "reinforcers" as external, hence observable and measurable causes to explain the dynamics of human behavior. Cognitively-oriented psychologists favor terms such as "expectancies," "anticipations," or "self-efficacy appraisals" and "outcome appraisals." Humanistic psychologists prefer to use internal constructs with a future orientation. They favor concepts such as values and goals, human strivings, or potentialities to be actualized. A potentiality is not merely an inert capacity. It is a dynamic tendency that seeks to be actualized. Potentialities are motives and motivating. The potential to love seeks to be realized. So does the potential to hate. That is why it is so important to understand our motives in order to direct what we actualize in our behavior.

Depending upon one's point of view, a motive may be construed physiologically as a drive, cognitively as an expectancy or a reason for doing something, affectively as a felt need or emotional inducement to act, behaviorally as reinforcement, or teleologically as purposeful striving. These are some of the common ways motivation is construed in the field of psychology.

The Will as a Motive

With a few exceptions,[13] the concept of "will" is used much less commonly in psychological theories to describe and understand human motivation. It is particularly unfortunate that the idea of "will" was banished from the lexicon of therapeutic terms and replaced by concepts such as instinct, drive, need, and motive. Human volition plays a central role in the course of psychotherapy, yet most theories of psychotherapy do not have a model of the mind to which volition can be attributed. Moreover, psychotherapy is about intentional change, hence human willing is inherent in the process. Finally, the therapeutic relationship involves not only resolution of conflicts between the client's unconscious wishes and conscious choices; it requires also resolution of conflicts between the client's will and the therapist's will.[14] The latter conflicts have been construed in psychodynamic theory as the issues of transference, resistance, and counter-transference. The issue is broader than the distorted perceptions implied by those terms.

The relative absence of the term "will" in psychological literature is probably related to the desire to separate science from religion, and to the ascendance of psychological and environmental determinism within both academic and clinical psychology. The notion of "will" carries with it religious associations as in "the will of God,"[15] and the connotation of free will or the freedom to choose. Additionally, the term "will" has ethical connotations of being responsible for one's decisions based on chosen values and aims. In applied psychology, a moral model has been largely rejected in favor of a psychological model that postulates other types of causes such as drives, needs, or environmental contingencies. Psychology has attempted to be descriptive, but it has been implicitly prescriptive.[16]

Another reason for rejecting the concept of "will" has been its associated meaning of willpower. In this connotation will is misconceived as merely power or the resolve to "grit your teeth and bear it." This limited meaning may have philosophical roots in Schopenhauer's concept of will as a blind striving power or a life force lacking any purpose and in Nietzsche's view of will as the power to command.[17] Regardless of its origin, efforts to change behavior by appeals to willpower have not yielded consistently favorable results. Furthermore, explaining counseling failures in terms of the client's lack of will (i.e., resistance) has seemed like blaming the victim or worse, an expression of a judgmental moralism contrary to the therapeutic virtues of empathic understanding and unconditional positive regard.

Finally, the concept of "will" has fallen into disfavor because it focuses attention upon the future rather than the past as a determinant of human behavior, and "will" conveys the teleological meanings of intention or purpose. By contrast, many psychologists are committed to logical positivism and psychological determinism expressed in their explanations of present behavior in terms of material or efficient causes evident in either individual past histories or present environmental circumstances. Consequently, they are not likely to accept teleological explanations based on formal and final causes, nor a voluntaristic psychology that emphasizes both freedom and the future.[18]

This rejection of the concept of will by scientific psychology seems to be as unfortunate as it is willful. The concept of will does as much and more than most other terms used to describe human motives. In most theories of personality, motives function in two ways. First, they energize behavior. In this respect motives function like a force, a source of energy or power that propels behavior. Second, motives guide behavior in one direction rather than another. As an example, the person who has not eaten for some time is motivated by hunger, both energized to act and directed toward the goal of food. The concept of will fulfills both of these theoretical functions. To will something is to be motivated to do it. By willing something, I am both energized and directed to act toward a particular goal.

Motivational Terms in the New Testament

One way to comprehend the views of motivation in the Christian tradition is to simply record the words used and their appearances in the Synoptics and the New Testament. Consulting *Nelson's Complete Concordance of the Revised Standard Version Bible*, I counted the occurrences of several concepts that are commonly used to address and express human motivation. A listing is provided in Table 2.

A review of this table indicates the future orientation of the majority of these terms (will, want, desire, choose, wish, value, purpose, decide, strive, intend, or goal). These terms and their various derivatives occur about ninety-five times in the Synoptics alone and a total of about 400 times in the entire New Testament. In contrast, terms that connote motives with either a past or present orientation (drives/needs/motives) occur only twenty-four times in the Synoptics and sixty-five times in the entire New Testament. This descriptive summary, however simplistic, suggests that in the teachings of Jesus and the New Testament writers, the future counts in human motivation more than the past or present.

The dominance of the future-oriented terms also suggests that Jesus taught a teleological theory of motivation. What explains human behavior is not simply or primarily the satisfaction of needs or the gratification of drives that push us; it is the human will, our wants and wishes, our desires and choices, our values and purposes, our decisions and strivings that energize us and guide us to act in the present and to create our future.

Of these teleological terms, the one used most frequently in both the Synoptic Gospels and in the New Testament as a whole is the concept of "will." Together with the related term of "want," these words appear more than twice as often as any other motivational terms in the Synoptics (47 times) and in the entire New Testament (179 times). What one wills is paramount. It is what people want and choose that enables one to predict what they will do and to explain why they do it. The most influential antecedents of behavior are behavioral intentions.[19]

A Linguistic and Existential Analysis of "Willing"

The term "conation" is defined as the power or act of willing or striving. The common meaning of "will" is the faculty or capacity of determining one's actions. It refers also to the act or action of willing. To will something is to desire it, to want it, to intend it, and to choose it. To will something is not only to wish for it, but to bring it about by a conscious choice. To will something is to select it among

Table 2
Motivational Terms in the Synoptics and New Testament

Motivational Terms	Synoptics	New Testament
will/s/ed/willing	27	115
want/s/ed/ing	20	64
need/s/ed	20	54
desire/s/ed/ings	13	68
choose/chose/n	12	46
wish/es/ed/ing	10	32
value/s/valued	6	13
drive/s/driven	4	11
purpose/s/ed	3	26
decide/s/decision/s	3	15
strive/s/ings	1	7
intend/ed/ings/intent/tion	1	15
goal/s	0	1
potential/potentiality	0	0
motive/s/motivate/ed	0	0

other alternatives, to exercise an option, to make a deliberate decision. To will something is to elect it, or to decide in favor of it. Willing is an act of self-direction and self-determination. That which one wills is usually described as one's goal or objective, or more generally as one's purpose or mission.[20]

A behavior that has been willed is presumed to have occurred because a person wanted it to occur and decided to make it happen. Human action is the consequence of a person striving freely to bring it about for some purpose, objective, or goal. Acts of this nature are described as intentional or "willful," that is, they are acts that occur according to one's own desire and decision, not accidentally nor determined by other persons or forces, not even by biological drives or by psychological needs. Other connotations of "willful" are to insist upon one's own way, or to be stubborn, disobedient, rebellious, or selfish. Sin is a willful act in this latter sense.

When we describe persons as willing to do something, we think of them as having agreed to do it. They have consented to comply or conform. A *willingness* to do something is having a favorable disposition toward it. To be willing is to be inclined to do something or disposed to do it freely.

The element of freedom is included in the idea that one who is willing has been persuaded of the merits of the goal, not coerced or brainwashed. To coerce people is to force them to act against their wills, that is, in a manner that denies their freedom and choice, as when an autocratic executive imposes his will upon others. In contrast, to be willing is to agree to do something, to consent to it, to give permission, to grant or approve it. Acts of will are products of internal deliberations and conscious choices rather than external reinforcements, and more a matter of conscience than conditioning because choices are based on value judgements.

When the voluntary nature of willing is emphasized, we speak of a person doing something of one's own free will, or acting of one's own accord or initiative. The freedom implied by the concept of free will is more than indeterminancy or chance. It is freedom in the sense of being able to determine one's future through conscious decisions and intentional acts. Though limited, this freedom is an innate and defining characteristic of being human.[21] One cannot act willingly without some degree of freedom.

Willingness may be construed somewhat negatively, however, as mere acquiescence or capitulation, a concession or yielding, as when one merely allows or permits something. In the latter cases, one is more likely to be described as doing something unwillingly or reluctantly; doing it, but not with a happy heart.

In other uses, to will means to wish something, as in the phrase, "do as you will" or "try as they will, they just don't succeed." In this connotation, willing is akin to longing for something. Synonyms include yearning or craving, or to hunger or thirst for something as in the phrase, "to hunger and thirst for righteousness." To will something is to hope for it, to aspire to something, and to want it. The antecedent wish prompts one to strive for the desired object. An example of the latter is Jesus' teaching to "strive first for the kingdom of God and His righteousness" (Mt. 6:33; Lk. 12:31).

The concept of will is also used to express one's *preference* or pleasure. Many company personnel manuals stipulate that persons are "employed at will," meaning of course, their employer's preference or will. It is a phrase that gives the employer the power to hire or fire anyone at any time without cause. Except for protected classes based on age, gender, disability, or other minority status, employees work subject to their employer's will. This condition reflects the imbalance of power and hierarchical structure evident in most economic organizations that is antithetical to a democratic culture. Such is the nature of enlightened human relations in corporate America.

When sexual pleasure is willed, we speak of *lust*. The latter term is sometimes used more generally, however, to express an intensity of willing, or willing something passionately, as when one speaks of a lust for life. When we want something someone else possesses, we speak of *coveting*.

Another synonym expressing intentionality is *interest*. Vocational interests are presumed to be motives for entering certain occupations. While some are considered inherited and others learned, vocational interests may be construed as the product of wishes and decisions, as in concepts such as career aspirations or vocational preferences. These are additional ways of expressing what a person wants or wills.

The past tense of will is "willed" or *"would."* The latter term is used at times to express a preference, as in the phrase, "I would like to finish this book." This meaning connotes a lesser degree of commitment than the present tense, to will. An even weaker commitment, if not an absence of motivation, is expressed by the phrase, "He is lacking will." Sometimes "would" is used to convey an element of uncertainty or doubt, as in the phrase, "That would appear to be the case." To say that something would have happened under certain circumstances is to express a probability more positively. Alternatively, the past tense of "would" may function simply as a request, as "I would like you to consider this matter," or "I would like to be a disciple of Christ." The phrase "would like" is weaker than "I want." The latter conveys a more definite desire rather than a mere preference or hope for something.

The *period of time* emphasized by the term "will" is the future. Willing is potentiality that projects one into the future as Rollo May noted.[22] It is not merely power or resolve. At times even the past tense of "would" is used to express the future indirectly ("He said he would come") or to express a future desire ("He's a would-be Christian" or "She's a wanna-be saint"). It may imply a future condition as in the phrase, "If only you would repent, you would enter the kingdom of God." Recall that Jesus' words in this verse are translated more confidently as "will" rather than would, implying not a mere probability, but a certainty of both the condition of repentance and its rewarding consequences.

To will something means to want it. At times a contrast is drawn between what we want and what we need. In this context, "want" is used to express a preference whereas *"need"* is used to convey a necessity. I may want to eat a delicious fresh lobster, but I don't need it to survive. The contrast is useful, as is Maslow's hierarchy of needs, but both are unnecessary. We can speak instead of a *hierarchy of wants* based on our values and their relative importance to both the psychological well-being and spiritual healing of ourselves, our relationships, and our communities.

In some uses of "will" the connotation is that of determination or resolve, as when we speak of the "will to win" or "will power." In this sense, a moral strength or energy is implied. "Strength of will," "an indomitable will," or "an iron will" are additional expressions that convey the force of will. In these uses, "will" is construed both as a force and forceful. At times this connotation is expressed by the term courage. Other expressions of this meaning are to will something in earnest, or willing it with all one's heart.

The synonym of *"shall"* expresses greater determination, and even an obligation or moral necessity as in the command, "Thou shalt not kill." This more definite term "shall" has been used to translate Jesus' teachings of the beatitudes. "Blessed are the pure of heart, for they shall see God" is one example (Mt. 5:8). The term "shall" is also used to express the future tense ("We shall see"). It connotes a decision or promise ("I shall see to it," or "I shall control myself").

Self-control over physiological functions, like self-control of one's overt behavior, is an act of will. In the fields of behavioral medicine and health psychology, the techniques of biofeedback, meditation, and hypnosis are described as forms of psychophysiological self-regulation.[23] Persons can and do learn to control their muscle tension, their respiration, and even their blood pressure and their experience of pain. The results from these procedures are generally explained in terms of reinforcement or cybernetic theory. They can be construed also as acts of will, that is, as conscious acts of intentional self-control.

Depending upon *the object willed*, one might speak of the will to live (Schopenhauer), the will to self-affirmation (Spinoza), the will to power (Nietzsche), the will to superiority (Adler), the will to pleasure (Freud's pleasure principle), the will to adapt (Hartman), the will to competence (Robert White), the will to achieve (McClelland's need to achieve), or the will to meaning (Viktor Frankl).

Frankl wrote in *The Will To Meaning*[24] that one is either content with power or intent on pleasure only if one's primary will to meaning has been frustrated. The more basic human motivation is striving to find and fulfill meaning and purpose. Like happiness, even self-actualization is an effect of fulfillment of the will to meaning.

What we will directs our destiny. We are not determined by our genetic dispositions (temperament), personality type, nor by historical events or present circumstances, not even by environmental disasters. We can transcend to some degree all such constraints and contingencies. In this sense, "will" is the opposite of fate. Fate expresses the idea of something happening to us, whereas will expresses the notion that we make things happen. To some extent I control my fate by my will. That is because my intentions guide and direct my thinking and behavior, just as my will influences what and how I feel. Emotions accompany our goal-directed behavior as Carl Rogers observed.[25] The nature and intensity of these feelings is a function of what we want, how important it is to us, and how successful we are achieving it.

To assert *the primacy of will* over intellect, emotion, and behavior is another way of emphasizing being over knowing, feeling, and doing. To be human is to be conscious of our experience. More than that, to be human is to consciously will certain outcomes. *Intentional consciousness* is a defining characteristic of human nature and human experience. I have concluded it is one of the most fundamental characteristics of being human, second only to our finitude and freedom, both of which it presupposes.

I agree also with philosophers such as Augustine, Duns Scotus, Boehme, Schelling, Schopenhauer, and Nietzsche that "will" is an ontological reality, not merely a psychological phenomenon. Striving toward something (*conatus*) is the essence of what it means to be. Willing makes a being what it is, so that if willing disappears, the thing itself disappears. Without willing, dynamic living is reduced to an inert existence. Thus the defining characteristic of being human is this dimension of willing or striving. What I will makes me what I essentially am; I am essentially my strivings. My willing is also the power of my being, my courage to be, and what gives my life its vitality.[26] It is my intentionality that defines my being. To will is to be and to be is to will. Hamlet's ultimate question, "To be or not to be?" indicates that even non-being may involve an act of will.

By *intentionality* phenomenologists mean that our awareness is always the awareness of something. There is always an object of our consciousness.[27] While I endorse that meaning, I am using intentionality in a different sense here as the experience of freely choosing to act in a specific way at a given time and place to accomplish a particular objective. In this respect, the object of states of consciousness is their aim.

This experience of willing is not a subjective illusion as Hobbes implied.[28] Neither is willing an "explanatory fiction" as B. F. Skinner claimed of all internal states. It is neither a figment of my imagination, a neurotic fantasy, a superstitious myth, a delusion, nor merely wishful thinking to assert that I have the experience of willing something. It is a very real experience, and a defining characteristic of the experience of being human empirically and ontologically.

This human experience of willing is also a major source of existential anxiety because we are responsible for what we will, and we cannot evade this responsibility nor the necessity of making decisions. Moreover, there are always consequences of our choices. There are also moral laws that stipulate causes and consequences, just as there are physical laws governing the universe. As an illustration, in contrast to a legalistic, behavioral interpretation of the Book of Proverbs, Donald Capps interprets Proverbs as providing a vision of reality ordered by moral laws comparable to empirical laws of cause and effect. Proverbs conveys confidence and trust in a moral world and encourages moral development and the formation of moral character.[29] One need not be Hindu to affirm a law of karma. Jesus taught that as we sow, so shall we reap (Lk. 19:21–22), albeit with a different meaning than the Hindu concept.

When we will something we have made a decision to bring it into being. We have decided to pursue one goal or path in lieu of another. To will some purpose is to make an ethical decision that it is desirable to strive for this specific end as a good to bring about. We make a choice among alternative values when we select a particular objective or a specific course of action. Along the way, we choose secondary objectives as steps to our ultimate goal, like a star by which to navigate our ship to the destination we want to reach.

Theories of ethics vary according to whether an act is considered ethical because it achieves a desired good (teleological ethics), because it fulfills an obligation or duty (deontological ethics), or because it expresses love (agapist ethics).[30] But they assume in common some degree of freedom in decision making, that is, some freedom of will.

Absolute freedom is not a prerequisite in order to make ethical decisions. Neither is it possible. Only if I were by nature infinite could I have absolute freedom. Contrary to the claim of the Hindu religion, I do not believe that my essential nature is infinite (Atman) identical with the divine (Brahman). I am essentially both finite and free. My finitude limits my freedom. Therein lies the source of both existential anxiety and the moral ambiguity of human existence. Human moral experience is the experience of willing limited by finitude. Our limited choices and conflicting intentions contribute to the stress of decision making.

To will something is to make up your mind, but not primarily in the sense of changing what you think. To will something is to make a decision, to embrace a mission, to take up a cause, to respond to a calling, or to fulfill one's destiny. What one is, one becomes through the cause to which one's life is devoted. It is always up to us to decide what to do. Decisions are inescapable, and we are responsible for our decisions to the degree we could have chosen otherwise.

The latter statement reaffirms that human freedom is conditional freedom, not absolute. One of the limiting conditions is one's level of awareness. To complement Otto Rank's notion that change in therapy occurs as a result of the client's conscious act of will, Leslie Farber spoke of both conscious and unconscious dimensions of willing.[31] The distinction between the two dimensions is suggested by such contrasts as being able to consciously will going to bed, but being unable to will oneself to sleep; or consciously to will to be assertive, but being unable to will courage; or to consciously will to be knowledgeable, but not being able to will wisdom. Appeals to effort and determination may influence conscious acts of will directed toward specific aims, but they are not effective with the unconscious dimension of willing. This insight about unconscious willing helps us appreciate the conditioning influence of unconscious wishes and desires on conscious choices and decisions.

Rollo May suggested that the first phase of the act of willing is a wish to influence the future in a meaningful way. One may not be aware of the antecedent wish, but the wish or desire is what initiates the process of willing. Commitment and choice are further stages in the act of willing that culminates in action.[32]

Building on the insights from both May and Farber, another existential psychotherapist, Irvin Yalom postulates two components or *two phases of willing*. Human behavior is initiated through unconscious wishing and it is subsequently enacted through conscious choice. Both wishing and choosing are stages in the complete experience of willing. The will is defined as the combination of desire and decision. Both are necessary antecedents of behavior. Stated another way, the direct cause of human behavior is an act of will that, in turn, is a function of both desires and decisions.[33] This definition implies that neither a desire nor a decision alone is sufficient to cause a human action. Conscious, intentional action ensues not simply because one wishes it or wants it, but also because one chooses it or makes a decision to do it. Self-directing deeds are prompted by both dreams and decisions.

The therapeutic implication of this biphasic conception of the experience of willing is that we need to attend to both unconscious wishes and conscious decisions. With respect to the former, it is important to recognize that *wishing and feeling* are related. Yalom writes: "One's capacity to wish is automatically facilitated if one is helped to feel. Wishing requires feeling. If one's wishes are based on something other than feelings—for example, on rational deliberations or moral imperatives—then they are no longer wishes but 'shoulds' or 'oughts', and one is blocked from communicating with one's real self."[34]

An unfortunate implication of this view is that my values and obligations are not a part of my real self, or that conscience is not a central part of authentic being. Instead, one's real self is defined by feelings. Perhaps this limitation could be overcome and Yalom's insight relating wishing and feeling appreciated by speaking of moral experiences of duty as an awareness of "felt obligations." Since feelings are meaningful or "felt meanings," one of the meanings of a feeling may be the sense of obligation expressed.

Yalom recognizes that while the experience of feeling may be prerequisite to wishing, the two are not identical. One can feel without wishing, and consequently, without willing.[35] Impulsive acts of a sensual nature and "crimes of passion" constitute examples of behaviors determined by feelings.

While it is important to evoke affect in psychotherapy, there is no evidence that the arousal of emotion per se is the active mechanism of change.[36] On the other hand, a purely cognitive or intellectual approach to therapy without affective engagement omits the "corrective emotional experience" that Franz Alexander noted as a necessary condition for a long term therapeutic outcome.[37] Since wishing includes an affective component as a motivational force, if affect is blocked, so is the experience of one's wishes, hence the entire process of willing cannot be initiated and the experience of willing remains unactualized. One may not feel like a genuine agent of action in part because one has stopped feeling anything, or because one has inhibited those feelings that prompt one to act humanly such as feelings of compassion, courage, and empathy.

The experience of willing is a unique domain of psychological experience. Willing cannot be reduced to feeling, thinking, or acting. Nor can willing be reduced to wishing. The *second* component of the experience of willing to emphasize is a conscious choice or decision. Between the desire and the act is the decision. Action ensues not simply because one wishes it, but because one makes a decision to act. "To decide means to commit oneself to a course of action."[38] The failure to act reflects that no genuine decision has been made. Ultimately the experience of willing is choosing among alternative courses of action.

As the second component of willing, deciding is a more conscious experience than wishing. Being more conscious, decisions may be influenced more by thoughtful deliberations and rational judgments, including moral reasoning and insights into the dimensions of experience of which one may be presently only dimly aware. Consequently, there is a direct link between *thinking and willing*, or between insight and decisions.

Insights may activate or liberate the decisional phase of willing. For example, believing that I need to change in order to meet my needs and others' needs, and that I have the power to change are both insights that facilitate decision-making. Similarly, recognition of the relative risks and gains of both changing and not changing, and knowing that I am the one who must change the situation I have partly created are insights that help me to make a decision.[39] Finally, insights from moral reasoning into one's obligations and responsibilities are important considerations that enable one to decide. Since most decisions involve criteria and standards by which they are made, and these standards function as guiding values, ethical reasoning will facilitate decision-making.

Nevertheless, while thinking and insight facilitate a decision, insight alone does not produce behavior change. In order to act, one must make a decision to trigger the action. What translates insight into action is the decision. The will accomplishes what the intellect alone cannot do. Since both desire and decision are elements of the experience of willing, we may speak of willing as the bridge between desire and behavior, between the dream and the deed. Thus, the will becomes the decisive factor in the process of behavior change. Self-directed change and self-regulating behavior are ultimately the consequences of an act of will.

This view of willing as both unconscious wishing and conscious choosing implies that a central mechanism of change in the therapeutic process is the client's eventual decision to commit to a course of action among available alternatives. In other words, it is as important to own one's decisions as it is to own one's feelings.[40] All behavior is not a function of self-determining decisions consciously made, but intentional and self-regulating behavior requires conscious choices and commitments to act.

Consequently, a strategic goal of psychotherapy is to liberate the will from those factors that could, would, and do determine or limit it and make one a victim of fate. A liberated will allows one to become a person who creates and directs one's future through deliberate decisions and free choices. Insofar as human willing is central to the change desired in therapy, then the therapist must attempt to influence the magnitude, direction, and duration of the client's willing. I concur with Yalom that therapy is effective to the degree it influences the client's will.[41]

While this may sound both logical and straight forward, the process of coming to a decision is neither simple nor easy. More often than not, significant life decisions, such as getting married or divorced, or changing careers, are difficult decisions fraught with conflict. The psychodynamic concept of *resistance* recognizes the difficulties involved in decision-making. An existential analysis helps one appreciate the numerous *obstacles to making decisions*. These include perceptions that one has very limited options or no alternatives whatsoever; the lack of clear criteria or values by which one can or should decide; feelings of guilt about wanting a change; the belief that one does not have the right or authority to decide; a lack of confidence in one's ability to make good decisions; the fear of failure that one will make the wrong decision; fears one will regret a decision after it is made; a felt incapacity to decide (a paralysis of will); the desire to be excused or rescued rather than accept personal responsibility for change; a perfectionistic attitude that there is only one right decision one must make; or the fear of losing the approval of others by deciding one way versus another. Moreover, a current decision to change implies that one could have decided otherwise before, hence it calls into question a previous decision that may have led to negative consequences or even to a wasted life for which one must assume responsibility and a burden of guilt that seems unbearable. Finally, the belief that there is no genuine forgiveness or that one can do nothing to atone for a mistake, not even by altering the present or future, are obstacles to making a decision to change. These are some of the factors that contribute to the stress of decision-making and to conflicted decisions.[42]

The conflicts and stress associated with decisions lead many persons to avoid them. There are many *ways of avoiding decisions*. One may give up making the decision and delegate it to someone else (a parent, spouse, friend, employer, clergy, therapist, government, church, etc.). By delegating decisions one can reduce or escape the risks involved and avoid being held accountable for the decisions made by another person or agency. Alternatively, one can give up one's freedom to choose by trusting fate, chance, karma, or some other impersonal force. One can also devalue the alternative rejected or excluded by the decision. Or one can settle for less by lowering expectations.[43] In these and many other ways persons attempt to avoid making responsible decisions both in and out of therapy.

In more extreme instances, persons develop decisional disorders that are described more commonly as "mental disorders." Examples are impulsive and compulsive disorders; passive dependent, narcissistic, or anti-social personality disorders; anxiety or depression over a felt inability to change so that one remains tied to what one loathes, or suffers guilt over wanting a change. These are volitional disorders, not merely aberrations of thought, feeling, or behavior. They are *disorders of the will* both in magnitude and direction.

Decisional Conflicts: What Do You Want?

Sometimes our decisions are based on calculations of costs and benefits. We apply a kind of hedonic calculus weighing various pleasures against potential pains. There are often trade offs required in our decisions. We may even want two things that are incompatible with each other. That is, we want both, but we can't have both ("You can't have your cake and eat it too"). Psychologists call this an approach-approach conflict.

Alternatively, we may want to avoid two things, neither of which is desirable, as expressed in the question, "Which is worse? The devil you know, or the devil you don't know?" This is an example of the avoidance-avoidance conflict. You'd like to avoid both, but you may have to accept one of the undesirable alternatives.

On the other hand, we may want to approach just one thing, but also avoid aspects of it. This situation is described as an approach-avoidance conflict. This state of being both attracted to and repelled by someone or something is called ambivalence. Mixed feelings and contradictory desires are very common in human experience. Alternatively, we may want two things, both of which have positive and negative aspects (a double approach-avoidance conflict).

All of these types of conflicts among wants may result in indecision, impulsive decisions, and emotional distress. They are manifestations of a conflicted will and conflicted decisions.[44] Our approach to God may be fraught with similar conflicts. Motives for a religious or spiritual life are often mixed. It is all a matter of what we want or will.

There is a connection between how we feel and what we want. Many persons are unhappy or angry because they don't get what they want. Others are unhappy because they do get what they want. The problem is that what they want cannot possibly bring them the sustained joy they desire. Still others are frustrated because they just don't know what they want. Or they may be afraid of the responsibility of making a choice, or too depressed to be able to decide.

What do you want out of life? Do you know? The very question betrays a somewhat egocentric orientation. We ask what we want, not what God wants. And usually we ask what we can get, rather than what we can give. Most human wants are like that. To expect otherwise is to deny the reality of human sin.

The question also betrays a kind of pride, as if we were fully conscious of all our strivings and completely in control. Dynamic psychology tells us we have unconscious wishes and aims. We have intentions and goals of which we are only barely aware, most of which are quite self-serving, and many even contrary to our conscious intentions. But that insight doesn't seem to keep us from frequently claiming that we know absolutely what we want. We may know what we want consciously, but not be aware of our other contradictory desires. Consciously, we may want to seek first the kingdom of God, but remain unconsciously unwilling to surrender. To be a disciple is a matter of both intellect and will, and it involves the reconciliation of conscious choices and unconscious wishes.

The direction one's life takes depends significantly upon what one wills. Three of the most *common human desires* are pleasure, success, and service. Some people think they want pleasure more than anything else. Since we only go around once in life, let's grab all the gusto we can. Most Christians don't believe we go around more than once, contrary to the idea of reincarnation, though if pressed, we could all probably think of someone who acts like he was once part of a horse.

It is the hedonistic paradox that tells us the conscious pursuit of happiness is the major obstacle to attaining it. Søren Kierkegaard characterized the pursuit of pleasure as the aesthetic life. He tried it for several years. It ended in the despair that he described as a sickness unto death in his book bearing that title to express its futility.[45] A life dominated by the *will to pleasure* ends in meaninglessness and despair. As Kierkegaard described it, despair is ultimately not willing to be oneself.

Instead of wanting pleasure, other persons have a strong *will to succeed.* They want worldly success with its attendant wealth, power, and fame. American capitalism is fed by these desires. It also feeds them. Yet the fulfillment of this desire for earthly success eludes us, like the carrot dangling at the end of a pole tied to the harness of the mule who keeps on straining toward it, never to attain it because it is a moving target. Some people go through life behaving like mules chasing elusive carrots.

While I may wish both pleasure and success for others, these two wants are most often selfish desires. What concerns me most is my own pleasure and my own success. As a result, I am very likely to see others as competitors and potential threats due to my egoistic perspective.

A more altruistic and noble desire is to focus upon others rather than solely upon self. This is expressed in the *will to serve,* and to serve something greater than self. The emergence of this desire signals the beginnings of a reconciled life, or at least a moral life. I may want to serve my family or friends, my employer or union or professional association, my church, my political party or country, even humankind. This is an ethical way of life that emphasizes duty in contrast to the philosophies of hedonism and materialism, the twin pursuits of pleasure and success.

A life of service has its rewards. These include expressions of esteem and gratitude from those whom we serve, and the satisfaction of making a meaningful contribution to the betterment of humankind. Yet even those who have lived an exemplary life of dedicated service may wonder, Was it all worth it? Really worth it? We may even despair as we face the end of a life of service and a future in which we will no longer be able to serve. Is there not more to life than this? It is an existential question about life's meaning that my father asked poignantly when he despaired about dying of cancer and realized he could no longer continue to work beyond his fifty-four years of service as a dedicated physician.

Most persons don't want to die. Among all human wants, that is probably among the least popular. Most of us hope for eternal life, just as we want infinite knowledge and endless joy. The Hindu faith affirms that what all persons really want is liberation from all that is finite. What we truly want is infinite being, infinite consciousness, and infinite bliss.[46] The claim of Hinduism is that we can get what we want, for these are all attributes of the transcendent god the Hindus call Brahman. These experiences are enjoyed by those who unite with Brahman by realizing one's true Self called Atman, who is the one god incarnate within all persons, the One in the many. In the Hindu faith, persons are understood as essentially the many manifestations of this "one infinite reality."

Seek First the Kingdom of God

Jesus taught that we can have what we want. But we must choose carefully, for most human desires end in disillusionment and despair. Infinite joy and eternal life are experienced by those who want the right thing. And what is that? Seek first the kingdom of God and his righteousness (Mt. 6:31–33/Lk. 12:31). Strive to do the will of God. That is the key to a reconciled life, the pathway to the good life.

Note that Jesus' view of the good life is an intentional life of commitment and action, not merely or even primarily a contemplative life of the mind. His teaching is in contrast to the philosopher Descartes who thought that what matters most is the intellect. The most unique endowment of persons, Descartes wrote, was their capacity to think ("I think, therefore I am"). Contemporary cognitive psychologists convey a similar message. So do Christian counselors who emphasize changes in beliefs as the condition of a therapeutic outcome.

Jesus of Nazareth was more of a spiritual genius than a philosopher. He taught that *the human will is paramount*, not the mind. The will symbolizes the uniquely human capacity to make commitments and choices. We define ourselves through our choices. We become who we are by our solitary decisions. We are therefore responsible for who we are and for what we become.

Jesus' message is clear. I am not reconciled with myself, others, or with God by what I know. When all that can be known is known, there still remains the necessity of decision. The will performs what the intellect alone cannot do. I must make a choice. I must choose to live in the light of knowledge or remain in the darkness of ignorance. I must make a commitment to act. It is through such commitments and decisions that I become fully human. And it is because I am responsible for my decisions and actions that I am accountable for their consequences.

Accountable to whom? To myself, to others, and to God. The most important of these is to stand right with God. We are what we are before God. And only before God do we realize how far we are from the person we ought to be and what we ought to want and will. Before God all persons are equal—equally responsible, and all need to repent. It is only as an individual face-to-face with God that repentance makes sense. It is alone before the Eternal that I realize my responsibility to become an individual through time.

To be aware of my eternal responsibility before God is to be conscious of living as an individual. I become an integrated personality, a whole and reconciled person by ultimately willing only one thing. I become fully human by willing the divine will. It is by loving God ultimately and serving God only that I resolve all my ambivalence and conflicting motives, correct my misplaced priorities, and resist compromises of conscience, the pressure of the crowd, and utopian promises of social salvation. It is by holding fast to God that my own reconciliation is actualized. Being reconciled with God, I can then become more reconciled with myself and an agent of reconciliation for others.

I have said previously that our relationship with God transforms us through love, faith, and hope. God changes what I think, how I feel, and what I do. I wish to add now that God effects all those changes by transforming my selfish desires into sanctified strivings. *God redeems my will.* God transforms what I want. God changes this intentional core of my being and consequently my thinking, feeling, and doing.

The Spirit of God works within us through love, faith, and hope to transform our motives and aims. Biological drives and psychological needs no longer predominate. Economic and social motives become secondary. Spiritual motives become primary. God's will becomes our will. We seek first the kingdom of God.

And the more we do, the less anxious we become about tomorrow (Mt. 6:33–34/ Lk. 12:31–32).

Reconciled with God, we become motivated to be servants of God rather than striving to be counted among the rich and famous (Mt. 6:24/Lk. 16:13; Mt. 6:11). We worship instead the Lord our God and we serve only God (Mt. 4:10/Lk. 4:8). In all that we do, we strive to serve God without fear, in holiness and righteousness (Lk. 1:73–75). Brother Lawrence expressed it this way: In everything you do, practice the presence of God. Be resolved to make loving God the purpose of everything you do.[47]

The truly reconciled person gives without expecting anything in return (Lk. 6:35). Jesus urged us to do good because it is good to do, not because it may bring us public recognition, prestige, or praise from others (Mt. 6:1–8). It is not finite aspirations such as prestige or power, or fame or fortune that claim the allegiance of the righteous. It is rather *to will the will of God*, to love the Lord my God with all my heart and soul and mind and strength. The result is reconciliation with myself and others and eternal life with God, a goal more worthy to be desired than all the glitter, glamour, and gold of this world (Lk. 10:25–28/Mt. 22:34–40/Mk. 12:28–31). Jesus cautioned us that we must not delight in riches or the comforts of earthly life, nor allow the cares of this world to choke the pathway through which the Spirit breathes into us the very breath of life, inspiring us to become fully human (Mt. 13:1–9/Mk. 4:1–9/Lk. 8:4–8).

The Call to Repentance: A Reconciled Will

Jesus cautioned us also about certain intentions or *motives that are unrighteous*. His own resistance to the tempting satisfaction of physical needs suggests that a materialistic philosophy of pleasure is unacceptable: "One does not live by bread alone, but by every word that proceeds from the mouth of God" (Mt. 4:1–4). His resistance to the temptation of power (Mt. 4:5–7) suggests that the will to power is rejected. And his resistance to the temptation for personal glory in exchange for the worship of false gods suggests this too is an unacceptable motivation (Mt. 4:8–10).

Jesus rebuked lovers of money and those who worshiped Mammon (Mt. 6:24/ Lk. 16:13), hence the pursuit of wealth or worldly success is unacceptable as an ultimate goal. Neither revenge nor retaliation is acceptable. When he was arrested, Jesus told his disciples to put away their swords (Mt. 26:47–56/Mk. 14:43–50/Lk. 22:47–53).

Neither did Jesus advocate freedom from suffering as an ultimate goal. Envy and hatred, pride and prejudice, these too are unacceptable motives. They are all examples of either destructive feelings or wanting the wrong things in life. They are symptoms of an unreconciled will.

Of course, God grants us the freedom to choose whatever we want. If you want to be angry, you can be bitter your whole life. If you want revenge, you can get that too. But if you get it, what have you gained, and what have you lost by getting it? If you want wealth, power, or pleasure, you are free to pursue those ambitions as well. And if you want to decline God's invitation to reconciliation, you are free to do that too. It is a choice many persons make in life. Comparing the kingdom of God to a marriage feast, Jesus said that many who were invited decided not to come (Lk. 14:15–24/Mt. 22:1–14).

Jesus taught that to be reconciled we must make a decision. We must *make a commitment and choose*. Divided loyalties create divisions within the human personality, not just between persons. Just as a house divided cannot stand, neither can a person who wants contradictory things (Mt. 12:22–26/Mk. 3:22–30/Lk. 11: 14–23). We cannot worship both God and greed (Mt. 6:24/Lk. 16:13; Lk. 16:14–15). Jesus said, "He who is not with me is against me" (Mt. 12:30/Lk. 11:23; Mk. 9:40; Lk. 9:50). This is a necessary choice. It is the most important decision of our lives.

Making a decision is one of the meanings of *repentance*. To repent is not merely to feel sorry or to feel remorse or guilt. Nor is it merely a change in one's thinking or behavior. Primarily it is a change of will, or metaphorically, a change of heart. To repent means that I decide to stop asserting my own will and start willing the will of God. Most of us don't need assertiveness training; we need training in humility and repentance. Jesus taught that repentance was the key to entry into the kingdom of God (Mk. 1:15; 6:12; Mt. 21:28–32).

The consequence of repentance is both holiness and peace. To be holy is to bear the fruits that befit repentance (Mt. 3:8/Lk. 3:8; Mt. 7:15–20; 12:33; 21:43). Holiness is the result of repentance. This is another way of saying that commitments have consequences. Motives matter. Intentions are important—what's in your heart, not just what's in your head or gut.

To be holy does not mean to be morally perfect. It does mean to be spiritually motivated. It means to hunger and thirst for righteousness (Mt. 5:6). Both hunger and thirst are physiological drives basic to our survival. By selecting these terms, Jesus meant to convey how critically important it is for us to make our aim in life the kingdom of God. To strive for righteousness is equally essential to both our survival and to our sanctification.

The Work of the Holy Spirit

Righteous behavior is evident in those who are inspired and guided by the Holy Spirit (Lk. 2:27) and baptized by the Holy Spirit (Lk. 3:16/Mk. 1:8/Mt. 3:11). To be inspired by someone is to be both energized and directed by them, that is, to be motivated by them. The Christian is motivated by the message and ministry of Jesus and by the divine Spirit working through love, faith, and hope.

The role of the divine Spirit in changing our desires is important to emphasize if we are to avoid the error of defining holiness as moral perfection and the destructive consequences of legalism and works righteousness. It also constitutes an antidote to superficial appeals to "will power" in order to effect behavioral change. The capacity to will the will of God is given by God to those who are inspired by God. Thus it is not solely or even primarily the result of an act that originates in human striving. Striving to do God's will is itself evidence of the movement of God in my life. To will the will of God is to be blessed by God with a gift, a reconciled life in harmony with the divine. Thus the appropriate response is gratitude, not pride. Faith is not a creation of the human will such as "a will to believe." Faith is a spiritual gift. So is the reconciled will.

Whole-Hearted Commitment

The term used most frequently by Jesus to express the conative dimension of human experience is the symbol of the "heart." Jesus counseled us to love God with all our heart, totally and completely, with our whole being (Mt. 2:34–38/Mk. 12:28– 30/Lk. 10:25–28). Our love for God is expressed through our commitment to will what God wills.

Jesus taught that just as evil thoughts come out of the heart, that is, from evil intentions, so also goodness comes from the heart (Mt. 15:18–19; Mk. 7:21–22; Lk. 6:45). One of the criticisms made of good-hearted people, usually by cynics, is that the road to hell is paved with good intentions. Perhaps, but more likely it is paved by selfish desires. It seems even more doubtful that the road to heaven is paved with evil intentions. Some people are evil, not merely maladjusted. They have a hardened heart. Others are deep down good. Their being has been transformed. They reflect the righteousness of God as reconciling persons who live according to God's reconciling will.

The point here is that what we do and how we act also influence our motives. Your heart will be where your treasure is located (Mt. 6:19–21/Lk. 12:33–34; Lk. 14:33, 18:22). If you want to know what your intentions are and what you are willing, look at your calendar and checkbook. How are you spending your time and money? By changing our behavior we can strengthen our will in one direction or another.

When I am honest with myself, I recognize that my behavior is inconsistent. The good that I would, I do not do. Similarly, fleeting thoughts enter my mind and leave as quickly as they came. Feelings come and go. It is only the human will that endures—our deepest commitments. It is by my acts of will that I steady myself. It is my commitment to God that I must hold on to in faith. Thus faith is not merely belief, nor primarily a feeling. It involves an act of will. Jesus confronts us with a decision. We either strive to follow his teachings or we don't.

It takes courage to commit our lives to become a disciple of Jesus of Nazareth. It requires a leap of faith across a chasm of so many competing philosophies of life and multiple causes for doubt and cynicism. It is also true, however, that our commitment to God gives us the courage we need, in addition to wisdom and compassion and the joy our heart desires.

While some individuals can point to a once-in-a-lifetime decision for Christ, for most individuals *conversion* is more like a gradual and continuous process rather than a momentary state. The spirit may be willing, but the "flesh" is weak. We need to practice daily those holy habits that sustain our commitment to will the will of God. These include our worship and prayer, study and service. It is especially through regular meditation on Scripture and contemplative prayer that God strengthens our will to do God's will.[48]

We express our will in what we pray for. Jesus taught us what to pray for in the Lord's Prayer (Mt. 6:9–13/Lk. 11:2–4). It includes petitions for our physical needs. We are not, after all, disembodied spirits. We are to pray to God not to be led into temptation and to be delivered from evil. In this prayer we express our repentance in the petition to be forgiven as we forgive others. And the Lord's Prayer is a petition that God's kingdom may come and God's will be done. Thus in the one prayer that Jesus taught, he taught us to pray to will the will of God, and to pray to God for the strength and the courage to accept God's will.

Usually what we pray for expresses what we consider to be most important in life. There are so many things in life we can take seriously and pursue passionately. That which we take most seriously functions as the object of our faith if it concerns us ultimately. What we care about reveals quite a bit about who we are and what our religion really is. That which concerns us ultimately defines our experience of the holy. That which I care about most passionately becomes my god, the ultimate cause for the sake of which I act.

Depending upon its nature, this god may either heal me or destroy me. Any preliminary goal that I choose will become destructive if I make it paramount. Any finite aim can become one of infinite passion and overwhelm me. Any relative value can become absolute and the cause of my undoing. Temporal purposes can function as if they were of eternal consequence, and particular cares can be treated as concerns of universal scope. Contingent strivings can become unconditional by claiming my total allegiance and promising me total fulfillment. Such is the human capacity for idolatry and the range of the idols of destruction.

Total devotion to any aim that is preliminary or particular, finite or temporal, relative or contingent causes human misery and ends in disillusionment if not despair. We must choose carefully, consciously, and intentionally the god we surrender to. After all, less important than the fact that we lived is what we lived for. That is the heart of the matter.

Purity of Heart

Søren Kierkegaard wrote that purity of heart means to will one thing—to will the good.[49] To will only the good means we do not will it for any other reason—not for any reward, nor out of fear of punishment. Nor do we will it half heartedly like double-minded people. Jesus said that we are to love God with all our hearts, souls, minds, and strength. Total allegiance and complete loyalty are needed to be fully reconciled with God. And to be reconciled with myself in the conative domain of my experience is to strive toward this one ultimate, unifying goal. All other strivings subside. All other concerns become secondary to my one ultimate concern to will the will of God.

If purity of heart is to will only one thing, namely, to will the will of God, then as we progress in this sacred striving we can expect to experience a greater sense of God's presence and power. Even more, we can anticipate the greatest of all joys, communion with God: "Blessed are the pure in heart for they will see God" (Mt. 5:8). Purity of heart is a beatitude. To want what God wants is to be truly blessed. Jesus encouraged us to remember always that God knows what we need before we ask. We are granted what we need according to God's will. But that may not be what we want, unless we want what God wants. God does not always grant us what we want; God gives us what we need.

Just as holy habits are an important part of the Christian life, so too are such holy hopes and sacred strivings. The most holy aim of all is to will the will of God. This is the true passion for excellence. This is the motive *summa cum laude*. This is the striving that is sacrosanct. There is no greater good than to will the will of God.

If we are truly ambitious and the high achievers we pride ourselves as being, let us strive first, foremost, and always for the kingdom of God and God's righteousness, for this is the most noble and challenging of all human aims (Mt. 6:33/Lk. 12:31; Mk. 1:15). The consecrated Christian strives toward this goal by emulating Jesus, as expressed in the hymn, "Lord I want to be like Jesus, in my heart." We become more like him as we are motivated by him and adopt his intention of willing the will of God. Not my will, O God, but Thine be done.

Other Views on the Concept of the Will

This emphasis upon the human will is really nothing new. It has historical roots in the synthesis of Aristotelian teleology and biblical faith achieved by St. Thomas Aquinas in the Middle Ages.[50] Strivings for sanctification through the power of God's Spirit were evident also in the Protestant ethic of the seventeenth century and in John Wesley's theology in the mid-eighteenth century.

In the eighteenth century this conative dimension was stressed particularly in Immanuel Kant's philosophy. Kant emphasized the sense of moral obligation and practical (ethical) reason. Based in part on Kant's moral philosophy, in the nineteenth century Albrecht Ritschl grounded religion in conscience and moral judgments of value. Religious beliefs are justified by religious experience, but this was a moral experience of an ethical will rather than Schleiermacher's "consciousness of absolute dependence." One's present experiences of forgiveness and reconciliation are primary and include the social dimension of creating on earth the kingdom of God through loving service and struggles for justice.[51] It is in and through my own ethical consciousness of making value judgments and moral decisions that I grasp and I am grasped by the will of God. From this perspective, to speak of Jesus as the Christ is to affirm that Jesus has the value of God. This is a Christology grounded in a theory of value and value judgments.

The emphasis upon this conative dimension finds additional support in existential philosophers such as Heidegger and Jaspers, in novelists as Sartre and Camus, in religious existentialists as Kierkegaard, Bultmann, and Buber, and in psychologists as Otto Rank, Roberto Assagioli, Viktor Frankl, Rollo May, Gerald

May, and Irvin Yalom. They share in common an emphasis upon human freedom and personal involvement as concrete individuals making value commitments and ethical decisions. They share an emphasis upon the central role of the human will.

Paul Tillich criticized this conative view of faith as a voluntaristic distortion.[52] My own reply is first that Tillich's criticism is justified concerning the examples of distorted faith he mentions. Second, his examples are relatively extreme, and a more moderate position taken here is that the experience of willing is primary, but not the exclusive domain of either faith or being itself. God transforms us preeminently, but not exclusively, through this intentional domain of experience. God transforms us primarily, but not solely, through this conative domain of conscience. God redeems my will. I become more reconciled with God by increasingly willing the will of God in grateful response to God's healing love. In this lifelong process my selfish goals are gradually overcome, though never replaced completely by sanctified strivings.

It is God who redeems my will. No human act of will can overcome our own existential estrangement. This is the meaning of the concept of the "bondage of the will."[53] It is another way of highlighting the need of human nature for divine grace and a way of avoiding the voluntaristic distortion of faith that Tillich rightly criticized as one of the forms of self-salvation.

As Tillich has shown, and I have noted previously, both thoughts and feelings presuppose being. So do intentions and acts of will. Intentionality must start with being; it cannot get behind it. An act of will is based on being, and it cannot leave this foundation. In order to will one must first be. Willing is a process attributable to only living beings. Only the behaviors of existing beings may be considered as intentional acts. We may attribute purpose to things, such as the purpose of a machine, but living beings have intentions.

Intentions become more conscious in human beings, hence subject to processes of self-reflection and critical evaluation. Consequently, human behavior becomes more self-determining, transcending, and free. Through the process of conscious deliberations of alternative courses of action, persons become capable of exercising their wills to choose one goal among several possibilities.[54] Once a decision is made, the selected goal becomes a final cause for the sake of which behavior is intended and enacted.[55] This perspective expresses both a teleological and voluntaristic psychology, upon which a theory of psychotherapy may be constructed that emphasizes the relationship between mental health and moral decisions. Psychotherapy becomes a process of deliberate decision-making based upon a model of persons as decision makers, who have conditional freedom which they exercise and maximize through their own conscious willing, choosing, and acting. Including the concept of the will ensures that one's theory of psychotherapy will preserve a degree of freedom in the process of change and affirm human agency and personal responsibility for change.

Jesus did not teach that the chief cause of human suffering was ignorance, or that our salvation was to be found through reason or corrected thinking. The basic problem is neither a learning deficit nor faulty learning. The basic problem lies in the human will. It is human self-centeredness and idolatrous commitments that cause so much unnecessary suffering. To become reconciled, persons need to be reoriented in values, goals, loyalties, and ultimate concerns. Self-will must be transformed to be reconciled with God's will.

Moreover, any truth gained through practical (ethical) reasoning and moral conscience is also ambiguous truth, with limited certitude and significance due in part to the conflicts within the cognitive element of acts of will, and because of the estrangement of the human will from the will of God.

Persons who emphasize the experience of willing are likely to view Scripture as a source of moral guidance and Jesus as a teacher of religious ethics. Another perspective is to appreciate Jesus as the one who revealed the will of God, and our Savior by virtue of his own inspiring example of a human will reconciled with the divine will. In this view, Jesus was unique by virtue of his decision to accept God's goal of reconciliation as his own life goal. Their relation is one of shared purpose rather than identical natures. This is an expression of a teleological Christology.

There is a danger, of course, that Jesus' revelations about the kingdom of God will lapse into mere ethical teachings or moral injunctions. What prevents that is the meaning of the kingdom of God as a symbol of the real objective acts of God in human experience.[56] God acts in human history—in yours and in mine. In this action, ethical guidelines are revealed, but so are an ontological reality and a transforming power experienced in our relationship with God. Similarly, God's love and majesty are revealed, which elicit affective responses of compassion, courage, joy, and thanksgiving. The kingdom of God is an experienced reality of divine and human reconciliation, not merely a depository of ethical wisdom.

By way of summary, the concept of will integrates both unconscious wishes and conscious decisions; it affirms enough freedom to make choices; sufficient rationality to make discriminating and moral judgments among alternatives; the capacity to envision a future determined in part by one's present decisions; and the ability to bring about outcomes one intends through conscious commitments and selected actions.

The will is not, however, the only domain involved in the psychological experience of reconciliation, nor are its effects unidirectional. As the wish is the initial phase of willing influenced by feeling, so conscious decisions as the second phase of willing are influenced by thinking and insight, and by encouraging, therapeutic relationships.

The reconciling therapist approaches clients as whole human beings, not as a homunculus known as the will. To ask a person "What are you doing?" is to focus upon their present behavior. To ask, "How are you feeling?" is to evoke the affective domain of experience. To ask a person, "What do you want?" is to elicit one's desires and wishes. To ask, "What do you intend to do?" is to activate their volitional capacity to will. All of these questions need to be addressed therapeutically in addition to exploring their interpersonal relationships and their ultimate concerns. By addressing these aspects one facilitates both a therapeutic encounter and holistic healing in the direction of a more reconciling life.

There is a structured meditation of the inner way[57] that expresses a similar thought. One asks repeatedly the question, "Who am I?", until one is awakened to the insight that I am neither my body, mind, nor memories, not my sensations nor my wishes, neither my thoughts, feelings, nor behavior. I am other than any of these, and more than the sum of them all. The Christian finds that something more in a reconciled relationship with God as a disciple of Jesus of Nazareth for the foundation for an authentic identity.

NOTES

1. For an archetypal perspective renewing the concept of the soul, see Hillman, J. (1975). *Re-Visioning psychology.* New York: Harper & Row, Publishers.

2. Adams, J. (1977). *Competent to counsel.* Nutley, NJ: Presbyterian and Reformed Publishing Company.

3. Practical theories of religion which define it essentially as ethics seem to support the emphasis upon behavior. Examples include the seventeenth century Deists' view of religion. See Livingston, J. (1971). *Modern Christian thought from the enlightenment to vatican II.* New York: Macmillan, pp.12–40. In the New Testament, the letter of James and 1 Corinthians 13 are classic statements of the primacy of love over faith, and of deeds over creeds.

4. Worthington (1986) concluded an exhaustive review of "religious counseling" with the following observation: "No support has been found that religious counseling has any more beneficial effects than does secular counseling in working with religious clients. In fact, little is known about what really makes religious counseling distinct from secular counseling." Commenting on that statement, Paul Giblin wrote seven years later: "Unfortunately I believe that Worthington's comment continues to ring true today, and that our profession [pastoral counseling] sorely needs increased research activity." Giblin, P. (1993). Research and pastoral counseling. In McHolland, J. (Ed.). (1993). *The future of pastoral counseling: Whom, how, and for what do we train?* (p. 134). Fairfax, VA: American Association of Pastoral Counselors. Rather than striving to demonstrate the superiority of religious counseling, perhaps it is sufficient to show it yields results comparable to secular psychotherapy.

5. Contrary to Ayn Rand's objectivist ethics, most religions do not consider selfishness a virtue. See Rand, A. (1964). *The virtue of selfishness.* New York: Penguin Books.

6. For discussion of the dynamics of work addiction, see Oates, W. (1971). *Confessions of a workaholic.* New York: World Publishing Co. Another book by a Christian psychiatrist which addresses addiction is May, G. (1988). *Addiction and grace: Love and spirituality in the healing of addictions.* San Francisco: Harper & Row.

7. Brother Lawrence (1975). *The practice of the presence of God.* Grand Rapids, MI: Baker Book House, p. 33.

8. Symptom substitution refers to the phenomenon that successful treatment of a symptom (e.g, a particular fear) without treating the psychological conflicts which are causing it may result in the appearance of another (substitute) symptom. This is a psycho-

dynamic proposition, which some behaviorists have tested and not confirmed empirically.

9. Rudolph Otto's phenomenological analysis of the religious consciousness led him to emphasize a sense of the noumenous (holy) as its essential structure. See Otto, R. (1923). *The idea of the holy.* London: Oxford University Press.

10. Tillich, P. (1951). *Systematic theology* (Vol. l). Chicago: University of Chicago Press, p. 215.

11. For an application of Taoist psychology, see Dreher, D. (1990). *The Tao of inner peace.* New York: Harper Perennial.

12. Rogers, C. (1951). *Client centered therapy.* Boston: Houghton Mifflin, p. 491.

13. Low, A. (1950). *Mental health through will-training.* Boston: The Christopher Publishing House; Rank, O. (1978). *Will therapy.* New York: W. W. Norton; May, R. (1969). *Love and will.* New York: Dell Publishing; May, G. (1982). *Will and spirit.* San Francisco: Harper and Row; Assagioli, R. (1965). *Psychosynthesis: A collection of basic writing.* New York: Arkana; and Assagioli, R. (1973). *The act of will.* New York: Arkana.

14. Yalom, I. (1980). *Existential psychotherapy.* New York: Basic Books, p. 301. It was Otto Rank who characterized the therapeutic relationship as a struggle of wills. His goal of therapy was to develop and strengthen the client's creative will (willing what one wants) in contrast to either a counter will (willing in opposition to another's will) and to a positive will (willing what one must). He spoke of the "a priori will" to emphasize it central role in therapy. (Ibid., pp. 16, 295–296.) Rank introduced the concept of will to modern psychotherapy as a correction to Freud's psychic determinism that functioned as a convenient excuse for a client to refuse responsibility, without which a positive therapeutic outcome is unlikely. In place of a model of a driven person, Rank emphasized the person as driver with a creative will. The creative will utilizes drives in addition to inhibiting them. See Rank, O. (1945). *Will therapy and truth and reality.* (J. Taft, Trans.). New York: Alfred A. Knopf, p. 111.

15. "Many psychologists believe incorrectly that if a theorist argues for freedom of the will in behavior, this must necessarily be a proreligion argument. A tough minded psychologist can be heard to say: 'If we let 'free will' get back into the description of behavior we will have to let 'God' back in too. And then 'there goes our science!'" Rychlak, J. (1981). *Introduction to personality and psychotherapy.* Boston: Houghton Mifflin Company, p. 294.

16. Psychology erroneously interprets many of its prescriptive biases as merely descriptive assertions about human behavior, according to Prilleltensky, I. (1994). *The morals and politics of psychology: Psychological discourse and the status quo.* Albany, NY: State University of New York Press, p. 25.

17. See Yalom, I. (1980). *Existential psychotherapy.* New York: Basic Books, p. 290.

18. In much of psychological literature the concept of will and free will are considered subjective illusions as Hobbes implied. (Cited by Yalom, I. [1980]. *Existential psychotherapy.* New York: Basic Books, p. 290). Some exceptions are Adler, A. (1964). *Social interest: A challenge of mankind.* New York: Capricorn Books;. Allport, G. (1961). *Pattern and growth in personality.* New York: Holt, Rinehart, and Winston; Allport, G. (1955). *Becoming: Basic considerations for a psychology of personality.* New Haven, CT: Yale University Press; and the concept of the "telosponse" in Rychlak, J. (1981). *Introduction to personality and psychotherapy: A theory construction approach.* Boston: Houghton Mifflin Company, pp. 754–808. Rychlak discusses the four types of causes used to explain human behavior and natural events (pp. 2–6). A teleological perspective based on final causes is necessary to preserve human freedom.

19. Empirical evidence for the central role of behavioral intentions as primary antecedents of behavior has been presented in considerable psychological research based upon Fishbein, M. (1972). A theory of reasoned action: Some applications and implications. In M. M. Page (Ed.), *1979 Nebraska Symposium on Motivation*. Lincoln, NE: University of Nebraska Press.

20. Roberto Assagioli suggested that the act of willing occurs in six *stages*: Intention, deliberation, decision, affirmation, planning and programming, and direction and regulation of execution. These stages reflect the *qualities* of the human will as determination and decisiveness, integrating and organizing. Insofar as purity of heart is to will one thing, Assagioli's phenomenology of the experience of willing and acts of will become relevant to understanding spiritual growth. Assagioli, R. (1973). *The act of will*. New York: Penguin Books, pp. 19–35, 135–199.

21. Here I affirm Tillich's view of "finite freedom" as the essential being of humans, hence also characteristic of our actual personality, though actualized in varying degrees. Tillich, P. (1952). *The courage to be*. New Haven, CT: Yale University Press, p. 52. For a psychological discussion of how human choice arises in behavior, see Rychlak, J. (1981). *Introduction to personality and psychotherapy*. Boston: Houghton Mifflin Company, pp. 286–300. Rychlak affirms free will as a central construct in his teleological theory.

22. May, R. (1969). *Love and will*. New York: Delta, p. 197.

23. Schwartz, M. (Ed.). (1995). *Biofeedback: A practitioner's guide* (2nd ed.). New York: The Guilford Press.

24. Frankl, V. (1969). *The will to meaning: Foundation and applications of logotherapy*. New York: New American Library, p. 35.

25. Rogers, C. (1951). *Client-centered therapy*. Boston: Houghton Mifflin, pp. 492–494.

26. Tillich, P. (1952). *The courage to be*. New Haven, CT: Yale University Press, pp. 20, 26, 33, 81.

27. Bettis, J. D. (Ed.). (1969). *Phenomenology of religion: Eight modern descriptions of the essence of religion*. New York: Harper & Row, pp. 10–11, 25–28. This is a position distinct from the state of pure consciousness without an object advocated in yoga psychology as a higher level of consciousness.

28. Cited by Yalom, I. (1980). *Existential psychotherapy*. New York: Basic Books, p. 290.

29. Capps, D. (1981). *Biblical approaches to pastoral counseling*. Philadelphia: The Westminster Press, pp. 107–114, 121–124.

30. Frankena, W. (1973). *Ethics*. Englewood Cliffs, NJ: Prentice-Hall.

31. Farber, L. (1966). *The ways of the will*. New York: Basic Books, p. 15.

32. Cited by Yalom, I. (1980). *Existential psychotherapy*. New York: Basic Books, p. 300.

33. Ibid., p. 302.

34. Ibid., p. 305.

35. Ibid., p. 307.

36. Ibid., p. 307.

37. Ibid., p. 309. Yalom notes that the purpose of affect arousal in Gestalt therapy is not merely catharsis, but to help persons rediscover their wishes. Emotional enemas are insufficient to produce sustained change.

38. Ibid., p. 314.

39. Ibid., p. 340–346.

40. Ibid., pp. 328, 331.

41. Ibid., p. 292.

42. Ibid., pp. 317–321.

43. Ibid., pp. 321–328.

44. A conflict model of decision-making was presented by Janus, I., & Mann, L. (1977). *Decision Making: A psychological analysis of conflict, choice, and commitment.* New York: The Free Press.

45. Kierkegaard, S. (1954). *Fear and trembling and the sickness unto death.* New York: Doubleday.

46. Smith, H. (1991). *The world's religions.* New York: HarperSanFrancisco, pp. 19–22.

47. Brother Lawrence (1975). *The practice of the presence of God.* Grand Rapids, MI: Baker Book House.

48. "Conversion is not a matter of prevailing arguments, but it is a matter of personal surrender" (that is, a matter of will). Tillich, P. (1957). *Dynamics of faith.* New York: Harper and Brothers Publishers, p. 125. Two practical books describing various forms of Christian spirituality are Mass, R., & O'Donnell, G. (1990). *Spiritual traditions for the contemporary church.* Nashville, TN: Abingdon Press; and Foster, R., & Smith, J. (1993). *Devotional classics: Selected readings for individuals and groups.* New York: HarperSan-Francisco.

49. Kierkegaard, S. (1938). *Purity of heart is to will one thing.* New York: Harper and Row.

50. Barbour, I. (1966). *Issues in science and religion.* San Francisco: Harper Torchbooks, pp. 16–23. Writing in the thirteenth Century, Aquinas identified Aristotle's First Cause with the personal and purposeful God of the Bible, the one whom Jesus called "Father." This God has various ways of accomplishing the divine will, including God's work through natural causes as well as miracles. I have suggested similarly that God's will to reconcile the world is accomplished through our natural experiences of reconciliation. Further insights into a psychology of the will and its relation to the mind, emotions, behavior, and human agency may be gleaned from Aquinas' anthropology. See McDermott, T. (Ed.). (1989). *St Thomas Aquinas: Summa Theologiae: A concise translation.* Westminster, MD: Christian Classics, pp. 126–129, 182–200, 260, 500–502, and xxv–xxxi.

51. Barbour, I. (1966). *Issues in science and religion.* San Francisco: Harper Torchbooks, p. 107.

52. Tillich, P. (1957). *Dynamics of faith.* New York: Harper Torchbooks, pp. 35–38. His position is based in part upon the notion of the bondage of the will. See Tillich, P. (1957). *Systematic theology* (Vol. 2). Chicago: University of Chicago Press, pp. 41, 63, 78–81.

53. Tillich, P. (1957). *Systematic theology* (Vol. 2). Chicago: University of Chicago Press, pp. 78–79.

54. Rychlak's definition of "will" is this: "To will is therefore to opt, decide, affirm one meaning-alternative from among the many possible." He notes that willful reasoning need not be entirely conscious as Freud observed in his concept of the unconscious "counterwill." Rychlak, J. (1981). *Introduction to personality and psychotherapy.* Boston: Houghton Mifflin Company, p. 294. This is an important insight which should help us avoid a judgmental moralism.

55. This is comparable to Rychlak's concept of the "telosponse." He defines telosponse as "a mental act whereby the person affirms and thereby predicates a meaningful premise encompassing a purpose for the sake of which behavior is then intended." Rychlak, J. (1981). *Introduction to personality and psychotherapy.* Boston: Houghton Mifflin Company, p. 793. From his Jungian perspective, behavior is more a function of formal and final causes than material or efficient causes. He presents a teleological psychology which

highlights the central role of human intentions and decisions as antecedents of behavior. Humans are self-determining agents of their actions because they have "both the freedom to select meanings (ideas) for the sake of which to behave and the resultant willful intention (psychic determinism) to enact them overtly in behavior." (Ibid., p. 297). Human freedom and intentionality are both necessary to consider one an agent of action. For further discussion of his central concept of human agency, see pp. 282, 285, 289, 294, 686, 791.

56. The theme of "God acting in history" is the principal motif of historical-biblical theologians such as Joseph Sittler and G. Ernest Wright, and among some Christian ethicists such as H. Richard Niebuhr and Paul Lehman. From this perspective, God's will is revealed more in human history than in nature, and one answers the ethical question, "What ought I to do?" by asking first, "What has God done?" and second, "What is God doing?" For a review and critique, see Gustafson, J. (1981). *Ethics from a theocentric perspective* (Vol. 1). Chicago: University of Chicago Press, pp. 42–56. My own emphasis on experiences of reconciliation in human history as revelatory events expresses a biblical theology and a theocentric ethic affirming the theme of divine action and presence in the world. God acts in and through human acts of reconciliation to reconcile the world.

57. A structured meditation defines what the inner activity is that one strives for in the practice of meditation. A meditation of the inner way focuses upon one's inner life and experience. The example given of "Who am I?" is found in Hindu, Buddhist, and Christian versions. See LeShan, L. (1974). *How to meditate.* New York: Bantam Books, pp. 41, 45, 69–72.

Chapter Seven

Conclusions and Future Directions

The purpose of this chapter is to provide a succinct summary and to indicate directions for further development of this theory of psychotherapy by placing it in an interdisciplinary context of philosophy, ethics, and science. Suggestions for theological development are also provided.

SUMMARY OF THEORETICAL PROPOSITIONS

The themes of this book can be summarized in the following set of propositions.
1. The points of both divergence and convergence between psychology and theology suggest that at a theoretical level (a) complete separation between these two disciplines is neither necessary nor possible, (b) they cannot and should not be unified into a single discipline, and (c) a greater degree of rapprochement between these disciplines is both possible and desirable (chapter two).
2. The dialectical method of critical correlation provides a basis for dialogue between psychology and theology in contrast to either their separation or integration (chapter three).
3. Any theory of psychotherapy must address the questions of its source, norm, and medium of knowledge. The concept of reconciliation constitutes the norm for the theory presented here. The source of this concept is the religious symbol of the kingdom of God taught by Jesus of Nazareth as recorded in the Synoptic Gospels. The medium through which this idea is known and becomes an empirical reality is human experience in its ontic, scientific, historical, spiritual, and moral dimensions (chapter three).
4. A linguistic analysis of the term "reconciliation" reveals that it is a comprehensive concept useful as a building block for a theory of counseling and as a bridge between psychology and theology. Based on that analysis,

reconciliation was defined as a multidimensional, unifying experience of resolving conflicts within and among alienated persons, whose being and relations are transformed through the power of forgiveness and the process of compassionate confrontation into a healing reunion of love, justice, and peace for the sake of which one decides to act (chapter four).

5. The purpose of counseling is to experience reconciliation in social, psychological, and spiritual dimensions through the process of compassionate confrontation of client incongruities in a Spirit-centered, therapeutic relationship (chapter four).

6. There are several reasons for favoring reconciliation as the purpose of counseling: it affirms that change is multidimensional and healing is holistic; that brokenness is real, but relationships heal; it affirms hope and the developmental nature of holiness; it serves as a norm for counseling decisions; it expresses the church's ministry and its pastoral functions; it is consistent with the church's confession of faith, and it is supported by a Christian theology of reconciliation; finally, it provides an even broader context for unification in ecumenical discussions as well as guidance on social issues (chapter four).

7. A phenomenological analysis of reconciliation discloses its essential structure as a multidimensional, unitary experience. Reconciliation occurs between persons, within individuals, and in relation to God. It has social, psychological, and spiritual dimensions (chapters four through six).

8. The psychological dimension reflects the impact of experiences of reconciliation in several domains. In the cognitive domain, knowledge is transformed into wisdom. In the affective domain, feelings of anger, fear, despair, and entitlement are transformed into compassion, courage, joy, and thanksgiving. In the behavioral domain, unethical conduct is transformed into righteous actions sustained by habits of holiness. In the conative domain of intentional decisions, selfish desires are transformed into sanctified strivings as one wills the will of God (chapters five and six).

FUTURE DIRECTIONS

There are at least four general directions in which the study of reconciliation may be advanced as it relates to a theory of counseling: philosophical, ethical, theological, and scientific.

Philosophical Directions

All psychological theories and theological systems depend upon philosophical assumptions. These are assumptions about how we know what we know (epistemology), about the nature of reality and the structure of being (ontology), and about who we should be and what we ought to do (ethics). As a result, both psychological theories and theological systems may be distinguished and evaluated as to the adequacy of their epistemology, ontology, and ethics.

Epistemological Assumptions. How do we know what we know? There have been several answers given to this question in both theological and psychological discourse. Orthodox Christian theologians have affirmed that religious knowledge of any consequence is *revealed knowledge,* partially through creation as a form of general revelation and fully through God in Christ and Holy Scripture as the media of special revelation. Others within both modernist Catholic and liberal Protestant traditions have affirmed the role of reason as a pathway to religious truths in the form of natural theology and moral theology, both of which constitute preparation for the truths of revealed theology. Within liberal Protestant traditions particularly, religious experience in either its subjective, moral, or historical dimensions has been emphasized, along with the authority of reason, and in some cases, an empirical, scientific theology has been derived.

Within the field of psychology, a *phenomenological epistemology* has been applied since William James explored the nature of human consciousness. This tradition constitutes a minority point of view in academic psychology. The dominant perspective at the present time continues to be a form of naturalism and logical positivism, both of which exclude religious and philosophical explanations in favor of statements that are empirically verifiable or falsifiable through controlled observations. Logical positivism has been challenged recently,[1] and I have rejected it as necessary to the development of a scientific theory of psychotherapy. I believe it is possible to develop a "religious-scientific" theory of psychotherapy as suggested in chapter three. More specifically, I am constructing a scientific theory of psychotherapy grounded in the religious construct of reconciliation. The epistemological assumptions of this theory warrant further examination and development, and particularly the phenomenological method of inquiry.

The aim of a phenomenological approach is to describe the meaning of a concept in order to understand the reality to which it refers. In terms of the theme of this book, one asks first, "What does reconciliation mean?" The methodological principle applied is that the meaning of a concept must be clarified and circumscribed before its validity can be tested through controlled measurements of scientific predictions. The initial step to determining meaning is to describe phenomena as they are "given" in experience without interference of theoretical explanations or restrictions concerning measurements. A satisfactory phenomenological description makes the reality that the ideas are supposed to reflect understandable to others and it illuminates other related ideas.

In a purely phenomenological approach to reconciliation, one would take an example of a typical reconciling event or experience and attempt to discern within it and through it the essential structure or universal meaning of reconciliation. But how does one know which concrete example to choose? A purely phenomenological approach does not provide the answer; however, this question can be answered by introducing an existential criterion to guide one's selection. The resulting epistemology is an *existential phenomenology.*

The existential criteria used in this analysis have been the concepts of ultimate concern and reconciliation.[2] Those examples that disclose ultimate concerns and the depth dimension of reconciliation are appropriate illustrations to investigate and explore. Using these criteria, I have selected Jesus' experience of reconciliation as the concrete and specific example in which to discover a more universal meaning of reconciliation. This approach seems best suited to provide a normative description of reconciliation, which includes the spiritual and moral dimensions as well as psychosocial dimensions.

In this book I have focused primarily upon the meaning of reconciliation. However, I have affirmed its actuality in human experience by attempting to point where and how it is actualized. Examples in the psychological dimension include the empirical changes occurring in such emotions as anger, fear, despair, and entitlement as they are transformed into compassion, courage, joy, and thanksgiving.

The phenomenology of reconciliation presented in this book is but one example of several approaches taken in the phenomenology of religion.[3] These various approaches share a common goal: each has tried to describe the essence of religion as an actual experience.

While they share a common goal, phenomenological studies of religion differ in terms of their focus. Some approaches have concentrated upon the object of religious experience; others have focused upon the subject. The *object* of religious experience has been described naturalistically as the experience of power (van der Leeuw), in supernaturalist terms as the experience of the Being of beings (Maritain), in transcendental terms as the experience of the holy (Otto), psychologically as a projection of ideal humanity (Feuerbach), and ontologically as the experience of New Being (Tillich).[4]

A second type of phenomenology of religion focuses upon the *subject* who has the religious experience. In this approach religious experience is understood as a quality of consciousness in contrast to either a body of knowledge (doctrine) or a code of conduct (ethics). In the history of Protestant theology, the noteworthy example is Friedrich Schleiermacher's description of religion as the awareness of absolute dependence, a consciousness of finite life in the Infinite and Eternal. For Schleiermacher the essence of religion is neither a matter of knowing or doing; it is neither theoretical nor practical, neither a revealed truth nor a prescribed lifestyle. Rather, the essence of piety is a conscious experience of belonging to God and being related with God. This view is rather near to my own, which emphasizes the conscious experience of being reconciled with God, self, and others. In both perspectives, being, consciousness, and relating are emphasized over knowing or doing.

Another example of this phenomenological emphasis upon the subject's religious experience is Paul Tillich's description of religion as a dimension of life. The religious dimension is not a separate compartment or part of life, but the depth dimension of every aspect of human existence. The spiritual dimension is the expression of ultimate concern. This is not limited to the conscious level (as

Schleiermacher emphasized); it includes the subconscious level of experience (consistent with Frankl's emphasis). For Tillich, religious experience is also an ontological experience of Being itself.[5]

I have adopted a *dimensional phenomenology* by distinguishing the social, psychological, and spiritual dimensions of reconciliation. While each of these dimensions is distinct, each is essentially related within the unity of experience. As the spiritual dimension is the most inclusive of these three, reconciliation cannot be reduced to a social experience of relations with other persons, nor to a psychological experience of personal integration. A corollary implication is that social and psychological dimensions of reconciliation cannot be excluded by a purely theological interpretation emphasizing the spiritual dimension. The experience of reconciliation includes both of these dimensions and more. Ultimately reconciliation is a religious experience, that is, an experience with a spiritual dimension.

What makes reconciliation a religious experience? The answer to that question depends upon the meaning one gives to the concept of religion itself. A phenomenological analysis suggests that the essence of religion is not found in its institutional forms, nor in its rituals of worship, fasting, or prayer. Nor is the essence of religion contained within a particular cosmology or creed. Neither is religion merely a mystical feeling, a spiritual aspiration, a code of conduct, or a social phenomenon. While religion is expressed positively in all of these domains— cognitive, affective, conative, behavioral, and interpersonal—the essence of religion is experiential. Religion is essentially a lived experience. Reconciliation is also a lived experience.

This is not a mysterious, supernatural experience of a "wholly Other" who comes from another world of invisible spiritual beings. Nor is this merely a natural experience expressed in the human desire for immortality, a conscious experience of belonging, a sense of the holy, or an experience of power. Religious experience is an existential phenomenon. It has to do with the meaning of our existence here and now. The proper question to ask is what makes existential experience religious? The religious a priori, that which defines human experience as religious, is the actual experience of reconciliation in the various dimensions of life. To be religious is to be reconciled socially, psychologically, and spiritually. Reconciliation is the depth dimension (i.e., the religious dimension) in all realms of human experience.

Common to all three dimensions of the experience of reconciliation is a relationship and an encounter. The social dimension emphasizes our relationships with others, the psychological dimension stresses our self-relatedness, and the spiritual dimension highlights our relationship with God. In all three dimensions, reconciliation is not conceived as either a substance or process, neither a thing nor an idea; rather, it is the experience of a relationship. Existentialists such as Martin Buber described this as an authentic I-Thou encounter. From this perspective, "to be" is to be related. To be religious is to encounter others, ourselves, and God in reconciling relationships.

The goals of a phenomenological inquiry are to describe a phenomenon *as it is experienced* in order to understand it. The focus of this analysis has been upon the phenomenon of reconciliation. Since reconciliation is not merely an idea, but an experience, this is an empirical approach that can and must be evaluated in terms of its treatment of the data of religious experience and psychosocial experiences of reconciliation. An accurate description of the experience of reconciliation is preliminary to an analysis of its causes and consequences.

A basic premise of the phenomenological method is that the meaning of an experience is not determined by its origin nor by knowing its antecedent causes. The question "What does reconciliation mean?" is not the same as "What causes it?" To inquire about what this experience is like, or how reconciliation is actually experienced is a different approach epistemologically from the question of the necessary and sufficient conditions for reconciliation to occur. Although both types of questions are important, the question of meaning precedes the question of cause and cannot be reduced to it.

Just as the meaning of reconciliation cannot be reduced to its origins or causes, neither can the meaning of reconciliation be restricted to its particular manifestations in concrete forms. A phenomenological analysis seeks to describe the essence of an experience, that which is disclosed as common in several concrete illustrations. Accordingly, while the priority of lived experience is affirmed, and reconciliation is always experienced in, by, and between individuals, this experience is not limited to any individual or historical expression of it. It follows that the Christian's experience of reconciliation is but one positive form that the experience of reconciliation takes. Nevertheless, a description of this particular form serves as a valid, empirical source (though not the sole source) for understanding the essential structure of the general experience of reconciliation. With this more general understanding of what reconciliation means, we may look to other religions, philosophy, science, and the arts for additional cultural expressions of the basic structure of reconciliation and for further clues to its content and form in human experience.

A phenomenological analysis of reconciliation has been necessary to construct a theory of counseling based on this Judeo-Christian concept and experience. Yet this constructivist mode of relating psychology and theology is only one potential form of interaction between them.[6] There is a *dialectical epistemology* evident in this theory as well. This is not a Hegelian dialectic of a thesis and antithesis reconciled in a synthesis of ideas, but a dynamic interaction characterized as a continuous dialogue involving questions and answers exchanged between these two disciplines in a method called critical correlation. Insofar as both disciplines serve both functions of raising questions and providing answers, a genuine dialogue between equals will be possible. And so it should be, since both are sources of truth relevant to the human condition in general and to counseling in particular.

To encourage such dialogue I emphasized in chapter two the points of convergence between psychology and theology. Among these similarities are the *rational and empirical epistemologies* these two disciplines share. In the present treatise, I have applied logical reasoning to reach semantic clarity by analyzing both secular and religious meanings of reconciliation in chapters four, five, and six. I have endorsed an empirical epistemology by selecting "experience" as a central construct, by stressing its role as the medium of both religious and scientific knowledge, and by insisting that this theory must lead to testable hypotheses. This I have done based on both religious and scientific convictions grounded in an empirical theology and in an experiential theory of counseling. The epistemological foundation is a dimensional, existential phenomenology, dialectical, rational, and empirical.

Ontological Assumptions. The present theory is based on certain assumptions about reality. These assumptions are expressed in a *multidimensional ontology of being, which is relational, existential, and realistic.* The fundamental elements and structure of being are those postulated by Paul Tillich in his *Systematic Theology.*[7] That particular ontology is not a necessary foundation, nor the only one possible; however, some theory about being and reality is necessary to ground both theology and psychology. The experiences of knowing, feeling, doing, willing, and relating are all modes of being and they presuppose it. Insofar as these modes of experience are not merely subjective or illusory, but are affirmed as real, some concept of both reality and its relation to human experience is required. We must go beyond a phenomenological description of reconciliation to ask the question of its truth and reality.[8]

This does not mean that either theology or psychology is reduced to philosophy, only that both depend upon it. Moreover, both disciplines employ language and concepts with ontic meanings, and these need to be made explicit. Examples include such constructs as substance and process, cause and purpose, being and time, and growth and meaning.[9] Salient ontic constructs in the present theory are being, consciousness, and meaning, self and world, essence and existence, experience and finite freedom, estrangement and reconciliation, and the multidimensional unity of human experience.

The concept of reconciliation is itself an ontological construct: it refers to both a state of being and a reality of becoming.[10] In the reconciled life the basic ontic elements of being that are separated in existence are reunited, albeit fragmentarily. These are the polarities of individuation and participation, dynamics and form, freedom and destiny. Reconciliation among these elements brings unity to the basic ontological structure of the self and world.[11] As a result, being reconciled means to experience more fully the unity of our existential being with our essential being; we begin to become who we truly are. In this respect reconciliation is both a saving and a healing experience ontologically and empirically.

There is another ontological category which can serve as a foundation for a theology and psychology of reconciliation. The philosopher, Martin Buber, suggested that in lieu of categories of "substance," "ideas," "process," or "experience," the idea of "*relation*" best serves as the primary category for understanding the nature of reality. In contrast to terms such as "being," or a "self and world" structure of being, Buber spoke of the "I-Thou relation" as the fundamental category. In my own view, "relation" presupposes "being," both logically and ontologically, but I wish to include the category of "relation" as an ontological term, and to suggest that future philosophical development of a theory of reconciliation will be enriched by a study of Buber's philosophy for some of the following reasons.[12]

As a Jewish philosopher, Martin Buber's central question was how to understand his experience of a direct relation with God. To "experience" something is to sense or perceive it, to feel or think it, to imagine or will it. In all instances, what is experienced is an object ("it") in an I-It relation.[13] In contrast, one knows another person, including the person of God, only in an I-Thou relation in which we meet or encounter another rather than objectify or analyze them. Consequently, knowing is not limited to intellectual knowledge; there is also an existential or relational knowing that occurs in genuine encounters with nature, other persons, and with spiritual being. In the face of the directness and immediacy of such relations, everything indirect becomes irrelevant.[14]

Both ontologically and epistemologically the category of "relation" is primary in Buber's philosophy. As a paraphrase of Jesus' statement about not living by bread alone (Matthew 4:4), Buber's position may be summarized as follows: "One does not live by experiences alone, but by relationships." The idea of "relation" is crucial to understanding that Jesus' symbol of the kingdom of God points to a realm of reconciling relationships.

The concept of "relation" has the further advantage of avoiding an exclusively intrapsychic conception of reconciliation as the experience possessed by an individual, or as something that can be reduced to a particular psychological domain within an individual's experience, whether cognitive, behavioral, affective, or conative. For example, though we may speak of the idea of reconciliation, the concept that describes it is not the same as the reality it describes, nor can a reconciling experience be reduced to the cognitive domain as changes in one's thinking. To label something is not the same as living it; humans do not live by their labels alone. An intellectual understanding of reconciliation is both essential and helpful, but we are not reconciled by our intellect, the claims of cognitive psychology and cognitive-behavior therapies notwithstanding.

Moreover, while we may speak of acts of reconciliation, the reconciling relationship cannot be reduced to its behavioral domain as merely something one does. Nor can the relationship be reduced to a feeling like love. In the moral dimension, the love that reconciles is a responsive and responsible relationship between persons, not merely a feeling of affection or even an act of love on the part of one toward the other. Like love, reconciliation exists *between* persons, not merely in one or both of them independently. The relationship is more than the sum of its two participants, though both are needed to create it.

Another advantage of Buber's ontic concept of "relation" is found in his theological notion that God relates to us as an "I" relates to a "Thou" even though we may not be aware of it. Our lack of awareness does not preclude God from relating in such a way as to help us actualize our own capacity to relate similarly as an "I" in an I-Thou relation.[15] This notion supports the psychological observation that experience is not always or solely a conscious experience. It suggests that experiences of reconciliation are not limited only to those of which we are aware. We may speak of *unconscious reconciliations*, including unconscious reconciling processes both within an individual and between persons. In theological language, the kingdom of God comes without our always knowing where, when, how, through whom, or with whom it comes (Mt. 13:33; Mk. 4:26–29; Lk. 17:20–21). Nevertheless, it is a present reality and a lived experience of reconciling relationships.

Although the theological concept of the kingdom of God functions in part as an ethical ideal in the present theory, this concept symbolizes primarily the real realm of reconciling relationships. Our relationships with God and other persons are both ontological and empirical realities. The kingdom of God is not merely a religious symbol, a theological concept, nor merely an ethical norm; it is an ontic reality humans experience with God and with one another in this present world characterized as an estranged existence: we are not the persons we were created to be and potentially are.

To affirm the kingdom of God as an experienced reality, not merely as a religious symbol or moral value, suggests a philosophical position of realism. In contrast to philosophical idealism, which affirms that reality is a subjective world of ideas, ideals, or forms, *ontological realism* affirms that the natural world, human experience, and being itself are objectively real, neither an illusion nor purely mental.

This is not, however, a naïve realism that asserts that facts exist totally apart from our interpretation of them, or that reality exists completely independent of our experience and perceptions of reality.[16] While reality consists in the basic polar structure of self and world, the two are interdependent and necessarily related.[17] To express this point I have adopted an existential and relational ontology, that is, an affirmation that reality is experienced as "being-in-the-world" or as a "self-world relation." In this manner, I have attempted to avoid the Cartesian split between subject and object and between self and world in favor of their essential interdependent relation.[18]

A naïve realism presumes that we can provide a literal representation of reality based on a one-to-one correspondence between a model of reality and reality itself, or between a subjective concept that functions as a sign and its objective referent. By contrast, the *critical realism* I am affirming here states that all language—both scientific and religious—is symbolic and selective, analogical and abstracting, and more or less useful for particular purposes.[19] A critical realism suggests that our concepts do not constitute the reality represented, but they do represent real events in the world. Furthermore, we encounter reality and being in our immediate experience, though neither one can be reduced to our experience.[20]

Viewed from this perspective of critical realism, reconciliation cannot be restricted to a subjective world of ideas. As a symbol, "reconciliation" points us to the reality it represents. Reconciliation is not a mere abstraction, nor merely a useful fiction in the service of the will to live as in Vaihinger's positivist idealism.[21]

Neither is reconciliation an illusion. Reconciliation is a real mode of being and a real way of relating that we actually experience in a real world.

While critical realism is a helpful ontology, more than a critical realism may be required. Paul Tillich advocated a *self-transcending realism* to express the transcendent or depth dimension of life as the real saving power of reconciling love.[22] This type of realism may help us to see that each experience of reconciliation is both unique and universal. It is unique in its concrete particularity in time, place, and persons; it is universal in its unconditional, inclusive nature and transcends persons, place, and time. In both its unique and universal dimensions, experiences of reconciling relationships are real ways of being and are lived in the present. In these real experiences we have an empirical sense of the sacred and the transcendent dimension of life.

To illustrate an empirical sense of the transcendent dimension of experience, I offer the following analogies. You cannot see the wind, and usually you cannot smell it or touch it, though you may sense it as the pressure and movement of air upon or across your skin. But you do not "see" the air or wind. You can sense its presence in its effects, such as the waves on the surface of a lake, or the rustling sounds of branches bending on tall pines in its path. You may "see" the wind even as a visual pattern on a weather radar screen in the form of swirling colors depicting clouds being moved by this invisible force. Yet none of these empirical indicators is the wind itself; they are all observable effects of the wind. From its visible effects we infer the reality of the wind.

In an analogous way, we cannot see God, but we can experience the effects of God's reconciling love in human acts of reconciliation and infer from our experiences of reconciliation the reality of the One who reconciles. But God is not the same as the experience of reconciliation any more than the wind is identical with its effects. Nevertheless, to us a mixed metaphor, human experiences of reconciliation function symbolically and empirically as observable indicators of God's presence like branches bowing in the breath of God.[23]

The image of breath suggests another analogy. I do not really see the ocean of air from which I draw my breath. Yet without it I would surely die. Similarly, I do not see Being itself (God), yet were I not part of it, I would not be. In my own breath and being I may experience the effects of Breath and Being through my participation in it and dependence upon it. Yet Being is not identical with my being nor is Breath limited to my own breathing. Nevertheless, my own breathing and being may serve as ciphers of the Breath and Being of God. The analogy is not so far-fetched when you appreciate that the Greek word *pneuma* translated as "spirit" also means "breath." To live a spiritual life is to breathe the Breath of God.

One more analogy. Experiences of reconciliation may function as the ground from which a figure emerges in human consciousness. From the ground of multiple reconciling events a pattern may emerge in the form of a figure of One who reconciles. But we must not confuse figure and ground. When we mistake the effects of God for the essence of God we are on the road to idolatry. Being itself as figure is more than our own experience of personal being as ground. The meaning and power of Being are its transcending depths, though also immanent in our relations to being and participation in being.

All analogies are limited and none of them constitute logical proof for the existence of God. Yet analogous reasoning raises the question and possibility of God, answered religiously by a transcending and transforming revelation.[24] Christians find this revelation in the life and teachings of Jesus.

The philosophical positions of critical and self-transcending realism just presented are two options among many alternative approaches, including those that deemphasize or even deny ontology. Consequently, this theory may be evaluated philosophically from other perspectives such as philosophical idealism, philosophies of life, value, or personal being, naturalism and positivism, pragmatism, phenomenology, logical empiricism, process philosophies, and other forms of theistic or atheistic existentialism.[25] It would be helpful to compare and contrast the present theory with these other approaches utilized to understand what is real and what it means to be.

Any one of these alternative worldviews could be used to provide a philosophical foundation for reconciliation as the purpose of psychotherapy, though some better than others. As an example, in contrast to an atheistic naturalism, a mythical supernaturalism, or a metaphysical dualism or monism, one may consider a theistic naturalism, theistic realism,[26] or an experiential idealism.[27] Alternatively one could justify reconciliation on purely pragmatic grounds, or as an empirical phenomenon apart from any theistic or atheistic ontology whatsoever. Those with a less ontological bent may be inclined to do so. I have not found the idea that something is true and good merely because it is useful to be a compelling argument for the validity of any proposition. But being useful is as important as being true, and a pragmatic test of meaning has a legitimate place in philosophical, theological, and psychological discourse. This is especially true for an applied field such as the practice of psychotherapy.

My main point here is that we cannot proceed either theologically or scientifically without clarification of our ontological assumptions about what reality is, what it means to be, and how self and world are related. However, I appreciate the right of others to disagree with this view, and I respect those who think through their positions in dialogue with other perspectives. Like many others, I am not persuaded by either theological fundamentalism or by scientific dogmatism.

Ethical Theories of Conduct and Character

Although ethics is properly one specialization within philosophy, I will discuss it separately here to emphasize that I am constructing a normative theory of psychotherapy. I shall proceed by asking the following questions: What are the ethical assumptions implicit in this theory? What type of ethical theory has been presented? and What justification can be provided for selecting reconciliation as the primary principle?

Ethical Assumptions. It is critical to the dialogue between theology and psychology that their ethical assumptions be made explicit and that these assumptions be compared and evaluated. Both theological systems and theories of psychotherapy are value-laden constructions. Neither one can be considered as a value-free or value neutral interpretation of the human condition.[28]

One of the legitimate criticisms of popular Christian ethics has been its restricted focus upon personal ethics to the exclusion of concerns and actions related to social justice and peace, and the lack of a prophetic, ethical critique of economic and political systems, public policies, and social programs. One of the moral ambiguities of psychological theories of counseling is that their prescriptive values are often disguised as descriptive statements: needs have replaced virtues, drives have replaced decisions, reinforcers and causes have replaced values and obligations. I have attempted to correct both types of error in this theory of counseling by stating explicitly that reconciliation functions as an ethical norm for evaluating both theological systems and psychological theories of psychotherapy.

Type of Ethical Theory. The question may be raised as to the type of normative theory that I have proposed. Is this a theory of moral obligation or a theory of moral value? In chapter six I suggested that reconciliation functions as both a normative concept for a theory of moral value and as a fundamental principle for a theory of moral obligation. Reconciliation is both a virtue of character and a principle of conduct.

This position implies that one need not choose between the two. An ethic of duty can be recast as an ethic of virtue. These two ways of using reconciliation as both a value and a principle are complementary rather than mutually exclusive. A satisfactory normative theory addresses both an ethic of being and an ethic of doing, and both types of ethical theory are needed.[29] Virtues of character provide the motivation for ethical conduct, and principles of conduct provide virtues with direction. In this two-fold manner reconciliation serves as the foundation for the development of my normative theory of psychotherapy as a moral philosophy.

By presenting the reconciled life as the purpose of psychotherapy I have opted for a *teleological* theory of moral obligation. In this type of ethical theory, reconciliation functions as the intrinsic, nonmoral value that psychotherapy is designed to bring into being.[30] Psychotherapy functions as an instrumental or extrinsic, nonmoral value; that is, psychotherapy is justified as a means to achieving the end of reconciliation. At the same time, a *rule-deontological* theory of moral obligation was expressed in the principle that in a given situation one ought to follow the rule to "do what reconciliation requires."[31] Here the determining construct is duty defined by a rule.

Grounded in a personal theism, this ethical theory of reconciliation could be construed also as a version of an *agapist* ethic, which emphasizes God's reconciling love. Since reconciliation is one meaning of love, as Tillich has noted,[32] Jesus' summary of the moral law in terms of love (Mt. 22:37–40) could be translated as an obligation to be reconciled with God and to be reconciling with one another. But one need not follow this moral principle either as a divine command or because one ought to imitate God's love. Gratitude for God's acceptance of us though we are unacceptable serves as the primary Christian motivation, not obedience, imitation, or fear.[33]

The two central principles of love and justice that constitute the content of the norm of social reconciliation must be applied reasonably through intermediate moral axioms to each unique situation.[34] Both values and facts must be considered and related logically, hence to some degree this is a contextual or situation ethic.[35]

As a *contextual ethic*, the moral principle of reconciliation could be applied as an act or as a rule. In act-reconciliation, one decides what to do by first getting clear about the facts of a situation, and then asking what is the reconciling or the most reconciling thing to do in light of the facts of this particular situation. In a rule-reconciliation approach, one determines what one ought to do, not by asking which *act* is the most reconciling, but by determining which *rules of action* are most reconciling, and then one follows these reconciling rules in particular situations whenever this is possible. Intermediate moral axioms are examples of rules of action that can be derived from the norm of reconciliation. Principles of psychotherapy and professional codes of ethics function similarly as rules guiding a therapist's actions.

Further ethical analyses of this theory would help to classify it as to the type of ethical theory it expresses. Such analyses would help to clarify its intrinsic versus instrumental values, the virtues and obligations advocated and to develop the meanings of the good life as a reconciled life, the good society as a reconciling society, and good psychotherapy as a therapy whose purpose is reconciliation and whose products are a reconciling personality and reconciled relationships.[36]

Implicit in these comments is the notion that like other theories of psychotherapy, this one needs to be evaluated as a moral philosophy. By presenting the concept of reconciliation as an intrinsic value[37] to be actualized through psychotherapy, I have moved intentionally from a phenomenological description to an ethical prescription. In my view, reconciliation is not merely a meaningful experience to be described and understood; it is a normative experience to be realized. Neither is reconciliation merely an experience or an idea; it is also a value and a goal, a moral obligation and a virtue.[38]

We need a moral philosophy to evaluate the relative worth of experiences described phenomenologically. Ethical concerns can be bracketed out for a descriptive analysis, but not permanently. We need ethical standards by which to make moral judgments, values and norms by which to make our decisions, and principles by which to define our purpose and to guide our conduct. Moreover, we need moral ideals embodied in concrete individuals to inspire us by demonstrating empirically that we are capable of becoming who we ought to be. The theory of reconciliation presented in this book is explicitly ethical in all these respects. It constitutes a moral philosophy about who we ought to be and what we should do individually and professionally.[39] We are to be agents of reconciliation who do what reconciliation requires. Further study is warranted to explore the broader social implications of reconciliation as an ethical norm from which intermediate axioms may be derived to guide social ethics and interpersonal relations.

An implication of this type of moral philosophy is found in my rejection of theories of psychotherapy that advocate a form of egoistic hedonism expressed in the goal of enlightened self-interest as a way of achieving personal pleasure, or expressed in the goal of satisfaction of an individual's needs in order to achieve personal happiness without regard for the needs and rights of others. I also reject various forms of nonhedonistic egoism reflected in such goals of therapy as personal awareness, mental health, or self-actualization when advocated without considerations for the welfare of significant others. Neither have I endorsed a utilitarian ethic of the greatest good (reconciliation) for the greatest number, though that would be a defensible theory of moral obligation. Nor am I advocating a new categorical imperative of reconciliation as a monistic form of a rule-deontological theory of moral obligation. Jesus' first commandment was to love God, not to love the experience of reconciliation. The Christian categorical imperative is to love God and to love justly one's neighbor as oneself. We must not transform the experience of reconciliation into another ethical absolute or into an idol of worship. Consistent with the ethical monotheism Jesus taught, I affirm that only God is absolute, but I also appreciate that others may doubt or deny this theological proposition and expression of faith.

Ethical Justifications. Additional questions to address concerning this normative theory of psychotherapy include the following: How are the moral values and ethical principles selected and justified? More specifically, why be a reconciling person or a reconciling counselor? Why should we do what reconciliation requires? Why strive for a reconciling society? These questions illustrate the more general issue of how moral judgments are justified.

Justifying ethical obligations and virtues is the proper task of meta-ethical discourse, beyond the scope of this book and beyond my own knowledge of philosophical ethics. Nevertheless, certain strategies of justification may be ruled out and a constructive direction can be suggested.

Neither meta-ethical relativism nor normative relativism is satisfactory, since these positions claim respectively either that (a) there is no objective, rational way to justify one basic ethical principle over another, or (b) while reconciliation may be good for one individual or society, it is not right or good for another. Both positions would deny any universal moral principles. In my view, the principle of moral obligation, "Do what reconciliation requires," can be generalized as a universal moral principle.

I would also reject nonrational justifications of reconciliation based on appeals to such authorities as an intuitive sense that reconciliation is good, that reconciliation feels right, or even that it is commanded by God.[40] Ethical principles and actions based on intuition, emotion, or divine commands may be either reasonable and relevant, or unreasonable, arbitrary and contrary to human experience. As an example, to follow literally the biblical injunction to forgive seventy-seven times (Mt. 18: 21–22) is both unreasonable and inhumane in the experience of battered women and abused children.[41]

Dissatisfaction with these forms of justification has led some to adopt a definist theory. In this approach one defines "ought" in terms of "is," or values in terms of facts. But a definist theory of justification is also problematic. To define what is good or right in terms of what is actually desired or factually conducive to happiness is to commit a logical error of defining values as if they were facts. This is not to say that a value judgment, such as "reconciliation is good," cannot be tested empirically to determine whether or not it is actually experienced as good; only that ethical assertions must not be derived from, equated with, or disguised as assertions of fact. This type of logical error is called the naturalistic fallacy.

A major shortcoming of most psychological theories of psychotherapy and counseling is precisely this kind of logical error: they function as disguised or implicit moral philosophies. An example is to postulate self-actualization as the primary human need or innate drive and to argue that therefore it should serve as the primary virtue, principle of action, or purpose of psychotherapy. Alternatively, one may define the ethical terms of what is right, good, or obligatory as fulfillment of the need for self-actualization, or as the satisfaction of some other human need such as the need for security, the need for love, and so forth. Are security, love, and self-actualization good simply because they are human needs? Is it right to act out our sexual and aggressive drives simply because they exist? That seems both logically and morally dubious. Ethical principles and moral values do not depend logically on facts, whether these are psychological facts of an empirical nature such as human needs or tendencies, or theological facts of a spiritual nature such as the gifts and fruits of the Spirit.

The latter statement suggests that the logical error of attempting to derive values from facts is not limited to naturalistic theories of psychotherapy. As an example of a theological version of a definist theory of justification, one might claim that "right" refers to the fact that it is "commanded by God." In this case, saying that reconciliation is right would be merely a shorter way of saying that reconciliation is commanded by God, or reconciliation is obligatory because it is actually the will of God.

This raises another question pertinent to the theory presented here. By deriving an ethical norm of reconciliation from a religious concept of the kingdom of God, have I committed the error of attempting to derive a moral "ought" from a theological "is," or moral values from religious facts? The answer to that question would be positive if no other grounds were offered to justify this ethic of reconciliation. I present other grounds from a moral point of view in the discussion that follows.

Whether one defines ethical terms such as "right" and "good" in psychological or theological terms, appealing to a definition to support an ethical principle such as reconciliation is not a satisfactory justification for at least three reasons: (a) the definition itself needs to be justified, (b) justifying the definition involves the same problems that justifying a moral principle involves, (c) both psychological "facts" and theological "facts" are debated, doubted, or denied in our pluralistic society, hence dialogue with those of other persuasions requires some other way of justifying the moral principle of reconciliation.[42]

Adopting a *moral point of view* is another way to justify reconciliation as the norm. A moral point of view requires that we are "free, impartial, willing to universalize, conceptually clear, and informed about all possible relevant facts. Then we are justified in judging that a certain act or kind of action is right, wrong, or obligatory, and in claiming that our judgment is objectively valid. . . . Our judgment or principle is really justified if it holds up under sustained scrutiny of this sort from the moral point of view on the part of everyone."[43] Furthermore, one is taking the moral point of view if one considers the good of everyone alike rather than only one's own good. Finally, a moral point of view is tolerant and open-minded about alternative candidates and rankings of what is good, right, and obligatory.

This is basically a rational point of view. It does not claim that the validity or rank of a particular norm such as reconciliation can be logically proven, but it does mean that we can justify reconciliation as a norm by providing a reasonable argument for its selection as a value and principle of moral obligation. More than that, this moral point of view implies we are obligated to justify our selection by providing rational arguments.[44]

I would commend the reconciled life as an intrinsic value (good as an end), as an inherent value (good as an experience), and as a contributory good as a part of the good life and an element of human happiness. I have presented reconciliation also as a moral value, that is, as a virtue to be cultivated by counselor and client alike, and as an intrinsic, nonmoral value as the "good" to be realized as the purpose of psychotherapy. My recommendations are not merely an expression of feeling, will, or decision, though these elements are certainly involved. Instead, I believe that commending reconciliation as a primary principle and cardinal virtue is rationally justifiable.[45] Acceptance of this principle and value is not a matter of blind impulse, an arbitrary decision, or just another "whatever." Neither must we accept the norm of reconciliation on blind faith.

Morality and Religion

The latter statement raises the question of the relation between morality and religion, or between ethics and theology. From the moral point of view just presented, the norm of reconciliation is logically independent of religion and independent of religion for its justification. As a Christian, I find justification for this norm in Jesus' gospel of reconciliation recorded in the Synoptic Gospels particularly in the religious symbol of the kingdom of God; however, I recognize that this is an appeal to a particular revelation and faith tradition that may not be persuasive to non-Christians. Doing the will of God is clearly not an obligation assumed by one who doubts or denies that God exists. For believers and doubters alike, a rational justification of reconciliation as the norm seems warranted, but especially with those of other faiths or with no formal faith.[46]

Consequently, I would not attempt to justify the norm of reconciliation solely in terms of my deeply held religious conviction that it is God's will to reconcile the world. In such a divine command theory,[47] the answer to the question "Why should we be reconciled with God and with one another?" is answered "Because God commands us to be reconciled, and we ought to be obedient to God's will or imitate God's reconciling love." While these reasons are compelling for me and others who find their identity within the Judeo-Christian tradition, they are not convincing to the remaining world that God seeks to reconcile. As agents of reconciliation, we who identify ourselves as disciples of Christ must seek ways to bridge the cultural and religious gaps between ourselves and others if the world is to be reconciled according to God's will.

I do not mean to imply there is no relationship whatsoever between morality and religion, nor that they ought to be completely separated. Jesus combined religion and morality in the single motive of loving God, neighbor and self. This is a religiously grounded moral injunction to love justly our neighbor as ourselves. I agree with Adolph von Harnack's interpretation of Jesus' commandment, namely that "in this sense religion may be called the soul of morality, and morality the body of religion."[48]

What nurtures the human soul is the Spirit of the living God, who provides the grace necessary to persevere in the pursuit of virtue by blessing us with spiritual gifts and fruits of the Spirit that sustain and animate the moral life.[49] Love from God and love to God provide the reason and power by which to love one another, and love of one's neighbor is the only practical proof that love of God dwells within the human heart.[50] While we do not need this particular religious vision either to justify reconciliation as a primary norm or to recognize its moral worth, nevertheless, a religious vision of life describes the kind of world in which reconciliation may emerge, and religious experiences of God's love motivate and empower us to help create that world.[51]

There is another connection between morality and religion suggested by the term "empowerment." Many persons with religious affections are inspired and motivated by the *moral ideal* personified by the spiritual founders and the saints of their faith.[52] Exemplary persons such as Jesus of Nazareth and Gautama Buddha, Mahatma Gandhi and Martin Luther King, Jr. play a central role in the moral education and moral development of their followers. As concrete illustrations of moral ways of being, they serve as empowering moral ideals.[53] The motivating power of Jesus as a moral ideal may explain why one of the most widely read books in the history of Christian spirituality is *The Imitation of Christ*.[54]

Having a moral ideal like Jesus means we want to be a person like him and we strive to emulate him.[55] Moreover, the embodiment in Jesus of the virtue of reconciliation encourages us to be like him because we see that insofar as we become reconciled with God like Jesus, we too may experience this beatitude and serve as agents of reconciliation to our alienated world. As a moral ideal Jesus shows us both what is desirable and what is possible with God, and also that what is desirable has been actually achieved in a human person (Jesus), hence it is achievable by us with God's grace as we become a person like Jesus. For those who are inspired by Jesus' example, and empowered by God's reconciling love, "ought" does imply "can" as Kant suggested.[56]

To speak of Jesus as a moral ideal is to speak of his character. To speak of character is to speak of *virtues*. Viewed in terms of a theory of moral value, reconciliation functions as a virtue. In general terms, a virtue is a habitual and firm tendency to do good. A virtue is not a personality trait like introversion, though a virtue could be construed as a moral trait. Human virtues are relatively stable dispositions of the intellect and will that govern our acts, order our passions, and guide our conduct in accordance with faith and reason.[57] According to this definition, the virtue of reconciliation manifested in the religious figure of Jesus of Nazareth serves a twofold function: this virtue shows us who we ought to become and moves us toward the moral ideal Jesus represents. In a more general sense, virtues embodied in moral ideals function as religious motives to both energize and direct us. Consequently, religious figures may function to motivate and inspire us to become responsible, reconciling people.

Since the concept of virtue functions in moral theory analogous to the concept of motive in psychological theory, theories and research on learning and personality development can contribute to the cultivation of virtues. In a similar way, psychological theories of motivation and personality dynamics may be informed by the concept of virtue and by the application of moral ideals. Construed in this manner, both human development and personality dynamics would emphasize the intentional and moral nature of human behavior consistent with teleological and voluntaristic perspectives. These perspectives interpret human conduct primarily, though not exclusively as a function of decisions made deliberately and of conscious goals chosen freely for the sake of which behavior is intended and enacted.

Moreover, a moral ideal can play a central role as both a construct in a normative theory of psychotherapy and as a guiding image in therapeutic practice. Through therapy individuals consciously experience their motives, and they learn to evaluate alternative goals and to apply new strategies for achieving them. Additionally, they become more free to direct their actions based on decisions made in light of values clarified and virtues embraced.[58] The psychological identification with moral ideals will facilitate these processes. In all three of these applied areas of psychology—human development, motivation, and psychotherapy—the use of a moral model such as Jesus of Nazareth is supported by the empirical evidence for the efficacy of observational learning involving the imitation of models.[59]

While I have derived the ethical norm of reconciliation from Jesus' religious concept of the kingdom of God, other foundations and justifications for this norm could be provided. Thus one could define the purpose of psychotherapy as reconciliation, and affirm the value of a reconciled life and the goal of a reconciled society all on humanistic grounds consistent with the worth and dignity of persons endorsed by a secular philosophy based on democratic principles of liberty, equality, and justice. However, since I have advocated the religious concept of the kingdom of God as the foundation for the ethical principle and virtue of reconciliation, further study of this theological construct will be important to the development of this theory.[60] Have I represented Jesus' teachings about the kingdom of God in an accurate manner? Does the concept of reconciliation express his teachings as a lietmotif? What is the religious meaning of reconciliation? How is it related to other theological terms such as justification and sanctification? Answers to these questions will help to shape the theological development of this normative theory of counseling.

Theological Directions

The biblical and theological foundations for this normative theory of psychotherapy have been summarized in the discussion of it's source and norm in chapters three and four. Since the normative construct is reconciliation expressed symbolically in Jesus' teachings about the kingdom of God, the Synoptic Gospels constitute the primary sources in which his message is recorded and interpreted. Numerous references from the Synoptics have been provided in chapters five and six to document Jesus' teachings about the reconciled life as the foundation for this form of biblical counseling.

Unlike conservative advocates of biblical counseling,[61] as the theological framework for this book I have adopted a position within the liberal Protestant tradition.[62] I will summarize here a few of its salient themes: (a) the centrality of the teachings of Jesus of Nazareth about the kingdom of God, (b) the theocentric religion of Jesus embedded within, yet distinct from the Christocentric religion about him, (c) a demythologized/de-Hellenized Christian faith, (d) a relational and teleological Christology, (e) the inspiring example of Jesus' reconciled and reconciling life, (f) the essence of Christianity as a transforming experience of reconciliation with God, self, and others, (g) the immanent and preeminent grace of God, (h) Christian realism, (i) Christian pluralism, (j) the use of Scripture, tradition, reason, and experience to validate theological propositions, and (k) both a theology of reconciliation and a reconciling theology. These themes warrant further exploration and development, including their implications for the social and spiritual dimensions of reconciliation.

Further clarification may occur by placing this theory in the context of some of the typologies which have been used to classify both theology and Christology. For example, in relating theology and psychology as expressions of Christianity and culture respectively, the present theory appears to be more consistent with H. Richard Niebuhr's category of "Christ transforming culture" than with other categories such as Christ against or above culture, the Christ of culture, or Christ and culture in paradoxical relation.[63] Thus, I have favored a theonomous psychotherapy (theology transforming psychology) in lieu of theology against psychology, theology over psychology, or a theology of psychology. By emphasizing critical correlation as a method for continuous dialogue between psychology and theology in lieu of either their synthesis or separation, I have adopted a revisionist approach[64] and a dialogical approach.[65]

My description of the human condition as an estranged existence which leads to the quest for reconciliation reflects an existential and empirical theology grounded in a universal human experience. This is a position contrary to the "postmodern" rejection of a shared human condition as expressed by cultural relativists. A theological anthropology illuminated by an existential analysis can provide an understanding of human existence that transcends cultural and historical limits and locations. By attempting to recover and revitalize the experience of reconciliation embodied within the Judeo-Christian tradition as a foundation for a theory of psychotherapy, I have adopted an inductive method rather than a deductive or reductive method.[66]

I have emphasized reconciliation over both justification and sanctification as the central theological metaphor subsuming both, and a theory of atonement which is more subjective than objective,[67] more inspirational than juridical, and both psychological and historical. Moreover, by emphasizing that reconciliation is accessible throughout history (including the present), and not exclusively at one point in time (either past or future), I have opted for a processive rather than a transactional perspective.[68]

My interest in, and dependence upon the contemporary quest for the historical Jesus, my emphasis upon his authentic message of reconciliation, and my description of his reconciling relation with God as the experience of a communion of love and wills reflect an historical, relational, experiential, and teleological Christology. By virtue of his reconciling relation with God, and his message and ministry of reconciliation, Jesus of Nazareth is a unique and definitive mediator of reconciliation, but neither the final nor exclusive medium. Consequently, with respect to other world religions, I favor a Christian pluralism in contrast to either an imperial exclusivism or a radical relativism.[69]

Like other liberal theologians I have grounded my Christian faith in human experience and in the historical message of Jesus recorded in Scripture. Human experience is the medium and realm of reconciliation in which the kingdom of God is actualized. The meaning of reconciliation is found in the life and gospel of Jesus of Nazareth. Jesus' gospel of reconciliation is a unique answer to the human dilemma of estrangement and that constitutes a sufficient claim for his messianic mission and for Christianity as a transforming faith.

The notion that faith is transforming suggests that spiritual growth is as important as theological development. It will be fruitful to explore further the spiritual dimension of reconciliation. By way of anticipation, the spiritual dimension may be construed as the realm of being, consciousness, and meaning experienced as ultimate concern in finite existence through time. The spiritual dimension involves becoming more fully human like Jesus of Nazareth through the experience of a transforming relationship with God. This is characterized as a life long process of growing awareness of God acting in and through my life, and by a communion with God in faith and love as one practices forgiving living sustained by a life of faithful meditation and prayer, dedicated study, and devoted service.

Scientific Directions

Since I am attempting to present not merely a philosophy or theology of counseling, but also an empirical theory relevant to practice, it is necessary to advance this theory scientifically beyond both a phenomenological description and a theological interpretation of reconciliation. To advance this theory scientifically will require the customary steps in theory construction. Theoretical constructs need to be developed along with hypothetical relationships specifying the relevant antecedents and consequences. Operational definitions of the constructs must be stated to permit measurements, including measures of independent, intervening, and dependent variables. Empirical data need to be collected through controlled research to test the hypotheses derived from a scientific theory of reconciliation, and the theory will need to be revised accordingly. Through these standard procedures, the fourfold goals of scientific investigation are pursued: to describe, understand, predict, and modify the phenomenon under investigation.

In this book I have made an initial attempt to describe and to promote under-standing of the experience of reconciliation through a linguistic analysis of its popular and biblical meanings and through a phenomenological analysis of the dimensions along which persons are expected to change as they live more reconciled lives. I selected Jesus' experience of reconciliation with God and others as the concrete example in which to discover the essence of reconciliation as a lived experience.

A next step is to conduct phenomenological research with other people who have experienced reconciliation to describe further the dimensions and dynamics of this experience, to understand it more fully, and to derive further hypotheses about its essential structure and determining functions.[70] Clues may be derived concerning its purpose and processes as well as its causes and consequences from both qualitative and quantitative research. One example is to use the semantic differential[71] or narrative analyses[72] to help determine the meaning and implications of reconciliation.

As noted earlier in chapter three, a useful model to guide empirical investi-gation of this experience of reconciliation is Carl Rogers' programmatic research on client-centered therapy.[73] One may begin by delineating the characteristics of the reconciling person, the stages of growth occurring through the process of therapy guided by the purpose of reconciliation, and the necessary and sufficient conditions to produce such growth toward a more reconciled life. Initial measures of this experience will be approximations, perhaps more qualitative than quanti-tative, but their applications will help to achieve greater conceptual clarity and construct validity.

This line of scientific research will help to answer some of the following important questions: what are the empirical indicators that a reconciled life is present or absent, and to what degree? What distinguishes a reconciled and reconciling personality from other types? Is this a personality type or a constel-lation of multiple traits? Do we need both a state theory and a trait theory of reconciliation? If reconciliation is a virtue, that is, a trait of character, is it possible to investigate it scientifically in a manner analogous to personality traits? That is, can we construct a multi-trait profile such as a Reconciled Personality Inventory? Among potential scales are the moral traits of wisdom, compassion, courage, joy, gratitude, and a reconciling will. A factor-analytic approach may help to determine whether these specific traits are included and may help us to discover others.

As an alternative to viewing reconciliation as a trait, it may prove equally fruitful to construe reconciliation as an attitude. The early tripartite view of attitude with cognitive, affective, and behavioral dimensions provides a heuristic model for investigating their interactions and the implications of inconsistency among these three dimensions of a reconciling attitude. One might adopt a functional theory to explore what needs or functions a reconciling attitude can serve for a person or group. Examples include a knowledge function, an ego-defensive function, a utilitarian function, or value-expressive function. Moreover, the bases and structure of a reconciling attitude in conjunction with other attitudes could be explored. Perhaps even more useful would be the application of social psychological research on attitude change through persuasion and other principles and strategies of social influence. Also relevant is social psychological research on aggression, prejudice, group processes, the formation of identity, social cognition, attribution and interpersonal perception, and the development of prosocial motivation such as helping others.[74]

Another line of psychological research is suggested by the motivating function of moral ideals. Since moral ideals function in a manner similar to motives, both to energize and to direct behavior, one could approach the study of reconciliation in terms of theories of motivation. How would one measure a "need for reconciliation"? Does the state of being reconciled constitute a form of positive reinforcement? Which motivational terms used in psychological theories are most helpful in understanding an individual who wants to become a reconciling person? Shall we speak of a drive toward reunion of the separated as Paul Tillich notes, or of the "will to reconcile" in a manner analogous to Viktor Frankl's "will to meaning"?

Additional research questions include the following: What are the respective functions of cognitions, feelings, intentions, behavior, and relationships in the process and experience of reconciliation? Does this process get started through an unconscious desire to reconcile? Is there such a phenomenon as unconscious reconciliation within and between persons? Is reconciliation ultimately a conscious choice and an outcome we bring about ourselves as volitional agents through deliberate decisions? How does this process occur through time? Does it move through identifiable stages or phases? The dynamics of reconciliation as a process through time could be expressed as a movement through such stages or phases as: union/separation/reunion, integration/disintegration/reintegration, attachment/detachment/reattachment, connection/disconnection/reconnection, or misidentification/disidentification/reidentification.[75]

Moreover, it is important to ask about the relationship between the experience of reconciliation and mental and spiritual health.[76] How is a reconciled life or a state of being reconciled related to concepts of mental health and to the indicators of social well-being specified in quality of life research,[77] to the stages of faith development and spiritual formation,[78] and to measures of spiritual well-being?[79] These and other questions need to be addressed and answered empirically and scientifically.

Empirical research is feasible because experiences of reconciliation transform human character and human relations. There are observable, measurable indicators of the experiential changes that occur as persons become more reconciled with

God, with self, and with others. By implication, there are also empirical tests to determine whether or not persons are changing and in what direction, just as there are empirical tests of the presence or absence of programs of social reform. As one empirical indicator of genuine faith is its fruits in action,[80] we may infer from an assessment of acts of reconciliation the potential presence of a reconciling faith.

Our scientific understanding of reconciliation may be advanced by asking a further set of questions: What are the antecedents and consequences of reconcili-ation? What causes it? What are its effects? What predicts and modifies reconciling behavior? These are the typical questions addressed in the scientific investigation of phenomena. A related question is this: What are the necessary and/or sufficient conditions for reconciliation to occur? Must blood be shed as a sacrifice, or can one be inspired by another's reconciling life to become more reconciled with God, self, and others?

Phenomenological investigations will be useful to describe and understand the meaning of reconciliation by interviewing persons for additional concrete examples from which we may infer the general structure and essential dimensions of this human experience. Is the experience of reconciliation itself an essential mechanism of change occurring in psychotherapy? Is the experience of forgiveness the "active ingredient"of reconciliation, or can reconciliation occur in other ways, for example, through the altered states of consciousness emphasized in Eastern religions as enlightenment or unitive experiences?

An information processing model may be useful to advance research as expressed by the following questions: What are the inputs, processes, and outputs of reconciliation? We may ask also about the purpose, process, and practice of reconciliation. And these six questions are also relevant: Who reconciles what with whom, when, where, how, and why.

As further illustrations of potential research, social scientists, including social psychologists, may contribute theory and research to help define the reconciling society. Industrial and organizational psychologists may explore the implications of this construct for corporate structures and human relations. Economic institutions must balance motives of service, profit, and quality in addition to achieving a fit between the individual employee's rights and goals with corporate needs and goals. In a system of democratic capitalism, what would a reconciling corporation be like? Would it have both similarities to and differences from a reconciling corporation in a system of democratic socialism? How is a reconciling corporation different from an alienating corporation? One may ask a comparable question about religious institutions: What are the markers of a reconciling community which gathers in a church, synagogue, or mosque? Finally, ecological psychologists may help us to understand what a reconciliation with our earth would entail.[81] Presumably this would be a change from an attitude of dominance and exploitation to one of cooperation to restore and save it, akin to the Native American attitude of reverence toward Mother Earth and Father Sky.

Within the field of science generally, and scientific psychology particularly, there are a number of criteria that have been used to evaluate the relative merits of theories. Those scientific theories are preferred that summarize best the current data pertinent to its field of inquiry and predict new knowledge. A desirable theory is comprehensive, parsimonious, logically coherent, precise and clear, operational and heuristic, empirically supported and practical.[82] Other soft criteria have included such standards as the elegance of a theory and its integration with other areas of inquiry.

Based on these criteria, this theory will need the contributions of many others to come to fruition. This process will be enriched by an interdisciplinary approach involving theologians, philosophers, and social scientists. I invite others to join me on this journey toward a more reconciling life. It is a journey begun centuries ago when Jesus of Nazareth called us to advance the realm of reconciling relationships. The kingdom of God is always at hand, but many hands are needed to actualize it on earth as it is in heaven.

NOTES

1. Jones, S. L. (1994). A constructive relationship for religion with the science and profession of psychology. *American Psychologist, 49*(3),184–197. Both logical positivism and nominalism constitute challenges to the ontology of "being" I have adopted in this book. See Tillich, P. (1951). *Systematic theology* (Vol. 1). Chicago: University of Chicago Press, p. 230. See n.3 in chapter two for additional references.

2. Tillich, P. (1951). *Systematic theology* (Vol. 1). Chicago: University of Chicago Press, pp. 106–108.

3. A phenomenological hermeneutic has been applied in theories of culture by Tracy, D. (1981). *The analogical imagination: Christian theology and the culture of pluralism.* New York: Crossroad, and by McFague, S. (1982). *Metaphorical theology: Models of God in religious language.* Philadelphia: Fortress Press.

4. The classification of approaches and illustrative theories are presented by Bettis, J. (Ed.). (1969). *Phenomenology of religion: Eight modern descriptions of the essence of religion.* New York: Harper & Row.

5. In contrast to a teleological view of spirit as the inner aim of life, Tillich prefers an ontological view of "spirit" as "the unity of the power of being with the meaning of being." Tillich, P. (1951). *Systematic theology* (Vol. 1). Chicago: University of Chicago Press, p. 249. His existential ontology is an alternative to supernatural, humanistic, dualistic, or monistic world views (Ibid., p. 65).

6. Another way of relating psychology and theology is in the critical evaluation mode. See Jones, S. L. (1994). A constructive relationship for religion with the science and profession of psychology. *American Psychology, 49*(3), 184–197.

7. Tillich, P. (1951). *Systematic theology* (Vol. 1). Chicago: University of Chicago Press.

8. For a discussion of criteria by which truth may be verified see Tillich, P. (1951). *Systematic theology* (Vol. 1). Chicago: University of Chicago Press, pp. 100–105.

9. The concept of "substance," which was popular in philosophy and theology up to the early twentieth century, has been deemphasized and replaced by concepts such as process and events, being and becoming, experience, relation, and function. See Macquarrie, J. (1988). *Twentieth century religious thought.* Philadelphia: Trinity Press International, p. 21.

10. The concept of "becoming" has equal ontic status as "being." Tillich, P. (1951). *Systematic theology* (Vol. 1). Chicago: University of Chicago Press, p. 181.

11. Taylor, M. K. (1991). *Paul Tillich: Theologian of the boundaries.* Minneapolis, MN: Fortress Press, p. 141. Tillich defines God as "Being Itself." This he asserts as the only non-symbolic statement we can make about God. The self-world structure of Being avoids a subject-object dualism and the errors of both positivism and idealism. It also suggests a fundamental category of "relation," though Tillich does not include it among the primary four: time, space, causality, and substance. In his discussion of the actuality of God, Tillich speaks of "being-in-relation" as one of the symbolic statements about God: God is being, living, creating, and related. Tillich, P. (1951). Systematic theology (Vol. 1). Chicago: University of Chicago Press, pp. 173–174, 235–290.

12. Buber, M. (1958). *I and Thou* (2nd ed.). New York: Macmillan. See also Schilpp, P., & Friedman, M. (Eds.). (1967). *The philosophy of Martin Buber.* La Salle, IL: Open Court.

13. Buber, M. (1958). *I and Thou* (2nd ed.). New York: Macmillan, pp. 3–5, 11, 18, 27. Buber's contrast between I-It and I-Thou relations is a helpful way of understanding the meaning of alienation in contrast to reconciliation. It implies also that the phenomenological view of consciousness as intentional, that is, as always having an object, may be an example of a construct in the I-It realm.

14. Ibid., pp. 6, 9, 12. Buber's I-Thou relation provides a philosophical and theological foundation for the clinical emphasis on assessment of interpersonal processes rather than an exclusive focus on intrapsychic dynamics. See Peterson, D., & Fishman, D. (1987). *Assessment for decision.* New Brunswick, NJ: Rutgers University Press.

15. Buber, M. (1958). *I and Thou* (2nd ed.). New York: Macmillan, p. 9.

16. Naive realism has been rejected in part as a result of the movement away from Newtonian mechanics to quantum physics. For a critique of naive realism, see Barbour, I. (1966). *Issues in science and religion.* New York: Harper Torchbooks, pp. 284–286.

17. This is Tillich's position. Tillich, P. (1951). *Systematic theology* (Vol. 1). Chicago: University of Chicago Press, pp. 168–204. He speaks of "Being-in-relation" as one of the metaphors for describing the actuality of God. Under this concept he discusses divine holiness, power, love, and God as Lord and Father (Ibid., pp. 271– 289).

18. The notion of an essential interdependence between subject and object has been advocated by several others. Examples include, Buber, M. (1958). *I and thou.* New York: Macmillan; and Sponheim, P. (1993). *Faith and the other: A relational theology.* Minneapolis, MN: Fortress Press. See also the discussion of process philosophers by Macquarrie, J. (1988). *Twentieth century religious thought.* Philadelphia: Trinity Press International, pp. 258–278; and Barbour, I. (1990). *Religion in an age of science.* New York: Harper-SanFrancisco. In his discussion of the actuality of God, Tillich refers to God as "Being-in-relation" as one of several symbolic statements. Tillich, P. (1951). *Systematic theology* (Vol. 1). Chicago: University of Chicago Press, pp. 271–289.

19. Barbour, I. (1966). *Issues in science and religion.* New York: Harper Torchbooks, p. 157.

20. Ibid., p. 168–171. A critical realism affirms that "despite the fact that descriptions of the world are in part our creation, the world is such as to bear description in some ways and not in others." (p. 169). One may affirm a critical realism without advocating a Whiteheadian process philosophy as Barbour adopts.

21. For a critical discussion of Hans Vaihinger's philosophy of 'as if' see Macquarrie, J. (1988). *Twentieth-century religious thought.* Philadelphia: Trinity Press International, pp. 80–82.

22. As an alternative to both a supernaturalism and naturalism, Paul Tillich advocates a "self-transcending realism'" to express the human experience of the transcendent as the real, saving power of reconciliation. See Taylor, M. K. (1991). *Paul Tillich: Theologian of the boundaries.* Minneapolis, MN: Fortress Press, pp. 67–82, 126–141.

23. Huston Smith noted that the name the Hindus give to the supreme reality is Brahman, which has a dual etymology, deriving as it does from both *br*, "to breathe," and *brih*, "to be great." The chief attributes to be linked with the name are *sat*, *chit*, and *ananda*: God is being, awareness, and bliss. Smith, H. (1991). *The world's religions.* New York: HarperSanFrancisco, p. 60.

24. Tillich characterizes the logical arguments for the existence of God as ways in which the question of God's existence is raised and as indications of the quest for revelation. It is the *analogia entis* (analogy of being) which makes it possible to speak of God nonsymbolically as Being itself. Tillich, P. (1951). *Systematic theology* (Vol. 1). Chicago: University of Chicago Press, pp. 131, 204–211, 239.

25. These various philosophical systems are summarized by Macquarrie, J. (1988). *Twentieth century religious thought.* Philadelphia: Trinity Press International.

26. Examples of theistic naturalism in Christian theology are Henry Wieman and Douglas Macintosh (cited by Livingston, J. [1971]. *Modern Christian thought from the enlightenment to vatican II.* New York: Macmillan, pp. 418–445. Examples in both philosophy and philosophical theology are the varieties of theistic realism presented by Franz Brentano, Samuel Alexander, Conway Morgan, the process philosophy of Alfred North Whitehead, Charles Hartshorne, and Ian Barbour, the panentheism of Teilhard de Chardin, the moderate realism of Neo-Thomism, and the Christian humanism of Jacque Maritain. (Cited in Macquarrie, J. [1988]. *Twentieth century religious thought.* Philadelphia: Trinity Press International, pp. 227–228, 258–300). Examples from psychology include the present work, the "theistic realism" advocated by Bergin, A. (1980). Psychotherapy and religious values. *Journal of Consulting and Clinical Psychology, 48*(1), pp. 95–105; and Richards, P., & Bergin, A. (1997). *A spiritual strategy for counseling and psychotherapy.* Washington, DC: American Psychological Association.

27. "Experiential idealism" affirms that ideas shape both human choices and social relationships, but the import and power of ideas is expressed in human experience, and ideals take shape in human life. Stackhouse, M. (Ed.). (1976). *James Luther Adams: On being human religiously.* Boston: Beacon Press, p. xix.

28. In contrast to views expressed in previous decades, the 1980s marked a significant change in that the vast majority of therapists were found to believe that values are embedded in psychotherapy and are a natural part of the change process. See Garfield, S., & Bergin, A. (1994). Introduction and historical overview. In A. Bergin & S. Garfield (Eds.), *Handbook of psychotherapy and behavior change* (4th ed., p. 12). New York: John Wiley & Sons.

29. Frankena, W. (1973). *Ethics* (2nd ed.). Englewood Cliffs, NJ: Prentice-Hall, pp. 61–67. Moral principles of conduct require moral virtues to become effective and actualized, and moral virtues require principles as guides. An ethic of principles expresses judgments of moral obligation or deontic judgments. An ethic of virtue reflects judgments

of moral value or aretaic judgments. (Ibid., p. 9).

30. Frankena, W. (1973). *Ethics* (2nd ed.). Englewood Cliffs, NJ: Prentice-Hall, pp. 80–83.

31. Frankena considers an act-deontology based upon either intuition or an existential decision as an untenable theory due to its absence of principles or rules by which to determine the validity of one's intuitions and decisions about what one ought to do. A rule-deontological theory provides such guiding principles. See Frankena, W. (1973). *Ethics* (2nd ed.). Englewood Cliffs, NJ: Prentice-Hall, pp. 23–28, 43.

32. Tillich's statement is that "the drive toward the reunion of the separated is love." Tillich, P. (1957). *The dynamics of faith.* New York: Harper and Brothers Publishers, p. 112. A paraphrase in voluntaristic terms is that love is the will to reconcile with that to which one belongs and from whom one is estranged.

33. The themes of grace and gratitude appear to have shaped Calvin's theology more than the notion of predestination, according to Gerrish, B. (1993). *Grace and gratitude: The eucharistic theology of John Calvin.* Minneapolis, MN: Fortress Press.

34. Two Christian writers who have advocated middle moral axioms are Ronald Preston and John Bennett, whose theories are summarized in Atherton, J. (Ed.). (1994). *Christian social ethics: A reader.* Cleveland, OH: The Pilgrim Press, pp. 129–156, 225–254.

35. Fletcher, J. (1966). *Situation ethics: The new morality.* Philadelphia: The Westminster Press.

36. I use the term "reconciling personality'" to connote that successful psychotherapy yields not only a more reconciled person, but one who contributes to reconciliation among others. In a somewhat similar manner, Alfred Adler stressed the importance of developing a prosocial motivation he termed "social interest." The term "reconciling" also connotes that past action is incomplete and continues in the present. For similar reasons the present progressive tense was selected for the UCC statement of Faith to emphasize God's on-going activity of reconciling the world. See Shinn, R. (1990). *Confessing our faith: An interpretation of the statement of faith of the United Church of Christ.* Cleveland, OH: United Church Press, pp. 72–74.

37. As an intrinsic value, reconciliation is good in itself or good because of its intrinsic properties. I would also argue that reconciliation is an inherent good as an experience, a contributory good as a part of the good life, and as a final good, that is, good on the whole. For definitions and discussion of these terms, see Frankena, W. (1973). *Ethics* (2nd ed.). Englewood Cliffs, NJ: Prentice-Hall, pp. 80–83.

38. Being a reconciling person may be considered a cardinal virtue either in addition to others or as one subsuming others. I would prefer to say that the reconciling individual possesses the traditional seven cardinal virtues in the Christian tradition: the three "theological" virtues of faith, hope, and love, and the four "human" virtues of prudence, fortitude, temperance, and justice. Like these religious virtues, reconciliation may be viewed as a fruit of the Spirit and sustained by spiritual gifts. (See The United States Catholic Conference. [1994]. *Catechism of the Catholic Church.* Mahwah, NJ: The Paulist Press, pp. 443–452.) Insofar as other human dispositions cannot be derived from the cardinal virtue of reconciliation, they could be considered either as other kinds of virtue or not a virtue at all (e.g., a trait of personality rather than a trait of character, or an intellectual ability or technical skill). See Frankena, W. (1873). *Ethics* (2nd ed.). Englewood Cliffs, NJ:

Prentice-Hall, p. 64.

39. The theory presented in this book may be considered as an example of a normative psychological theory grounded in moral philosophy. See Browning, D. (1987). *Religious thought and the modern psychologies: A critical conversation.* Philadelphia: Fortress Press, pp. xi, 125, 238.

40. Frankena, W. (1973). *Ethics* (2nd ed.). Englewood Cliffs, NJ: Prentice- Hall, pp. 102–105, 28–30, 57. The theory of moral obligation evident in the current Catholic Catechism expresses a divine command theory. Moral obligations are defined by the Decalogue recorded as the Ten Commandments in Exodus 21:1–17 and Dueteronomy 5:6–22. These moral commands are considered the revealed will of God. From these divine commands, additional duties and rights are derived. (See the United States Catholic Conference. [1994]. *Catechism of the Catholic Church.* Mahwah, NJ: Paulist Press, pp. 496–504, 534–544.)

41. Luke 17:4 records Jesus' teaching to forgive seven times, not seventy-seven times. In either case, to focus on the number is to miss Jesus' point about the preeminence and healing power of forgiveness.

42. Further criticisms of a definist theory are provided by Frankena, W. (1973). *Ethics* (2nd ed.). Englewood Cliffs, NJ: Prentice-Hall, pp. 97–102.

43. This is the theory of moral justification proposed by Frankena, W. (1973). *Ethics* (2nd ed.). Englewood Cliffs, NJ: Prentice-Hall, pp. 110–114. Basically in a moral point of view (a) one makes normative judgments, (b) one is willing to universalize these judgments, (c) one's justifications include facts about the consequences in terms of promoting or distributing nonmoral good and evil, and (d) in judging one-self or one's own actions, one's justification includes an assessment of the impact upon others, if others are affected (Ibid., p. 113).

44. A comparable position was taken by D. Browning. He advocated the norm of "mutuality" as the "inner rational core of morality." By that he meant the norm of "mutuality" can be rationally justified apart from a particular scientific, philosophical, or theological paradigm. See Browning, D. (1987). *Religious thought and the modern psychologies: A critical conversation.* Philadelphia: Fortress Press, pp. 131– 132, 138–140.

45. Rational justification for the objective validity of moral principles may include appeals to other nonmoral values, such as its benefits for individuals and for society as a whole. Appeals of this type are illustrated in chapter four of this book and by Frankena, W. (1973). *Ethics* (2nd ed.). Englewood Cliffs, NJ: Prentice-Hall, pp. 113–116.

46. Whether defined as ultimate concern or as confidence and loyalty, faith is a universal human experience. A challenge to one faith is always based upon another faith, whether it takes a secular or religious form. See Niebuhr, H. R. (1960). *Radical monotheism and Western culture. With supplementary essays.* Louisville, KY: Westminster/John Knox Press, pp. 16–23.

47. For a critique of the divine command theory, see Frankena, W. (1973). *Ethics* (2nd ed.). Englewood Cliffs, NJ: Prentice-Hall, pp. 28–30, 57.

48. Von Harnack, A. (1957). *What is Christianity?* Philadelphia: Fortress Press edition, 1986, p. 73.

49. In Catholic theology, seven spiritual gifts and twelve fruits of the Spirit sustain and perfect the seven cardinal virtues. See United States Catholic Conference. (1994). *Catechism of the Catholic Church.* Mahwah, NJ: Paulist Press, pp. 443– 452.

50. Love for others does not preclude love of self. Love of self remains a fundamental principle of morality. Therein lies moral justification for self-defense even if it means the use of lethal force against one's aggressor. See the *Catechism of the Catholic Church* (1994), p. 545.

51. D. Browning takes a similar position with respect to his proposal of mutuality as the rational core of morality: mutuality is right independent of whether God commands it or not. But religious belief in God provides a "full embodiment" of morality by providing a deep metaphor of the kind of world in which mutuality and justice can take place. This is a more theoretical contribution of religion to morality than the psychological and existential emphasis I have given to it. Browning, D. (1987). *Religious thought and the modern psychologies: A critical conversation.* Philadelphia: Fortress Press, pp. 131–132.

52. It is particularly in the gospel of Luke that the life of Jesus is presented as the model for Christians to imitate.

53. Frankena, W. (1973). *Ethics* (2nd ed.). Englewood Cliffs, NJ: Prentice- Hall, p. 67. In the history of liberal Protestant theology, Albrecht Ritschl stressed that justification and reconciliation were accomplished through the moral influence of the historical Christ and through the Christian community. It was particularly in his more practical book, *Instruction in the Christian Religion*, that he defined faith itself as a value judgment, and emphasized the ethical dimension of the reconciled life as working for the kingdom of God on earth. See Livingston, J. (1971). *Modern Christian thought from the enlightenment to vatican II.* New York: Macmillan, p. 254–255, and Jodock, D. (Ed.). (1995). *Ritschl in retrospect: History, community, and science.* Minneapolis, MN: Fortress Press.

54. á Kempis, T. (1486). *The Imitation of Christ.* Chicago: Moody Press Edition, 1958.

55. In psychological language, a moral ideal functions like an "ego-ideal" or "ideal-self," not merely the incorporation of parental values as in Freud's concept of the "superego." A moral ideal forms one's conscience and provides it content.

56. What one does is influenced in part by what one believes he can do. Bandura terms this belief as self-efficacy, which is enhanced through imitation of observed models. See Bandura, A. (1977). Self-efficacy: Toward a unifying theory of behavior change. *Psychological Review, 84,* 191–215.

57. United States Catholic Conference. (1994). *Catechism of the Catholic Church.* Mahwah, NJ: Paulist Press, p. 451. The Catholic Church utilizes the inspiring power of moral ideals in its veneration of saints as faith-filled, human examples of inspiring virtue.

58. The therapeutic value of a moral ideal is recognized and applied in the approach developed by Assagioli, R. (1965). *Psychosynthesis: A collection of basic writings.* New York: Arkana, pp. 166–177.

59. Bandura, A. (1960). *Principles of behavior modification.* New York: Holt, Rinehart and Winston; Bandura, A. (1977). *Social learning theory.* Englewood Cliffs, NJ: Prentice-Hall; and Bandura, A. (1986). *Social foundations of thought and action: A social cognitive theory.* Englewood Cliffs, NJ.: Prentice Hall.

60. There is a very extensive theological literature on the concept of the kingdom of God. A few references are provided in n.52 and n.82 in chapter three.

61. A contemporary example is MacArthur, J., & Mack, W. (1994). *Introduction to biblical counseling: A basic guide to the principles and practice of counseling.* Dallas, TX: Word Publishing. Consistent with Jay Adams' nouthetic counseling, upon which this book

is based (pp. 49–55), the authors reject attempts to develop any integrated Christian psychology in favor of the principle of Scripture's sufficiency which is used to justify a "separate and unequal" relation between theology and psychology (pp. 16–20).

62. Historical figures in the liberal Protestant tradition since the nineteenth century include Friedrich Schleiermacher, Albrecht Ritschl, Adolph von Harnack, Ernst Troeltsch, Hosea Ballou, William Channing, Theodore Parker, Matthew Fox, Rufus Jones, Horace Bushnell, William Adams Brown, Arthur C. McGiffert, Walter Rauschenbusch, Henry Wieman, Douglas Mcintosh, and James Luther Adams.

63. Niebuhr, H. R. (1951). *Christ and culture.* New York: Harper & Row. Niebuhr's typology and others discussed here are summarized by Cowdell, S. (1996). *Is Jesus unique? A study of recent Christology.* New York: Paulist Press, pp. 10–13. According to M. Stackhouse, " . . . the United Church of Christ still believes, with the Niebuhrs, Tillich, and King, that the proper direction for us is Christ transforming culture." Stackhouse, M. (1986). Obedience to Christ and engaged in the world. *Prism, 1*(2), 7.

64. Tracy, D. (1975). *Blessed rage for order.* San Francisco: Harper & Row.

65. The dialogical category is specified by Dulles, A. (1976). Contemporary approaches to Christology: Analysis and reflections. *Living Light, 13,* 119–144.

66. Berger, P. (1979). *The heretical imperative.* New York: Doubleday.

67. Aulen, G. (1931). *Christus Victor: A historical study of the three main types of the atonement.* London: SPCK.

68. Rupp, G. (1974). *Christologies and cultures: Toward a typology of religious worldviews.* The Hague: Mouton.

69. Cowdell, S. (1996). *Is Jesus unique? A study of recent christology.* New York: Paulist Press, pp. 15–17. Christian pluralism is more dependent on the Christian tradition than the broader religious pluralism of Unitarian Universalist theology. See Buehrens, J., & Church, F. (1989). *Our chosen faith: An introduction to Unitarian Universalism.* Boston: Beacon Press, p. 114. See also Marshall, G. (1991). *Challenge of a liberal faith* (3rd ed.). Boston: Skinner House Books, pp. 99–141; and Robinson, D. (1985). *The Unitarians and Universalists.* Westport, CT: Greenwood Press, pp. 87–122.

70. For discussion of phenomenological research methodology, see Polkinghouse, D. (1989). Phenomenological research methods. In Valle, R., & Halling, S. (Eds.). *Existential-phenomenological perspectives in psychology* (pp. 41–60). New York: Plenum Press. An earlier discussion is Kruger, D. (1979). *An introduction to phenomenological psychology.* Pittsburgh, PA: Duquesne University Press, pp. 113–139.

71. Osgood, C., Suci, G., & Tannenbaum, P. (1957). *The Measurement of meaning.* Urbana, IL: University of Illinois Press.

72. Friedman, J., & Combs, G. A. (1996). *Narrative therapy: The social construction of preferred realities.* New York: W. W. Norton and Company; White, M., & Epston, D. (1990). *Narrative means to therapeutic ends.* Adelaide, South Australia: Dulwich Centre; and Toukamanian, S., & Rennie, D. (Eds.). (1992). *Psychotherapy process research: Paradigmatic and narrative approaches.* Newbury Park, CA: Sage. The stories of the Exodus and return from exile are examples of narratives of reconciliation in the history and faith of Israel.

73. Rogers, C. (1961). *On becoming a person: A therapist's view of psychotherapy.* Boston: Houghton Mifflin. Additional theological models are the empirical theology of Douglas Macintosh and the theological naturalism of Henry Wieman, both discussed in

Livingston, J. C. (1971). *Modern Christian thought from the enlightenment to Vatican II.* New York: Macmillan, pp. 418–446, and the critical realism grounded in process theology by Barbour, I. (1990). *Religion in an age of science.* New York: HarperSanFrancisco.

74. For a current summary of theory and research in these areas see Tesser, A. (1995). *Advanced social psychology.* New York: McGraw-Hill.

75. The latter terms refer to yoga psychology which suggests the fundamental cause of human suffering is the incorrect identification with the ego as one's true nature and personal center. One must become dis-identified with this illusion and re-identified with the Self (Atman) who is God (Brahman) incarnate as the One in the many. See Swami Ajaya (1983). *Psychotherapy East and West: A unifying paradigm.* Honesdale, PA: The Himalyan International Institute of Yoga Science and Philosophy of the USA, pp. 127–182. The application of the disidentification process in psychotherapy is also found in Assagioli, R. (1973). *The act of will.* New York: Viking Press, pp. 214–217.

76. The challenge of defining mental health continues to occupy the attention of psychologists. A recent example is Gorenstein, E. (1984). Debating mental illness. *American Psychologist, 39*(1), 50–56.

77. A review of quality of life research is provided by Hollandsworth, J. G., Jr. (1988). Evaluating the impact of medical treatment on the quality of life: A 5-year update. *Social Science and Medicine, 26,* 425–434. More recent references are Frisch, M., Cornell, J., Villanueva, M., & Retzlaff, P. (1992). Clinical validation of the Quality of Life Inventory: A measure of life satisfaction for use in treatment planning and outcome assessment. *Psychological Assessment, 4,* 92–101; and Lawton, M. (1997). Measures of quality of life and subjective well-being. *Generations, 21,* 45–47.

78. Fowler, J. (1981). *Stages of faith: The psychology of human development and the quest for meaning.* New York: HarperSanFrancisco.

79. A source for measures of spiritual well being is Fitchett, G. (1993). *Assessing spiritual needs.* Minneapolis, MN: Augsburg Press.

80. For a discussion of the relation of faith and action see Niebuhr, H. R. (1988). *The kingdom of God in America.* Hanover, NH: Wesleyan University Press, p. 113.

81. See Clinebell, H. (1996). Greening pastoral care. *Journal of Pastoral Care, 48*(3), 209–214; and Clinebell, H. (1996). *Ecotherapy: Healing ourselves, healing the earth.* Minneapolis, MN: Fortress Press.

82. Similar criteria have been suggested for a satisfactory philosophical theology: it is (a) reasonable, (b) comprehensive, (c) contemporary (relevant), and (d) in process and leaves room for development. (Macquarrie, J. [1988]. *Twentieth century religious thought.* Philadelphia: Trinity Press International, pp. 449–452.) Three related criteria by which to evaluate both theological and scientific statements are their (a) coherence, (b) comprehensiveness, and (c) relation to data. See Barbour, I. (1966). *Issues in science and religion.* New York: Harper & Row, pp. 252–255.

Selected Bibliography

SCIENCE AND RELIGION

Ashley, D., & Orenstein, D. (1990). *Sociological theory: Classical statements.* Boston: Allyn and Bacon.

Barbour, I. (1966). *Issues in science and religion.* New York: Harper Torchbooks.

Barbour, I. (1990). *Religion in an age of science: The Gifford lectures, 1989-91* (Vol. 1). New York: HarperCollins.

Bettis, J. B. (Ed.). (1960). *Phenomenology of religion: Eight modern descriptions of the essence of religion.* New York: Harper & Row.

Bevin, W. (1991). Contemporary psychology: A tour inside the onion. *American Psychologist, 46,* 475–483.

Bube, R . (1971). *The human guest: A new look at science and the Christian faith.* Waco, TX: Word Books.

Campbell, A. (1997). *Health as liberation: Medicine, theology, and the quest for justice.* Cleveland, OH: The Pilgrim Press.

Ferre, F. (1961). *Language, logic, and God.* New York: Harper and Brothers.

Foster, J. D., & Ledbetter, M. F. (1987). Christianity and psychology and the scientific method. *Journal of Psychology and Theology, 15,* 10–18.

Harding, S. (1991). *Whose science? Whose knowledge?* Ithaca, NY: Cornell University Press.

Heim, K. (1953). *Christian faith and natural science: The creative encounter between twentieth century physics and Christian existentialism.* New York: Harper Torchbooks.

Jeeves, M. (1971). *The scientific enterprise and Christian faith.* Downers Grove, IL: InterVarsity Press.

Kiresuk, T., Smith, A., & Cardillo, J. (Eds.). (1994). *Goal attainment scaling: Applications, theory, and measurement.* Hillsdale, NJ: Lawrence Erlbaum Associates.

Kruger, D. (1979). *An introduction to phenomenological psychology.* Pittsburgh, PA: Duquesne University Press.

Lapsley, J. (1972). *Salvation and health: The interlocking processes of life.* Philadelphia: Westminster Press.

Lund, N. (1980). *A common call to care for the whole person: An argument for the reconciliation of the Christian faith and medical science in a wholistic approach to health care.* St. Paul, MN: (s.n.).

Manicas, P., & Secord, P. (1983). Implications for psychology of the new philosophy of science. *American Psychologist, 38,* 399–412.

Miles, T. R. (1959). *Religion and the scientific outlook.* London: George Allen and Unwin.

Morris, T. (1994). *God and the philosophers: The rconciliation of faith and reason.* New York: Oxford University Press.

Osgood, C., Suci, G., & Tannenbaum, P. (1957). *The measurement of meaning.* Urbana, IL: University of Illinois Press.

Peacock, A. (1993). *Theology for a scientific age: Being and becoming—natural, divine, and human.* Minneapolis, MN: Fortress Press.

Robinson, D. N. (1985). *Philosophy of psychology.* New York: Columbia University Press.

Russell, B. (1972). *A history of Western philosophy.* New York: Simon & Schuster.

Smith, H. (1991). *The world's religions.* New York: HarperSanFrancisco

Tesser, A. (1995). *Advanced social psychology.* New York: McGraw-Hill.

Toukamanian, S., & Rennie, D. (Eds.). (1992). *Pychotherapy process research: Paradigmatic and narrative approaches.* Newbury Park, CA: Sage.

Valle, R., & Halling, S. (Eds.). (1989). *Existential phenomenological perspectives in psychology.* New York: Plenum Press.

PSYCHOLOGY AND THEOLOGY

Adler, A. (1964). *Social interest: A challenge of mankind.* New York: Capricorn Books.

Allport, G. (1950). *The individual and his religion: A psychological interpretation.* New York: Collier Macmillan Publishers.

Allport, G. (1955). *Becoming: Basic considerations for a psychology of personality.* New Haven, CT: Yale University Press.

Allport, G. (1961). *Pattern and growth in personality.* New York: Capricorn Books.

Assagioli, R. (1965). *Psychosynthesis: A collection of basic writings.* New York: Arkana.

Assagioli, R. (1973). *The act of will.* New York: Viking Press.

Bergin, A. (1980). Psychotherapy and religious values. *Journal of Consulting and Clinical Psychology, 48*(1), 95–105.

Bergin, A., & Garfield, S. (Eds.). (1994). *Handbook of psychotherapy and behavior change* (4th ed.). New York: John Wiley & Sons.

Bergin, A., & Jansen, J. (1990). Religiosity of psychotherapists: A national survey. *Psychotherapy, 27*(1), 3–7.

Brazier, D. (1995). *Zen therapy: Transcending the sorrows of the human mind.* New York: John Wiley & Sons.

Browning, D. (1987). *Religious thought and the modern psychologies: A critical conversation in the theology of culture.* Philadelphia: Fortress Press.

Burns, J. P. (Ed.). (1981). *Theological anthropology.* Minneapolis, MN: Fortress Press.

Campbell, A. (1997). *Health and liberation: Medicine, theology, and the quest for justice.* Cleveland, OH: Pilgrim Press.

Capps, D. (1993). *The depleted self: Sin in a narcissistic age.* Minneapolis, MN: Fortress

Press.

Capps, D. (1995a). *Agents of hope: A pastoral psychology.* Minneapolis, MN: Fortress Press.

Capps, D. (1995b). *Hope: A pastoral psychology.* Minneapolis, MN: Fortress Press.

Clinton, S. M. (1990). A critique of integration models. *Journal of Psychology and Theology, 18,* 13–20.

Dreher, D. (1990). *The Tao of inner peace.* New York: Harper Perennial.

Farber, L. (1966). *The ways of the will.* New York: Basic Books.

Farnsworth, K. (1982). The conduct of integration. *Journal of Psychology and Theology, 10,* 308–319.

Farnsworth, K. (1985). *Wholehearted integration: Harmonizing psychology and Christianity through word and deed.* Grand Rapids, MI: Baker Book House.

Feuerbach, L. (1989). *The essence of Christianity.* New York: Prometheus Books.

Fleck, J. R., & Carter, J. D. (Eds.). (1981). *Psychology and theology: Integrative readings.* Nashville, TN: Abingdon.

Fowler, J. (1981). *Stages of faith: The psychology of human development and the quest for meaning.* New York: HarperSanFrancisco.

Fowler, J. (1984). *Becoming adult, becoming Christian.* New York: Harper and Row.

Frankl, V. (1975). *The unconscious God: Psychotherapy and theology.* New York: Simon and Schuster.

Freud, S. (1961). The future of an illusion. *Standard edition of the complete psychological works of Sigmund Freud, 21,* 1–56. London: Hogarth Press. (Original work published 1923).

Gorsuch, R. (1988). Psychology of religion. *Annual Review of Psychology, 39,* 201–221.

Hillman, J. (1975). *Re-visioning psychology.* New York: Harper and Row.

Ingram, J. (1995). Contemporary issues and Christian models of integration: Into the modern/postmodern age. *Journal of Psychology and Theology, 23*(1), 3–14.

Jahoda, M. (1958). *Current concepts of positive mental health.* New York: Basic Books.

Jones, E. S. (1994). A constructive relationship for religion with the science and profession of psychology. *American Psychologist, 49*(3), 184–197.

Kierkegaard, S. (1954). *Fear and trembling, and sickness unto death.* Garden City, NY: Doubleday.

Kirwan, Wm. (1984). *Biblical concepts for Christian counseling: A case for integrating psychology and theology.* Grand Rapids, MI: Baker Book House.

Lapsley, J. (1972). *Salvation and health: The interlocking processes of life.* Philadelphia, PA: Westminster Press.

Lasch, C. (1978). *The culture of narcissism.* New York: W. W. Norton.

Lauer, E., & Mlecko, J. (Eds.). (1982). *A Christian understanding of the human person: Basic readings.* New York: Paulist Press.

Malony, H. N. (Ed.). (1983). *Wholeness and holiness: Readings in the psychology and theology of mental health.* Grand Rapids, MI: Baker Book House.

Malony, H. N., Papen-Daniels, M., & Clinebell, H. (Eds.). (1988). *Spirit centered wholeness: Beyond the psychology of self.* Lewiston, NY: Edwin Mellen Press.

Macquarrie, J. (1988). *Twentieth century religious thought.* Philadelphia: Trinity Press International.

Macquarrie, J. (1996). *Mediators between human and divine: From Moses to Muhammad.* New York: Continuum.

Marty, M., & Peerman, D. (1984). *Handbook of Christian theologians.* Nashville, TN: Abingdon.

May, G. (1982). *Will and spirit.* San Francisco: Harper and Row.

May, R . (1969). *Love and will.* New York: Dell.

McDermott, T. (Eds.). (1989). *St. Thomas Aquinas: Summa Theologiae: A concise translation.* Westminster, MD: Christian Classics.

McGaa, E. (1990). *Mother earth spirituality: Native American paths to healing ourselves and our world.* New York: HarperSanFrancisco.

McGinn, M. (1996). *Psychology, theology, and spirituality in Christian counseling.* Wheaton, IL: Tyndale House.

Meehl, P., Klann, R., Schmieding, A., Breimeier, K., & Schroeder-Slomann, S. (1958). *What, then, is man? A symposium of theology, psychology, and psychiatry.* St. Louis, MO: Concordia.

Menninger, K. (1973). *Whatever became of sin?* New York: Hawthorn Books.

Mowrer, O. H. (1961). *The crisis in psychiatry and religion.* Princeton, NJ: D. Van Nostrand.

Mowrer, O. H. (Ed.). (1966). *Morality and mental health.* Chicago: Rand McNally.

Myers, D. (1978). *The human puzzle: Psychological research and Christian belief.* New York: Harper and Row.

Narramore, B. (1974). Guilt: Where theology and psychology meet. *Journal of Psychology and Theology, 2,* 18–25.

Neihardt, J. (1979). *Black Elk speaks: Being the story of a holy man of the Oglala Sioux.* Lincoln, NE: University of Nebraska Press.

O'Donohue, W. (1989). The (even) bolder model: The clinical psychologist as metaphysician- scientist-practitioner. *American Psychologist, 44,* 1460–1468.

Otto, R. (1923). *The idea of the holy.* Oxford, London: Oxford University Press.

Perry, J. (1988). *Tillich's response to Freud: A Christian answer to the Freudian critique of religion.* Lanham, MD: University Press of America.

Prilleltensky, I. (1994). *The morals and politics of psychology.* New York: State University of New York Press.

Reiff, P. (1987). *Triumph of the therapeutic: Uses of faith after Freud.* Chicago: University of Chicago Press.

Richards, P., & Bezgin, A. (1997). *A spiritual strategy for counseling and psychotherapy.* Washington, DC: American Psychological Association.

Shafranske, E. P. (Ed.). (1996). *Religion and the clinical practice of psychology.* Washington, DC: American Psychological Association.

Sheikh, A., & Sheikh, K. (Eds.). (1989). *Eastern and western approaches to healing: Ancient wisdom and modern knowledge.* New York: John Wiley and Sons.

Surgerman, S. (1976). *Sin and madness: Studies in narcissism.* Philadelphia: Westminster Press.

Swinomish Tribal Mental Health Project. (1991). *A gathering of wisdoms. Tribal mental health: a cultural perspective.* LaConner, WA: Swinomish Tribal Community.

Tracy, D. (1975). *Blessed rage for order.* New York: Seabury Press.

Vande Kemp, H. (1984). *Psychology and theology in western thought (1672-1965): A historical and annotated bibliography.* Mill Wood, NY: Kraus.

Vande Kemp, H. (1986). Dangers of psychologism: The place of God in psychology. *Journal of Psychology and Theology, 14,* 97–109.

Vande Kemp, H. (1996). Historical perspective: Religion and clinical psychology in America. In E. P. Shafranske (Ed.), *Religion and the clinical practice of psychology.* Washington, DC: American Psychological Association.

Wulff, D. (1991). *Psychology of religion: Classic and contemporary views.* New York: Wiley.

THE NEW TESTAMENT

Bartsch, H. W. (Ed.). (1961). *Kerygma and myth: A theological debate.* New York: Harper and Row.

Bultmann, R. (1956). *Theology of the new testament* (Vol. 1). New York: Charles Scribner's Sons.

Harrington, D. (1988). Second testament exegesis and the social sciences: A bibliography. *Biblical Theology Bulletin, 18,* 77–85.

Kee, H. C. (1983). *Understanding the new testament* (4th ed.). Englewood Cliffs, NJ.: Prentice-Hall.

Macquarrie, J. (1960). *The scope of demythologizing: Bultmann and his critics.* London: SCM Press.

Neill, S., & Wright, T. (1988). *The interpretation of the New Testament, 1861-1986* (rev. ed.). Oxford, England: Oxford University Press.

Perrin, N., & Duling, D. (1986). *The New Testament: An introduction* (2nd ed.). New York: Harcourt Brace Javanovich.

Smith, W. C. (1993). *What is scripture? A comparative approach.* Minneapolis, MN: Fortress Press.

Wehrli, E. (1993). Biblical interpretation in the United Church of Christ. *Prism, 8*(2), 97–103.

THE SYNOPTIC GOSPELS

Bultmann, R. (1963). *The history of the synoptic tradition.* Oxford, England: Basil Blackwell.

Funk, R., Hoover, R., & The Jesus Seminar. (1993). *The five gospels: The search for the authentic words of Jesus.* New York: Macmillan.

Nickle, K. (1988). *The synoptic gospels: An introduction.* Atlanta, GA: John Knox Press.

Perrin, N., & Duling, D. (1982). *The new testament: An introduction.* New York: Harcourt Brace Jovanovich.

Throckmorton, B. (1992). *Gospel parallels: A comparison of the synoptic gospels.* Nashville, TN: Thomas Nelson Publishers.

Vermes, G. (1993). *The religion of Jesus the Jew.* Minneapolis, MN: Fortress Press.

THE KINGDOM OF GOD

Beasley-Murray, G. R. (1986). *Jesus and the kingdom of God.* Grand Rapids, MI: Wm. B. Eerdmans.

Borg, M. (1994b). *Meeting Jesus again for the first time.* New York: HarperSanFrancisco.

Bornkamm, G. (1960). *Jesus of Nazareth.* New York: Harper & Row.

Brown, T., & Gray, D. (1994). *Parables of the Kingdom.* Quaker Home Service. Available through Friends General Conference, 1216 Arch Street, 2B, Philadelphia, PA, 19107.

Chilton, B. (1996). *Pure kingdom: Jesus' vision of God.* Grand Rapids, MI: Wm. B. Eerdmans.

Dodd, C. H. (1935). *The parables of the kingdom.* London: Nisbet and Co.

The interpreter's dictionary of the bible. (1962). (Vol. 3, pp. 17–26). New York: Abingdon.

Jeremias, J. (1971). *New testament theology: The proclamation of Jesus.* New York: Charles Scribner's Sons.

Kaylor, R. D. (1994). *Jesus the prophet: His vision of the kingdom on earth.* Louisville, KY: Westminster/John Knox Press.

Mitchell, S. (1993). *The gospel according to Jesus.* New York: Harper.

Niebuhr, H. R . (1988). *The kingdom of God in America.* Hanover, NH: Wesleyan University Press.

Patterson, S. (1996). Shall we teach what Jesus taught? *Prism, 11*(1), 40–7.

Perrin, N. (1963). *The kingdom of God in the teachings of Jesus.* Philadelphia: Westminster Press.

Perrin, N. (1967). *Rediscovering the teaching of Jesus.* London: SCM Press.

Reiser, M. (1997). *Jesus and judgment: The eschatological proclamation in its Jewish content.* Minneapolis, MN: Fortress Press.

Song, C. S. (1993). *Jesus and the reign of God.* Minneapolis, MN: Fortress Press.

Steinberg, M. (1975). *Basic Judaism.* New York: Harcourt, Brace & Co.

Vermes, G. (1993). *The religion of Jesus the Jew.* Minneapolis, MN: Fortress Press.

von Harnack, A. (1986). *What is Christianity?* Philadelphia: Fortress Press.

Weiss, J. (1985). *Jesus' proclamation of the kingdom of God.* Chico, CA: Scholars Press.

Willis, W. (Ed.). (1987). *The kingdom of God in twentieth century interpretation.* Peabody, MA: Henrickson Publishers.

THE HISTORICAL JESUS

Borg, M. (1987). *Jesus: A new vision.* San Francisco: Harper and Row.

Borg, M. (1994a). *Jesus in contemporary scholarship.* Valley Forge, PA: Trinity Press International.

Borg, M. (1994b). *Meeting Jesus again for the first time.* New York: HarperSanFrancisco.

Borg, M. (1994c). Reflections on a discipline: A North American perspective. In B. Chilton & C. Evans (Eds.), *Studying the historical Jesus: Evaluations of the state of current research.* Leiden: E. J. Brill.

Bornkamm, G. (1960). *Jesus of Nazareth.* New York: Harper & Row.

Bultmann, R. (1958). *Jesus and the word.* New York: Scribner's.

Bultmann, R. (1958). *Jesus Christ and mythology.* New York: Charles Scribner's Sons.

Charlesworth, J. (1986). From barren mazes to gentle rappings: The emergence of Jesus research. *Princeton Seminary Bulletin, 7,* 221–230.

Chilton, B., & Evans, C. (Eds.). (1994). *Studying the historical Jesus: Evaluations of the state of current research.* Leiden: E. J. Brill.

Cowdell, S. (1996). *Is Jesus unique? A study of recent Christology.* New York: Paulist

Press.

Crossan, J. D. (1991). *The historical Jesus: The life of a Mediterranean Jewish peasant.* New York: HarperSanFrancisco.

Crossan, J. D. (1995). *Jesus: A revolutionary biography.* New York: HarperSan-Francisco.

Eckardt, A. (1992). *Reclaiming the Jesus of history: Christology today.* Minneapolis, MN: Fortress Press.

Evans, C. (1989). *Life of Jesus research: An annotated bibliography.* Leiden: E. J. Brill.

Evans, C. (1992). *Jesus.* Grand Rapids, MI: Baker Book.

Funk, R. W. (1996). *Honest to Jesus: Jesus for a new millenium.* New York: Harper-SanFrancisco.

Funk, R. W., Hoover, R. W., & The Jesus Seminar. (1993). *The five gospels: The search for the authentic words of Jesus.* New York: Macmillan.

Hare, D. A. (1990). *The son of man tradition.* Minneapolis, MN: Fortress Press.

Harrington, D. (1988). Second testament exegesis and the social sciences: A bibliography. *Biblical Theology Bulletin, 18,* 77–85.

Jeremias, J. (1971). *New testament theology: The proclamation of Jesus.* New York: Charles Scribner's Sons.

Nolan, A. (1992). *Jesus before Christianity.* Maryknoll, NY: Orbis Press.

Perrin, N. (1967). *Rediscovering the teaching of Jesus.* London: SCM Press.

Sanders, E. P. (1985). *Jesus and Judaism.* Philadelphia: Fortress Press.

Sanders, E. P. (1993). *The historical figure of Jesus.* New York: Penguin Books.

Shanks, H. (Ed.). (1994). *The search for Jesus: Modern scholarship looks at the gospels.* Washington DC: Biblical Archeology Review.

Vermes, G. (1993). *The religion of Jesus the Jew.* Minneapolis, MN: Fortress Press.

Witherington, B. (1995). *The Jesus quest: The third search for the Jew of Nazareth.* Downers Grove, IL: InterVarsity Press.

Wright, W. T. (1996). *Jesus and the victory of God: Christian origins and the question of God* (Vol. 2). Minneapolis, MN: Fortress Press.

RECONCILIATION

Aridas, C. (1987). *Reconciliation: Celebration of God's healing forgiveness.* Garden City, NY: Image Books.

Arrington, F. (1980). *The ministry of reconciliation: A study of II Corinthians.* Grand Rapids, MI: Baker Book House.

Augsburger, D. (1996). *Helping people forgive.* Louisville, KY: Westminster/John Knox Press.

Balou, H. (1853). *A treatise on atonement.* Boston: A. Tompkins.

Barth, K. (1956). *The doctrine of reconciliation* (G. W. Bromiley, Trans.). New York: Scribner's.

Barth, K. (1958). *Church dogmatics* (Vol. 4: Parts 1, 2, 3a, & 3b). Edinburgh, Scotland: T. & T. Clark.

Basetti-Sani, G. (1974). *Louis Massignon (1883-1962): Christian ecumenist prophet of interreligious reconciliation* (A. H. Cutler, Trans.). Chicago: Franciscan Herald

Press.

Battle, M. (1997). *Reconciliation: The Ubuntu theology of Desmond Tutu.* Cleveland, OH: The Pilgrim Press.

Beer, J., Stief, E., & Walker, C. (1996). *Mediator's handbook.* Philadelphia: Philadelphia Yearly Meeting [of The Society of Friends].

Brennan, P. (1986). *Penance and reconciliation.* Chicago: Thomas More Press.

Bromiley, G., & Torrance, T. (Eds.). (1936-1969) *Church dogmatics by Karl Barth* (Vols. 1-4). New York: Scribner's.

Buzzard, L., Buzzard, J., & Eck, L. (1992). *Readiness for reconciliation: A biblical guide.* Annandale, VA: Christian Legal Society.

Chacour, E. (1990). *We belong to the land: The story of a Palestinian Israeli who lives for peace and reconciliation.* New York: HarperSanFrancisco.

Crabtree, A. (1963). *The restored relationship: A study of justification and reconciliation.* Valley Forge, PA: Judson Press.

Cuschieri, A. (1992). *The sacrament of reconciliation: A theological and canonical treatise.* Lanham, MD: University Press of America.

Dallen, J. (1986). *The reconciling community: The rite of penance.* New York: Pueblo Publishing Co.

Dallen, J., & Favazza, J. (1991). *Removing the barriers: The practice of reconciliation.* Chicago: Liturgy Training Publications.

Denner, J. (1985). *The biblical doctrine of reconciliation.* Minneapolis, MN: Klock & Klock.

De Young, C. (1997). *Reconciliation: Our greatest challenge—our only hope.* Valley Forge, PA: Judson Press.

Dunn, S., & Longergan, A. (Eds.). (1991). *Befriending the earth: A theology of reconciliation between humans and the earth.* Mystic, CT: Twenty-Third Publications.

Fernandez Gazcia, D. (1992). *The father's forgiveness: Rethinking the sacrament of reconciliation* (Palmo Olmedo, Trans.). Collegeville, MN: Liturgical Press.

Habermas, R., & Issler, K. (1992). *Teaching for reconciliation: Foundations and practice of Christian educational ministry.* Grand Rapids, MI.: Baker Book House.

Hedquist, P. M. (1979). *The Pauline understanding of reconciliation in Romans 5 and II Corinthians 5: An exegetical and religio-historical study.* (microform). Ann Arbor, MI: University Microfilms International.

Hefner, P. (1966). *Faith and the vitalities of history: A theological study based on the work of Albert Ritschl.* New York: HarperCollins.

Helling, M. (1982). *Sign of reconciliation and conversion: The sacrament of penance for our times.* Wilmington, DE: M. Glazier.

Henchal, M. (Ed.). (1987). *Repentance and reconciliation in the church: Major presentations given at the 1986 national meeting of the Federation of Diocesan Liturgical Commissions.* Collegeville, MN: Liturgical Press.

Hennelly, A. (1993). *Signs of the times: Theological reflections of Juan Luis Segundo.* Maryville, NY: Orbis Books.

Herman, H. J. (1993). *Faith and order: The reconciliation of law and religion.* Atlanta, GA: Scholars Press.

Hoffman, G. (1995). *No royal road to reconciliation.* Pendle Hill, PA: Pendle Hill Pamphlets.

Hunter, M. (1996). Ritual of reconciliation—another way. *The ISTI Sun, 2*(2), 3.

Published by the Interfaith Sexual Trauma Institute at Saint John's University and Abbey in Collegeville, MN, 56321-2000.

Kraybill, R. 5. (1981). *Repairing the breach: Ministering in community conflict.* Scottdale, PA: Herald Press.

Lachmund, M. (1979). *With thine adversary in the way: A Quaker witness for reconciliation* (F. Likite, Trans.). Wallingford, PA: Pendle Hill Publishing.

Lloyd Jones, D. (1972). *God's way of reconciliation* (studies of Ephesians, chp. 2). Grand Rapids, MI: Baker Books.

Lochman, J. (1980). *Reconciliation and liberation: Challenging a one-dimensional view of salvation* (D. Lewis, Trans.). Philadelphia: Fortress Press.

Martin, R. (1981). *Reconciliation: A study of Paul's theology.* Atlanta. GA: John Knox Press.

McCollough, C. R. (1991). *Resolving conflict with justice and peace.* New York: Pilgrim Press.

McCullough, M., & Worthington, E. (1994). Encouraging clients to forgive people who have hurt them: Review, critique, and research prospectus. *Journal of Psychology and Theology, 22*(1), 3–20.

McCullough, M., & Worthington, E. (1994). Models of interpersonal forgiveness and their applications to counseling: Review and critique. *Counseling and Values, 39*(1), 2–14.

Meninger, Wm. (1996). *The process of forgiveness.* New York: Continuum.

Mitchell, M. (1991). *Paul and the rhetoric of reconciliation: An exegetical investigation of the language and composition of I Corinthians.* Tubigan, Germany: J.C.C. Mohr.

Muellez, D. L. (1991). *Foundation of Karl Barth's doctrine of reconciliation: Jesus Christ crucified and risen.* New York: E. Mellen Press.

Osborne, K. (1990). *Reconciliation and justification: The sacrament and its theology.* New York: Paulist Press.

Pannell, W. (1993). *The coming race wars: A cry for reconciliation.* Grand Rapids, MI: Zondervan.

Patton, J. (1985). *Is human forgiveness possible: A pastoral care perspective.* Nashville, TN: Abingdon.

Polner, M., & Goodman, N. (1994). *The challenge of Shalom: The Jewish tradition of peace and justice.* Philadelphia: New Society Publishers.

Presbyterian Church, U.S.A. (1991). The Confession of 1967. *Book of confessions.* Louisville, KY: The Office of the General Assembly.

Rader, W. (1989). Just peace and revolutionary nonviolence. *Prism, 4*(2), 48–61.

Ritschl, A. (1872). *A critical history of the Christian doctrine of justification and reconciliation* (J. S. Black, Trans.). Edinburgh, Scotland: Edmonston and Douglas.

Ritschl, A. (1901). Instruction in the Christian religion (A. T. Swing, Trans.). In A. T. Swing (Ed.), *The theology of Albrecht Ritschl.* New York: Longman's Green, and Co.

Ritschl, A. B. (1902). *The Christian doctrine of justification and reconciliation: The positive development of the doctrine* (2nd ed.). (H. R. Mackintosh & A. B. Macaulay, Trans.). Edinburgh, Scotland: T. & T. Clark.

Roberts, J. (1971). *Liberation and reconciliation: A Black theology.* Philadelphia: Westminster Press.

Sande, K. (1991). *The peacemaker: A biblical guide to resolving personal conflict.* Grand Rapids, MI: Baker Book House.

Sano, R. (1985). A theology of evangelism. In T. Runyon (Eds.), *Wesleyan theology today: A bicentennial theological consultation.* Nashville, TN: Kingswood Books—An imprint of the United Methodist Publishing House.

Schlicket, J., Zimmermann, M., Hari, A., & Messner, F. (Eds.). (1984). *Penance and reconciliation: International bibliograhy, 1975-1983.* Strasbourg, France: Cerdic Publications.

Schreiter, R. J. (1992). *Reconciliation: Mission and ministry in a changing social order.* Maryknoll, NY: Orbis Books.

Scott, N. (1952). *Rehearsals of discomposure: Alienation and reconciliation in modern literature: Franz Kafka, Ignauzio Silone, D. H. Lawrence, and T. S. Eliot.* New York: King's Crown Publishers.

Smedes, L. (1996a). *Forgive and forget: Healing the hurts we don't deserve* (rev. ed.). New York: HarperSanFrancisco.

Smedes, L. (1996b). *The art of forgiving: When you need to forgive and don't know how.* Nashville, TN: Moorings.

Taylor, V. (1952). *Forgiveness and reconciliation: A study in new testament theology.* London: Macmillan.

Tillich, P. (1957/1963). *Systematic theology* (Vos. 2 and 3). Chicago: University of Chicago Press.

United Church of Christ. (1986). Order for reconciliation of a penitent person, and order for corporate reconciliation. *Book of Worship.* New York: Office for Church Life and Leadership, pp. 268–288.

United Church of Christ. (1996). *History and program of the United Church of Christ.* Cleveland, OH: The United Church Press.

United States Catholic Conference. (1975). *Eucharistic prayers for masses of reconciliation: Arranged for celebration.* Washington, DC: Publications Office.

United States Catholic Conference. (1984). *Reconciliation and penance: Post-synodal apostolic exhortation, reconciliatio et paenitentia of John Paul II to the bishops, clergy, and faithful on reconciliation and penance in the mission of the Church today.* Washington, DC: Office of Publishing and Promotion Services.

United States Catholic Conference. (1986). *Penance and reconciliation in the church.* Washington, DC: Office of Publications and Promotion Services.

United States Catholic Conference. (1994). *Catechism of the Catholic Church.* Mahwah, NJ: Paulist Press.

Van Leeuwen, M. S. (1993). *After Eden: Facing the challenge of gender reconciliation.* Grand Rapids, MI: Wm. B. Eerdmans.

Washington, R. (1993). *Breaking down walls: A model for reconciliation in an age of racial strife.* Chicago: Moody Press.

Wilson, K. (1982). *How to repair the wrong you've done: Steps to restoring relationships.* Ann Arbor, MD: Servant Books.

THEOLOGY AND ETHICS

Atherton, J. (Ed.). (1994). *Christian social ethics: A reader.* Cleveland, OH: The Pilgrim Press.

Aulen, G. (1931). *Christus Victor: A historical study of the three main types of atonement.* London: SPCK.

Barth, K. (1958). *Church dogmatics* (Vol. 4: Parts 1, 2, 3a, & 3b). Edinburgh, Scotland:

T. & T. Clark.

Barth, K. (1959). *Protestant thought from Rousseau to Ritschl.* (Brian Cozens, Trans.) New York: Harper.

Braaten, E. E. (1990). *Justification: The article by which the church stands or falls.* Minneapolis, MN: Fortress Press.

Bratton, F. (1968). *The legacy of the liberal spirit.* Gloucester, MA: Peters Smith Publishing.

Bretall, R. (Ed.). (1963). *The empirical theology of Henry Nelson Wieman.* New York: Macmillan Co.

Bromiley, G., & Torrence, T. (Eds.). *Church dogmatics of Karl Barth (1936-1969).* New York: Scribner's.

Buber, M. (1970). *I and thou.* New York: Scribner's.

Buber, M. (1985). *Between man and man.* New York: Collier Books.

Buehrens, J., & Church, F. (1989). *Our chosen faith: An introduction to Unitarian Universalism.* Boston: Beacon Press.

Bultmann, R. (1969). *Faith and understanding.* Philadelphia: Fortress Press.

Cahill, L., & Childress, J. (Eds.). (1996). *Christian ethics: Problems and prospects.* Cleveland, OH: Pilgrim Press.

Church, F. (Ed.). (1967). *The essential Tillich: An anthology of the writings of Paul Tillich.* New York: Macmillan.

Eisenbeis, W. (1983). *The key ideas of Paul Tillich's systematic theology.* Washington, DC: University Press of America.

Fairweather, A. M. (Ed.). (1964). *Aquinas on nature and grace.* Philadelphia: Westminster Press.

Fletcher, J. (1966). *Situation ethics: The new morality.* Philadelphia: Westminster Press.

Frankena, W. (1973). *Ethics.* Englewood Cliffs, NJ: Prentice-Hall.

Gazvie, A. (1899). *The Ritschlian theology: Critical and constructive.* Edinburgh, Scotland: T. & T. Clark.

Gerrish, B. A. (1992). *Grace and gratitude: The eucharistic theology of John Calvin.* Minneapolis, MN: Augsburg Fortress Press.

Gunnemann, L. (1987). *United and uniting: The meaning of an ecclesial journey.* New York: United Church Press.

Haan, N., Bellah, R. N., Rabinow, P., & Sullivan, W. (1983). *Social science as moral inquiry.* New York: Columbia University Press.

Heyward, I. (1982). *The redemption of God.* Washington, DC: University Press of America.

Hicks, J., & Hebblewaite, B. (Eds.). (1980). *Christianity and other religions.* Philadelphia: Fortress Press.

Jodock, D. (Ed.). (1995). *Ritschl in retrospect: History, community, and science.* Minneapolis, MN: Fortress Press.

Johnson, D., & Hambrick-Stowe, C. (Eds.). (1990). *Theology and identity: Traditions, movements, and polity in the United Church of Christ.* Cleveland, OH: United Church Press.

Johnson, E. (1992). *She who is: The mystery of God in feminist theological discourse.* New York: Crossroads.

Kierkegaard, S. (1938). *Purity of heart is to will one thing.* New York: Harper and Row.

Kierkegaard, S. (1954). *Fear and trembling, and the sickness unto death.* New York:

Doubleday.

LaCugna, C. (1991). *God for us: The trinity and Christian life.* New York: Harper-SanFrancisco.

Langford, T. (Ed.). (1991). *Doctrine and theology in the United Methodist Church.* Nashville, TN: Kingswood Books.

Livingston, J. (1971). *Modern Christian thought from the enlightenment to vatican II.* New York: Macmillan.

London, P. (1964). *The modes and morals of psychotherapy.* New York: Holt, Rinehart, and Winston.

Macquarrie, J. (1988). *Twentieth century religious thought.* Philadelphia, PA: Trinity Press International.

Macquarrie, J. (1996). *Mediators between human and divine: From Moses to Muhammad.* New York: Continuum.

Marshall, G. (1991). *Challenge of a liberal faith* (3rd ed.). Boston: Skinner House Books.

Marty, M., & Peerman, D. (1984). *A handbook of Christian theologians.* Nashville, TN: Abingdon.

McDermott, T. (Ed.). (1989). *St. Thomas Aquinas: Summa Theologiae: A concise translation.* Westminster, MD: Christian Classics.

McFague, S. (1982). *Metaphorical theology: Models of God in religious language.* Philadelphia: Fortress Press.

Mendelsohn, J. (1995). *Being liberal in an illiberal age: Why I am a Unitarian Universalist.* Boston: Skinner House Books.

Miller, A., & Arthur, D. C. (Eds.). (1975). *Paul Tillich's systematic theology: A philosophical analysis of being human and an apologetic theology of the divine life.* St. Louis, MO: Eden Publishing.

Mueller, D. L. (1991). *Foundations of Karl Barths doctrine of reconciliation: Jesus Christ crucified and risen.* New York: Mellen Press.

Niebuhr, H. R. (1951). *Christ and culture.* New York: Harper and Row.

Niebuhr, H. R. (1960a). *Radical monotheism and Western culture. With supplementary essays.* Louisville, KY: Westminster/John Knox Press.

Niebuhr, H. R. (1960b). *The meaning of revelation.* New York: Macmillan.

Niebuhr, H. R. (1963). *The responsible self: An essay in Christian moral philosophy.* New York: Harper and Row.

Niebuhr, R. (1940). *The nature and destiny of man: A Christian interpretation.* New York: Charles Scribner's Sons.

Niebuhr, R. (1964). *Schleiermacher on Christ and religion.* New York: Charles Scribner's Sons.

Ogden, S. (1969). Present prospects for empirical theology. In B. Meland (Ed.), *The future of empirical theology.* Chicago: University of Chicago Press.

Orr, J. (1903). *Ritschlianism: Expository and critical essays.* London: Hodder and Stoughton.

Phillips, R. P. (1964). *Modern Thomistic philosophy* (Vols. 1 and 2). Westminster, MD: The Newman Press.

Presbyterian Church, U.S.A. (1991). *Book of confessions.* Louisville, KY: The Office of the General Assembly.

Prilleltensky, I. (1994). *The morals and politics of psychology: Psychological discourse and the status quo.* Albany, NY: State University of New York.

Rademacher, R. (1968). *A Tillich glossary.* Dubuque, IA: Wartburg Theological Seminary.

Robinson, D. (1985). *The Unitarians and the Universalists.* Westport, CT: Greenwood Press.

Runyon, T. (Ed.). (1985). *Wesleyan theology today: A bicentennial theological consultation.* Nashville, TN: Kingswood Books.

Rupp, G. (1974). *Christologies and culture. Towards a typology of religious worldviews.* The Hague: Mouton.

Schilpp, P., & Friedman, M. (Eds.). (1967). *The philosophy of Martin Buber.* La Salle, IL: Open Court.

Schleiermacher, F. (1958). *On religion: Speeches to its cultured despisers.* New York: Harper and Row.

Schleiermacher, F. (1989). *The Christian faith.* Edinburgh, Scotland: T. & T. Clark.

Shinn, R. (1990). *Confessing our faith: An interpretation of the statement of faith of the United Church of Christ.* Cleveland, OH: United Church Press.

Smith, H. (1991). *The world's religions.* New York: HarperSanFrancisco.

Sponheim, P. (1993). *Faith and the other: A relational theology.* Minneapolis, MN: Fortress Press.

Stackhouse, M. (Ed.). (1976). *James Luther Adams: On being human religiously.* Boston: Beacon Press.

Swing, A. T. (1901). *The theology of Albrecht Ritschl.* New York: Longmans, Green, and Co.

Taylor, M. K. (Ed.) (1987). *Paul Tillich: Theologian of the boundaries.* Minneapolis, MN: Fortress Press.

Tillich, P. (1951). *Systematic theology* (Vol. 1). Chicago: University of Chicago Press.

Tillich, P. (1957a). *Dynamics of faith.* New York: Harper and Row.

Tillich, P. (1957b). *Systematic theology* (Vol. 2). Chicago: University of Chicago Press.

Tillich, P. (1963). *Systematic theology* (Vol. 3). Chicago: University of Chicago Press.

Tracy, D. (1975). *Blessed rage for order.* San Francisco: Harper and Row.

Tracy, D. (1981). *The analogical imagination: Christian theology and the culture of pluralism.* New York: Crossroad.

Troeltsch, E. (1991). *The Christian faith.* (Garrett E. Paul, Trans.). Minneapolis, MN: Fortress Press.

von Harnack, A. (1986). *What is Christianity?* Philadelphia: Fortress Press.

Weidman, J. (Ed.). (1984). *Christian feminism.* San Francisco: Harper and Row.

Wogaman, J. (1993). *Christian ethics: A historical introduction.* Louisville, KY: Westminster/John Knox Press.

Zachman, R. (1993). *The assurance of faith: Conscience in the theology of Martin Luther and John Calvin.* Minneapolis, MN: Fortress Press.

PASTORAL COUNSELING

Adams, J. (1970). *Competent to counsel.* Nutley, NJ: Presbyterian and Reformed Publishing Company.

Adams, J. (1979). *More than redemption: A theology of Christian counseling.* Phillipsburg, NJ: Presbyterian and Reformed Publishing Co.

Backus, W. (1985). *Telling the truth to troubled people.* Minneapolis, MN: Bethany House.

Bonthius, R. (1948). *Christian paths to self-acceptance.* New York: King's Crown Press.

Capps, D. (1979). *Pastoral care: A thematic approach.* Philadelphia: Westminster Press.

Capps, D. (1981). *Biblical approaches to pastoral counseling.* Philadelphia: Westminster Press.

Capps, D. (1990). *Reframing: A new method in pastoral care.* Minneapolis, MN: Fortress Press.

Ciarrocchi, J. (1994). *The doubting disease: Help for scrupulosity and religious compulsions.* Mahwah, NJ: Paulist Press.

Clinebell, H. (1984). *Basic types of pastoral care and counseling.* Nashville, TN: Abingdon Press.

Clinebell, H. (1995). *Counseling for spiritually empowered wholeness: A hope-centered approach.* New York: Haworth Pastoral Press.

Clinebell, H. (1996). *Ecotherapy: Healing ourselves, healing the earth.* Minneapolis, MN: Fortress Press.

Crabb, L. (1977). *Effective biblical counseling.* Grand Rapids, MI: Zondervan.

Crabb, L., & Allender, D. (1984). *Encouragement: The key to caring.* Winona Lake, IN: Zondervan.

Fowler, J. (1987). *Faith development and pastoral care.* Minneapolis, MN: Fortress Press.

Gartner, J., Larson, D., & Vaclar-Mayberry, C. (1990). A systematic review of the quantity and quality of empirical research published in four pastoral counseling journals, 1978-1984. *Journal of Pastoral Care, 44,* 115–123.

Gilbert, M., & Brock, R. (Eds.). (1988). *The Holy Spirit and counseling. Vol. 2: Principles and practices.* Peabody, MA: Hendrickson Publishers.

Hughes-McIntyre, M. F. (Ed.). (1979). *Abstracts of research in pastoral care and counseling.* Richmond, VA: Joint Council on Research in Pastoral Care and Counseling.

Hulme, Wm. (1981). *Pastoral care and counseling: Using the unique resources of the Christian tradition.* Minneapolis, MN: Augsburg Publishing House.

Hunter, R. J. (1990). *Dictionary of pastoral care and counseling.* Nashville, TN: Abingdon Press.

Johnson, E. (1992). A place for the Bible within psychological science. *Journal of Psychology and Theology, 20*(1), 346–355.

Johnson, W. (1993). Outcome research and religious psychotherapies: Where are we and where are we going? *Journal of Psychology and Theology, 3*(2), 297–308.

Joy, D. (Ed.). (1983). *Moral development foundations: Judeo-Christian alternatives to Piaget/Kohlberg.* Nashville, TN: Abingdon Press.

Kelsey, M. (1973). *Healing and Christianity.* New York: Harper and Row.

Kirwan, W. (1984). *Biblical concepts for Christian counseling: A case for integrating psychology and theology.* Grand Rapids, MI: Baker Book House.

Lester, A. D. (1995). *Hope in pastoral care and counseling.* Louisville, KY: Westminster/John Knox Press.

Liebert, E. (1992). *Changing life patterns: Adult development in spiritual direction.* New York: Paulist Press.

MacArthur, J., & Mack, W. (1994). *Introduction to biblical counseling: A guide to the principles and practice of counseling.* Dallas, TX: Word Publishing.

Maddock, M. (1990). *The Christian healing ministry.* London: SPCK.

May, G. (1988). *Addiction and grace: Love and spirituality in the healing of addictions.* San Francisco: Harper and Row.

McHolland, J. (Ed.). (1993). *The future of pastoral counseling: Whom, how, and for what do we train?* Fairfax, VA: American Association of Pastoral Counselors.

McNutt, F. (1974). *Healing.* Notre Dame, IN: Ave Maria Press.

Milazzo, G. T. (1991). *The protest and the silence: Suffering, death, and biblical theology.* Minneapolis, MN: Fortress Press.

Oates, W. (1971). *Confessions of a workaholic.* New York: World.

Oglesby, W. (1980). *Biblical themes for pastoral care.* Nashville, TN: Abingdon.

Propost, L. (1988). *Psychotherapy in a religious framework.* New York: Human Sciences Press.

Soelle, D. (1975). *Suffering.* Minneapolis, MN: Fortress Press.

Strunk, O. (1988). Research in the pastoral arts and sciences: A reassessment. *Journal of Pastoral Psychotherapy, 2,* 3–12.

Tillich, P. (1952). *The courage to be.* New Haven, CT: Yale University Press.

Wicks, R. J., & Parsons, R. D. (Eds.). (1993). *Clinical handbook of pastoral counseling* (Vol. 2). New York: Integration Books.

Wicks, R. J., Parsons, R. D., & Capps, D. (Eds.). (1993). *Clinical handbook of pastoral counseling* (Vol. 1). New York: Integration Books.

Wimberly, E. P. (1994). *Using scripture in pastoral counseling.* Nashville, TN: Abindgon.

PSYCHOTHERAPY

Bandura, A. (1977). Self-efficacy: Toward a unifying theory of behavior change. *Psychological Review, 84,* 191–215.

Bandura, A. (1977). *Social learning theory.* Englewood Cliffs, NJ: Prentice-Hall.

Bergin, A. (1980). Psychotherapy and religious values. *Journal of Consulting and Clinical Psychology, 48*(1), 95–105.

Bergin, A., & Garfield, S. (1994). *Handbook of psychotherapy and behavior change* (4th ed.). New York: John Wiley and Sons.

Brazier, D. (1995). *Zen therapy: Transcending the sorrows of the human mind.* New York: John Wiley and Sons.

Corsini, R., & Wedding, D. (1989). *Current psychotherapies.* Itasca, IL: F. E. Peacock.

Doherty, Wm. (1995). *Soul searching: Why psychotherapy must promote moral responsibility.* New York: Basic Books.

Drakeford, J. W. (1967). *Integrity therapy.* Nashville, TN: Broadman Press.

Fishbein, M. (1972). A theory of reasoned action: Some applications and implications. In H. E. Howe, Jr., & M. M. Page (Eds.). (1979). *Nebraska Symposium on Motivation, 27,* 65–116.

Fitzgibbons, R. (1986). The cognitive and emotive uses of forgiveness in the treatment of anger. *Psychotherapy, 23*(4), 629–633.

Frankl, V. (1984). *Man's search for meaning: An introduction to logotherapy* (3rd ed.). New York: Touchstone Books.

Frankl, V. (1988). *The will to meaning: Foundations and applications of logotherapy.* New York: Meridian.

Friedman, J., & Combs, G. A. (1996). *Narrative therapy: The social construction of preferred realities.* New York: W. W. Norton.

Frisch, M., Cornell, J., Villanueva, M., & Retzlaff, P. (1992). Clinical validation of the

Quality of Life Inventory: A measure of life satisfaction for use in treatment planning and outcome assessment. *Psychological Assessment, 4,* 92–101.

Herink, R. (Eds.). (1980). *The psychotherapy handbook: The A to Z guide to more than 250 different therapies in use today.* New York: Meridian.

Janus, I., & Mann, L. (1977). *Decision making: A psychological analysis of conflict, choice, and commitment.* New York: The Free Press.

Johnson, W., Devries, R., Ridley, C., Pettorini, D., & Peterson, D. R. (1994). The comparative efficacy of Christian and secular rational-emotive therapy with Christian clients. *Journal of Psychology and Theology, 22*(2), 130–140.

Kelly, G. (1955). *The psychology of personal constructs.* New York: W. W. Norton.

Lawton, M. (1997). Measures of quality of life and subjective well-being. *Generations, 21,* 45–47.

Lee, R. R., & Martin, J. C. (1991). *Psychotherapy after Kohut: A textbook of self psychology.* Hillsdale, NJ: The Analytic Press.

Lipsley, M., & Wilson, D. (1993). The efficacy of psychological, educational, and behavioral treatment: Confirmation from meta-analysis. *American Psychologist; 48,* 1181–1209.

Lowry, L. R., & Meyers, R. W. (1991). *Conflict management and counseling.* Dallas, TX: Word Publishing.

Mahrer, A. H. (Ed.). (1967). *The goals of pychotherapy.* New York: Appleton-Century-Crofts.

May, R. (1983). *The discovery of being.* New York: W. W. Norton.

Messer, S. B. (1987). Can the tower of Babel be completed? A critique of the common language proposal. *Journal of Integrative and Eclectic Psychotherapy, 6,* 195–199.

Mowrer, O. H. (1964). *The new group therapy.* Princeton, NJ: Van Nostrand.

Mowrer, O. H. (1966). *Abnormal reactions or actions.* New York: William C. Brown.

Norcross, J., & Goldfried, M. (Eds.). (1992). *Handbook of psychotherapy integration.* New York: Basic Books.

Patterson, C. H. (1985). *The therapeutic relationship: Foundations for an eclectic therapy.* Monterey, CA: Brooks/Cole.

Patterson, C. H., & Hidore, S. (1997). *Successful psychotherapy: A caring, loving relationship.* Northvale, NJ: Jason Aronson.

Peterson, D., & Fishman, D. (Eds.). (1987). *Assessment for decision.* New Brunswick, NJ: Rutgers University Press.

Phillips, L., & Osborne, J. (1989). Cancer patients' experiences of forgiveness therapy. *Canadian Journal of Counseling. 23*(3), 236–251.

Pingleton, J. (1989). The role and function of forgiveness in the psychotherapeutic process. *Journal of Psychology and Theology, 17*(1), 27–35.

Propst, R., Ostrom, R., Watkins, P., Dean, T., & Mashburn, D. (1992). Comparative efficacy of religious and nonreligious cognitive-behavioral therapy for the treatment of clinical depression in religious individuals. *Journal of Consulting and Clinical Psychology, 60,* 94–103.

Rank, O. (1945). *Will therapy and truth and reality.* (J. Taft, Trans.). New York: Alfred A. Knopf.

Rogers, C. (1951). *Client-centered therapy.* Boston: Houghton Mifflin.

Rogers, C. (1961). *On becoming a person: A therapist's view of psychotherapy.* Boston: Houghton Mifflin.

Rychlak, J. (1981). *Introduction to personality and psychotherapy: A theory construction approach* (2nd ed.). Boston: Houghton Mifflin.

Schwartz, M. (Ed.). (1995). *Biofeedback: A practitioner's guide* (2nd ed.). New York: Guilford Press.

Smith, M., & Glass, G. (1977). Meta-analysis of psychotherapy outcome studies. *American Psychologist, 32,* 752–760.

Swami Ajaya. (1983). *Pychotherapy East and West: A unifying paradigm.* Honesdale, PA: The Himalyan International Institute of Yoga Science and Philosophy of the U.S.A.

White, M., & Epston, D. (1990). *Narrative means to therapeutic ends.* Adelaide, South Australia: Dulwich Centre.

Yalom, I. (1980). *Existential psychotherapy.* New York: Basic Books.

SPIRITUALITY/SPIRITUAL DIRECTION

Brother Lawrence. (1975). *The practice of the presence of God.* Grand Rapids, MI: Baker Book House.

Brother Roger of Taize. (1987). *Awakened from within: Meditations on the Christian life.* New York: Doubleday.

Cloud, F. (1970). *Prayers for reconciliation.* Nashville, TN: Upper Room.

Foster, R., & Smith, J. (1993). *Devotional classics: Selected readings, for individuals and groups.* New York: HarperSanFrancisco.

Hassel, D. J. (1990). *Healing the ache of alienation: Praying through and beyond bitterness.* New York: Paulist Press.

Higgins, J. (Ed.). (1975). *Thomas Merton on prayer.* New York: Image Books.

Hinson, E. G. (Ed.). (1993). *Spirituality in ecumenical perspective.* Louisville, KY: Westminster/John Knox.

Liebert, E. (1992). *Changing life patterns: Adult development in spiritual direction.* New York: Paulist Press.

Mass, R., & O'Donnell, G. (1990). *Spiritual traditions for the contemporary church.* Nashville, TN: Abingdon Press.

Merton, T. (1957). *The silent life.* New York: Farrar, Straus, & Giroux.

Merton, T. (1961). *New seeds for contemplation.* New York: New Directions.

Steere, D. (1984). *Quaker spirituality: Selected writings.* Mahwah, NJ: Paulist Press.

United Church of Christ. (1986). Order for reconciliation of a penitent person, and order for corporate reconciliation. *Book of worship.* New York: Office of Church Life and Leadership, pp. 268–288.

United States Catholic Conference. (1975). *Eucharistic prayers for masses of reconciliation: Arranged for celebration.* Washington, DC: Publications Office.

Index

reason, 205; of Scripture, 61, 78;
    of theology, 33
autonomous disciplines, 31
autonomous psychology, 33
autonomous theology, 33
autonomy, 130
avoidance-avoidance approach, 187
avoiding decisions, ways of, 187

Babylonian exile, 67
Barth, Karl, 31, 98, 107
beatitudes, 65, 162, 182, 195, 219
becoming, process of, 122
behavior, covert, 167
behavior change, 186
behavior therapy, 168
behavioral approaches, 32, 37, 163
behavioral changes, 173, 192
behavioral domains, 55, 99, 121, 123,
    153, 156, 167, 204, 207, 210, 224
behavioral intentions, 178
behavioral mĕdicine, 182
behavioral psychologists, 74
behavioral psychology, 168. *See also*
    psychology
being, 56, 59, 99, 123, 129–30, 163,
    175, 183, 189, 196, 204, 206, 209,
    212, 213, 222; ethic of, 105, 214;
    existential concept of, 54;
    multidimensional ontology of,
    209; nature of, 32, 40, 41; ontic
    elements of, 209; ontological
    concept of, 54
Berkeley, George, 71
Bethany, 63
Bhagavad Gita, 7, 59
bhakti yoga, 163
Bible, 6–7, 12, 59–61, 65, 68, 130,
    148, 154
biblical exegesis, 60
biblical literalism, 65
biblical sources, 36
biblicism, 79
bibliolatry, 60, 65
biological drives, 120–21, 124, 190
biopsychosocial dimensions, 29;
    theories of, 44
biopsychosocial model, 1, 4
blessed life, 139, 140, 146–49

Boehme, Jacob, 182
"bondage of the will," 196
Book of Acts, 57
Book of Job, 128. *See also* Job
Book of Proverbs, 183. *See also*
    Proverbs
Borg, Marcus, 4–5, 7, 57, 67
Bornkamm, Günther, 58
Brahman, 184, 189
Breath, 212
Brother Ego, 171
Brother Lawrence, 171, 191
Browning, Don, 16
Brunner, Emil, 31
Buber, Martin, 31, 42, 98, 195, 207,
    209–10
Buddha, Gautama, 9, 125–26, 138, 219
Bugenthal, James, 42
Bultmann, Rudolph, 4–6, 12, 31, 42,
    57–58, 195
Bunyan, John, 141

Calvin, John, 5, 68
Camus, Albert, 195
Cana, 63
capitalism, democratic, 225
Capps, Donald, 7, 183
Cartesian split, 33, 211
catharsis, 10
Catholicism, 107
Catholic moral theology, 77
Catholic tradition, 107
causal judgments, 43
changed life style, 173
character-conduct therapy, 78
Christ, 31, 46, 54, 75, 107, 218, 221
Christian anthropology, 168
Christian counseling, 69, 105, 168. *See
    also* counseling
Christian counselor, 124
Christian courage, 137. *See also*
    courage
Christian discipleship, 145, 161, 169,
    174
Christian ethics, 214
Christian existentialist, 107
Christian experiential approach, 12
Christian faith, 69–70, 106, 163, 168,
    172, 221, 222

ontological construct, 99
ontological dimensions, 163
ontological meaning, 97
ontological reductionism, 35
ontological reality, 72, 182
ontology, 40, 71, 174, 204–5; atheistic,
    213; theistic, 213
operant conditioning paradigm, 74
organizational psychologists, 225
Orthodox Christian theologians, 205
Otto, Rudolph, 42, 106
overt behavior, 182

pantheistic monism, 68
parables, 63, 65, 121, 125, 128, 144,
    159, 173
paralysis of will, 186
Parsons, Talcott, 12
pastoral care, 106, 108
pastoral counseling, 8, 12, 30, 42, 73,
    102; theology, 42. *See also*
    counseling
pastoral counseling journals, 30
pastoral functions, 101, 204
Patterson, Charles, 7
Paul, 5–7, 57, 68, 72, 105, 128, 132
Pauline principle, 14, 59, 169
penance, 104, 107–8, 127
personal experience, 2
personal reconciliation, 63. *See also*
    reconciliation
personality: dynamics, 220;
    psychological theories of, 42, 44;
    reductionist theories of, 9;
    religious typology of, 163;
    structure, 42; theory of, 10–11, 16,
    98, 120, 124
personality structure, theory of, 9
personal transformation, 128, 160
person-centered theorists, 132
"perspectivalist" approaches, 32
Peter, 59, 158
pharisaical religion, 126, 169
Pharisees, 37, 135
phenomenological analyses, 16, 208,
    223
phenomenological approach, 18, 205
phenomenological descriptions, 215,
    222

phenomenological interpretation, 109
phenomenological investigations, 225
phenomenological philosophy, 168.
    See also philosophy
phenomenological research, 101, 223
phenomenological theories, 42
phenomenology, 213
philosophers, 226
philosophical theology, 75. *See also*
    theology
philosophy, 32, 52, 71, 108, 203, 209,
    222; moral, 214–15
physical dimension, 121
physiological drives, 176, 192
pluralism: Christian, 221–22;
    psychological, 39; religious, 39
pneuma, 212
polity, 106
Pollyanna, 139
popular psychology, 152. *See also*
    psychology
"possibility thinking," 138
positivism, 213
positivist philosophy 168. *See also*
    philosophy
potentialities, 176
pragmatism, 213
prayer, 148, 161, 174
primacy of being, 130, 163, 174
primacy of will, 182
primary will to meaning, 182. *See also*
    will
processive perspective, 222
programmatic research, 73
prophecy, 106, 168
Protestant Christian theologians, 98
Protestant theology, 107, 206. *See also*
    theology
Protestant work ethic, 33, 195
Proverbs, 7, 59, 65, 128, 183
Psalms, 7, 59, 131, 153
pseudo-happiness, 139. *See also*
    happiness
Psyche, 34; Logos of the, 31. *See also*
    Logos
psychoanalysis, 74
psychoanalytic therapy, 74
psychodynamic approaches, 32
psychological change, 121
psychological counseling, 102. *See*

About the Author

R. PAUL OLSON is a Professor at the Minnesota School of Professional Psychology, where he teaches psychotherapy and spiritual direction, religious anthropologies, integrative psychotherapy, health psychology, and professional ethics. He received an M. Div. from Yale Divinity School, and his Ph.D. in clinical psychology from the University of Illinois-Urbana.